THE DISARTICULATE

The Disarticulate

Language, Disability, and the Narratives of Modernity

James Berger

NEW YORK UNIVERSITY PRESS

New York and London

NEW YORK UNIVERSITY PRESS
New York and London
www.nyupress.org

References to Internet websites (URLs) were accurate at the time of writing. Neither the author nor New York University Press is responsible for URLs that may have expired or changed since the manuscript was prepared.

For Library of Congress Cataloging-in-Publication data, please contact the Library of Congress

ISBN: 978-0-8147-0846-0 (cloth)
ISBN: 978-0-8147-2530-6 (paper)

New York University Press books are printed on acid-free paper, and their binding materials are chosen for strength and durability. We strive to use environmentally responsible suppliers and materials to the greatest extent possible in publishing our books.

Manufactured in the United States of America

10 9 8 7 6 5 4 3 2 1

Also available as an ebook

CONTENTS

ACKNOWLEDGMENTS

Writing, as all writers know, is generally a solitary, often a lonely pursuit. This project seemed especially so. I wrote most of my first book in grad school, and so had the support and good company of a faculty committee and assorted fellow students. I didn't have a full-time job, didn't have children. We were all there together working on our books. Then, if we were fortunate, we got academic jobs. Perhaps our families expanded. It took more effort and ingenuity to create and sustain social and professional communities. I didn't do such a good job of that. My book about disarticulation—in its linguistic and social senses—was written in something of a disarticulated condition. It became a ten-year struggle to articulate.

I was not entirely alone, of course. My colleagues in the English Department at Hofstra University, where I taught from 1997–2007, were enormously supportive and contributed significantly to my thinking. Let me mention with particular gratitude Lee Zimmerman, Tom Couser, John Bryant, Shari Zimmerman, and Sabina Sawney.

During my time at Hofstra, I received a National Endowment for the Humanities Fellowship (2002–2003), which helped me greatly in my writing.

Thanks also to my new colleagues in American Studies and English at Yale. This new job—teaching courses that expand my thinking, replacing a two-hour commute on I95 with a fifteen-minute bike ride, and a semester research leave not stipulated in the standard senior lecturer's contract—has greatly assisted me in finishing the book.

And my heartfelt thanks to the following, whose help in the form of comments on drafts, conversation about the project, or general encouragement has been invaluable: Jeffrey Bernstein, Avital Ronnell, Tobin Siebers, Richard Deming, Nancy Kuhl, Jean-Jacques Poucel, and all the members of the Yale Working Group in Contemporary Poetics (our conversations always helped unclog my articulations); Ed Ryan, Rachel Adams, and the Future of Disability Studies project at Columbia University(for our discussions and, especially, for making me feel welcome in this field); Joanna Klink, Henry Sussman, Mark Osteen, Sheila Blumstein, Eileen Boris, Lisa Zunshine, and Porter Abbott.

Thanks especially to Graham Cassano for the most intellectually stimulating and challenging conversations of the past dozen years—and, of course, for the music.

Thanks to students and faculty at University of Pennsylvania and University of California-Santa Barbara for allowing me to present portions of this project and providing insightful commentary.

Thanks to Robert McRuer and another, anonymous, reader for NYU Press. I am profoundly grateful for their very serious readings and comments; to my editor at NYU, Eric Zinner, for his enthusiasm and encouragement; and to Michael Bérubé for his interest in my work over the years, as well as for encouraging me to submit this book to the Cultural Front series.

A special thanks to my parents, Arthur and Jean Berger, for asking me continually, "Now *what* is your book about?"; for showing me how to respond ethically and politically to society's disarticulated; and for their extraordinary devotion to their daughters.

Let me thank also those who have distracted me from writing, but enriched me immeasurably. Thanks to my political comrades in New Haven—at the Connecticut Center for a New Economy (CCNE), Communities Organized for Responsible Development (CORD), and most recently, New Haven Rising—in solidarity to Adam, Hugh, Janis, Mike, Cristina, Lisa, Gwen, Ian, Scott, and the whole gang. We've accomplished some amazing things, and there's a lot of work still to come. And thanks to my musical pals—to the Skamatix, the NMS Premier Jazz Ensemble, Blue Pontiac, and the Lyric Hall Orchestra (you know who you all are). I need to do politics and I need to play music; otherwise, nothing else can happen.

In 2007, I received my most massive new portion of distraction and inspiration: the birth of my daughters, Hannah Lily and Teya Samara. I've seen them grow from tiny infants in incubators to solid, curious, beautiful, and very loquacious and articulate little girls. Perhaps I could write a book about them, but a sentence now seems beyond me. In any event, they draw, dance, know the meanings of "soporific" and "exquisite," can tell you the story of *The Magic Flute* (and mimic the Queen of the Night's arias), climb trees, can't quite bicycle without training wheels—no, wait, they just learned last week!—, are not convinced, I don't think, that there's no crying in baseball. I am exhausted all the time. I want only to be present for them and out of their way, and let them exhaust me till I'm one hundred.

Finally, thanks to my wife, Jennifer Klein—my best friend, closest comrade, colleague, and true love; a wonderful mother, a superb scholar, and developing into a pretty good jazz drummer. Jennifer, like her father, the late Ted Klein, is an exemplar of integrity and moral courage. Jen and I were working on our books over most of the same years, and she beat me to publication by a year—thus, I get to footnote her rather than the other way round! We both write about care—in very different but overlapping senses—so we've been able to help each other a great deal. We next plan to do a writing project together. We'll see if we can; I won't spell it out here, but if we pull it off, it will be a good one. Anyway, thank you, Jen, from the bottom of my heart, for everything.

* * *

Portions of this book have, in differing versions, appeared elsewhere, and I am grateful to the original publishers for permission to reprint. Part of chapter 3 appeared in *PMLA* 120 (2005) as "Falling Towers and Postmodern Wild Children: Oliver Sacks, Don DeLillo, and Turns Against Language." Part of chapter 4 appeared in *JAC: A Quarterly Journal for the Interdisciplinary Study of Rhetoric, Writing, Multiple Literacies, and Politics* 24 (2004) as "Trauma Without Disability, Disability Without Trauma: A Disciplinary Divide"; and part appeared in *American Book Review* 26.6 (2006) as "Models of Uncaring." Part of chapter 5 appeared in *Autism and Representation*, ed. Mark Osteen, as "Alterity and Autism: Mark Haddon's *Curious Incident* in the Neurological Spectrum."

Introduction

Disarticulate and Dysarticulate

The real title of this book is not "The Disarticulate"; it is "The Dys-/Disarticulate." My excellent and sensible editor at New York University Press, Eric Zinner, and series editor Michael Bérubé both advised me to keep it simple, lose the slash, and pick one title so as to avoid confusion. Let me now—now that my reader has picked up the book, opened it, and started to read—reintroduce the slash, the double title, the stutter, the confusion.

Why does a book about representations of cognitive and linguistic impairment require a neologism and, further, an awkward compounded one? Its components are homonyms, which form the most seductive and meaningless relations in language. Like other arbitrary combinations of sound and meaning (like rhyme and alliteration), homonyms remind us that language stands always in relation to the non-linguistic, and that the sharp outlines of meaning still shake off the loose sod of nonsignificance from which they emerged. My topic—the figure of cognitive or linguistic impairment; the figure outside the linguistic loop—is unstable and conglomerate. Its social and theoretical location slides from the domestic and personal through medical, scientific, and sociological discourses, religious metaphors of redemption, theories of genetic and cultural degeneration, and more recent theories and practices of neuroscience; and intermittently it bears a reader across the divide between language and all that is not language. The dys-/disarticulate is the figure at the boundary of the social-symbolic order, or who is imagined to be there, and at that liminal place, there is no adequate terminology. One cannot even quite determine whether he is an object of desire or revulsion.

What is certain is that his articulation is negated, doubly or multiply. "Dysarticulation" is a term in speech pathology denoting the confusion of phonemes. "Disarticulation" is a term used in surgery, butchering, and cooking, meaning the separation or amputation of limbs at the joint. As *disarticulate*, the figure is forcibly severed from the social fabric, stigmatized, silenced, possibly physically dismembered. There are intimations of sacrifice, thus of redemptive violence, the severing that makes whole, the suturing that may be the basis of ideology; and the term contains as well the critique of such violence and suturing. As *dysarticulate*, the figure is blocked from language, standing at the convergence of all of language's impasses: those of injury, trauma, neurological variation, sociopolitical silencing, and the working of language itself as language plots its own aporias. But the "dys" also renders the figure pathological, an object of diagnosis and treatment, and this, obviously, is a problem, for where truly does the pathology lie, and what would be required for its cure? The pathology entailed in "dys" is as much social as individual. Yet, as the dysarticulate figure is disarticulated, he remains at the center of the story, testifying to the injustice of his disfigurement.

The negated term, "articulation," remains—negated but active. It is always language we are concerned with, even when we study discourses of its limits, failures, or exclusions. The dys-/disarticulate is the figure for the outside of language figured in language. But he is also a representation of a human being living as an individual subject in a social world. And as a person perceived and figured as "other," he becomes the focus of ethical considerations. The texts to be discussed here consistently foreground and problematize these ethical questions, and in particular, issues of care. There is in these texts a dynamic of centripetal and centrifugal moral forces, as the dys-/disarticulate figure is thrust away from and drawn back toward the social order.

* * *

I came to this project, or it came to me, primarily along two trajectories, one professional and one personal. My first book, *After the End:*

Representations of Post-Apocalypse, explored, among other things, the status of language after some traumatic, definitive event—after, as Yeats put it, a world was "changed, changed utterly." If we imagine—for one of a number of psychological, historical, and ideological reasons—the world ending, and thereby imagine the ends also of our means of representing or imagining, what would constitute our symbolic system for that imagined cataclysm? The question applies also to actual historical catastrophes. After trauma, after "apocalypse"—which is, I argued, a hyperbolic projection of some trauma—what will be the symbolic remainder? After the world, *a* world, ends, what is left, and what words will we have to articulate what seems a state of absolute damage and loss? The book was concerned with the limits of language and the relations between language and all that is *not*-language; it took its cue from Wittgenstein's well-known remark that "in order to be able to draw a limit to thinking, we should have to be able to think both sides of the limit (we should therefore have to be able to think what cannot be thought). The limit can, therefore, only be drawn in language and what lies on the other side of the limit will be simply nonsense" (*Tractatus* 27).

Yes, but what vital, crucial, and significant nonsense!—as Wittgenstein himself was quite aware. The traumatic, the sacred, the sublime, the abject, the material (and maternal), the feminine, the queer, the dark, the transcendent, the obscene—all the unspeakables have their places here. This is where the post-apocalypse is at work, and also where we find the dys-/disarticulate. So my thinking on the limits of language continued, and I began to realize that, with a differently calibrated prism, all these rays began to focus on figures in modern fiction who had difficulty articulating: on central figures, for instance, in *Billy Budd*, *The Sound and the Fury*, *The Secret Agent*, *Nightwood*, and *White Noise*. I read further and discovered Richard Powers and Jonathan Lethem. A colleague suggested Wordsworth. I became interested in Helen Keller and took a year away from this project to edit a new edition of *The Story of My Life*. I pursued Wild Children into their textual forests. I sat on panels on naming with Adam, Cratyllus, and Walter Benjamin. I had to learn and relearn everything I knew or pretended to know about language, modernism, post-modernism, neuroscience, narrative, disability theory, ethics, and all possible relations among them. It took a long time, and when I wasn't agonizing over the slowness, difficulty, and loneliness, it was the most fun I've ever had doing research. And so this study of portrayals of characters with cognitive or linguistic impairments came into being.

But to answer the question, why *this* direction, and not some other, in pursuing questions about the limits of language, I would look toward my biography. I am the oldest of three children, all of us born in the mid- to late 1950s. My two younger sisters, Susan and Claudia, both have serious developmental disabilities (the general condition I grew up calling "mental retardation"; genetic evaluations have pointed somewhat uncertainly toward a condition called Angelman's Syndrome). They cannot speak. I, on the other hand, grew up to become a college English professor and eternal student of modern literature and literary theory. There is clearly a connection between these disparate conditions, and this book is part of it. But I don't know how to say exactly what it is. Our family handled our situation the way most families in the 1950s and 1960s would have. Susan, who has more difficulty communicating and caring for herself, was enrolled in a residential school—quite an excellent, nurturing institution—when she was quite young—perhaps seven or eight, as I remember. Claudia lived at home until she was about thirteen, then went to the same school Susan attended. This separation affected us all very deeply, but it seemed to be the best way to go. At any rate, it was the norm for the time. We visited the girls almost every weekend. My parents, now in their eighties, continue to see them at least once a month (now they live in group homes in residential neighborhoods).With my career, and distance, and now a young family, I am able to visit only once or twice a year, which makes me sad and ashamed, but it's difficult to remedy the situation. I've always been very close to Claudia, with whom I lived through most of high school. And Claudia was always the more vivacious and communicative. Susan has had more emotional and physical difficulties, and our relationship has been more distant. It's strange to think we're all in middle age now, and about to turn the corner past that epoch. When our parents die, I'll be responsible for my sisters.

It was always conveyed to me as I grew up—and I use the passive voice advisedly, for I don't remember how directly or actively it was conveyed; it seemed often in the manner of a tacit understanding—that I should live my life as I wanted, and should not feel obligated to choose a college, job, career, or residence nearby in order to help care for Susan and Claudia. We all recognized, I suppose, that this obligation would come to me eventually. But it was to be postponed until truly necessary. Till that time, I should live like any other boy or man with normal siblings. And so I did. I did not devote myself to my sisters, but rather to my own life, my experience, the directions of my thinking. This seems very modern, perhaps very American. I don't know, in retrospect, if it was the right approach to life. I'm not sure, if I were a parent in my parents' circumstances, I would try to convey quite the same understanding, though I very much appreciate what my parents wanted to do for me. For my own part, living with the independence that I've had—and not taking on a role of care-giver—has certainly broadened and enriched my life. But it must, in some ways, have impoverished it too. I developed, I think, acertain carelessness together with a fear of forming close relations. These qualities are being rectified now that I, at last, have young children of my own. I hope in the coming years that I'll be able to form closer relationships with my sisters again.

These experiences of separation, my parents' difficult decisions, questions of home and institution, and the responsibility of siblings helped bring into focus for me the overarching issue of care for those with cognitive impairments. And my personal concerns soon coincided with my literary choices, for in many of the texts I studied, siblings relationships were of central importance. I can still remember reading *The Sound and the Fury* for the first time in high school and being most deeply affected by Caddy's feelings for Benjy, which so paralleled mine for Claudia. Almost all the fictions examined here involve care, and point to the tensions between private or familial and public provision of care. The family can provide more steadfast love, but usually lacks resources. As Joseph Conrad puts it in *The Secret Agent* (and as I shall quote several times in this book), the private remedy has "the only one disadvantage of being difficult of application on a large scale." As I worked on this project, my wife, the historian Jennifer Klein, was at the same time working with Eileen Boris on a book on home health-care-workers who, as a labor force, form a kind of interface between private, familial care and care provided by the state—and yet are themselves vastly underpaid and unrespected. And as I worked to understand the literary texts and discussed the history of home care with my wife, I came also to read philosophical accounts of care by Eva Kittay and Martha Nussbaum, and to immerse myself in disability studies writings which often regarded care as a more problematic, hierarchical activity.

The Disarticulate (or "Dys-/Disarticulate") is, then, like most books, I suspect, an overdetermined mix of articulations and dys-/disarticulations. As in my family life, some things are uttered and some things are silent. My career and the intellectual trajectories that now converge in this book are both expressions and evasions of my experience with my sisters. Let me quote myself briefly, from a poem I wrote a few years ago:

> I've established that my poetry's
> principal quality
> is evasion.
> I've always thought I was
> exploring the edges of language,
> where language meets
> not-language—
> sensation, neurology:
> the unsayable, not just as trauma
> or the sublime or the sacred
> but as experience
> in all regards
> untranslatable,
> a massive
> bundle unable
> to be carried across intact
> the boundary not a boundary—
> uncontiguous,
> not on the same plane.
>
> Or such was my theory.
> Of course it has
> occurred to me
> that my most deeply
> defining experience of language
> was the fact
> of my two sisters' inability to speak—
> their mental retardation,
> as we
> used to call it.

It has occurred to me
that my sisters are almost entirely
missing from my poetry—

   like a great centripetal shove,
   as if an orchestral composition
   explicitly calls for a certain instrument,
   say a somewhat unusual one,
   maybe a euphonium,
   and then for the entire piece
   marks it "tacit." (Prior 58–59)

What I wrote about my poetry applies also to my academic work—though with more generic appropriateness since one does not expect to see family dramas played out in a scholarly monograph. But the generic convention has loosened somewhat in recent years, and so, in the interests of an intellectual-affective genealogy, I present a bit of my drama here. Some such mixture of experience, thought, and form must lie at the root of any human, symbolic expression. (Let me note also in passing that I play the euphonium.)

* * *

The Disarticulate has five chapters which trace historical and theoretical trajectories in the representation of cognitively or linguistically impaired characters in modern fiction. Let me say clearly at the outset that this is not in any way a comprehensive history of cognitive impairments and disabilities, social attitudes, clinical approaches, etc. For such histories, see excellent work by James Trent, Patrick McDonagh, C. F. Goodey, and R. C. Scheerenberger.

    Chapter 1, "The Bearing Across of Language: Care, Catachresis, and Political Failure," focuses first on a prehistory, describing impasses of language in the *Epic of Gilgamesh* and parts of the Hebrew Bible. As language comes to define the status of the human, the obstruction of language—for instance, at the revelation at Sinai—comes to figure the divine. The chapter then describes the distinction between the Old Testament prophet as a partly dys-/disarticulated purveyor of divine instruction and the fool as depicted in the wisdom literature (e.g., Proverbs and Ecclesiastes). In the Hebrew Bible, divine ordinance and normative social order are not intrinsically in conflict. The prophet comes to return the divine and social to their proper relation; the fool is one who fails to comply both with divine mitzvot and social convention—which are, essentially, the same. This is in contrast to the subsequent delineation of the sacred fool of Christian thought, wherein the divine and social contexts are seen to have diverged. Insofar as the fool possesses divine knowledge, he is dys-/disarticulated and rendered radically other in the social world.

Sacred fools in their secular variations in modernity occupy the remainder of the chapter. In Wordsworth's "The Idiot Boy," we see how cognitive impairment points both toward a radically new poetics and a renewed ethics, not explicitly Christian, in which the vulnerable must be cared for. Melville's *Billy Budd* and Carson McCullers's *The Heart is a Lonely Hunter* emphasize the role of desire in the cultural imagining of figures at the margins of language. Those who cannot speak for themselves are imagined in the cultural-ideological shapes that are adequate to the symbolic resources available at the time. In *Billy Budd*, this imagining results in an astonishing overdetermination of the figuring of Billy as he is pieced together by a range of allusions, preconceptions, and wishes that preclude any knowledge of who he might actually be. McCullers's *Heart*, with less allusion and more wishful projection, performs a similar constructive process with John Singer. In both McCullers and Melville, the dys-/disarticulate figure stands as an alternative to the prevailing social order, yet at the same time has neither clear definition nor power. Finally, it is notable that the desire to imagine a dys-/disarticulate other can be entwined with sexual desire, but that sexual desire in these texts is also dys-/disarticulated. The imagination of the dys-/disarticulate seems ideologically linked to a vision of radical, desexualized innocence. Any introduction of sexual desire, even covertly, as in the case of Claggert in *Billy Budd*, results in catastrophe.

Chapter 2, "Linguistic Impairment and the Default of Modernism," places dys-/disarticulate figures in Faulkner, Conrad, and Djuna Barnes in the context of anxieties about totalizing, systematizing energies of modernity—the sense that in epistemological and administrative terms, the modern world sought to define and control all phenomena.

The dys-/disarticulate here is that which cannot be accounted for and which thus has some undetermined subversive power. And yet, as is clear in *The Sound and the Fury*, *The Secret Agent*, and *Nightwood*, modern science and social thought very much sought to place cognitively impaired people in a clinical and bureaucratic category, that of the "feeble-minded," "idiot," or "degenerate"—persons who, if they reproduced, would constitute threats to a well-ordered, democratic polity and who therefore had to be both cared for and controlled. The imagining of Faulkner's Benjy and Conrad's Stevie coincided with the expansion of state power into the lives of cognitively impaired people and their families in the forms of compulsory institutionalization and sterilization. Benjy and Stevie constitute imperatives for genuine forms of care outside the totalizing practices of modernity. But while in no way "degenerate"—and both novels critique the premises and consequences of this notion—the characters are genuinely impaired, and they require care. Yet neither novel can indicate any viable means for resisting modernity's encroachments.

There is a problem here. If the forces of modernity are conceived as systemic and all-pervasive, then the critique of modernity must be total as well. The dys-/disarticulate other must embody some radical, unaccountable alterity in relation to the social-symbolic order; must occupy some utopian, apocalyptic, purely negative position and detach itself from any practical political program. The totalizing, dys-/disarticulated critique of modernity-as-totality paints itself into an epistemological-political corner. And there is the problem, again, of desire. To maintain the still-sacred innocence of the secular "idiot," adult sexuality (especially adult female sexuality) must be banished. Care for the impaired boy comes from the sister, and so any emergence of sexual desire would encounter numerous taboos and stigmas. In *Nightwood* we see, among other things, the consequences of open desire for a dys-/disarticulate figure—a world in which all human definition slips into obscurity, and language falls into ever-more imbricated analogies whose only referent may finally be individual pain and social collapse.

The problematics of the critique of a totalizing modern social-symbolic order continue in chapter 3, "Post-Modern Wild Children, Falling Towers, and the Counter-Linguistic Turn." In novels by Paul Auster, Jerzi Kosinski, and Don DeLillo, we see the old Enlightenment figure of the wild child reinvoked and reimagined. In the modernist texts discussed in chapter 2, descendents of the sacred fool contended with ideologies of degeneration and eugenics. In the post-modern texts of chapter 3, the biologistic ideologies have fallen into disrepute. This post-1960s moment contains Rousseauean, utopian echoes of primal, innocent man who will challenge the fallen social-linguistic order. The modern sacred fool gives way to the post-modern wild child, imagined to have not merely diagnostic but redemptive powers. These are necessary because the world in these texts is portrayed as broken or fallen. Auster's *City of Glass* conflates a post-Babel linguistic condition of shifting signifiers with the economic and social crises of New York in the 1970s. In Kosinski's *Being There*, the Edenic, unfallen garden merges with the blankness of television broadcast, and Chance, the wild child, emerges from that mixed but homogenous domain. In DeLillo's *White Noise*, American consumer culture is presented as a Baudrillardian simulation whose surface cannot be punctured even by death. The drug Dylar restores an Adamic connection between word and thing, and Wilder, the wild child, appears to embody a deeper relation between post-modern media and some primal lack of mediation. All these post-modern wild children are, however, explicitly presented as sites of fantasies of unmediated, prelapsarian life—in instances of, we might say, a counter-linguistic turn in post-modern thought. While these post-modern dys-/disarticulations bear close resemblances to the modernist instances discussed in chapter 2, they differ chiefly, I argue, in the more explicitly fantastical and projective nature of their exclusions from language. Wilder differs from Benjy, for example, in large part because the sacralizing language connected with him is spoken by his father while that connected to Benjy is voiced by the purportedly objective narrator of Part IV. Finally, these fictional wild children are further contextualized through a discussion of some case studies of cognitively and linguistically impaired people written by the neurologist Oliver Sacks. Sacks's "cases" appear to be wild children, too, figures possessing vision surpassing the capacities of language even as they have difficulty living in the "normal" social-symbolic world. Sacks is an enthusiastic supporter of his subjects as he tries to reveal a deeper humanity beneath their dys-/disarticulations. Insofar as Sacks's moving narratives lack the ironic undercutting that characterize the fictions discussed in this chapter, they render more clearly the late twentieth-century longing for the innocent and revelatory dys-/disarticulate wild child—a longing, and an ideology, that the post-modern fictions place in question.

Chapter 4, "Dys-/Disarticulation and Disability," turns to a question that builds over the course of previous chapters: it concerns the relation between this project and some of the projects of literary and cultural disability studies. Clearly, there are important overlaps. Not only are disabled characters at the centers of the fictions analyzed here, but the fictions tend to be critical of the stigmatizing and oppressive treatments often visited on these characters and to insist on at least some degree of agency for them, even though it may prove ineffective. My arguments regarding dys-/disarticulation differ from certain well-established directions in disability theory in three main areas: metaphor, trauma, and care. I argue against what I see as an iconoclastic tendency in disability theory that regards all metaphorical use of disability as suspect. This seems to me an impossible position to maintain. It is legitimate to criticize representations of disability that are clearly hostile and derogatory, but it is not always easy to know when this occurs. Moreover, as virtually all sophisticated views of language agree, it is impossible to avoid the use of tropes; there is no language that might depict disability, or anything else, "as it really is." Metaphor—or, as I have argued, catachresis—is how language emerges out of not-language, and we should encounter it with the cognitive, aesthetic, and ethical tools at our disposal. The problem of metaphor leads into a discussion of the incongruous gap between theories of disability and those of trauma. While pursuing overlapping topics, the two fields have little to do with each other, and, I argue, the consequences for both are deleterious. Trauma theory, with its apocalyptic tendencies and its emphasis on the obliterating effects of traumatic events, often appears to be, in effect, a theory of catachresis—of how terms are constructed for events that seem to be beyond linguistic expression. Thus, it has no interest in events that may be merely disabling. Conversely, disability theory, in its adherence to a social (rather than a biological or medical) model of disability, often rejects the notion of damage or pain altogether, except what is caused by social barriers. Thus, as I argue, disability theory seems marked by an inability to mourn while trauma theory suffers from an inability to stop mourning. With regard to care, I argue that disability studies' emphasis on autonomy and independence, though in many ways correct, can also make it difficult to account for vulnerability, pain, and the need for care on the part of disabled subjects, particularly those with cognitive impairments. Like its rejection of the notion of trauma, this ambivalence toward care (and with it, the realities of universal vulnerability, interdependence, and the lives of people who cannot live without care) limits disability theory's effectiveness.

Finally in this chapter, I discuss what seem to me the more promising recent directions in disability theory suggested by work by Michael Davidson, Robert McRuer, Tobin Siebers, and Tom Shakespeare. More accepting of metaphorical transformations, these approaches take into account the imperatives of care and, as Siebers put its, the "blunt, crude realities" of life with disability and, indeed, of all corporeal mortal life.

In the final chapter, "Alterity Is Relative: Impairment, Narrative, and Care in an Age of Neuroscience," I describe the shift in representations of figures with cognitive or linguistic impairments that comes with the enormous acceleration of knowledge in neuroscience. The imaginings of radical alterity that were so crucial to modernist and post-modern imaginings no longer seem so relevant in the context of late-twentieth- and early twenty-first-century neuroscience in which all differences in brain function and dysfunction are seen as falling across a spectrum of abilities. At the same time, neuroscience, in its guise as one of the most powerful contemporary ideological constructs, insists that knowledge of brain processes ultimately holds the key to understanding all aspects of human thought, feeling, behavior, and culture. If true, this would signal a massive epistemological shift. The traditional means of understanding the human soul, social relations, and cultural products—i.e., religion, philosophy, literature, psychoanalysis—would be obsolete, or mere addenda to the more fundamental understanding given to us by neuroscience. As ideology, neuroscience is successor to the totalizing ideologies of modernity discussed in chapter 2, and again portrayals of dys-/disarticulate figures provide a critique of this sense that some final, unambiguous knowledge of the mind is possible. At stake, I argue, is a "defense of narrative," or even, more broadly, of language in the face of methodologies that claim to bypass narrative's and language's intrinsic ambiguities and contingencies. Texts like Mark Haddon's *The Curious Incident of the Dog in the Night-Time*, Jonathan Lethem's *Motherless*

Brooklyn, and Richard Powers's *The Echo Maker* draw heavily on neu-roscientific knowledge and present precise clinical descriptions of the impairments at the centers of their stories—in contrast to the far vaguer depictions in modernist and post-modernist fictions. These are, as one critic called them, "neuronovels," but they understand neuroscience in an expansive, not a reductive, sense, one in which the complex, pro-ductive-receptive, and irreducible structure and function of the brain finds its most characteristic expression in human language use with all its indeterminacies. And this sense, I argue, is closer to the *science* of contemporary neuroscience than is the ideological fantasy of total explanation.

*   *   *

The figure and concept of the dys-/disarticulate as I have described it is as old as our oldest recorded uses of language, but is also peculiarly modern. At each historical moment, representations of some figure out-side of language will serve as a point of intersection and conflict for the most powerful discourses of its time—of theology, politics, semantics, ethics, science, and aesthetics. Each points in its own way to some place beyond all discourse that would provide a final affirmation or negation to the social-symbolic world. The dys-/disarticulate is that place, relo-cated among us. The figures discussed here thus serve, I think, as reveal-ing sites of social fantasy, pointing as directly as any cultural production we could name toward our utopian, dystopian, apocalptic, traumatic, and healing projections. At the same time, these dys-/disarticulate fig-ures are portrayals of human beings in particular social circumstances and thus embody ethical challenges that remain unanswered.

1

The Bearing Across of Language

Care, Catachresis, and Political Failure

Adam and Enkidu

The problem of how to speak with the non-speaking, with those in some sense outside the loop of language, has occupied users of language since at least some of the earliest documentations of language—the *Epic of Gilgamesh* and the Hebrew Bible. Since then, both in narrative and in the more abstract discourses of religion, philosophy, and, more recently, science and medicine, there has been a continuing dialogue, or an imagined dialogue, with those sited beyond, or just on the borders of language: with animals, infants, angels, the dead, the inanimate objects of nature, and the inanimate (or animate) constructions of human-kind. This dialogue has extended also to human beings who lack (or are, or were, presumed to lack) the use of language, or whose linguis-tic capacity is impaired: those with stutters, developmental cognitive impairments, and the range of conditions now understood by the term "autism"; those who are deaf; and those growing up apparently without socialization or language—the so-called "wild children."

These discourses point to a relation between the linguistic world and some realm outside it or adjacent to it. The child coming into language is fascinated by animals and by infants, and recognizes his affinity with them and his distance from them. This astonished relation and non-rela-tion is never lost. Language and the forms of rationality it structures, or is structured by, and transmits, shapes subjectivity and social relations. In Genesis, Adam's act of naming is the first political act, establishing a hierarchy in which the namer assumes authority over those he names.

But this power is unstable. That first, Adamic, language was, according to tradition, a perfect language, purveyor of the true names of things. The unity of unambiguous understanding created by the perfect language was later the vehicle of rebellion against the power that had underwritten it. The fall of Babel, the second fall, was the fall into language as we know it—into ambiguity, duplicity, multiplicity, jokes, puns, lies, translations, fictions, and truths in the plural. It marked the division between, as Walter Benjamin put it, "language as such" and the "language of man." It marked the distinction Charles Peirce noted between the indexical sign that points toward and is ineradicably linked to its referent and the symbol whose significance can shift and is always dependent on a third term (which then, in its turn, can only be understood through further semantic triangulation). This is the distinction made also by Plato in "Cratyllus" between the word which truly means the thing and the word whose meaning is merely conventional. Babel marks as well the infinite regress toward the ever-receding referent-trace that Derrida termed "differance."

According to such construals, we have been falling for a long time. And in all these tales and theories, we can register a nostalgia for a mode of being that is not human in our familiar social and linguistic senses. The indexical language of Adam and Cratyllus is a language of fullness, of truth in the singular. Its plenitude and precision is angelic, almost like having no language at all. As the hero Gilgamesh was half human and half god, his friend Enkidu was half human and half animal. Initially, his animal side was dominant. He ran with the animals and possessed no language. Nor did he have a human, social, ethical sense; in his animal adventures, he caused extensive property damage, and people appealed to Gilgamesh to bring this human beast under control. But Enkidu as animal was too fast, and as human was too clever to be caught. In the end, it was sexual desire—the animal urge that, in humans, has such sweeping and intertwining social and symbolic permutations—that brought him into society and into language. A woman taught him human sexual behavior and language simultaneously, and from that time on, he was human. He had entered the social and symbolic world through desire and love. This was a gain, of course. He could now perform conscious, purposeful, ethical actions; he could become heroic. His sexuality now was social and symbolic, and thus, properly, erotic. He now began his lifelong friendship with Gilgamesh. As a user of symbols, he now had an understanding of time, of the negative, and of death. Indeed, according to the logic of the tale, Enkidu can die only after, and indeed, as a result of, his entry into language and his friendship with Gilgamesh. Now that Enkidu is gendered, symbol-using, and mortal, he is fully human.

But he can no longer run with the animals or communicate with them. It is not possible to live in both worlds; to enter one means forever to leave the other. Nor can he even remember what it was like to be an animal. And this is an infinite loss—and a consistent theme in theories of language. To learn language is to gain everything, to become cognizant in all recognized ways. And yet, this tradition of thinking about language that spans the entire recorded history of language reserves—or claims to remember—a space for an other of language, for an alterity that can be heard only before language or after language or outside of language or in the breakdowns and impairments of language. It reserves this space of alterity, desires it, and is terrified of it.

In biblical tradition, this outside of language is the sacred. Before the prophet can speak, he must be forcibly silenced—Isaiah by the coal to his lips, Ezekial by the vision of animate wheels within wheels, Jonah through his gestation inside a whale. Moses, of course, was "slow of speech" and spoke with "uncircumcized lips." The utterance of prophecy, as Herbert Marks argues, arises out of a moment of blockage, a stammer, in which the prophet is overcome by the force of divinity. The Hebrew word for "oracle," Marks notes, is also the word for "burden," for something that must be suffered or carried. The repeated use of this term in both nominal and verbal forms in the prophetic books indicates an ambivalence regarding the relation of language to the divine commission. As Marks writes of Ezekial's vision of the divine chariot, its "superabundance . . . defies assimilation" (8). This incommensurability of the divine with human language is apparent also in the revelation at Sinai. Here, the biblical text states that the people of Israel saw both the lightning coming from the mountain and also the thunder and the voice of the shofar (Exodus 20:15, 20:18 in some editions). They did not hear the thunder or the voice of God; they saw them—a revelation as "deafened moment" in Lennard Davis's sense, a meaning conveyed not through voice or phonetic language but through physical gesture, and therefore with greater immediacy. How can this sensory confusion be explained? The Talmudic commentator Rabbi Ishmael (90–135 C.E.), apparently in a mood of common-sense irritation, dismissed the question: "They saw what was visible and heard what was audible." But other commentators insisted on maintaining the paradox, arguing that the divine voice, as that which was at that moment supremely present, could only be seen and not heard; that it, one might say, disabled the auditory faculty, or that human hearing was already an impaired sense when confronted with divinity. As Philo of Alexandria wrote, hearing "is but a sluggish sense, inactive until aroused by the impact of the air, but the hearing of the mind possessed by God makes the first advance and goes out to meet the spoken words with the keenest rapidity." The voice of God, wrote Philo, was a flame of articulate speech, "and so clearly and distinctly were the words formed by it that [the people] seemed to see rather than hear them." This difference between the human and the divine voice—by which "the voice of men is audible, but the voice of God truly visible"—exists because the divine voice is directly creative and effective: "whatever God says is not words but deeds, which are judged by the eyes rather than the ears."[1]

Human language, in this view, is impaired in relation to divine content. Rabbi Ishmael makes a similar point in glossing God's statement to the Israelites that "you yourselves have seen [that I spoke to you from the heavens]." For Rabbi Ishmael, there can be doubt or deception with regard to a spoken communication, but regarding vision there can be no uncertainty. Vision requires presence; voice and hearing entail mediation and distance. But this point regarding the intrinsic impairment of human language is already familiar from the complementary stories in Genesis about language's origin and fall. The original language created by Adam was one of naming, and thus, presumably, of perfect correspondence between word and object. Each name that Adam bestowed was, in effect, a proper name, not a generic name. Language, in this view, could possess no generalizing and no systemic function, and thus could have no slippage of signifiers, no ambiguity. As Walter Benjamin wrote in his paean to Adamic language, "Name is not only the last utterance of language, but also the true call of it. Thus in name appears the essential law of language, according to which to express oneself and to address everything else amounts to the same" ("On Language as Such and the Language of Man," 319). In a language of this sort, the naming of the divine would not be problematic. At the same time, it would not be needed. God does not offer a name for himself until Exodus 3:14, and then as an almost stuttered tautology: "I will be what I will be."

We need not accept this premise of a language of perfect naming; indeed, to do so would be a sign of derangement. A language of pure naming sounds like a Wittgensteinian thought exercise from *Philosophical Investigations* ("It is easy to imagine a language consisting only of . . . ," etc. [8e]). But there are related theses that may retain greater plausibility. One can reject the notion of a perfect language, but still maintain that the representational functions of language work well enough until they are faced with some radical alterity: God, the sublime, an overwhelming trauma, some principle of universal disruption like the Lacanian "real." Or one can accept that perhaps what language principally does is not correspondence or representation, but something else—a form of action, or of thinking; a social bonding; the working of ideology. Hence, naming is one thing language does, but one thing among others. And one can then have several attitudes toward this view: pleasure at contemplating language broken free (not fallen) from the mistaken strictures of "adequacy"; or nostalgia for the imagined loss of true reference, for the loss of the indexical and entry into the symbolic.

This last thought brings us back to Enkidu and to an entirely different mode of response to the fantasy of Adamic language. Or, first, to a response that follows from those in the preceding paragraph, and then to one that indicates a different direction. First, we might say that Enkidu's story suggests that the animal, the non-human, is another object beyond the power of language to name or depict; that the animal can be added to the list of god, sublime, trauma, real and "other": unknowable because unsayable. Enkidu in this reading cuts in line to become one of the first ancestors of the long and invaluable genealogy of catachresis— the term invoked because no true name is known. And this book is, to a considerable degree, an account of the workings of catachresis. But in other ways, Enkidu points toward an escape from these same agonies and pleasures. The language that Enkidu enters is not at all a language of correspondence or naming, but rather of sociality and desire. Once Enkidu enters language, it is a matter of indifference to the story what exactly is the nature or the origin of that language. Language is simply what human beings do and what animals don't do. What is beyond that language is not some realm that a better language would be able to represent. Nor is it a place of sublime terror, ecstasy, divinity, or obscenity.

It's just a place. Animals live there in their way, and humans live within language in their way. The gods speak fluently to both. Nor is there the sense, as in Adam's language of naming, that the act of speaking is an act of power and dominance. In Enkidu's entry into the symbolic-social world, both sex and language are mutual acts. Enkidu was other, someone to be feared; and the beautiful woman selected to lure him in to the social-symbolic world must have been afraid, and had reason to be. But he was persuaded—demonstrating, in this story, the erotic character of language and the symbolic, communicative character of human sex. Language, in this story, is ordinary. It is functional, playful, sociable, capable of double meanings (and, we can assume, double entendres). It does not aspire to towers and perfect correspondence. It can be mistaken, misused, or impaired; but it cannot "fall" and be broken.

Enkidu does not lose entirely his alterity when he enters the social-symbolic-erotic world, but he conveys a different notion of alterity. He can no longer run with or, in their own terms, communicate with the animals, but he still is half animal. The Gilgamesh story is an allegory of human composition and dividedness. The range of modes of being portrayed in Gilgamesh and Enkidu— from god to human, from human to animal—is the range of possibility for all human being. There is a spectrum of being, and the human is not just one isolated point on the spectrum, but is composed, blended, and so contains the alterities both of the divine and the animal. The entirely, solely human part of the human would be the part that makes, uses, and depends on language, but there is neither surgery nor philosophical analysis capable of delimiting the purely human (and linguistic) from its surrounding alterities.

To recognize the other both in the interlocutor and in oneself is the basis of an ethics. If the self contained no other—which is to say, if language could entirely comprehend and define one's being—then the self would be self-sufficient. The possibility of self-knowledge would be complete, and the self could entirely comprehend the discourse of another self who would be likewise self-sufficient. Ethics among such beings would take a very different form than that with which we are familiar. It would be the ethics of angels, the ethics peculiar to beings who have no needs or lacks. Or perhaps it would be the ethics of stoics or of neoconservatives.[2] But the ethics of composite beings suffused with otherness must recognize the incomprehensibility and the vulnerability of the other. This is Emmanuel Levinas's lesson, as amended by Eric Santner. Ethics, for Santner, begins in the recognition of the other who is other to himself, by another who is also other to himself (81). This is a necessary correction, I think, to Levinas, who places all responsibility on the self and all alterity (seen as opaque and vulnerable) in the other. Levinas seems at times to assume that the self is transparent to himself, of a piece and self-sufficient. But this could not be the case, and the implausibility of this scenario is implied in Levinas's depictions (in *Totality and Infinity*) of language and of eroticism. Levinas consistently warns against projecting the self onto the other—against thematizing, or, in Heideggerian terms, which are congenial here to Levinas's intent, against enframing the other. There is an implied iconoclasm in this argument, for it seems to call into question any form of representation. Especially if one regards the other as entirely other (*tout autre*), then what form of discourse would not be a thematizing, a projection? But to form the question this way assumes a language of correspondence, a descendent of Adamic/Cratyllic language, and this is not Levinas's view. He is more a descendent of Enkidu. The self must not thematize the other, and yet language is the only way in which one addresses the other. But language as conversation, as relation, does not (or need not) colonize the other. In its spontaneity, its improvisatory quality, in its attentiveness and responsiveness, language in this social sense allows the other to be what it may be—other and other to itself, resisting totalization from all sources. Moreover, precisely because (as Philo of Alexandria pointed out in a negative sense with regard to revelation) spoken language maintains a distance between speakers, because it is mediated, because it is subject to errors and ambiguitites, it can better maintain and preserve the alterities of the speakers. Language's inadequacy (in Adamic terms) is, for Levinas and Santner, its value (*Totality and Infinity* 40, 51–52).

The Prophet and the Fool

The moment of revelation portrayed in Exodus resulted in a universal impairment, and subsequent enhancement, of linguistic-cognitive capacity. Overwhelmed, deafened by divinity, the Israelites see God's voice—perhaps as script within a flame, or perhaps as some sequence of divine gestures, some natural-sacred signing which provides an "in-hearing" comparable to the more familiar Greek trope of insight. But the contents of that revelation—the Torah and its mitzvot, God's commandments for personal and community life—are exceedingly normative. As unsystematically assembled in the narratives and legal codes of the Tanakh and then as glossed in rabbinic commentaries, the revelation at Sinai inscribes a set of legal practices and norms of behavior pertaining to all areas of social life: property, debt, marriage and divorce, labor, and the state, as well as more specifically religious practices. It is noteworthy in itself that this exceedingly norm-driven prescription for life is said to derive from a moment of mass linguistic trauma and impairment. After Sinai, however, the universal experience of impairment, trauma, and revelation is restricted to the prophets, with Moses, who facilitated the revelation at Sinai, as prototype.

The prophet is a reminder and a renewal of revelation, a metonymic emissary bearing its original trauma and impairment. Himself linguistically impaired, he serves a disruptive, stammering social function, making apparent the disjunction between the trauma of revelation and the comfort of the social norms that derived from it—a comfort that extends further to the easing of those norms into new norms increasingly distanced from their painful introduction. The prophet's intention is to make life difficult, to condemn the normativity of ordinary life insofar as it has, inevitably, strayed from the rigors of those norms' original, revelatory inscription. While some of the Old Testament prophets exhibited foolish behavior—Ezekiel playing in the dirt, Jeremiah wearing an ox's yoke, Job sulking when Ninevah is not destroyed, Hosea's marrying a prostitute—in general, the Tanakh makes a clear distinction between the prophet and the fool. The prophet's proximity to revelation impairs his relation to language, but does not affect his intellect. Fools are mentioned prominently in the Tanakh's wisdom literature, the books of Proverbs and Ecclesiastes, but in these instances, the fool is, simply, a fool. He is continually being seduced by "forbidden" women (Proverbs 7:6–27); he ignores good advice (Proverbs 1:22; Ecclesiastes 4:13); he tries to persuade others to follow the path of folly (Proverbs 9:13–18). But the fool is always punished: "He whose speech is foolish comes to grief (Proverbs 10:9); "a rod is ready for the back of the senseless" (Proverbs 10:13). In this genre of wisdom literature, there is no overlapping of wisdom and folly. God created the world on a foundation of wisdom (Proverbs 3:19, 8:22), and wisdom consists simply in living according to prevailing social norms. Folly is a dangerous, self-destructive deviation from social norms. There is no sense, as in William Blake's reinterpretation of wisdom literature in *The Marriage of Heaven and Hell*, that "if the fool would persist in his folly, he would become wise."

The sacred fool is a Christian innovation, embodying a position entirely inimical to prevailing norms. Christian sacred folly exists in a world in which both revelation and prophecy have ceased and in which social norms have fallen away entirely from divine ordinance. Christ has come and gone, and the world can be truly redeemed only when he returns; but he does not return. All prophecies have been uttered—for, in Christian terms, they referred to the coming of Christ—and all revelation has been revealed, even the final one that removes the veils concealing the world's ending. And yet the world, in this middle moment of time between revelation and apocalypse, impossibly continues.[3] As an embattled, ridiculed group of believers holds to the truth of salvation through the crucified Christ, Paul lays out the social-theological context that makes the sacred fool both possible and necessary:

> Divine folly is wiser than the wisdom of man, and divine weakness stronger than man's strength. . . . [God] has chosen things low and contemptible, mere nothings, to overthrow the existing order. (Corinthians I.1:18–29)

In the depictions of revelation and prophecy that we examined in the Old Testament, there is a disjunction between ordinary language and the sacred. But the practice of religion and the practice of life are not so disjunct, and the contents of revelation and prophecy are normative and mundane. To live by the mitzvot revealed at Sinai does not require further excursions into alterity, as is made clear late in Deuteronomy:

> Surely, this instruction which I enjoin upon you this day is not too baffling for you, nor is it beyond reach. It is not in the heavens, that you should say, "Who among us can go up to the heavens and get it for us and impart it to us, that we may observe it?" Neither is it beyond the sea, that you should say, "Who among us can cross to the other side of the

sea and get it for us and impart it to us, that we may observe it?" No, the thing is very close to you, in your mouth and in your heart, to observe it. (30:11–14).

As in the wisdom literature, wisdom and adherence to the divine will are synonymous and synchronic with normative religious practice. When these norms are threatened, whether by a foreign power or domestic corruption, the prophet enters bearing the power of the alterity of the original revelation in order to renew the norms. In Paul's depiction, however, the smoothly functioning norm is itself the crisis, and so "wisdom" is the opposite of the "wisdom" of Proverbs and Deuteronomy. Divine wisdom is not close, not obvious, nor normative. It is possessed only by a few, and they will be regarded as fools. Indeed, since, for Paul, "fool" is a socially constructed category, they will be fools. In the context of prevailing norms, the Christian is cognitively disabled. He does not know what others know, and his knowledge is not considered knowledge. In such a scenario, it will take more than prophecy to set the world right. Paul's perspective is not prophetic, it is apocalyptic: his goal is the "overthrow" of "the existing order." "Ruin" is not the fate of the fool, as in Proverbs ("the mouth of the fool is an imminent ruin" [10:14]), but of the entire regime of what passes for sense and worldly wisdom. Only a fool would wish this, but, for Paul, divine alterity has departed definitively from the larger world and now can be perceived only as a form of cognitive impairment.

In the prophet and the sacred fool, we see two instances of linguistically or cognitively impaired figures embodying a society's relations between a symbolic-theological order and a nonlinguistic, or super-linguistic realm that is believed to ground that order. There is not space here to narrate the long history of the sacred fool, but his influence has been extensive even into the modern period.[4] It is fair to say, however, that the fool gradually absorbed the functions of the prophet. Why? The prophet stammered his imprecations toward a homogeneous community and toward a state dedicated to fulfilling the dictates, both spiritual and mundane, of the original revelation—a state, in fact, conceived by the first and most significant prophet and founded by his immediate successor. The prophet is usually in conflict with the state, but he is not of a fundamentally different order; he comes to remind, to rectify, not radically to transform. And because the divine and the worldly are not perceived to be completely at odds, the prophet is attended. His impaired speech is the socially recognized sign that he must be listened to. The fool, however, occupies a place outside the civic order. Even if his derangement is a pose, he wields no authority, and his real or assumed folly is a sign that the divine has no place in this world. The ultimate sacred fool in literature is Dostoevski's—not Myshkin, but Christ in Ivan Karamazov's parable. The church itself, in this tale, has established an efficient, modern, secular order, and Christ must be executed again in order to preserve it.

Can there, then, be degrees of alterity? Does otherness look different, or, indeed, is otherness different under different historical circumstances, or from different ideological perspectives? Certainly, it does, and is. Derek Attridge argues that the singularity, the uniquely literary quality of literature consists in its task of reimagining language so that alterity can be encountered. But alterity, otherness, the other is not some stable thing beyond representation that then enters language through various innovative tropic twists. Rather, each social-symbolic configuration requires and conceives its own others. Otherness, for Attridge, "is that which is, at a given moment, outside the horizon provided by the culture for thinking, understanding, imaginging, feeling, perceiving." Thus, otherness "is not simply 'out there' but is produced by the same operations that constitute what is familiar" (19). It is not "what is 'ineffable' or 'inexpressible' in a general sense, only . . . what cannot be thought or said in a particular culture at a particular time" (30).

But we must add to Attridge's thesis, what cannot and must be thought or said. Both the imperative and the impossibility will be specific to each culture. The conception of a divine that speaks through prophets is different from that of a divine that speaks through fools; and different from the conception of negative theologians of the middle ages; and different from the "wild child" constructed by Enlightenment philosophes; and from the modern incarnations of the wild child; and from the late-nineteenth- and early twentieth-century socio-medical constructions of the "idiot" or the "feeble-minded." And yet, all of these "others" and makers of others are in the position of Faulkner's Benjy who is "trying to say." So, in this way, we read, or compose our reading, as Gertrude Stein advises in the glorious extended stammer of "Composition as Explanation":

This makes the thing we are looking at very different and this makes
what those who describe it make of it, it makes a composition, it confuses, it shows, it is, it looks, it likes it as it is, and this makes what is seen
as it is seen. Nothing changes from generation to generation except the
thing seen and that makes a composition. (497)

There is another sense in which we might say that alterity is relative.
Research in neuroscience, going back to Broca and Wernacke in the
nineteenth century, but accelerating exponentially since the late twentieth century, has sought to describe mental functioning as electro-chem-
ical transactions in the brain. Understood in these terms, cognitive and
linguistic capacities and impairments fall along spectrums of ability,
and no human being can be regarded as other in a neurologically meaningful sense. This book's project, then, would seem to come to an end
when it reaches the present age of neuroscience. But it does not. The
notion of a spectrum calls into question older ideas of absolute alterity—the impaired figure as vessel of divinity, or of primal innocence or
animality—but it reinforces the perspectives seen in psychoanalysis and
in Santner and Harpham of a subject who is other to himself. Matthew
Belmonte writes of the autistic individual that he is "human, only more
so"—that is, possessing, though in differing proportion and emphasis,
the same powers and limits as people at other regions of the spectrum;
and at those limits, engaged likewise with an otherness now newly conceptualized as part of the human neuronal makeup.

We must distinguish in neuroscience between ideology and practice. The ideology of neuroscience claims that all of what we think of as
activities or products of mind are now, or will soon, or will ultimately be
explained entirely and without remainder as activities of the brain. As a
character in Jonathan Franzen's novel *The Corrections* explains, what we
thought we knew through philosophy or art or psychology, we now really
know through neuroscience. But the practice of neuroscience in both
its research and clinical tracks proves that the brain is too complicated
for this ever to be the case. The firing of mirror neurons or the brain's
capacity for constructing the points of view of others will not explain
fully how representation happens in any medium or genre, for these
neurological factors cannot take into account the histories of media or
genres, or the ideological tensions at work in any given representation.

Human physical evolution, after all, including the evolution of the brain, was complete at least a hundred thousand years before any narrative of human culture or history can be started. To the neuroscientist, the brains that executed the paintings at Lascaux, or the brains that first began to use symbols, are the same as the brains that composed *Gilgamesh*, *The Divine Comedy*, and *Finnegan's Wake*. Brains work in certain ways to manipulate symbols, to perceive human agency and imitate it in language, to organize events in time, to imagine situations as different from what they are, to lie, or to empathize, to give backrubs, to gossip, to sing, to coo to infants. Physically, neurologically, we have not evolved further. Our societies and social lives, our subjectivities, cultural products, technologies, genres, and ideologies, however, have changed. To say that all our cultural products are made possible by particularities of brain anatomy is to say at the same time everything and nothing. Obviously this is the case. But to say anything meaningful about cultural products, we must focus attention on the histories and social contexts of those products, since brain anatomy has remained the same. And to this we must add that now, when studying representations of cognitive and linguistic impairment, the new understandings indicated by neuroscience will be part of these histories and contexts.[5]

Catachresis as Character

As Wittgenstein pronounced, "in order to draw a limit to thinking we should have to be able to think both sides of this limit (we should therefore have to be able to think what cannot be thought). The limit can, therefore only be drawn in language and what lies on the other side of the limit will be simply nonsense" (*Tractatus* 27). This is true if one's primary desire is to establish a limit, to establish a set of terms that will determine a conceptual terrain, a totality. The goal, the limit, is the terminological terminus. The word is the ending, and beyond the terminal lies wilderness. But the reverse of Wittgenstein's dictum is also true. If one's primary desire is to conceive an unthinkable, bring an alterity into the lexicon, then one first must build a terminal where all the trains of the unspeakable can discharge their passengers. The negation must have something to negate; alterity requires a place from which to differ. The impaired figure is that point, transient and porous, just beyond terminology's terminal. It might be sitting on a wall, though the wall has encroached on territory that does not belong to its builders; it stands on a stolen boundary, perhaps for security purposes. Or it might be perched on a ladder about to be discarded— not at the top, but perhaps midway. It stands on no one's shoulders and has no vantage, but clings to the imagined waist of the structure.

The strange thing is that wherever it is, the impaired figure appears to be at the center. In a text, a verbal medium, a place composed entirely of words, the figure without words or with distorted words, the one outside the symbolic loop is placed at the moral, political, significatory center. Language is all. What became dogma in literary theory and some social science thinking was always a suspicion. How can there be thought, consciousness, a self, an other, or a social order without language? But with every linguistic turn (and Rorty's was far from the first), comes a counter-linguistic turn. Language is not all; it does not go "all the way down." There is more, there is matter, there is mother—and all that might follow from those beginnings: the body, the real, the abject, the semiotic, the divine, the sublime, excrement, death, angels animals infants, the stupid,[6] the echoing pulse of the circadian.[7] What could be more evident than that "I incorporate gneiss and coal and long-threaded moss and fruits and grains and esculent roots, and am stucco'd with quadrupeds and birds all over" (Whitman 55)? Utterance seems to mouth itself around the mute, even as every utterance takes its position in a synchronic and diachronic flux that, when forced to stay still, reveals the properties of a system.

If language is tropic, catachresis is the foundation of language, and the linguistically impaired figure in literature is the catachresis as character.[8] The problem of catachresis emerges in the act of defining it. In classical rhetoric and in dictionaries today, "catachresis" is an abuse of language: the use of the wrong word or of a word with a standard usage in one context dragged into a use against usage in another. "The sun sowed its rays." "I see a voice." *Kata*: against; *chresis*: use. But Quintillian enlarged this definition, making "catachresis" mean a word which "adapts to whatever has no proper term" (Par. 34). But what exactly is a "proper term"? After Babel, once we have abandoned or been deprived of a language of naming, we are left with a language of use in which terms can be appropriate, but no term can be precisely proper. The things of the world are precise, each object properly itself. But language is general. Each word—and not only nouns, but all parts of speech—stands for whole categories of things, actions, and qualities.[9] The only non-catachretic word could be a proper name, and even these designations lead to confusion. The opening half hour of James Cameron's *The Terminator* depicts the frustrations of searching for someone with a common name in a metropolitan phone book. And, of course, objects can shift from category to category. Melville's Ishmael considered whether a whale could be called a fish and concluded that it could, since it, apparently, quacked like a fish. A tomato is, according to biological categories, a fruit, but most of us prepare and eat it as a vegetable. Usages collide, and proper use in one vocabulary is an abuse in another.

If there are no proper terms, then catachresis is a general condition of language and, as Dumarchais wrote, "it rules in some fashion over all other figures," indeed, "over language itself" (q. in Parker 65). Seen in this way, catachresis and the tropes it rules are not luxuries or ornaments. As Cicero observed, they arise out of need, out of language's "poverty and deficiency" (q. in Parker 66). If truth, as Nietzsche expressed it so trenchantly, is a mobile army of metaphors, the catachrestic character of language ensures that we do not have to go into combat with only the Rumsfeldian army that we have. It ensures the possibility of innovation and makes language's poverty of proper reference its strength. To signify kata-chresis, against usage, can, of course, mean merely what Aristotle meant by metaphor: to summon a term from one context to signify in another. But in the more pervasive sense we have been exploring, catachresis is not just rearranging the verbiage in either a witty, illuminating, or ridiculous way. It means rather to extend the implied function of metaphor to its limits—to "bear across" not just from one verbal context to another, but from the inexhaustible, and inexhaustibly desired, realm of not-language into language. Catachresis refers to the wish enacted in language—in poetic language especially, but somehow in all language—to reach toward some place, some piece of consciousness or non-consciousness, outside of language. It is felt sometimes as nostalgia, sometimes as vertigo, or as ecstasy, or terror, or peace. This linguistic place is not enough, but how does one leave it? And how leave a note saying where you've gone?

I would cite three theoretical topoi—among many other possible ones—to provide analogous contexts for this discussion of catachresis.

Julia Kristeva's categories—"semiotic," "chora," or "abject"—propose ways of thinking the passage from non-language into language. Kristeva's semiotic is a rumbling, a babbling, the preverbal cooing and chirping exchanged with caresses between mother and baby (and so, in Kristeva's Lacanian psychoanalytic frame, in contrast to, and preceding, the Oedipal, paternal drama and sacrifice experienced in entering the symbolic). Kristevan catachresis is always a straddling, a bearing across of non-signifying elements into and out of language. The semiotic "can pass over, can be codified within the language of communication . . . constructed in grammar and logic." As this happens, however, "we reach a moment of distortion, a moment of rhetorical figures, rhythms and alliterations," which Kristeva refers to as "poetic language," but which to some degree occurs in all language (*Interviews* 212). At this moment of distortion, the moment of trope—of catachresis—Kristeva, we might say, "goes Adamic." The nonsymbolic elements of language "attempt to dissolve . . . the bar between signifier and signified," which Kristeva describes as "the first social censorship" and "first guarantee of the subject's position" (*Revolution* 50). That is to say, if translated to theology (and it is not too difficult a translation, even though Kristeva claims poetic language to be "atheological" [*Revolution* 49]), the semiotic in language reverses the Fall. The very processes, relations, and modes of identity that language removes us from are embedded in language. Even as it mediates and distances, language, for Kristeva, brims with immediacy and proximity.

This is the case as well in new work by Mutlu Konuk Blasing and Daniel Heller-Roazen. Both these writers stress language's simultaneous remembering and forgetting of the nonsymbolic. For Blasing, lyric poetry in its non-sensical materiality—which is to say, its form—is a conduit to the time before the acquisition of language. It is, she writes, "a culturally sanctioned discourse that allows us to remember—without remembering—the history that we are. In poetry, we recognize ourselves in an uncanny return of something long forgotten, our origins in the passage into symbolic language" (16). Through poetry, which "exploits the affective qualities of sounds, remembering the history of the production of speech sounds . . . the necessary ground of symbolic language may be 'retrieved'—remembered or imagined—out of the 'amnesia' of referential language, whose stability depends on infantile amnesia" (49). Heller-Roazen writes of the infant's babbling as the for-gotten source of all enunciation, indeed of an infinitude of languages that never came to be. To remember the infant's speech "would be only an echo, of another speech and of something other than speech: an echolalia" that made all speech possible (12). Writing of exclamations, "the unwelcome yet inalienable members of every phonological system that no language can do without and that none shall recognize as its own" (17), Heller-Roazen concludes that "a language in which one can-not cry out would not be a truly human language at all. . . . Nowhere is a language more 'itself' than at the moment it seems to leave the terrain of its sound and sense, assuming the sound shape of what does not—or cannot—have a language of its own. . . . It is here that one language, gesturing beyond itself in a speech that is none, opens itself to the non-language that precedes it and that follows it" (18). Heller-Roazen con-cludes his book by situating all of us in the ruins of Babel.

"The Idiot Boy"

More than any other literary text, Wordsworth's "The Idiot Boy" brings the portrayal of cognitive impairment into contact with the dys-/disar-ticulating discourses of modernity. As Alan Bewell and Avital Ronell have described, Wordsworth was deeply engaged with Enlightenment thinking regarding the "wild child" and the "idiot" as living Lockean blank slates who could serve as test cases of the presence of innate moral and intellectual features or the determining influence of socialization and language. In the figure of Johnny, the poem's "idiot" protagonist, Wordsworth presents a secular version of the sacred fool, in whom the sacred is transformed into ethical and aesthetic manifestations. Unlike contemporaneous thinking on wild children, Wordsworth's concerns are not primarily anthropological or epistemological. The boundary of language in "The Idiot Boy" is uncrossable by means of conventional language. The encounter with Johnny is an impasse of traditional forms of representation, but also provides access to a new poetic form whose foundation is a metaphorical or catachretic friction with alterity. Thus, "The Idiot Boy" concludes with an entry into an aesthetics of the sub-lime or avant-garde. And this new aesthetics, which eludes traditional genres, is located in a social class position that, for Wordsworth, also implies an ethical position. Wordsworth, in effect, confronts traditional poetics with a modern poetics, but confronts modern philosophy with what he sees as a more traditional ethics.

Johnny, the developmentally disabled son of Betty Foy, though not altogether outside of language, is inaccessible to prevailing discourses. At two points in the poem, Johnny is the object of conjectures that proceed along well-traveled paths. As she searches for her son, Betty anxiously speculates as to what might have become of him. Perhaps, she thinks, he drowned in trying "to hunt the moon within the brook" or perhaps he climbed into a hollow tree or perhaps he has joined the gypsies or was carried by his pony to a hall of goblins (212–31). Later, the poem's narrator likewise wonders what his protagonist might be doing, again prefacing his conjectures with a series of "perhapses." Perhaps, on top of a hill, Johnny has grasped a star and put it in his pocket; perhaps he now rides backwards on his pony, "all silent as a horseman ghost" (325); perhaps he is hunting sheep, "a fierce and dreadful hunter he" (328); or "Perhaps, with head and heels on fire, / And like the very soul of evil, / He's galloping away, away" (312–36). These conjectures, of course, are of different types. Betty's are quite serious, while the narrator's are part a humorous self-deprecation that ends with his berating the muses for abandoning him at the crucial moment of his story. But both sets of conjecture attempt to place Johnny in some generic occult or heroic narrative, whether earnest or comic, and all these conjectures fail. Johnny is outside of genre and beyond the reach of the muses.

Nevertheless, or, rather, because of this discursive inaccessibility, Johnny's entry into language at the end of the poem creates poetry of a new kind. His impairment transforms conventional language into a troped, indexical poetics. It points and twists at the same time. Johnny pulls the non-linguistic experience across its boundary into a language that misnames and by misnaming conveys a truth. When the non-linguistic is borne across into language, if it is to maintain its truth it must create an impaired language. "The cocks did crow to-whoo, to-whoo, / And the sun did shine so cold!" (449–50). Johnny's language here resembles the sensory confusion of Biblical revelation, but refigured as an experimental poetics. Ronell makes this point succinctly: "Poetry is the idiot boy" (275). The idiot in Wordsworth cannot be reached by the muse because he is the muse.

Wordsworth's impaired figure is, then, the focus of a new poetry of radical metaphor that drags otherness into language. The impaired figure is able, in poetry, to fulfill the role in which he was cast, but was unable to play in philosophy: "to occupy," as Alan Bewell put it, "the threshold between nature and man"—or, we might say, between the non-linguistic and language—"a figure linking the two states" (57), a figure, thus, intrinsically catachretic. But Johnny as catachresis is located, and problematized, in precise social and ethical contexts. Betty, Johnny, and Susan live in a setting of rural poverty and isolation in an England beginning its transformation into an urban, industrial society. Economic, political, and scientific ideological tendencies sought to render into discourse and to regulate the mentally impaired figure that Wordsworth portrayed as outside of discourse. Already Blake could write of walking through London's "chartered streets" beside a "chartered Thames." The impulse in Locke, Condillac, and other Enlightenment thinkers—quite evident in most philosophical responses to wild children and the developmentally disabled—was to regard language and socialization as the primary, or even the sole, determinants in subjectivity, as thus establishing the charter, the grid, for all social relations. There is a thematic line—swerving, varied, but inexorable—from Blake's chartered streets of Enlightenment Urizen to Heidegger's world picture, Levinas's totality, Althusser's version of Lacan's symbolic order, Adorno and Horkheimer's dystopic reading of Enlightenment, and early twentieth-century ideologies of eugenics. The theme is the elimination of alterity through the creation of a thoroughly rationalized world. The agent of that aspiring rationality in "The Idiot Boy" is the doctor whom Johnny goes to fetch but never finds, who dismisses Betty's desperate query with "The devil take his wisdom! . . . What, woman, should I know of him?" (258–60).

"The Idiot Boy" is a key founding text in a modern counter-discourse that seeks to maintain and elaborate a catachretic relation with otherness, and not allow it to be absorbed into philosophical, scientific, or political languages of rationality. In "The Idiot Boy," alterity (as non-language) is embodied in Johnny and uttered through his impaired, catachretic poetics. But of equal importance, alterity is maintained, is allowed to exist and to flourish owing to Johnny's acknowledged place in a family and community. The aesthetics he creates and embodies is made possible by an ethics—by the fact that he is loved and cared for. The poem as a whole is oriented around care, its actions motivated by care. Old Susan Gale, "she who dwells alone," is not alone. When she is ill, her neighbor Betty attends her and sends Johnny, "him whom she loves," to bring the doctor. When Johnny does not return, Betty is compelled to search for him. "Consider, Johnny's but half-wise," Betty tells Susan; "We must take care of him" (188–89). Susan, then, recovers from her ailment because of her care, manifested as anxiety, for Betty and Johnny: "And as her mind grew worse and worse, / Her body—it grew better" (415–16). Johnny, finally, can announce his impaired-poetic disclosure only because he has been found by his mother.

Wordsworth, in a letter of 1802, expressed his sense of the position of the cognitively impaired in contexts of family, ethics, spirituality, and social class. Referring to attitudes of "loathing and disgust" that upper-class people in particular felt toward the cognitively impaired, Wordsworth wrote that these attitudes were evidence of "a false delicacy" and, more fundamentally, "a certain want of comprehensiveness of thinking and feeling." People of the lower classes, Wordsworth continued, do not share this lack in moral sensibility. "If an Idiot is born in a poor man's house it must be taken care of and cannot be boarded out, as it would by gentle folks, or sent to a public or private receptacle for such unfortunate beings." In fact, a cognitively impaired person was often considered a blessing to a family since, as Wordsworth put it, "their life is hidden with God." Ultimately, for Wordsworth, the treatment of cognitively impaired people represented the supreme test of moral behavior: "I have indeed often looked upon the conducts of fathers and mothers of the lower classes of society towards Idiots as the great triumph of the human heart. It is there that we see the strength, disinterestedness, and grandeur of love" (q. in Bewell 54–55).

"The Idiot Boy" is oriented toward and grounds its aesthetics in care as bestowed in family and community relationships in a particular historical and class setting. These relationships of care, however, are presented as threatened and tenuous. Care for Johnny is expressed largely as anxiety as he leaves the home and travels into the larger world. His linguistic dysarticulation continually threatens to become a social disarticulation, and his eventual discovery by his mother—the poem's happy, comic ending—has a certain magic, improbable air. It is wished for, both by Betty and by the reader, but one feels that a tragic outcome might, in reality, be more likely. Again, the threats of social or familial severing and of physical harm as he leaves the home correspond to the ideological and social changes with regard to mental impairment that Wordsworth sees as products of a new era. If Johnny is not found by his mother, he will quite likely be taken by civil authorities and institutionalized or will blend into the growing ranks of urban poverty, ultimately to be destroyed. An ethics of care, for Wordsworth, means to resist these forces of modernization, to maintain a traditional, familial, and sentimental relation to cognitive impairment. It means also to resist the philosophical violence in which Wordsworth himself partly participates in this poem by making the impaired figure the poetic conduit for the non-linguistic. As Avital Ronell argues, Enlightenment discourses of the non-linguistic make muteness a form of mutilation and the figure of the idiot "a kind of holding pen for linguistic violence." The Enlightenment's non-linguistic other, in Ronell's reading, as manifested in the wild child or the idiot, "commences in disfigurement, as the mutilation over which the philosophers tried to write in an attempt to restore the proper, the literal, what is proper to man" (253). What is proper to man for Wordsworth, however, is not the propriety expressed in reason but the "great triumph of the human heart" as shown in caring for the most vulnerable. In Wordsworth's ethics, the mutilation, or disarticulation, that would be practiced on the idiot by the discourses and institutions of modernity is instead directed toward those very discourses, indeed toward language itself. The dys-/disarticulation of language by the being outside of language creates an avant-garde poetics which, while secular, resembles the language of revelation—and has religious implication insofar as the idiot's life is "hidden with God." And this poetics is grounded in a traditional, even Christian ethics: "That which you do to the least of my brothers you do to me."

But care, in this text and in others that we will examine, has an interesting restriction. In care with regard to the dys-/disarticulate, there can be no place for the erotic. In "The Idiot Boy," care is a mother's domain. The father is a woodcutter who spends the week away in the forest. The bond between mother and son, and the feelings of the mother for her son, are intense. Some erotic feeling would seem to be implied, especially since the Oedipal drama has apparently been resolved in the son's favor, the father being gone. But for care to work in the ethical sense that the poem intends, any erotic implication must be suppressed. Johnny is a non-sexual or pre-sexual being. Betty has no sexual relation, indeed, no relation at all, with her husband that we can see. Susan Gale dwells alone. In modernist texts like Conrad's *The Secret Agent* and Faulkner's *The Sound and the Fury*, the central ethical relationship is between a cognitively impaired brother and his sister, and "The Idiot Boy" could be transposed to this form quite easily. Betty, in effect, has no husband, and the elderly Susan Gale could be read as mother to both Betty and Johnny. The ethical question, after all, is not how a parent treats a child—that much should be obvious—but how one treats one's brother. The original biblical crime was fratricide, and Christ's moral challenge concerned the treatment of brothers. In Wordsworth and in the modernist texts, the mother/sister is wholly invested in the impaired son/brother, and in this almost fused relationship, the erotic, incestuous component is bypassed and reinvested in care. There is a singleness, a desperateness, a jealousy of devotion even when its object is not yet lost which resembles erotic fixation. But for the ethical to function in these texts, and thus for the catachretic function to become active, the otherness of language to emerge, the erotic must be suppressed, and it is.

Or it reemerges in the catachresis; it is carried across along with the rest of the alterity into a troped, transfigured language. That seems to be the case in "The Idiot Boy." First, Johnny's repeated prelinguistic noise—his "burring," "the noise he loves" (100)—seems akin to Kristeva's presymbolic, maternal semiotic or to Heller-Roazen's infantile echolalia, the sounds made by infants that are not later incorporated into any language, or to Blasing's depictions of the origins of lyric in the material, non- or pre-symbolic parts of language. All these versions of the non-symbolic, sonic sources or exteriors of language stress its rhythmic, repetitive character, conveying a sense of infantile eroticism; and there seems likewise in Johnny's burring and his joyous expectation of his journey a sense of erotic anticipation. Further, in keeping with the mock-heroic tone of the poem's narration, the pony on which Johnny rides is a humble kin to Pegasus, the steed of poetic flight, and there seems at least a sexual germ in the narrator's imagining of Johnny's contorted manner of horsemanship—"his face unto the horse's tail" (323). Finally, in poetic language itself, achieved through escape from and return to motherly or sisterly nurture, the transgressive eroticism suppressed in that relation is released with a more general address. To whom did the cocks (owls) crow? ("To-whoo, to-whoo")?

An ur-text of modern depictions of cognitive and linguistic impairment, "The Idiot Boy" illustrates clearly features that will occupy this book's subsequent analyses. We see first the inaccessibility of the impaired figure to discourse and at the same time his overdetermination by numerous discourses—of philosophy, science, religion, aesthetics, sociology, for example. The representation of the impaired figure becomes a site of conflict among the discourses that construct it. As part of this conflict, as both empty and overly filled, the impaired figure is an object of projection of the wishes and fears of other characters and of readers. There is never a moment at which someone does not want the impaired figure to be or to signify one thing or another, and thus to further contribute to his overdetermination. These representational tensions contribute furthermore toward an ethical content which then rebounds back toward the representations. This occurs in two ways. First, as I just described with regard to "The Idiot Boy," issues of care are crucial to all the texts under discussion. And the concept of care is not unproblematic, as we have seen already in its relation to sexuality and as we will see further in other ways. Second, in all these texts, we face questions of the ethics of representation. Are there limits to how a cognitively impaired person ought to be represented, and, if so, how does one determine those limits?

Project and Overdetermine: Dis-/Dys- Articulation and Modern Literature

As we have seen, Wordsworth's "Idiot Boy" combines tendencies found in the sacred fool and the wild child, and introduces as well ways of thinking and writing more characteristic of modern literature: the impaired figure's location in a marginal social setting; his inaccessibility to the symbolic, and thus his availability both to projection on the part of the other characters and the narrator, and to a textual overdetermination as a result of these projections; his languages's potential to function as an avant-garde poetics; his position as figure of opposition to (and potential victim of) the modern world-as-system; and his role as an object of care. Though the lost boy is at last found by his mother, their reunion is miraculous. The poem's logic is one of dys-/disarticulation as a catachretic impasse of language is conflated with a real or threatened social severing. Let me now turn to two texts that will clarify these tendencies and prepare the way for the chapters that follow. Carson McCullers's *The Heart is a Lonely Hunter* illustrates the problematics of the projection of desire onto a "mute" figure presumed to understand and thus redeem individual subjects. This presumption, of course, is the central projection, and all the projection onto the deaf character, John Singer, is made necessary by McCullers's presentation of the failure of sociality in general and political action in particular.

> How Singer had been before was not important. The thing that mattered was the way Blount and Mick made of him a sort of home-made God. Owing to the fact he was a mute they were able to give him all the qualities they wanted him to have. Yes. But how could such a strange thing come about? And why? (232)

That is the book in a nutshell, in both its assertions and its questions. It is a simple premise, told in simple language, as if it were a fable or some lost chapter from Genesis. But the novel's complexity comes, first, in the nature of the fantastic identifications projected onto Singer and, second, in the text's relation to itself—that is, in the text's own fantasies of sociality and isolation, the possibilities of politics, and the work of language. The novel, as I will argue, engages in a conflict against its narrative. It began, as we see from an earlier draft, with a strong and central political impulse and, in the end of the published version, returns to that impulse. But the bulk of the narrative—that is, the story of the characters' relations with John Singer—not only abandons but disparages political action, and identifies failures in social relations as manifestations of some universal, existential aporia. McCullers's novel, published in 1940, was conceived as a novel of the 1930s—contemporaneous in time and spirit with the work of Steinbeck and Wright—but delivered as a novel of the 1950s, closer in tone and tendency to Malamud and O'Connor.[10]

The Heart is a Lonely Hunter is, most obviously, about the need for genuine communication and social contact. The characters speak repeatedly of their need for some other "who will understand" their deepest feelings and aspirations. But some force or forces—it is not clear what—block communication and understanding. Dialogue is impossible; what occurs instead are a series of monologues with a non-speaking other who is presumed to understand all. Mick, Blount, and Dr. Copeland see in John Singer a listener exactly attuned to their deepest concerns. Indeed, the entire town experiences Singer as a repository of identificatory fantasies, as "the Jews said that he was a Jew. The merchants . . . claimed he received a large legacy and was a very rich man. It was whispered in one browbeaten textile union that the mute was an organizer for the C.I.O. A lone Turk . . . claimed passionately to his wife that the mute was Turkish . . . [and] that when he spoke his language the mute understood" (200). Singer, analogously, regards his friend Antonopoulos in the same way: "This was the friend to whom he told all that was in his heart. . . . He watched the things that were said to him. And in his wisdom he understood" (204).

No one requires any actual confirmation of this understanding. The individual voice comes out of solitude and is received in silence; dialogue in this novel results in dissension. The other who understands can only be someone at the margins of language, a magic, transcendent presence, or, in the psychological terms the novel suggests, an imaginary, projected site of fulfilled desire. And the novel's central and obvious irony is that the one presumed to understand in fact understands very little. Singer's lip-reading skills are imperfect, and he misses a great deal of the language directed at him. His limitations in understanding Mick's passionate discussions of her love of music are obvious. "She knows I am deaf but she thinks I know about music," he writes in an unsent letter to Antonopoulos (215). Similarly, though less obviously, Singer's naive, conventional notions of politics prevent him from understanding either Jake Blount's Marxist explanations of class conflict or Dr. Copeland's views on race. And the emptiness of these investments in the linguistically impaired figure is reinforced in Singer's relationship with Antonopoulos. This friend whom Singer addresses as "you who understand" is, as McCullers presents him, a grotesque, self-absorbed man with minimal linguistic abilities in any mode, whose primary interests are food and masturbation.[11]

Even when a possibility for communication seems to arise, it cannot materialize. Copeland and Jake attempt quite sincerely to arrive at a

political consensus that will bring together struggles for racial and economic justice, but they end in bitter argument. And Singer, after Antonopoulos's death, finds a possible community with other deaf people he
meets in a pool hall, but cannot join with them. In fact, at this moment,
he unconsciously mimics the anti-social style of Antonopoulos, behav-
ing so peculiarly that the others shun him. Yet while this impossibility of
sociality and communication is the narrative's central theme and is presented in the clearest terms, with the deaf Singer as its pivotal figure, it is
not a stable or coherent category, and nor is Singer stable or coherent.

Sociality is impossible in *The Heart is a Lonley Hunter* for two quite
separate and sufficient reasons, and in the separation of these reasons
lies the text's instability. Genuine social relations are impossible because
of flaws in the political-economic system. And genuine social relations
are impossible because of some universal or existential condition. These
explanations are mutually incompatible, and the linguistically impaired
figure stands in the gap between them. In the first case, the impasse is
amenable to reform; in the second, it is not. And in the second case,
John Singer functions as a clear synecdoche for the universal condition, while in the first case, he is a catachresis for a condition that cannot properly be uttered or heard. Paradoxically, the universal or existential—presumably more vague and nameless—condition achieves a
precise naming in this novel, while the political and economic conditions are rendered unutterable. The linguistically impaired figure here
is a mistake, an abuse of language (catachresis in its purest etymologi-
cal sense) in that Singer's role in the novel is to miscarry the narrative
from a political impulse to an existential or spiritual one—to render
the universal precise and localized, and the political unspeakable and
incomprehensible.[12]

Given the novel's initial and subsequent reception, it is easy to forget
that *The Heart is a Lonely Hunter* is a novel of the 1930s, a novel of the
Depression. Even Richard Wright, in a review of 1940, praised McCuller's depiction of Dr. Copeland as the most fully realized, most human,
portrayal of an African American ever written by a white author. But
the author of *Native Son* did not mention McCullers's depiction of the
Marxist labor organizer, Jake Blount. What has seemed most evident
about this text is the universal pathos of frustrated human striving for
community, or, in more sophisticated readings, the underlying striving

for broader conceptions of gender and sexuality. But more thoroughly closeted than queerness in this text is politics. In the proposal she submitted to Houghton Mifflin in 1938 ("Author's Outline for 'The Mute'"), McCullers's political concerns are paramount. "Human beings are innately cooperative," McCullers wrote, "but an unnatural social tradition makes them behave in ways that are not in accord with their deepest nature" (124). Jake's goal in her outline was to change the prevailing "predatory, unnatural social conditions" (131). Regarding Mick, McCullers explained that "her tragedy does not come in any way from herself. She is robbed of her freedom and energy by an unprincipled and wasteful society" (128). And in the proposal's greatest single divergence from the novel, McCullers described Jake and Dr. Copeland achieving a genuine understanding: "Their dialogue comes from the marrow of their inner selves. They both lapse into the rhythmic, illiterate vernacular of their early childhood. The inner purpose of each man is seen fully by the other. In the course of a few hours these two men, after a lifetime of isolation, come as close as it is possible for two human beings to be" (143). In the novel, of course, Blount and Copeland's efforts at dialogue fail bitterly, and they find no way to link the politics of race and of class.

At the same time, however, McCullers's description of the communion achieved by Blount and Copeland allows us to see both the novel's original political emphasis and its circumvention through the figure of Singer. Each man sees the other's "inner purpose," which is political. But their dialogue, as McCullers describes it, stands outside of language and ideology. They are united not in language but in "the rhythmic, illiterate vernacular of their early childhood"—that is, in some equivalent of Kristeva's chora, Heller-Roazen's echolalia, or Blasing's lyric—in some necessary precursor of language that extends into language but that is not, properly speaking, language, not part of the social-symbolic order, not attached to ideology. The conciliation of these two deeply committed political minds is of an order deeper than politics and does not appear to be, in fact, political at all. It is, rather, spiritual, elemental, beyond and beneath language and symbolic usage. And this is the direction McCullers ultimately took, except that the sub- or super-verbal communion was shifted from a status of achievement to one merely of desire. And thus we get Singer, the one who understands—who is presumed, desired to understand—without the use of language.

But McCullers does not just circumnavigate her original impulse toward social justice in favor of a desired though fictitious spiritual-emotional communion represented in the linguistically impaired figure of John Singer. *The Heart is a Lonely Hunter* notably disparages political action. Blount is not merely "unwilling to compromise," does not merely "vacillate between hate and the most unselfish love," as McCullers put it in her "Author's Outline (131). He is egregiously ineffective as a political organizer—frequently drunk, irascible, and utterly unable to meet people on their own terms and then move them from inertia, despair, or anger toward political action. Similarly, Dr. Copeland is a signally ineffective advocate for racial justice. To say, as McCullers did in her proposal, that "the great flaw in all his theories is that he will not admit the racial culture of the Negro" (133) is a vast understatement. Copeland cannot communicate with anyone. His intellectual and ethical model is Spinoza who, in his mind, merges both with John Singer and with Christ. Copeland seeks to emulate an excommunicated apostate who seeks to liberate the thinking of his people but can only express himself in a highly specialized, generally incomprehensible language. Political action is impossible insofar as political activists share in the same communicative impasses that characterize society as a whole. The problem, then, is not so much the "predatory and unnatural social conditions" to which McCullers alluded in her proposal as it is a general problem of language, or the human communicative apparatus, itself. The problem is the human condition, whose most salient aspiration is for communion without dialogue, for a deep sociality without the mess of an actual society.

One might point out that McCullers's depiction of the failure of racial and class struggles in the South in the late 1930s is not historically inaccurate, but failure is not the whole story. Delma Eugene Presley suggests that Jake Blount is partly based on Fred Beal, an organizer for the National Textile Union, who helped plan an unsuccessful strike at the Loray Mill in Gastonia, North Carolina, in 1929. McCuller lived in Charlotte in 1937 and heard then about the Loray strike and Beal's role (Presley 106). It is true that the Loray strike failed, and that it resulted in serious violence; the police chief of Gastonia and one of the leading local labor activists, Ella May Wiggins, were both murdered over the course of the strike. But it is not the case that the strike failed, or that the labor movement in the South as a whole was stymied because the organizers were ineffectual Jake Blounts. Beal and the other NTU organizers were described as "a flamboyant lot" (Whalen 29), but did a creditable job given the physical violence and ideological aggression from local press and politicians that opposed them. Beal, according to historian John Salmond, was "first and foremost an organizer, with little patience for theoretical or ideological concerns" (18). And, much unlike Jake Blount, Beal had great tolerance for people's failures and frailties. He understood, as Salmond put it, that "the scab of today was the striker of tomorrow" (68). Moreover, even in the difficult times of the late 1930s in the South—with violent union-busting, a seemingly eternal system of racial oppression, and continuing economic depression—the failure of social reform and the abandonment of political action were not foregone conclusions. Katherine Du Pre Lumpkin, a southern liberal associated with New Deal policy makers, expressed cautious optimism in *The South in Progress* (1940) that local activists backed by the ideological, political, and financial power of the federal government could significantly improve economic and racial conditions. The South, Lumpkin insisted, "has been moving toward the threshold of great progress" (233) and cited as "one of the most encouraging signs of change" the willingness of "progressive white Southerners" to welcome the participation of African Americans in progressive causes (227). Lumpkin noted with satisfaction the success of an interracial Conference for Human Welfare held in 1938 in Birmingham, Alabama, where representatives of labor and civic groups discussed progressive tax codes, voting rights, and broader application of the National Labor Relations Act (230). As historians Robin Kelly and Glenda Gilmore have documented, there was a great variety of political activism centered on union organizing and racial justice in the South in the late 1930s. The fact that these efforts largely failed need not be attributed either to the personal incompetence of the activists or to universal failures of language. These failures, rather, seem to bear out the warning Lumpkin issued tempering her optimism, that if the "essentials of sound public policy are circumvented or, worse, flouted, the door of progress will have been slammed in the South's face" (233).

McCullers's disparaging depiction of political action, then, was a thematic choice, not a concession to a self-evident historical reality. The central role of the linguistically liminal John Singer as a universal site of projected desire necessarily results in a problematizing of language and thus of the purposeful use of language in political action. Singer as character emerges out of a perceived impasse of language and politics and then becomes such a compelling character that he further facilitates these impasses. Each further investment in Singer as "home-made god," as Biff calls him (232), continues the novel's movement away from its earlier political commitments. And it is not just the characters (including, of course, Singer himself, in Antonopoulos) who make these investments, but the text itself. Even as the text explicitly, to the point of obviousness, indicates the emptiness of its characters' projections, the text remains enthralled to their emotional logic and can present no alternative to them. The site outside of language—that object of deepest hope revealed as an empty space, further revealed as circumlocution or catachresis for a language of social reform—is, in the end, again the object of deepest hope. Its catachretic otherness stands, not balanced but somehow suspended, on the same language that debunks its authority.

But at the end of the novel, political concerns return. Owing to economic pressures on her family, Mick is forced to quit high school, abandon her after-school musical studies, and take a job at Woolworth's. Her dilemma prompts her to issue a mystified critique of capitalism: "It was like she was cheated. Only nobody had cheated her. So there was nobody to take it out on. However, just the same she had that feeling. Cheated" (354). What had cheated her, of course, was the "predatory and wasteful" economic and political system that she is too deeply submerged in to recognize. A Fred Beal might now be able to move her toward a more conscious and radical politics, though Jake Blount probably could not. But this powerful, though preliminary, intuition can occur only after John Singer is dead. Singer's disarticulation from the novel creates space for political perception to reemerge. Yet it seems that the narrative deck still is stacked and its reasoning circular, for the social and symbolic conditions that made Singer necessary are still in force. "It was like she was cheated. Only nobody had cheated her." The oppressive work of the social-symbolic order still is unarticulatable. Mick's use of the negative is Odyssean. Who had cheated her? "Nobody"—just as, previously, that same "nobody" had sustained her. The place of the "mute" "Singer," the one who understands, is finally taken by the ideology of capitalism—which it had earlier displaced. Both, in this novel, are posited as unknowable, unspeaking, and unspeakable. To understand and to cheat become the same. All catachretic terminologies ultimately converge.

Such convergences are even more powerfully present in *Billy Budd*. As *The Heart is a Lonely Hunter* shows, the linguistically impaired figure is a site of projected desire—for his fellow characters, for the author, for readers, and for the text itself. Going further, *Billy Budd* demonstrates what McCuller's text hints at but does not explore explicitly: that this desire is projected amid widespread, already existing, and often long-standing textual contexts and traditions of literature, religion, science, philosophy, and politics. The figure outside or at the borders of language functions as a cipher; any desire can be projected onto him. But he is also, simultaneously, overfull, a site of textual overdetermination. *Billy Budd* presents exceptionally clearly the modern sense that all phenomena have been discursively accounted for, whether by science or in some philosophical system; that there is nothing that does not conform to some antecedent or archtype; that this discursive overdetermination is oppressive and deceptive, and must somehow be shattered. Billy, with his stutter that places him at crucial moments outside of discourse, is then both the object and emblem of overdetermination and the source of the violent blow that would puncture the social-symbolic-ideological order. The violent catachresis of that blow, however, is instantly reintegrated into the discursive system by Captain Vere and the narrator.

To read *Billy Budd* is to enter a world of massive allusiveness. Billy is first placed under the general category of the "handsome sailor," a term carrying its own range of allusion—the star Aldebaran and the descendents of Ham (since the initial example of the handsome sailor is African). Billy thereafter is referred to as "Baby" (4), an Irish priest (6), "my peacemaker" (7), "like the animals . . . a fatalist" (9), "all but feminine in purity of natural complexion" (10), a statue of Hercules (11), a dog (12), a barbarian (12), Caspar Hauser (13), a beautiful woman in a Hawthorne story (13), David (36), a young horse (42), Hyperion (45), "young Adam before the fall" (52), a vestal priestess buried alive (56), an "angel of God" (58), a dog again (64), Isaac before his sacrifice (71), a sleeping child (75), a barbarian again (76), an angel—with reference to the early word for the English, the "angles"—(76), a beautiful English girl (77), a pre-Christian savage (77). Even as we read Billy as in some sense outside the symbolic order—as animal, child, feminine, barbaric, angelic, pre-lapsarian—we encounter him through symbolic markers of his outside status, each with long textual traditions. Susan Mizruchi is right to observe that Billy is "the most overdetermined character in American fiction" (149), and this overdetermination applies in lesser degrees to Claggart and Vere, and as well to the novel's plot.

But reading *Billy Budd* today entails another level of overdetermination, for to read this text means also to encounter at least some of the extensive commentary that has been written on it since its publication in 1924. The text's ambiguity now is part of an interpretive history, and that history of commentary is now, in effect, part of the text—just as, in normative Judaism, Talmudic commentaries on the Torah have become part of the Torah: an "oral Torah" revealed at Sinai, according to some traditions, along with the written text. To read the text today is to find oneself gravitating toward already established interpretive positions: the tale is conservative or radical, told straight by a reliable narrator or ironically by an ideologically limited narrator; or the text establishes such distinctions in order to show their inevitable blurring (cf. Cameron); or the mingling of theological and sociological or historical references indicates the anthropological underpinnings of Melville's thought, especially with regard to ideas of sacrifice (cf. Mizruchi); or these very interpretive differences serve in the text to manifest the problematics of interpretation, and so *Billy Budd* is, most fundamentally, the story of a conflict between approaches to reading (cf. Johnson). Finally, since Eve Sedgewick's monumental essay in *Epistemology of the Closet*, this novel has been an exemplary instance for queer readings.[13] Thus, to read *Billy Budd* is to step into the discursive histories that precede the text and form the logic of Melville's vast allusiveness and to step into the discursive histories that have followed the text's publication.

But at the center of this overdetermined text that demands such concern with textuality and interpretation is the moment when language is interrupted—the stutter—and, in that momentary absence of language, Billy's fatal blow to Claggart. The stutter, the interruption, the violent punctuation before the resumption is, as Barbara Johnson emphasizes, "the pivot on which the entire story turns" (94). The point is not, however, as Johnson argues, to illustrate how "language conveys only its own mechanical functioning" (94)—a position we can now, in retrospect, recognize as a standard deconstructive position from the time Johnson wrote her essay. Nor, I think, is it to show, as in Sharon Cameron's argument, how the rhetoric of Billy Budd, like a stutter, continually "asserts and retracts assertion" (183). Johnson and Cameron each spell out important aspects of the aporetic character of language in Melville. I would like to show further how Billy's linguistic impairment develops Melville's longstanding concern with the relation between language, or a symbolic-social order, and some other to that order. Melville's work, at crucial moments, thematizes the distinction between social convention, or human law and justice, and some indistinct, barely nameable thing outside the discursive realm.[14] For Ahab, the white whale serves as emblem for all that is unnameable and antithetical to human order—an alterity wholly other that inspires terror and must be extirpated. This alterity, however, is also translated—carried across—into the symbolic order in the mode of ambiguity or polysemeity. To extirpate the other, which traumatically transformed Ahab into a mixed, prostheticized, hybrid being, would be to restore a desired singleness of meaning. But then *Moby Dick* is a prolonged essay against Ahab's views on alterity. The whale, in all probability, is just a whale, an animal lacking symbolic capacity, and his malevolent spiritual properties are Ahab's projections. The true "other" in *Moby Dick*, we might say, is the narrator, "Ishmael," who claims the name of the alien wanderer who is also the first-born son.

But in later work, the wholly other, the other as outside the social-symbolic, comes closer to social life, so close as to merge with it. One need not seek for radical alterity in the South Seas; it may, like Bartleby, take up residence in your office. The relation with alterity is spelled out most explicitly and problematically in the pamphlet in *Pierre* on the distinction between the categories of the horological and the chronometric. A true chronometer, the pamphlet explains, keeps true Greenwich time no matter where in the world it is carried. This absolute time- keeping corresponds to divine morality which is invariable across all places and epochs. In contrast to chronometric time is horological time—that is to say, local time. And while chronometric time is true, it cannot be adhered to. It would involve one in "all manner of absurdities:—going to bed at noon, say, when his neighbors would be sitting down to dinner" (*Pierre* 212). The same absurdity, the pamphlet argues, applies in the realm of moral chronometrics and horologicals. Christ, the prime example of a chronometric soul, insisted that one turn the

other cheek when struck or give all one has to the poor, but clearly such
behaviors are impossible in the world we live in and so cannot be reasonably expected. Rather, the pamphlet concludes, "in things terrestrial
(horological) a man must not be governed by ideas celestial (chronometrical)," and in consequence, "a virtuous expediency . . . seems the
highest desirable or attainable earthly excellence for the mass of men"
(214). Any person who attempts to live chronometrically "will but array
all men's earthly time-keepers against him, and thereby work himself
woe and death," as "plainly evinced in the character and fate of Christ"
(212–13). And, the pamphlet adds, the case of Christ was unique, since
he was "entirely without folly or sin"; "inferior beings" who attempt a
chronometric life will inevitably involve themselves in "strange, unique
follies and sins, unimagined before" (213).

    This astonishing blending of prudence and cynicism forms the envi-
ronment for much of Melville's most important work. The lawyer-nar-
rator in "Bartleby, the Scrivener," Amaso Delano in "Benito Cereno,"
and Captain Vere in Billy Budd are perfect instances of the virtues and
consequences of the horological life. Bartleby, Babo, and Billy appear to
be crushed embodiments of the chronometrical.

    In "Bartleby," the lawyer-narrator is, like Vere, thoughtful and flexible
in his conservatism; compassionate, essentially good-hearted, but firm
in his ultimate commitment to the horological—to the social order as it
is. The lawyer, finally, is baffled by the rigidity of Bartleby's adherence to
the negation of the worldly order. Ordinary, socially sanctioned caritas
is insufficient. Some higher, ultimate order of care is required in the case
of Bartleby, but it cannot be given. How can it be? What more can the
lawyer do? His lament at the end of the tale, "Ah Bartleby! Ah humanity!" prefigures Vere's death-bed repetition of Billy Budd's name. The
legal, financial, political, horological order represented with increasing
discomfort by the comfortable narrator cannot account for or sustain a
being like Bartleby, a visitor from the chronometric.

    The incompatibility of human law with a deeper conception of justice
is presented again in "Benito Cereno." Babo's silence, his removal of himself from discourse, is another model of Bartleby's refusal and Billy's stutter. Justice has vacated itself from law, and Babo, the law's object or target,
removes himself from language. And in "Benito Cereno," as in Billy Budd,
we encounter at the end of the narrative an official discourse—a final,

definitive affirmation of the horological which we know to be entirely at odds with the truth. Melville repeatedly asserts that truth and justice can exist only outside the social-symbolic order, whether in Bartleby's eccentric negations or in Babo's anti-imperial silence.

As readers like Johnson and Cameron would point out, though, the situation in *Billy Budd* is more complex, the lines of discourse more blurred. These protagonists with the initial of "B" all follow after and diverge from the "A" of Ahab. All, it might be, precede the "C" that would be Christ—left by Melville unwritten—or, which might, on the other hand, or on another articulation of the same hand, be Claggart, another "man of sorrows" (*Billy Budd* 46). Billy presents us with an unfallen, chronomentric innocence; he presents also an identity outside of symbolization altogether—the animal, angel, savage, or wild child. But even so, he remains in the alphabet. There is, after all, a recognized place in the symbolic order for the unsymbolizable—the place of the catachresis. What is carried across from the non-linguistic is always mistranslated and becomes an abuse, an impairment. Billy's stutter, in this context, is not a flaw in his perfection—the work, as the narrator puts it, of "the envious marplot of Eden" (13)—but the audible, non-signifying signature joining and distorting all the categories of authenticity and innocence in which the text involves him. And as a non-signifying signature, the stutter presents as well Billy's notion of language as single, non-duplicitous, and thus, not really language at all. When we read of Billy that "double meanings and insinuations [were] quite foreign to his nature" (9), we realize that his language is Adamic, the Benjaminian "language as such," and not our post-Babel "language of man." Billy's innocent, chronometric inability to interpret is his true linguistic impairment, for which the stutter is an emblematic echo.

Vere has a strong recognition of what the text so overdetermines. After Billy kills Claggert, Vere calls him "an angel of God" (58). When Billy at his trial asserts his innocence, Vere responds, "I believe you, my man" (63). No one in the text (with the exception, perhaps, of Claggert) believes more strongly than Vere in Billy's essential innocence. Chronometric justice would demand that Billy be freed, or apotheosized, and Vere, recognizing this, insists that horologic law be strictly enforced. He could not insist so rigidly on this strict enforcement were he not so entirely persuaded of the horological/chronometric dichotomy. As

Vere succinctly explains to the drumhead court, "natural justice" cannot be the criterion for adjudicating Billy's case. Do their military uniforms, asks Vere, "attest that our allegiance is to Nature? No, to the King. Though the ocean, which is inviolate Nature, though this be the element where we move and have our being as sailors, yet as the King's officers lies our duty in a sphere correspondingly natural? So little is that true, that in receiving our commissions we in the most important regards ceased to be natural free agents." Their duty, then, is to administer martial law "however piteously that law may operate" (67). At the Last Judgement, Vere concludes, Billy will be acquitted. "But how here? We proceed under the law of the Mutiny Act" (68).

In Vere's rejection of the chronometric in favor of the horological, in his absolute belief that "forms, measured forms are everything" (83), and in Billy's dying blessing of Vere, emerge simultaneously the book's ostensible conservatism and the ironic critique of that conservatism. Thus, Barbara Johnson's insight that *Billy Budd*'s central performance is of a conflict between types of reading remains intact. But within this aporetic framework, or perhaps pushing beyond it, what, again, is the function of the stutter, and of Billy specifically as a character with an impairment of language? The blow resulting from the stutter is a chronometric violence intruding into the horological world. And here Ahab, Melville's other great disabled character, returns to the discussion, for Billy's blow works in obedience to Ahab's injunction to "strike through the mask." In felling Claggert, Billy strikes down language as language—"the language of man," fallen language, polysemous language, language as we know it. The stutter is a metaphor for the disabling of metaphor, the disabling of textuality, the disabling of the textual overdetermination that is the distinguishing feature of this text and from which, nevertheless, Billy cannot escape. "He foully lied to my face and in presence of my captain," Billy explains, "and I had to say something, and I could only say it with a blow" (63). The life-ending blow appears the appropriate chronometric response, for to respond to a lie using language would be to enter the linguistic system of the lie, which Billy cannot do. But this appropriateness, as with Ahab, is apocalyptic—is world-ending. Christ in the Book of Revelation appears to John with his tongue transformed into a sword.

If Billy's blow is a striking through the mask, is Claggert, then, the white whale? Yes, certainly in an Ahabian view. Claggert presents a blank surface that conceals an absolute malevolence. And though he is named and his malevolence defined as "natural depravity," this definition is tautological, for "natural depravity" turns out to be nothing other than "a depravity according to nature" (34). Claggert, like the whale, is ultimately beyond category, resembling just before Billy strikes him "certain uncatalogued creatures of the deep" (56). In Melville's later narrative, however, the malevolent force is no longer cosmic or natural (though it takes on these tropes), but now is social and political. Claggert is Vere's subordinate, the ship's officer of enforcement and surveillance, an agent with a distinct place in the symbolic and material system of empire. Finally, it is not Claggert who plays the whale's role in Billy Budd, but the Bellipotent. The imperial warship is the home of duplicity, horological calculation, and the disciplines of the modern, capitalist, militarized state. In whatever sense his statement is uttered or received, Billy is correct upon his impressment to bid farewell by name to his old ship, the Rights-of-Man (9).

2

Linguistic Impairment and the Default of Modernism

Totality and Otherness: Dys-/Disarticulate Modernity

I wander through each chartered street / Near where the
chartered Thames does flow.
William Blake, "London."

Blake's famous poem lauds the triumphs of modern urban planning
and natural science. Both city and nature have been placed under the
charter of rational knowledge and guidance, and a just and fecund
society prospers through this knowledge. Oh! Sorry! I was looking at
the wrong note card! Of course, "London" is a bitter condemnation
of modern forms of knowledge and their effects on nature and social
life. But this mistaken conflation points toward the central epistemological and moral tensions of modernity, which can be summed up as
the problem of knowledge as system or model. As Isaiah Berlin argued,
the epistemological premise of the Enlightenment was that knowledge is potentially total, that "all genuine questions can be answered"
by means of rational, empirical inquiry (21), that knowledge takes the
form of propositions that are compatible with each other (64), and that
the totality of the world would form a "closed, perfect pattern" (105).
Michel Foucault described this approach to knowledge in more detail
in *The Order of Things*. Enlightenment thinkers sought to achieve "an
exhaustive ordering of the world" which could be "displayed in a system contemporary with itself" (74)—which is to say, that the means of
representation would be entirely adequate to the objects represented,
failing neither through lack nor excess. The ideal of knowledge entailed
an ideal of language, of "signs, a syntax, and a grammar in which all
conceivable order must find its place" (84). Such a language would
"gather into itself . . . the totality of the world."Crucially, though, for

such a possibility to be realized, "the world, as the totality of what is representable, must be able to become, in its totality, an Encyclopaedia" (85). Knowledge, in this view, relies on a language evidently surpassing the capacities of natural language (the language of common use). And, as Foucault continues this history, the project of knowledge thereby becomes increasingly entwined with problematics of representation. If knowledge is potentially total, but the symbolic means of knowing are necessarily flawed, then the modern natural and human sciences must create symbolic processes that will make knowledge actually knowable. Thus, Foucault writes of the "positivist dream" of a perfect scientific language which would be the "unmisted mirror of a non-verbal knowledge" (296), an unshakeable linkage of *les mots et les choses* (*The Order of Things*' original French title). And this connection of words and things, or of a symbolic system and the natural and social worlds, would not be a gnostic return to an Adamic, pre-Babel language of divine correspondance. It would serve as the mechanism for a secular, practical, technical ordering of the world. It would give the world its charter.

This modern project of knowing, charting and controlling the world has taken many forms: the Hegelian system; Weber's theory of instrumental reason, bureaucratization, and the "iron cage" of modern capitalist development; Wittgenstein's effort in the *Tractatus* to construct a symbolic network that would state as "atomic facts" all "that is the case"; the industrial-administrative techniques of Taylorism; emerging theories in biology from the mid-nineteenth through the early twentieth centuries of the organism and environment as homeostatic, self-regulating systems; Saussure's theory of language as self-referential system, and its descendents in structuralism and post-structuralism; Lacan's postulating of a symbolic order in which individual consciousness and social ideologies are formed; modern systems theories of Parsons and Luhmann; the cybernetics of Wiener; the dominance of quantitative models in economics and the social sciences. Implicit or explicit in these theories is an understanding of language, as Fredric Jameson put it, "as a total system . . . complete at every moment" (*Prison House*, 5). Linguistics would then become, as Saussure predicted, "the master-pattern for all branches of semiology"—that is, for all uses of signs (68). Seeing this prediction being fulfilled, Roland Barthes could describe culture as "a general system of symbols, governed by the same operations" and assert that "there is a unity in the symbolic field, and culture, in all its aspects, is a language" ("To Write," 13).[1]

This modern conflation of knowledge-representation-language-sys-tem-model-production-administration-culture-ideology seeks to portray a social-symbolic world without an exterior. It is all there; and what is there, is . . . what is. What is not known is simply not yet known—an empirical, not a systemic lack.

Running parallel to, and within, these articulations of totalizing sys-tems of knowledge, representation, and power have been the practices and discourses of dys-/disarticulation. As Michael Lemahieu wrote, "because the modern worldview acknowledges no limits to its discur-sive reach, there is no metalanguage that would escape its discourses and consequently no external perspective from which" to conduct a cri-tique (74). If a system is presumed to be total and without exterior or remainder, opposition must take the form of a failure of articulation (the dysarticulate) or forcible exclusion—dismemberment—from the social-symbolic order (the disarticulate). In response to this dilemma, we see the creation of the modern radical other, conceived specifically as other to symbolization. And just as the development of modernity's concept of system involves a conflation of linguistic, epistemologi-cal, economic, and political categories, so the development of modern alterity brings together a variety of incongruous entities "beyond repre-sentation." The older theological-political functions of the prophet and sacred fool are often retained, but joined now with the workings of the sublime, the primitive, the unconscious, the body, the traumatic, the abject, the ethically infinite other (e.g., of Levinas), entities that have "neither word nor concept" (Derrida, "Difference," 3; i.e., Heidegger's Being and appropriation, Derrida's differance, cendres, and shibboleth), Lacan's "real," as well as a variety of socio-political others: the woman, the racial other, the colonized, the proletarian, the Jew, the homosexual. Note that the exalted others are close kindred to the excluded, debased others, and that the socio-political "others" who have been disarticu-lated from the polity often partake of the dysarticulations of radical philosophical or theological alterity—e.g., Spivak's subaltern who can-not speak or Coetzee's Friday whose tongue has been cut off.

"The relief of speech," declared Kierkegaard's Johannes de Silencio in Fear and Trembling, "is that it translates me into the universal." Thus,

Abraham "cannot speak" (137). The "universal," for Kierkegaard, is Hegel's vision of a dialectical totality moving toward ultimate transparency and articulation, and of which ethics is a crucial part. But Abraham's act, the sacrifice of Isaac, cannot be articulated in any language of ethics. The ethical, as Kierkegaard writes, is "suspended" in Abraham— that is to say, in his direct relationship with God (85). Regarding his attempt to kill his son, there is nothing he can say, or there are no linguistic categories in modernity in which he might say it. He is indistinguishable from the psychotic individual on the evening news who murders his family because God tells him to. There are, of course, languages of psychopathology, social deprivation, religious fanaticism, stress, and so on—all of these being categories within the universal. But, Kierkegaard emphasizes, there can be no language of Abraham, only silence, nonsense, circumlocution, or catachresis. And Abraham, for Kierkegaard, is the limit case of a condition actually true for all—that is, true for all, yet not universal because incommensurably different in each case. "The individual is higher than the universal" (84). This proposition implies that incommensurability will always puncture totality; the system must collapse whenever it genuinely confronts experience—"the paradox that cannot be mediated" (95).

This opposition reappears in remarkably similar forms in many of the central documents defining the contours of modernity. In Derrida's pivotal critique of structuralism in "Structure, Sign, and Play," his principal object is structuralism's claim of a universal commensurability among cultures and symbolic systems—the presumed ability to occupy a coherent center amid social-symbolic flux. Derrida argues instead that such a presumed center is available for a process of infinite substitution, and so is not a center—a "fixed locus" that would ground all meaning and value—but is rather a "function by means of which meaning and value are continually shifting" (280). The "center" is an ideological not an epistemological place, and the structure that follows from it derives from contingencies of social power. As Burke would put it, the center is the "god-term," the term bearing the power to determine; or, in Lacan's terminology, the center is the "quilting point" (*point de capiton*) where the inherently unstable, incomplete symbolic order is woven into seeming, ideologically motivated, wholeness. And the "real," the unsymbolizable, traumatizing, and inevitable failure of the symbolic order and its ideologies generates ever anew those paradoxes "that cannot be mediated"—or, as Kierkegaard writes elsewhere, "keep[s] the wound of the negative open" (q. in Baker, 269).

But what is it that for Derrida will move us out from the ideology of the center? For the problem always, in these kindred critiques of the totalizing system, is how to get out of it. It is not enough to demonstrate that the system is theoretically untenable, to note, with Wittgenstein, that "the modern system tries to make it look as if everything were explained" (*Tractatus* 6.372), but that "at the bottom of well-founded belief lies belief that is not founded" (*On Certainty* 253). Even after one reveals centrality and its totalizing reach to be a linguistic construct serving some concentration of power, the power to totalize remains in place. Genuine destruction of structure can only be the work of some other of structure, some other of language—the return of the dis/dys-articulated. And this is what Derrida tries to usher in with his essay's final words:

> Here there is a sort of question, call it historical, of which we are only glimpsing today the conception, the formation, the gestation, the labor. I employ these words, I admit, with a glance toward the business of child-bearing—but also with a glance toward those who, in a company from which I do not exclude myself, turn their eyes away in the face of the as yet unnameable which is proclaiming itself and which can do so, as is necessary whenever a birth is in the offing, only under the species of the non-species, in the formless, mute, infant, and terrifying form of monstrosity (293).

In this astonishing mix of metaphors, the biological merging with the historical, the historical with the apocalyptic, and all converging in the figure of the not-yet-existing, unrepresentable, and unspeaking other, we see a vivid instance of the longstanding effort to conceive of alterity in relation to an intellectual-technical-economic totality that would assimilate, sublate, and colonize all others to its knowledge and method. And yet, one can certainly conceive the situation differently, imagine a more genial birth than that of the rough, apocalyptic beast that Derrida seems to have borrowed from Yeats. One need not, as in models under discussion, imagine language as "iron cage," "world picture," "totality," closed system, symbolic order as ideology, etc. To critique a social-symbolic order by means of some figure of radical alterity means to have accepted the premise of language/knowledge/representation as closed, imprisoning, and containing no terms for its own internal critique and reform. The problem, again, is how to get out. How is change possible? But is this not a pseudo-problem? Is change possible? Clearly, it is. One of the key features attributed to modernity by both its proponents and critics is the pervasiveness and rapidity of change. To which the response would be, certainly change occurs, indeed vertiginously, but consistently in the direction of greater totalization, and moves toward potential freedom quickly are reappropriated into the ideological, hegemonic whole. Empirical evidence is mixed on this point.

One can, nevertheless, proceed from different premises on how language or a social-symbolic order works, whether that ominous sounding term is even relevant, and whether some radical other of language is necessary as a utopian-apocalyptic point of opposition to the world as it is. While Kierkegaard required the non-speaking, anti-universal identity of Abraham to subvert the Hegelian system, and while Levinas, similarly, theorized the radical, unframeable, infinite other to stand in opposition to a social-symbolic totality, William James repudiated entirely that opposition between system and alterity. The urge toward totality, James argued, is a psychological trait, a personal impulse for "generalizing, simplifying, and subordinating" (14). Particular portions of knowledge are valid, but bits and pieces of reality will "remain outside of the largest combination of it ever made" (20), and this location outside does not render something radically other. Outside of one discourse is another discourse, perhaps a set of terms outlining things not known. We do not need, he writes, that "habit of thinking only in the most violent extremes" (40). One can imagine, rather, a universe "connected loosely, after the pattern of our daily experience" (39).[2]

This Jamesian pluralism and kindred approaches entail very different premises regarding language and its social consequences, including the location from which, and the tone in which, social critique can be directed. One need not, in this view, seek to get outside of language. There is no barrier, such as Wittgenstein invoked in the *Tractatus*, between language and nonsense (3). The social-symbolic order produces its own oppositions, and alterity is revealed through dialogue, or even conflict, but not through silence, folly, madness, sublimity, abjection, or apocalyptic shattering. Arguing against Saussure's view of language as a self-referential system, Valentin Voloshinov wrote of language's "inherent semantic openness, corresponding to a still active social process, from which new meanings and possible meanings can be generated" (q. in Raymond Williams 75).[3] Similarly, for Jean-Jacques Lecercle, it is "no longer possible to think of [language] as a system of signs—we must view it rather as a locus for contending forces. It is not a structure, but an unstable and potentially violent institution" (45). In such views of social-symbolic *life*—as distinct from social-symbolic *order*—the exclusion of an "other" can be regarded only as a political act, not as a necessity following from structural constraints. To be excluded from a hegemonic discourse is not to be an other of language. In these views of language, the conflation of dys-/disarticulation can be disentangled. One is not irretrievably trapped in a structured totality of representation, knowledge, production, and administration; and an external, radical other is conceptually unnecessary, for otherness is always present in language and in subjectivity. If certain language practices threaten to become hegemonic, they can be opposed with other language practices, or, as is probable, can be opposed using alternate modes existing within the same practice. And this is the case because, as Geoffrey Galt Harpham expresses it, "language is not just an autonomous formal system but rather a medium whose formal elements permit an unformalized excess to become legible, a medium saturated with otherness, and thus with ethics" (*Getting* 61). By this, Harpham means that insofar as language cannot be totalized (and so generates excesses, contradictions, incoherences, and other forms of resistance to composition and communication), interlocutors must work in order to understand each other—and, indeed, to understand themselves. Linguistic indeterminacy entails a practice that is both interpretive and ethical. In this sense, the imagined "fall" of language from Adamic, pre-Babel purity of meaning was a fall really into the recognition of others as subjects capable of speaking for themselves, not just as being correctly named and thus fixed into a linguistic totality. In this sense, the unnameable radical other is simply the reversed face of the perfectly named other. The first cannot speak at all; the second cannot speak for himself because his language has no interstices in which he might find his own voice.

This sense of language as imperfect, unsystemic, open, not totalizing seems at least as plausible as the sense that it opposes, and would seem to provide social, psychological, and political advantages: It allows both for autonomy and for psychological and social limits to autonomy, and does not reify either self or other; it is able to imagine ethical relations arising from the limits, flaws, and vulnerabilities of language and self, rather than seeking some perfect language or completely autonomous self, then despairing at their failures. This is the view shared, in broad terms, by Bakhtin, the later Wittgenstein, and Habermas, in addition to the theorists cited above. Why then hold a view that seems counter-intuitive, hyperbolic, and paranoid? Why not dispense with the radical dys-/disarticulate other and return to the actual, familiar (if also somewhat uncanny) intersubjective lifeworld of language which, as Habermas puts it, would diagnose "Western 'logocentrism' . . . not as an excess but as a deficit of rationality" (*The Philosophical Discourse of Modernity* 310)—with rationality here defined as something discovered through the unconstrained communication among different subjects, not as a mono-logic imposing foundational truths?

There seem to be several problems. First, it might appear that while the views of linguistic and societal openness are plausible and desirable, they are somehow illusory. All the apparent mobility in terms of technology, demographics, geographies, political regimes, economic development, and social mores may be construed simply as complex forms of stasis. Dominant ideological and economic power cannot be overthrown, and precisely for the reason that this power controls what is recognized as knowledge or sensible opinion. Dissent, too, has its place in this system, at least in its more liberal versions. And more sophisticated versions of systems theory, like those of Talcott Parsons and Niklas Luhmann, attempt to insert openness into their theories and to account for relations between the system and what transpires outside it. Parsons stresses that society consists of multiple systems, and that no single system can be studied apart from its relations with other systems. Moreover, he acknowledges the abstract and selective nature of any social theory. Systems are porous, theories are partial, totality is an illusion. Likewise, Luhmann theorizes communication as providing the means for a system "to maintain closure under the conditions of openness" so that systems can code novelty into their reproduction (13). System, for Luhmann, does not imply predictability. On the widest scale, no conceivable world system could be predictable owing to the particular internal evolutions of its subsystems. There is no external other to the system—all discourse is systemic—but there is an autonomy, or at least a sense of contingency in the evolution of subsystems, and thus of the larger system. Given these possibilities of openness and change that Parsons and Luhmann build into their notions of system, we might ask, why theorize a system at all?[4]

One might answer that it *appears*, at any rate, that the stronger imperative of even the most open, non-paranoid theory of system is to explain continuity and reproduction, not change. There seems to be an innate conservatism to the impulse to integrate all phenomena into a comprehensible, and thus predictable, whole. The paranoia I have referred to in reference to critiques of totality—the tendency to describe the system in the most unambiguous, hyperbolic sense—is matched by the systematizers' own terror of chaos, or, more modestly, of contingency. All must be subject to knowledge, thus control—even chaos itself!—or else all will be lost. We need not appeal to fears of actual castration to see in the threats to totality an echo of Freud's famous description of conservatism: "In later life, grown men may experience a similar panic, perhaps when the cry goes up that throne and altar are in danger" ("Fetishism," 153).

Why such tenacity of belief on the parts of both proponents and critics? Theoretical impossibility and empirical failure do not seem to be obstacles. Modernity, as Henri Lefebvre wrote, "is best characterized not as an already established 'structure,' nor as something which clearly has the capacity to become structured and coherent, but rather as a fruitless attempt to achieve structure and coherence" (187). Thus, every new set of discoveries or terminologies in the sciences or social sciences provokes new initiatives of totalization and, consequently, new visions of dys-/disarticulation—alterity, incoherence, abjection and impairment—to counter them. Such are many of the central statements of, or comments on, aesthetic modernism:

> The language of poetry is, then, a difficult, roughened, impeded language. (Victor Shklovksy, "Art as Technique")

> My propositions are elucidatory in this way: he who understands me finally recognizes them as senseless. (Ludwig Wittgenstein, *Tractatus Logico-Philosophicus*)

"The primary work" of western modernism "consists in strenuous acts of unknowing." (Philip Weinstein, *Unknowing: The Work of Modernist Fiction*)

Modernism's focus and method reflect "the nebulous consciousness of an idiot . . . its obsession with the morbid and the pathological." (Georg Lukács, *The Meaning of Contemporary Realism*)

Stupidity, the indelible tag of modernity, is our symptom. (Avital Ronell, *Stupidity*)

And if there is one hellish, truly accursed thing in our time, it is our artistic dallying with forms, instead of being like victims burnt at the stake, signaling through the flames. (Antonin Artaud, *The Theater and Its Double*)

It is to be hoped the time will come, thank God, in some circles it already has, when language is best used when most efficiently abused. (Samuel Beckett, letter to Axel Kaun, 1937)

But the matter of alterity is not just theoretical and aesthetic. Let me add one more quotation of very different provenance, that of social policy, to show more fully the working of modern dys-/disarticulation:

Among the social tasks that confront state governments today, none is more pressing than the care of the feeble-minded. . . . It is because they, at least as much as any other social class, complicate and involve every social problem, and because they, more than any other class, tend to increase on our hands. (Q. in Noll, 1)

The question, then, is not just how to conceive of an alterity that might confront a totalizing social-symbolic order, but how the modern state should treat mentally impaired people who could not function under modern economic and political conditions. The mentally impaired often could not work in modern industry (while they had been able to perform tasks in a traditional agricultural economy), and they could not fully participate as citizens in a democratic polity (while they could maintain a valued status in traditional family and community settings). The question, or the problem, of mental defectiveness was transferred from the private, familial setting to public sites of science and administration, a process which, in Great Britain, culminated in the Mental Deficiency Act of 1913. This law provided for the institutionalization of the mentally defective on both humanitarian and eugenic grounds. The mentally defective were regarded as both helpless and dangerous, requiring both care and control. Regarded now as scientific, clinical, and administrative objects, British subjects deemed mentally defective were simultaneously brought into public discourse and excluded from the polity. In the United Kingdom, anxieties concerning mental deficiency reverberated with anxieties about class. In the United States, these anxieties also brought in questions of race and immigration.[5]

Degeneration, Biology, and Literary Modernism

"'You would call that lad a degenerate, would you?' . . . 'That's what he may be called scientifically. Very good type too, altogether, of that sort of degenerate. It's enough to glance at the lobes of his ears. If you read Lombroso—'" (77). This brief passage from Conrad's *The Secret Agent* may serve to introduce the quasi-scientific discourse of the "degenerate" in turn-of-the-century thinking. From the late nineteenth through the first decades of the twentieth century, the category of "degenerate" took in a broad swath of cognitive, class, and racial others. Both biological and social, "degeneracy" defined both a status and a process. The degenerate individual occupied a particular place on the evolutionary ladder, a place made legible through physical features. And those who, for reasons both of heredity and environment, had devolved to a more primitive evolutionary state were, according the the widely influential theories of Cesare Lombroso, far more prone to criminal behavior than were normal persons. Furthermore, for Lombroso, degeneracy and hereditary atavism were racial characteristics.[6] Those with African or Asian features were regarded as less evolved. Indeed, Lombroso wrote, "there exist whole tribes and races more or less given to crime" (139).

The individual degenerate with his tendencies toward crime was an obvious threat to social order, and concerns regarding degeneracy articulated powerfully, and with apparently scientific apparatus, in Lombroso's ideas worked in tandem with specific anxieties surrounding the "feeble-minded" or "mental defectives" thought to be prevalent in Europe and America. The American psychologists Walter Fernald and Henry H. Goddard proposed the term "moral idiocy" to describe the inability of most cognitively impaired people to make adequate moral judgments.[7] But these anxieties regarding "mentally defective" individuals or families, though severe, could be assuaged through the clinical and social remedies recommended by Goddard and others: the institutionalization and, in many cases, sterilization of cognitively impaired people. More apocalyptic in import were fears of degeneration on broader societal or even global levels. This terror took two broad and intersecting forms. One, eugenic and Darwinian, feared that the more advanced races and social groups—i.e., upper-class northern Europeans—would be physically and genetically submerged by more the fertile populations of inferior races and lower classes. The racialist political scientist Lothrop Stoddard (satirized as "that man Goddard" in *The Great Gatsby*)[8] described the possibility of power shifting from the white to the "colored" races as "the supreme crisis of the ages" (299). Warning against the "seductive charm" of the "dangerous fallacies" of human equality, Stoddard assured his readers that "fortunately, we now know the truth" that heredity is "paramount" in all human endeavors (305), and that white civilization must prevent migrations of "lower human types" and "take in hand the problem of race-depreciation, segregation of defectives, and abolition of handicaps penalizing the better stocks" (308).

The anxieties over degeneration, however, pertained also to Western civilization itself. The individual pathologies diagnosed by Lombroso were akin in racialist ideology to Stoddard's depiction of colored others overwhelming white Europe and North America. But there was a sense too that, owing to the pressures of modern life, Europe was degenerating on its own. Francis Galton, a friend of Darwin and an early advocate of eugenics, wrote in 1865 that the modern forces of "centralization, communication, and culture" were beyond most people's capacities, that "our race is overweighted and appears likely to be drudged into degeneracy by demands that exceed its powers" (q. in Friedlander 66). This was the starting point also for Max Nordau, author of the most comprehensive *fin de siècle* account of cultural degeneration. "All conditions of life," Nordau wrote, "have, in this period of time, experienced a revolution unexampled in the history of the world" (37). Degeneration, for Nordau, resulted from the fatigue occasioned by modern life, a consequence "of the excessive wear and tear suffered by the nations through the immense demands on their activity and through the rank growth of large towns" (43). Hysteria and neurasthenia were among the organic symptoms affecting individuals, but Nordau devoted most of his analysis to broader cultural forms, almost all of which were, for Nordau, symptomatic of degeneration and contributing to its spread. Nordau was particularly critical of modern art and literature. "Their word," he wrote, "is no ecstatic prophecy, but the senseless stammering and babbling of deranged minds . . . the convulsions and spasms of exhaustion" (43).

These Larmarckian depictions of degeneration in which new physical and psychological traits are rapidly acquired, somehow translated into the genetic material, and transmitted to offspring emerge from reactionary political positions, yet seem to echo Marx's famous and ambivalent paean to capitalism in the *Communist Manifesto*:

> All fixed, fast frozen relations, with their train of ancient and venerable prejudices and opinions, are swept away, all new-formed ones become antiquated before they can ossify. All that is solid melts into air, all that is holy is profaned, and man is at last compelled to face with sober senses his real condition of life and his relations with his kind. (83)

And all this—industrialization, urbanization, globalization—Marx adds, takes place "to the great chagrin of reactionaries" (83). For Marx, modernity's turbulence is a necessary passage toward humanity's true articulation, for the injustices, dislocations, and contradictions of the age are exactly what indicate the absolute insufficiency of the existing social order. This uncanny convergence of vision and language among radicals and reactionaries suggests the political and ethical stakes in the discourses of degeneration. What exactly is degenerate? The racial other, the sexual deviant, the criminal, the anarchist, the artist, the genius, the proletarian, the "promiscuous" woman, the "mentally defective"? Or the statesman, the capitalist, the general, the police officer, the time-motion specialist, the publicist, the patriarch, the psychologist and diagnostician? The articulate or the dys-/disarticulate? As Daniel Pick summarizes the intellectual atmosphere of the late nineteenth century, "degeneration became the veritable common sense of innumerable scientific and cultural investigations" (67).

The modernist fictions under discussion in this chapter present all these possibilities. The language of degeneration and eugenics pervades these texts, but the rhetorical aim consistently is turned around, away from its usual objects. In *The Secret Agent*, Stevie, as we observed, is classified by the anarchist Ossipon, citing Lombroso, as a degenerate. And yet all the novel's characters, not least Ossipon, are characterized physiognomically. The novel is a circus of Lombrosian depiction, but the constant layering and overlaying of physiologic "readings" of character serve finally to parody and delegitimate the method. We can, I think, take as one of the few unironized statements in the book the anarchist Yundt's judgement that "Lombroso is an ass" (77). Degeneracy in *The Secret Agent* is universal and stems not from heredity but from systemic injustice, hypocrisy, and cruelty. Or, it may be more accurate to say that the trope of degeneracy is used to describe a world governed by injustice, hypocrisy, and cruelty, but that degeneracy itself is a ruse, an invention that both reveals and deflects from the real problems. As Joseph Conrad wrote regarding his characters in *The Secret Agent*, "they're all imbeciles . . . including an Embassy Secretary, a Minister of State, and an Inspector of Police" (q. in McDonagh 313). Similarly, *The Sound and the Fury* presents a cast of characters familiar to adherents of degeneration theories: Benjy, the "idiot," is son, brother, uncle, and object of care to an alcoholic, a neurasthenic, a suicide, a promiscuous young woman (and her promiscuous daughter), and a family of illiterate African Americans. The Compson family is on one hand a descendent of some doomed gothic clan, like Poe's Ushers, and on the other, a cousin of the objects of contemporary sociological studies like the Jukes or Kallikaks.[9] The Compsons may be said to be degenerating, but degenerating from what? From the corrupt and violent slaveholders we encounter in *Absalom, Absalom*. Or, we might say that the South is degenerating, but, in Faulkner's view, the moral and cultural status of the South was always questionable. As I will argue later, the novel's critique of degeneration is directed toward a rejection of *generation*: that is, of sexuality, especially female sexuality, and more broadly of humanity's biological status as sexed and mortal. And, concomitant with generation, the novel emphasizes the significance of care as a force opposing the denials and inhumanities of modernity. The novel's moral compass is the treatment of Benjy, "the least of my brothers," and the society's and family's true degeneration lies in the failure of care. Finally, in *Nightwood*, with its assorted Jews, homosexuals, circus performers, abortionists, false aristocrats, and tatooed negroes, we see the very groups who soon would be the targets of the hyperbolic and murderous eugenics of Nazism. Matthew, Nora, Jenny, Guido, Felix, and the subcultures they inhabit all fall under the same leveling diagnosis of degenerate. But in the terms of the novel, none is really anything other than human—insofar as they suffer and try to understand and articulate their lives as they live in historical, political, gendered structures of discourse and power. Whatever their apparent differences from sexual and racial norms, and however oblique the novel's language, these characters fall easily within the emotional range of humanity, neither more nor less degenerate than anyone else. If they and their brethren face extermination, "degenerate" will be a term applied not to them but to their killers. But Robin is something different, someone, as the novel insists in many ways, "outside the human type." How this exteriority, or dys-/disarticulation, is to be read is the central interpretive question the novel poses.

In each of these texts, the central "degenerate" figure is also cognitively or (in the case of Robin) linguistically impaired, which is not surprising given the close relation of discourses of degeneration to those of "feeble-mindedness" or "mental deficiency," and both with discourses of eugenics. But these central dys-/disarticulated figures also are placed within contexts of extreme, extravagant linguistic innovation and experimentation, and this presence of dys-/disarticulation in the most sophisticated and novel uses of language leads us to one of the most critical features of literary modernism.

In his polemic against modernism in *The Meaning of Contemporary Realism*, Georg Lukács complained that cognitive impairment, the "consciousness . . . of an abnormal subject or of an idiot," was the characteristic and determining feature of modernist style (26). "Psychopathology," he wrote, had become the "goal" of modernist writing (29), and "perversity and idiocy" were adopted as "types" of the human condition (32). The flaws in Lukács's evaluation of modernism are easy to find. To begin with, his insistence that a literary text provide some social and psychological norm against which the presumed abnormal can be measured in order accurately to reflect existing social dynamics and contradictions indicates a misunderstanding of the status of the text both as a formally self-contained object and as an intervention in a social field. Nevertheless, this particular observation, framed as mockery, that figures of cognitive and linguistic impairment are critical to the ideologies and styles of modernism carries a more important truth. Linguistically and cognitively impaired characters are indeed central to major modernist texts, and the problems that arise in trying to understand these characters can help us rethink the central problems of modernism. The mentally impaired figure in modernism is a point of convergence at which aesthetic, philosophical, ethical, political, medical, and scientific discourses come together and which, further, is immersed in deep anxieties associated with these discourses and their intersections. In texts like Conrad's *The Secret Agent*, Faulkner's *The Sound and the Fury*, and Barnes's *Nightwood*, we see how practices of modernist aesthetic excess collide with contemporaneous discourses of heredity, eugenics, and degeneration; how the early twentieth-century fascinations with the primitive converge with the pursuit of symbolic usages that might bypass mediation; and how innovations in institutional clinical treatment of mentally impaired people conflict with traditional religious and sentimental ideas and practices of care. These concerns, anxieties, and collisions cannot be reconciled. They were not reconciled historically—they remain unreconciled to this day—and they appear before readers in a disquieting tension in the literary texts of the period.

Why, after all, during a period of sustained and explosive innovation in literary language, should the most powerful writers of the time invest their energies in creating characters with radically limited capacities for language? What does it mean, in a verbal medium, to construct characters who function largely outside the linguistic loop? Furthermore, how can we account for the emotional investment that seems apparent in these characters, for they clearly are more than epistemological experiments? Other characters are deeply engaged with the impaired characters; these engagements form the bases of the narratives. It seems that the texts themselves are in love with the impaired. And, given that portrayals of linguistic and cognitive impairments have a history that reaches back to the Bible, in what specific, historical ways might we understand the portrayals we find in literary modernism?

The Secret Agent: Unaccountability and the "Current Words"

Winnie refers to her brother, Stevie, as the "'presiding genius'" (220) of their family, and I believe he serves that function for the novel as a whole. He is the moral center of a text that, given its style, cannot have a moral center. Irony in this novel performs a totalizing, leveling function, rendering all ethical-political positions equivalent, and eliminating the possibility of alterity. The world presented in *The Secret Agent* is a closed system. There can be no alternative because there is no outside. The rival state powers, the police and the anarchists, all share the same attitudes, the same carelessness, the same dedication to self-interest and self-per-petuation. As the Professor claims, "'the terrorist and the policeman both come from the same basket. Revolution, legality—counter moves in the same game; forms of idleness at bottom identical'" (94). It is, apparently, impossible even to imagine or find the language for some other ethical-political structure. Thus, in a moment that defines the novel's discursive attitude and atmosphere, the anarchist Ossipon responds angrily to the Professor's verbal quibbling over the use of the word "crime" with "'How am I to express myself? One must use the current words'" (95). This is the ideological dilemma Conrad presents in this novel: One can employ only the vocabulary that one finds at hand—the "current words"—and social reality is entirely defined by this vocabulary.

Conrad's sense here of the power of the "current words" expresses an attitude characteristic of modernity: the sense of possibility—expressed sometimes as hope, sometimes as fear—that the world, as a totality, can be systematically conceptualized and represented. The hope is for rational understanding and rationalized practice. As I indicated earlier, this hope was expressed across a wide range of scientific, philosophi-cal, sociological, and political forums. According to these, the natural world and human social practices can in their entirety ultimately be represented and thus controlled. Remaining pockets of irrationality and alterity will be assimilated to the discursive whole. The fear, of course, is that this process is indeed taking place—that the world is a closed, self-referring system, that possibilities for personal and social freedom have been foreclosed, and that language is a principal agent for these fore-closures. Concurrent with the philosophical, economic, and political projects aiming toward systemization have been an equally disparate set of resistances, including, I would argue, much of the modernist experimentation with aesthetic form.[10] The positing and the shattering of a totalizing discursive system can even be achieved simultaneously. Lacan, for example, describes a symbolic order whose effect on the psyche is absolutely defining, but insists also on the "real," the absolute other of symbolization which traumatically reveals the insufficiency of the system. At stake in all these projects, as in *The Secret Agent*, is the authority and dominion of "the current words" and the possibility of speaking or thinking outside their definitions.

Thus the importance of Stevie. He is the only character in *the Secret Agent* with a sense of altruism. His relationship with his sister, Winnie, is the only relationship characterized by care. In these ways, Stevie presents an alternative to the grotesque, callous, self-interest that animates and inhabits the social-symbolic order that Conrad depicts as apparently allowing for no alternative. And yet, as "presiding genius," as ethical alternative at the boundaries of discourse, Stevie obviously is problematic. His cognitive impairment identifies him as a version of the "sacred fool," a figure which in Christian tradition finds it origin in First Corinthians: "Divine folly is wiser than the wisdom of man" (I.25). The sacred fool stands apart from the secular order as an intrusion of an incommensurable divinity; his folly is the inevitable misrecognition of divinity in an unredeemed world. Stevie is most directly a descendent of Dostoevski's Myshkin. But he differs crucially from Myshkin, and from most of the lineage of sacred fools. Unlike Myshkin, he is not a highly educated aristocrat living with epilepsy and social ineptitude. Nor is he a shrewd satirist in the manner of a Shakespearean or Erasmasean fool. He is not even a crazed prophet as in the Russian tradition (cf. the end of *Boris Godunof*). Stevie is, in fact, mentally retarded (or developmentally disabled, to use the most current parlance). Whatever conclusions we draw regarding his folly, its sources are physiological.[11]

Stevie, as a recognizably mentally retarded person, is a "sacred fool" seen in the context of modernity, and the status of the mentally retarded in the early twentieth century was quite different than it had been through much of the nineteenth. Removed from religious and sentimental narratives, the "feeble-minded" or "mentally defective" became objects of scientific inquiry and classification—folly became a problem for modernity. What had previously been perceived as alterity now increasingly was charted by terminologies of science and social administration. Cesare Lombroso, of course, is an important referent in the novel. Ossipon identifies Stevie according to Lombrosian categories as a "degenerate," a "perfect type." But here the novel points in two directions. First, Lombroso is dismissed. Ossipon, his acolyte, is the novel's most loathsome character, and Yundt's rebuttal of Osspion's Lombrosian position seems entirely on point. At the same time, nevertheless, the Lombrosian perspective permeates the narrative; Lombroso's categories of physiological-cognitive-moral relations are a set of "current words" that evidently cannot be escaped.[12] By the time Conrad was writing, Lombroso's theories had largely been discredited in the scientific community, though in wider, more popular circles, versions of them were still current. Moreover, the sociological and political effect of Lombroso's thinking continued to be felt powerfully in the crafting of social policy regarding people with cognitive impairments.[13] While cognitive impairment was no longer regarded as a form of atavism or literal degeneracy, it was increasingly regarded as a serious threat to the British polity. Thus, the question, or the problem, of mental defectiveness was transferred from the private, familial setting to public sites of science and administration. As Matthew Thomson argues, these anxieties regarding the identification and treatment of the mentally defective arose from specific social and economic conditions of early twentieth-century Britain. People like Stevie who might be quite capable of a productive life in an agrarian economy could not work effectively in an urban, industrial economy. The mentally defective were regarded as both helpless and dangerous, requiring both care and control. Regarded now as scientific, clinical, and administrative objects, British subjects deemed mentally defective were simultaneously brought into public discourse and excluded from the polity. Mental defectiveness thus became the focus, as Thomson wrote, for "anxieties about regulating the boundaries of responsible citizenship and managing an increasingly sophisticated network of welfare institutions" (34).

Conrad, then, created Stevie at a moment when the cognitively impaired subject was being definitively inscribed in the "current words" of scientific and social discourses. In Stevie, we see the sacred fool detached from his alterity by Lombroso and his successors. Just as Conrad's text situates the anarchists fundamentally inside the system—their actions and beliefs merely a counter-move within, not a real alternative to, the dominant order—so Stevie too has his place and is accounted for.[14]

And yet, this discursive containment is not complete. If Ossipon's remark concerning the "current words" might be considered one motto for this novel, the other would be Chief Inspector Heat's response to the Assistant Commissioner's question regarding the discovery of Stevie's address label. "'How do you account for this?' The Assistant Commissioner nodded at the cloth rag lying before him on the table. 'I don't account for it at all, sir. It's simply unaccountable'" (140). And it is not just his address label, but Stevie himself who remains unaccountable, even in the midst of a social-symbolic order that has devised a set of terms intended precisely to account for him. The book attempts to render this unaccountablility in several ways.

First, most obviously, there is his impairment itself, which places him not entirely outside, but at a boundary of symbolic usage. Indeed, Stevie's relation to prevailing discourses is always partly within and partly without. Stevie can speak, can even read (thanks, the narrator informs us, to "our excellent system of compulsory education" [49]), but he has difficulty articulating his thoughts and is prone to stutter at moments of stress. His understanding of language is, if anything, overly literal, especially as he fails to grasp the anarchists' metaphoric usages—fails, more pertinently, to understand their emptiness. "'He believes it's all true'" is Winnie's complaint (86). And yet, in fact, Stevie is right. The anarchists' critiques of the social order are true; it is the anarchists themselves who do not believe them enough to act on them.[15] Stevie wants language always to be realized as action. The moves and counter-moves of language in the discursive order of this novel always constitute stasis. Action—whether of compassion or destruction—breaks the discursive order. And taking language literally, as Stevie does, means, paradoxically, to take it as something other than language: to take it as a kind of absolute congealment of fact. Thus, Stevie's struggle to articulate the moral-political problem embodied in the scene with the cabman and his horse (in which Stevie objects to the horse's being beaten) is not an effort merely to locate a correct or adequate phrase; Stevie, rather, is forced to remake language entirely: "muttering half words, and even words that would have been whole if they had not been made up of halves that did not belong to each other" (168). And his result, grammatically amputated, without a verb or an agent, and arrived at through a torturous process that resembles the transformative fragmentations of modern art, is a marvelous, accurate, empathetic condemnation of the social-symbolic order. "'Bad world for poor people'" (168). As soon as he utters this remark, Stevie "became aware that it was familiar to him already in all its consequences." That is, as a true assemblage of word, feeling, and fact, the utterance is a moral force, and the situation it describes requires redress.

Stevie does not understand that in the social-symbolic world shared by the police, the great powers, and the anarchists alike, moral pronouncements are sufficient in themselves. Stevie actually cares about human and animal suffering, a quality that distinguishes him from all other characters in the novel, with the exception of his sister, who, however, cares only about him. "'He can't stand the notion of any cruelty,'" Winnie says of him (87). The text suggests that Stevie acquired his sense of care from the care his sister provided him when they were children— "the consolation administered to a small and badly scared creature by another creature nearly as small" (219). This description suggests a notion of care rooted in empathy and personal experience, and Stevie's exercise of care extends this view. Listening to Yundt's account of the branding of prisoners, Stevie stood "rooted suddenly to the spot by his morbid horror and dread of physical pain. Stevie knew very well that hot iron applied to one's skin would hurt very much. His scared eyes blazed with indignation: it would hurt terribly" (79). The progression of Stevie's reaction is significant. He first responds viscerally, paralyzed by the horror and fear provoked by Yundt's description of the torture, and while provoked by words, these words reach a deep, nonverbal level of feeling. But then Stevie performs an act of cognition. His empathetic horror is translated into thought: He "knew very well" what the branding would feel like. Finally, out of that knowledge comes an ethical response signified by his eyes blazing with indignation. Stevie's ethical response, his caring, comes from a cognitive transformation of an immediate feeling of compassion. The same process occurs when he sees the cabman beat his horse and when he then hears the cabman tell of his own poverty and suffering. Stevie knows what suffering feels like. He has felt it himself and so feels a personal, experiential relation to the suffering of others. And this ethical response grounded in empathy is situated outside the social-symbolic order depicted in this novel.

Unable fully to grasp the symbolic codes of the dominant social order (an order presented as totalizing and determining all possible utterances) and deriving his sense of compassion and active care from personal, experiential sources, Stevie and his enactment of care constitute an alterity in relation to the dominant ethical frame presented in the novel. Viewed through the discursive resources available to the other characters, Stevie is, indeed, unaccountable.

And yet, viewed with another set of discursive resources, Stevie can be quite readily accounted for. Or rather, there are two such sets. We can point first to the romantic-modernist aesthetic tradition of the sublime. Stevie's circles, a "rendering of cosmic chaos, the symbolism of a mad art attempting the inconceivable" (76), signal Stevie's position at the boundary not just of this novel's social-symbolic order but of symbolization itself. This liminal symbolic place we saw also in Conrad's description of Stevie's fragmentary process of articulating his moral-political judgement, his words "made up of halves that did not belong to each other" (168). Conrad attempts through his portrayal of Stevie to reinscribe alterity in a modern world that claims entirely to have contained and assimilated it. Secondly, we can point to the discursive frame of Christianity. As noted before, the figure of the sacred fool has Christian sources. Stevie's ethics of care, especially given his status as a brother who is an object of care, also points toward a Christian referent, the admonition in Matthew 25.40 that "Inasmuch as ye have done it unto one of the least of these my brethren, ye have done it unto me." This Christian ethics relies on a sense of reciprocity rooted in empathy. The injunction of Luke 6.31 to act toward others as one would want them act toward oneself assumes that an ethical subject knows what it feels like to be mistreated and knows that others feel the same pain or humiliation. Moreover, this ethical perspective constitutes a critique of a dominant social order that does not recognize or act on these principles—thus, the emphasis on the oppressed, on "the least of my brothers." This is exactly the basis of Stevie's ethics.

As the novel makes hideously clear, however, Stevie's Christian ethics have no place in the modern world. They can be uttered only in a stammered form. Their chief proponent is genuinely cognitively impaired. Moreover, as the novel presents it, care in every instance is ineffectual. Though she devotes her life to her endeavor, Winnie cannot protect her brother. Stevie's moral indignation produces only explosions—first of the fireworks on the stairway, then of himself—and in this regard, his ethics of alterity bears an unlikely resemblance to the destructive politics of the Professor, the only other character portrayed as existing outside the symbolic loop. When Stevie attempts to imagine a way to make effective his care for the cabman and his horse, the only action he can imagine is "the bizarre longing to take them to bed with him," a wish which even Stevie recognizes as impossible. This ethical response, like his others, is based in personal experience; as he fantasizes about caring for the cabman and his horse, he recalls his sister carrying him "off to bed with her, as into a heaven of consoling peace" (165). To Stevie's experiential and empathetic moral imagination, "to be taken into a bed of compassion was the supreme remedy," to which the ever-corrosive narrator adds, "with the only one disadvantage of being difficult of application on a large scale" (166).

The ethics of care, then, as depicted in *The Secret Agent* is a form of genuine alterity. Originating in personal, private experience, associated with mental and linguistic impairment, with an aesthetics of the incommensurable, and with the archaic religious perspective of Christianity, opposed to modern techniques and ideologies of science and social administration, care, by all construals of modernity's "current words," is radically "unaccountable." Care has no place; it is impossible. And even were it conceptually possible, it would be impracticable. As we see from the text's ironic addendum to Stevie's notion of the "bed of compassion," the personal, experiential quality that gives Stevie's ethical sensibility its force at the same time limits its application. Care is private, familial, and cannot be transferred to the public realm. Located outside modernity's ideological frame, ethics can be represented only as cognitive impairment. And impairment, like all of modernity's "others," is continually engaged in a cyclical process of assimilation to modern terminologies and repositing as radical alterity. The ethics of care is a genuine alternative to the totalizing, self-interested ideologies of modernity, but it is archaic and powerless. A degenerate modernity rejects it, detonates it, throws it overboard.[16]

What remains at the end of *The Secret Agent* are only the current words—the newspaper article in which Ossipon reads of Winnie's anonymous death, another account of the unaccountable: "an impenetrable mystery seems destined to hang forever over this act of madness or despair" (266). As with Stevie and the ethics of care, this language simultaneously posits an "impenetrable" alterity and drags that otherness into a comprehensible symbolic frame: As the narrator notes, Ossipon "was familiar with the beauties of [the article's] journalistic style" (266). The available rhetorical choices appear to be cliché or nonsense. Irony, in The Secret Agent, is the language that is most fully conscious of this unresolvable modern tension between the current words and the unaccountable. Irony is the disabled, or the detonated, form of alterity. And Stevie, in his inarticulateness, his distinct impairment, personifies the novel's linguistic as well as its ethical position.

Authority, Language, and Sexual Agony
in *The Sound and the Fury*

Benjy (nee Maury) Compson is the best known, or most recognized, cognitively impaired character in modernist fiction, perhaps in all American literature. But what do we know? What do we recognize? Barbara Johnson's comment regarding Billy Budd applies equally to Benjy: the two are comparably overdetermined, both within their respective texts and in their interpretive histories. Benjy is situated at a social-historical confluence of attitudes toward cognitive impairment and of the broader ideological forces from which these attitudes emerged. He is argued over within the novel and in subsequent critical debates, and as he serves as a moral touchstone in his social relationships, so he is a hermeneutic touchstone among his interpreters. He cannot be heard, cannot make himself understood—he is continually and unsuccessfully "trying to say." The language Faulkner constructs for him confuses time and causality. One critic contends that it is not a language at all, but rather, "a direct objective correlative to Benjy's physical and visual sensations" (Polk 105). To have access to Benjy, one must climb through sets of contending discourses about him, while simultaneously encountering his own words, which are, as it were, granted to us by a modernist telepathy, an idiologos translated into some circuitous version of common parlance.

The Sound and the Fury displays a history of attitudes toward cognitive impairment. The African American characters regard Benjy in traditional religious or superstitious terms. Dilsey sees him as a living

instance of divine simplicity, "'de Lawd's chile'" (317), while Roskus and
Versh ascribe to him supernatural powers of prophecy. Benjy's responses
to Reverend Shegog's sermon in Part IV reinforce the sense of his close
affiliation with divinity and alterity. For Caddy, Benjy is an object of
intensely pleasurable and meaningful care; and through his relationship
with his sister, Benjy is portrayed as innocent and closely aligned with
nature. Mrs. Compson, taking an attitude more typical of the late nineteenth century, while also placing Benjy in a religious perspective, sees
him as evidence of some harsh divine "'judgement on me'" (5). Caddy's
suitor Dalton Ames casually refers to Benjy as "the natural'" (160), figuring him as a non-socialized wild child. And we hear the more modern opinions, which are influenced by changing clinical practice and
social science that came to regard the cognitively impaired as social
and sexual threats and to advocate institutionalization and sterilization.
"'Why don't they lock him up?'" (49) asks a townsperson, articulating
what was becoming contemporary conventional wisdom. Jason—with
his characteristic mean-spirited humor—is emphatic in this regard,
referring to Benjy's continued residence at home as "'robbing the state
asylum of its star freshman'" (230). We know that the family has Benjy
castrated after a misunderstood attempt to make contact with a school-
girl who was walking along the same route that Caddy used to take.
And in his 1945 appendix to *The Sound and the Fury*, Faulkner tells us
that Benjy is ultimately placed in the State Hospital in Jackson. Caddy,
of course, pleads with her brother Quentin not to allow Benjy to be sent
to an institution. But Quentin kills himself, Caddy is forced to leave the
family, and Dilsey lacks the legal authority to protect Benjy.[17]

The text, then, provides an overview of the attitudes and practices
regarding the cognitively impaired in the early twentieth-century
United States. James Trent, Stephen Noll, Penny Richards and, much
earlier, Stanley Powell Davies have all described the shift in attitudes
and practices from the sentimental and religious to those informed
by Darwinian thinking and emerging understandings (and misun-
derstandings) about genetics and heredity. In fiction of the 1860s, we
see an emphasis on care for cognitively impaired family members ("all
the love of humanity contained in the father's heart was centered on
his afflicted child" ["The Squire's Son"by Miss T. Taylor, q. in Richards
76]) and also on guilt felt by parents for producing "afflicted offspring,"

perhaps through their own vices. Edouard Seguin, a French physician who immigrated to the United States in 1848, was the most influential figure in conceiving of new medical and educational approaches for treating "idiocy," and thus of transforming cognitive impairment from a local, familial concern to a broader scientific and social concern. In effect, Seguin developed the first "medical model" for cognitive impairment and lay the groundwork for the widespread popularity and use of institutionalization of the cognitively impaired, though Seguin also wrote of the "angel spirit" of a mother caring for her mentally retarded daughter (q. in Brockley 136). By the late nineteenth century, the cognitively impaired population was seen increasingly in the United States, as in Great Britain, as a social and genetic threat. Richard Dugdale's 1877 multigenerational study of the "Jukes" family convinced many of links between low intelligence, heredity, crime, and vice. Walter Fernald wrote in 1909 that "every imbecile is a potential criminal" and that "the unrecognized imbecile is the most dangerous element in the community" (q. in Trent 160–61). The psychologist Henry H. Goddard was the most prominent figure in the theorizing and treatment of cognitive impairment in the first quarter of the twentieth century. Using the newly developed Simon-Binet intelligence test, Goddard found, to his and subsequently others' alarm, that between 40 and 50 percent of immigrants could be classified as "feeble-minded" and that Native Americans fared little better (Trent 168). A similar study showed that the average southern white male volunteering for the military tested as an "imbecile" (Noll 9). Goddard's 1912 study of the "Kallikak" family showed feeble-mindedness, vice, and criminality pervading one half of a New England family in every generation since the Revolution. In Goddard's view, the cognitively impaired person was "a form of undeveloped humanity," "the wild man of today" (q. in Trent 78), and the condition was endemic among the poor and working classes, immigrants, and African Americans. Moreover, unlike Seguin, Goddard did not believe that education or training provided much remedy, even for the more highly functioning "morons"; indeed, the "moron" posed the gravest social threat because he or she could more easily blend in with the general population. Goddard believed firmly in the necessity and efficacy of eugenics, and so urged the segregation in institutions and the sterilization of "mental defectives." If these measures were undertaken, he wrote, "we could, in a generation or two, reduce the number of our dependent classes enormously and save from a fourth the a half of the expense" of poverty, crime, and prostitution (q. in Trent 165).[18]

By the mid- to late 1920s, however, scientific attitudes regarding cognitive impairment were shifting. Both the data and the conclusions of Goddard's Kallikak study were increasingly regarded as dubious, and Goddard himself confessed that he had "gone over to the enemy" (q. in Kevles 148). The shift, as Davies described it, was toward a definition of "feeble-mindedness"— that "mother of crime, pauperism, and degeneracy," as Fernald put it (q. in Davies 87)—based more on social adaptation than on intelligence testing or heredity. Davies even cited Binet and Simon writing in 1908 that "a peasant, normal in ordinary surroundings of the fields may be considered a moron in the city. In a word, retardation is a term relative to a number of circumstances" (q. in Davies 7). But Davies's conclusion was that the feebleminded should not be considered a threat because the data regarding the procreation of further generations of "morons" was inconclusive and that higher-functioning "morons" could, in fact, be trained and integrated into the social-economic order. Davies envisioned a caste system governed by intellect (which he still considered, in a broad sense, hereditary) in which the feeble-minded would be adequately trained to do the repetitive and menial tasks that a modern, industrial society required. This "Brave New World" vision of social hierarchy informed Goddard's recantation:

> If moronity is only a problem of education and the right kind of education can make out of them happy and useful hewers of wood and drawers of water, what more do we want? It may still be objected that moron parents are likely to have idiot or imbecile children. There is not much evidence that this is the case. The danger is probably negligible. (Q. in Davies 377)[19]

Goddard and Davies try to leave behind the terror of hereditary and racial degeneracy as embodied in the cognitively impaired, locating this population instead at the bottom of a more or less static social hierarchy. What replaces eugenic panic for Goddard and Davies is an embrace of modern capitalism and the recognition that all but the most impaired intellects can, with training, have a place in it, and this level of comfort with the cognitively impaired in the modern economy may be linked to the severe restrictions on immigration enacted in 1924. The opposition to immigration, especially from southern and eastern Europe, stemmed in part from the anxieties over the supposed influx of the "mentally deficient." Curtailing immigration in part relieved these anxieties.[20]

Anxieties over degeneracy, in both genetic and cultural senses, nevertheless are central to *The Sound and the Fury* and reveal the gaps in Goddard's and Davies's ostensible solution to the panic over mental deficiency and its links to race, ethnicity, gender, and sexuality. Part III, Jason's monologue, shows us the leveling effects of modern capitalism as Jason, the would-be patriarch trying to maintain his family's name and dignity, works on more or less equal terms with his erstwhile social inferiors—for instance, his employer and his African American co-worker. Everyone Jason encounters in this part of the novel—his African American servants, his niece, Quentin, his boss, his co-workers, the telegraph operator, and quite possibly even himself—everyone with the exception of Caddy would likely score poorly on the Stanford-Binet scale. This little outpost of early twentieth-century capital, with its deteriorated aristocracy, freed slaves, racial castes, retail commerce, commodity trading (the plantation owner no longer grows cotton, he now buys and sells its "futures"), and major league baseball fans is a community, in Goddard's terms, of "morons." But all are able to function well, or well enough, as hewers, drawers, stock boys, and sales clerks. As Job responds to Jason after being called a fool, "'I don't spute dat neither. Ef dat uz a crime, all chain-gangs wouldn't be black'" (231). But what of Benjy? Even having rehabilitated and apprehended in comic form the community of "morons" that had so panicked psychologists and policy makers of the first two decades of the century, Faulkner still gives us Benjy—with Caddy—dys-/disarticulated at the novel's formal and ethical hinges.

What of Benjy? What *is* Benjy? How do we read him? Eventually, all thinking about *The Sound and the Fury* returns to these questions. Faulkner parades before us a parody of historical, cultural, and biological degeneration. The patriarch is an alcoholic nihilist, and his sons are a suicide, a sadist, and an "idiot"; the mother is a helpless and ridiculous hypchondriac; the daughter is promiscuous, bears an illegitimate daughter, and that daughter replicates her mother's promiscuity while lacking her mother's powers of sympathy. Every generation descends, in both senses, from its progenitors. Generation is degeneration, with the proviso (explored more fully in *Absalom, Absalom*) that even at its height, the world of the slave-supported southern aristocracy must be seen without nostalgia as a world erected and sustained through violence and hypocrisy. The Compsons seem to provide a case study as grotesque as the Kallikaks. In this context, then, Benjy is the most extreme and emblematic case of degeneration, as in Fernald's and Goddard's dys/eugenic fantasies. Jason's narrative slides Benjy into this slot, and he is castrated and finally shipped to the State Hospital in Jackson.[21]

This movement toward Benjy's disarticulation is continued in some of Faulkner's retrospective comments. His absolute removal would logically be necessary because of his absolute psychic and linguistic distance. In his 1933 introduction to *The Sound and the Fury*, Faulkner extends certain implications traced in Part IV in the description of Benjy's bellowing: "It was nothing. Just sound. It might have been all time and injustice and sorrow become vocal for an instant by a conjunction of the planets" (288). In that introduction, Faulkner wrote that Benjy was "without thought or comprehension; shapeless, neuter, like something eyeless and voiceless which might have lived, existed merely because of its ability to suffer; half fluid, groping: a pallid and helpless mass of all mindless agony under the sun" (231). Faulkner appears to base his description on the "omniscient," external perspective of the final section—a highly problematic basis—and then projects that external, cosmic view back into Benjy's consciousness, thus begging the question of how to read the novel's opening section. Faulkner seems to recollect Benjy through an odd combination of an apotheosis of sacred folly together with a modern, "scientific" contempt for the Goddardian "idiot." As he related in an interview in 1956, "the only emotion I can have for Benjy is grief and pity for all mankind. You can't feel anything for Benjy because he doesn't feel anything. . . . He no longer had Caddy; being an idiot he was not even aware that Caddy was missing. . . . If Caddy had reappeared he probably would not have known her" (233). These last comments seem especially obtuse, as if, at this point, Faulkner had finally adopted the perspective of Jason, the last "sane Compson," as Faulkner wrote, with an uncertain level of irony, in his appendix of 1945 (212).[22] One might best respond as Dilsey does to Frony regarding whether Benjy can recognize Caddy's name: "'You just say it and see if he don't'" (31). Benjy clearly is bigger than Faulkner's subsequent reductive apotheoses allow. And April 8th and April 6th cannot account for April 7th.

But April 7th cannot account for April 7th either. It portrays a linguistic event that cannot occur. Benjy's section is an extended catachresis from start to finish. Benjy has consciousness. Modern neuroscience, evolutionary psychology, and the study of animals all concur that consciousness can exist without language, and, in any case, Benjy does have some linguistic ability, albeit very limited. He recognizes names; he knows the word "hush" and probably some other words, but evidently not many. As many readers have noted, his consciousness is largely sensory—visual, aural, tactile, olfactory—mnemonic, and emotional. Yet while we are to assume that Benjy possesses little language, Faulkner has created for him an exquisite language of poetic immediacy. For example:

> Versh set me down and we went into Mother's room. There was a fire. It was rising and falling on the walls. There was another fire in the mirror. I could smell the sickness. It was on a cloth folded on Mother's head. Her hair was on the pillow. The fire didn't reach it, but it shone on her hand, where her rings were jumping. (61)

When critics note that Beny does not interpret his experience, that he represents "perception prior to consciousness, prior to the human need to abstract from events an intelligible order" (Kartiganer 329) or that he "records speech verbatim, like a tape recorder, whether or not he understands its meaning" (Ross, q. in Burton 210), they attribute these qualities to Benjy's status as an "idiot"—a judgement toward which Faulkner pointed when he claimed that "the only thing I can feel about him personally is concern as to whether he is believable as I created him" (233). But the principal question here cannot be whether Benjy is credible as a cognitively impaired person—that is, whether a person presumed to be like Benjy might possess a mind that actually thinks in the way that Benjy is shown to think. The answer to this question would obviously be no. The language of Benjy's section is not at all some supposed inner language of a cognitively impaired person. It is the language of literary modernism. As such, it is a language that calls the conventions of language into question, and more than that, calls into question the representational or epistemological functions of language altogether. What would language be once it is dys-/disarticulated? Rendered material, rendered traumatic, cut off from meaning, alienated from social reference, returned to innocence and abjection, returned to pure consciousness, returned to the senses, damaged, degenerated, and redeemed?

To use a language of cognition in a social-symbolic order of the sort that Faulkner imagines is intolerable. All centers of authority have collapsed, and so we begin with the voice of Benjy: a voice that is not a voice, a set of words that cannot be his words; words that stand for the metamorphosis of not-language into language—which is to say, metaphor as catachresis, the bearing across, the universal margin on which symbolization has always lost its balance and dragged its matter into the nets of sense.

What is called into question? First of all, the name itself, the act of naming. Names are doubled, changed, and removed. There are two Jasons and two Quentins. Benjy was originally named Maury, then renamed when his impairment became evident; his mother calls him Benjamin; Jason and the third-person narrator of Part IV call him Ben. Caddy is also Candace and misperceived by Benjy as caddie. And Caddy, of course, is banished, her name forbidden to be spoken, as a result of her sexual misconduct. Her name shares this fate with the word "funeral," perhaps even the word "death." Caddy's sexuality shares with death a common unspeakability, a link made explicit in Caddy's recollection of the death of one her dogs: "And when Nancy fell in the ditch and Roskus shot her and the buzzards undressed her" (33). The name embodying female sexuality is dys-/disarticulated; death cannot be mentioned. Furthermore, the funeral, as Frony says, is "'where they moans'" (33), thus identifying the unintelligible sound of mourning with Benjy's extra- or pre-linguistic bellowing, and with the sound of sexual pleasure. Through these alignments of cognitive impairment, the banishing and silencing of female sexuality, and the linguistic disfigurements of sex and death, all biological processes, from conception to birth to maturation and death, are problematized; and problematized as well is the passage of time in which these processes occur and can be narrated.

Naming is linked with patriarchy: that power with the power to name, the power to legitimate or delegitimate procreation and progeny. And so the patriarch, Jason the father, is directly—that is, through the destabilizing of his authority—connected to Benjy, the often-named who has no power to name. In Part I, the father delegates his authority to Caddy, creating confusion that prefigures much of the novel's further confusion, as Caddy claims authority ("'Let them mind me tonight, Father'" [24]), young Jason rejects the delegation, saying he will mind only Dilsey, and the father simultaneously gives authority to Caddy and to Dilsey ("'You all mind Caddy, then. When they are done, bring them up the back stairs, Dilsey'" [24]). Father's granting authority to Caddy is, of course, the gesture of a tired father acceding to the wish of a willful little girl, but in this fragmenting of paternal authority we see the novel's narrative strategy and political posture. All authority is delegated, fragmented, or usurped. Quentin continually refers, or defers, to his father's authority. His narrative is a constant refrain of "Father says." And what Father says is an ironic dirge of witty and hopeless platitudes and genteel misogyny, all to the effect that time would be more bearable if it were dys-/disarticulated and that life's most unbearable feature is its incessant tendency toward procreation, with particular focus on women's central role in this. "Because women so delicate so mysterious Father said. Delicate equilibrium of periodical filth between two moons balanced" (128), which might be considered a subset of "Father was teaching us that all men are just accumulations dolls stuffed with sawdust swept up from the trash heaps" (175). This is Quentin's paternal legacy, a "mausoleum of all hope and desire" (76), or, more prosaically, a watch which Quentin breaks on the morning of his suicide.

The father defers, Quentin clings to a nihilistic reflection, and Jason the son usurps, claiming authority for himself. Quentin's repetition of "Father says" becomes, in Jason's mouth, "I say." "'Once a bitch always a bitch what I say'" (180), thus in one phrase making more vulgar and violent his father's misogyny and stopping the periodical (or progressive) wheel of time with himself, as he wills it, on the top. Jason's misogyny is accompanied by his racism and anti-Semitism, his contempt for Benjy, his enthusiastic though unsuccessful participation in capitalist speculation, and his general greed and meanness. Jason's is the authority of money, power, and self-assertion. Jason's "sanity," as Faulkner termed it in his "Appendix," represents the logic of a modernity seen as degenerate. In moral terms, the chief "degenerate" in the novel is certainly Jason, not Benjy. Conversely, the "last sane Compson" would have to be Caddy, if by sanity we mean a capacity for empathy and care.

David Mitchell and Sharon Snyder remark correctly that "all of the Compson family members are explicitly judged in relation to their ability to imagine Benjy's humanity" (167). I would amend this comment so as to emphasize that the ethical judgement is not just of characters' ability to imagine his humanity but actively to nurture and care for it. As in *The Secret Agent*, the ethical vision of *The Sound and the Fury* emerges out of the relation of care between a sister and her cognitively impaired brother, and, as in Conrad's novel, this private relation of care is insufficient to oppose the totalizing and degenerate forces of modernity. In *The Sound and the Fury*, however, the failure of care is presented in more explicitly gendered terms. Caddy's banishment and erasure is a function of the family's and society's general inability to come to terms with mature female sexuality—thus with procreation, thus with mortality. Time, in Faulkner's modernity, is an empty, economic and rational time, from which any real understanding or experience of sexuality, procreation, and mortality—in other words, of life—have been removed. As Jason says, *correspondence*, in both literal and figurative (or economic and corporeal) senses, with women is permitted; but the physical trace of the correspondence must be burned after use. Therefore, modern time is traumatic time: characterized by the violent removal of what might have given it meaning, apart from the infinite commensurability of economic exchange and the implacable asymmetries of power.

Banished with Caddy are sexuality and care. These appear in the novel to be incompatible. Even Benjy recognizes, through the smell of her perfume, Caddy's transition into adult sexuality. Does the novel imply a biological, foundational separation between Caddy's innocence, associated in Benjy's mind with the smell of leaves, and her sexual maturity? Or has Benjy detected and internalized the ideological dichotomy we see also in Quentin's thinking—and which, indeed, informs the whole novel. Faulkner certainly was conflicted on this point, as we see in his retrospective comments. The young, innocent Caddy, as he said many times, was his "heart's darling," and the image of the young girl with the muddy drawers provided the first impetus for writing the novel. The grown-up Caddy, Faulkner informs us in his "Appendix," was last seen as the mistress of a Nazi officer. The novel itself, though, is less clear on the presumed gulf between Caddy's innocence and her sexual experience.

Caddy's care for Benjy consists significantly of her efforts to re-articulate him into family and social life. She does not see him as other, as without sense or feeling, or even as entirely without language. Through her care for Benjy, Caddy combats the entire modernist trope of the radical, symbolically inaccessible other that grounds so much of the narrative working of the very novel she is in. As we see in Part IV, Benjy's bellowing as inscrutable cosmic suffering and his affiliation with Reverend Shegog's attempts to induce a "communion beyond the need for words" (294) fall precisely within the modernist project described earlier in this chapter to oppose the totalizing functions of modernity through imagining a radical alterity that would shatter or bypass it. Caddy contests the premises of this dualism. Her view of the world does not require, and her experience with her impaired brother does not permit, the identification of him as some other radically exterior to the social-symbolic order, or outside the "current words." Still less does she regard him as an object of pity, contempt, superstitious awe, or scientific condescension. She regards him as her brother who is unable to care for himself and needs her help. When their mother refers to Benjy as "'my poor baby,'" Caddy responds, "'You're not a poor baby. Are you. Are you. You've got your Caddy. Haven't you got your Caddy'" (9). Caddy recognizes, moreover, that Benjy intends to communicate but finds it exceedingly difficult to make known even his simplest wishes. On several occasions, she asks Benjy what he is trying to say, most notably and successfully when he cries when she is wearing perfume. "'So that was it. And you were trying to tell Caddy and you couldn't tell her. You wanted to, but you couldn't, could you'" (42). We know that this perception is not just a projection of her own wishes, since, when Benjy later "assaulted" the girls outside his gate, his inner report of his action was that he was "trying to say" (53). Only Caddy, however, makes the effort to understand. Just as crucially, Caddy respects Benjy's feelings and his point of view. When one of her suitors tries to kiss her in Benjy's presence and she resists, he reminds her that Benjy can't talk. "'Are you crazy,'" Caddy replies. "'He can see'"

(47). Charlie the suitor is concerned presumably about Benjy informing Caddy's parents about their kissing. Caddy is concerned about Benjy's feelings at seeing her kissing Charlie.[23]

In this last example, we see again the suggestion of a fundamental incompatibility between care and sexuality—an incompatibility suggested also in our readings of *Billy Budd* and *The Secret Agent*. Claggart's betrayal of Budd, which results in Budd's killing of Claggart, seems to originate in part in Claggart's repressed erotic fascination with Budd. Lacking the sexual component, Claggart's "handsome is as handsome does it" would stand without its ironic and fatal implication. And Captain Vere's urgent need to try and execute Billy—for whom he cares deeply—appears as well to stem from the force of Billy's physical beauty and an innocence that exerts a destabilizing erotic power. In *The Secret Agent*, we see the rigorous enforcement of a divide between care and sexuality. Winnie enters into an apparently nonsexual marriage with Verloc so that she will be able to care for her brother. Winnie thus does what Caddy is unable or unwilling to do: She remains entirely her brother's sister and care-giver, at the cost of any erotic life for herself. Only after Stevie's death does she make any gestures toward the erotic, with her desperate flirtation with Ossipon, an attraction she had previously felt, but deliberately pushed away. Even with this separation from sexuality, care in *The Secret Agent* is powerless against the totalizing forces of modernity. Care fails also in *The Sound and the Fury*, but differently, for in Faulkner's novel we see the full ideological force of modernity—or, rather, of a historical moment in transition between pre-modern and modern—directed against a female sexuality that is not necessarily inimical to care. Caddy is written out of the social-symbolic order when she tries to overcome the separation between sexuality and care. And by the end of the novel, it is Caddy who is "trying to say," who is reduced to greater and greater incoherence, as she tries to provide the means to care for her daughter, but lacks the power to overcome Jason's resistance. The erasure of female sexuality represented in Caddy's banishment is a masculine, and largely modern, horror of procreation, physicality, time, and, finally, of life. It is the banishing also of care, and the replacement of care with the scientific, rational, institutional, administrative procedures of the modern world. Caddy's banishment is of a piece with Benjy's castration and institutionalization. They join each other in unspeaking and unspeakable otherness.

Once they are both outside, the symbolic order must account for their loss and reorganize itself around the traumatic space they occupied. There must be a vocabulary for alterity that allows the social-symbolic order to achieve a new coherence, a coherence of tragedy, mourning, and love for the other whose own vocabulary has been erased. This is what Faulkner provides in Part IV: the omniscient narrator who knows nothing, for whom the world is distant, like a picture, and in a constant state of dissolution or corrosion—a traumatized world whose trauma is contained and raised up in its representation. So, at last, we *see* characters whom in previous sections we had only heard. We see Dilsey's fallen flesh, "as though muscle and tissue had been courage or fortitude which the days or the years had consumed until only the indomitable skeleton was left rising like a ruin or a landmark above the somnolent and impervious guts" (266). We see Benjy, "a big man who appeared to have been shaped of some substance whose particles would not or did not cohere to one another or to the frame which supported it" (274). We see the church where the Easter service is held, lifting its "crazy steeple like a painted church, and the whole scene . . . as flat and without perspective as a painted cardboard set upon the ultimate edge of the flat earth" (292). This clearly is vision of a peculiar order. As John Matthews has pointed out most forcefully, the presumed authority of this third-person, objective narration is illusory.[24] Moving from the partiality of the subjectivities of the novel's first three sections, the final section sets out to give us the big or the full picture, but really gives us only the world *as* picture, as Heidegger put it; that is, the world understood as complete, with every piece accounted for, precisely because it has been rendered objectively, as the object of representation.

Omniscience is modernity's great aspiration, and the final section of *The Sound and the Fury* illustrates both the power and the fragility of this narrative-epistemological goal. We see Benjy, but what do we know of him? The narration of Part IV gives us Benjy as radical other in a way that his own narrative, for all its difficulties, leaps, and switchbacks, does not. The radical, cosmic-tragic alterity ascribed to Benjy in Part IV is by no means necessitated by Part I. "It was nothing. Just sound. It might have been all time and injustice and sorrow become vocal for an instant by a conjunction of planets" (288). Why is this the case? How do we know this? On whose authority? Benjy's discourse in Part I indicates the farthest reach of modernist language, an extended catachresis of unknowing aimed at all the totalizing, systemic knowledge claims of modernity, including the rational, scientific programs that would victimize Benjy. Benjy's discourse is not intended to represent the consciousness of a severely cognitively impaired person; but it is intended to validate his social and ethical position—through the catachretic rendering of a largely non-linguistic subjectivity, to render Benjy a full human subject. But he is still a dependent subject, and so the linguistic, modernist tearing apart of narrative is inseparable from the use of care as another counter to modern totalization.[25] And the vision of care expressed through Caddy is especially notable in that it combines the Christian ethos of ethical action toward "the least of my brothers" with an incipient and then realized sexuality. Furthermore, the profound and extravagant linguistic performance ascribed to Benjy's voice, as well as Caddy's treatment of him, problematizes the condescending force of the Christian "least." As we observed earlier, Benjy is not anyone's "poor baby," and while he cannot talk, "he can see."

Thus, while Benjy is certainly "other" in some degree in the novel's opening section, he is not the radical other depicted in the last section. From what, then, has Benjy as the avatar of cosmic nullity and tragedy been conjured? We must recognize first that while Part I constructs Benjy as a human subject living in a society of interdependencies (though, pointedly, of failed ones), that section is *organized*; its temporal leaps and gaps are centered on the trauma of Benjy's loss of Caddy. His bellowing is indeed an indicator of time and sorrow. But the "moaning" and "bellering" of Part I refer to a specific, biographical loss. Benjy cannot escape from that loss and its consequences. His consciousness is engaged in a never-ending "Fort-Da" exercise—Caddy is here; Caddy is gone—which he is never able to master. But only in Part IV, through the totalizing omniscience of objective narration, is specific loss transformed into universal, cosmic absence.[26] There is significant ambivalence at work here. Part IV, with its emphases on the visual and the spiritual, on the need to transcend language and achieve a "communion beyond the need for words," indicates the futility of even the most brilliant and innovative uses of language—that is, the formal experiments of Parts I through III. But Parts I through III have already unmasked the claims of Part IV, and these cannot convincingly be recuperated. Nevertheless, claims to a totality of knowledge continue, and

Part IV is an ambivalent document of those claims. And so the radical alterities of Benjy and Shegog in that section are responses *both* to the limited alterities of the three subjective monologues and to the overwhelming knowledge claims of the final, omniscient narrator. The radical other is invented out of modernity's efforts at totalization; it seeks to serve as a sign of their failure. The cognitively impaired character here again is the vehicle of this alterity because of specific cultural traditions of the sacred fool and wild child and because of the new dis/dys-articulation of the "idiot" or "mental defective" in early twentieth-century eugenic thinking and its applications by practioners like Goddard. As I argued earlier, the radical other, posited as entirely outside the symbolic loop, can exist only in the conceptual context of a social-symbolic order perceived as closed and totalizing.

This is the drama played out in Part IV, in which Benjy loses subjective and biographical specificity, becomes identified with cosmic absence and translingustic "communion," and is firmly aligned with an African American community portrayed, particularly in the person of Dilsey, as Christian, peasant, and pre-modern. Dilsey, of course, is the one character who decisively rejects the shifting quality of names that is such a signal instance of the novel's crisis of authority.

> His name's Benjy now, Caddy said.
>
> How come it is, Dilsey said. He aint wore out the name he was born with yet, is he.
>
> Benjamin came out of the bible, Caddy said. It's a better name for him than Maury was.
>
> How come it is, Dilsey said.
>
> Mother said it is, Caddy said.
>
> Huh, Dilsey said. Name aint going to help him. Hurt him, neither. Folks dont have no luck, changing names. My name been Dilsey since fore I could remember and it be Dilsey when they's long forgot me.
>
> How will they know it's Dilsey, when it's long forgot, Dilsey, Caddy said.
>
> It'll be in the Book, honey, Dilsey said. Writ out.
>
> Can you read it, Caddy said.
>
> Wont have to, Dilsey said. They'll read it for me. All I got to do is say Ise here. (58)

The novel's logic is here in miniature. Cognitive impairment dis/dys-articulates Benjy from the family name; Caddy invokes two sources of failed authority: the Bible and her mother; Dilsey insists on the stability of names from a divine, eternal perspective and invokes the authority of a book whose power resides in the immediacy of voice, not in writing or reading, and so overrides Caddy's skeptical objections.

By the end of the novel, Benjy and Dilsey are linked, physically, thematically, and in narrative style: "Dilsey sat bolt upright, her hand on Ben's knee. Two tears slid down her fallen cheeks, in and out of the myriad coruscations of immolation and abnegation and time" (295). Dilsey's face becomes an echo of Benjy's voice: "time and injustice and sorrow." But the claims, or desires, for Dilsey's permanence will of course be disappointed. She is near the end of her life, and the next generation of African Americans, Frony and Luster, are quite different from her. Frony shares the common disdain for people like Benjy. Dilsey, the African American, will join Caddy, the sexually mature woman, and Benjy, the "idiot" in dis/dys-articulation. As the novel ends, it is modernity—Jason and his racism, anti-Semitism, and misogyny, Jim Crow, financial speculation, xenophobia, false omniscience and systems of knowledge, the oppression of every form of the weak and vulnerable (especially those who cannot speak for themselves), the deterioration of all tradition both good and bad—that will endure.[27]

"Outside the Human Type": *Nightwood* and the Tribulations of Analogy

"'You have been unwise enough to make a formula; you have wrapped the unknowable in the garments of the known'" (*Nightwood* 136). Matthew O'Connor, the false doctor, joins Ossipon, the pseudo-anarchist. "'How am I to express myself? One must use the current words.'" But in *Nightwood*, the other is more other. Robin is exclusively catachretic. Barnes constructed her precisely in the gaps between all formulas and existing vocabularies. And I mean "precisely" here to mean *precisely*. Where a terminology comes into being, Robin will not be found. She is always lost, no garments fit her, no enigmatic address label will guide the authorities or her lovers to her residence. So, then, I don't mean "precisely." There is nothing precise about Robin, and "precisely" is the least precise word among all our current critical terms. When one sees the word "precise" used in any analysis, it is a sure portent that some vague, unspeakable intimation is approaching, and that is the word's only precision. The garments of the known are loose and flowing, beautiful and, with or without intention, dissembling; not even the most careful Kierkegaardian circumnavigation can tell us the shape of their unknown inhabitant(s), much less its (their) features or characters. Benjy and Stevie can be labeled—cruelly, oppressively—as feeble-minded, mentally defective, idiot, or moron. The work of their texts is to use and contest these vocabularies. We understand the functions of Benjy and Stevie and of the characters who interact with them better insofar as we understand the historical significance of the current words that seek to determine them. But Robin? She is evidently not developmentally disabled or mentally retarded or feeble-minded (to work back chronologically through sets of current words and their various ideologies). She apparently *can* use language, but does so only very seldom. Her "rigour," as Felix says, reveals itself "in her silence, as if speech were heavy and unclarified" (119). From start to finish, Robin is "unable or unwilling to give an account of herself" (49), and no vocabularies, not even the scientistic, reductive, oppressive terms we are all too familiar with, come close to fitting her even according to their own crude diagnoses.

We could say she is "degenerate," a term broad enough to enclose any trait or activity judged by early twentieth-century norms to be deviant: Robin's sex lives, her alcohol consumption, her parenting skills, the mental status of her son, the downward trajectory of her consciousness toward that of the animals. Discourses of biological and cultural degeneracy are of course highly relevant to *Nightwood*, with its assemblage of homosexuals, Jews, tattooed Africans, abortionists, and feeble-minded aristocrats. As Jane Marcus observes, this novel, with its peculiar characters and obsessions, can be read as a prologue to the racialist-biologistic violence that the Nazis would inflict on Europe in the following decade. The novel's characters and the culture they inhabit and help create are all degenerate according to the emerging fascist sensibility of the 1930s. Yet, even as Robin may serve as touchstone in critical debates over the role of fascism in the novel—is Robin, with her indeterminate identity, a radical force against the rigid definitions of fascism (as

Marcus and Rohman argue) or does her embodiment of the radically irrational and libidinal energies of the night represent fascism itself (as Carlson in part suggests)?—she seems unfitted for these terms as well.

And yet, this is not entirely true. If the boots do fit—and they seem to slide on and off quite smoothly at times—then Robin is the Cinderella of fascist sensibilities: "The girl lost, what is she but the Prince found? . . . We were impaled in our childhood upon them. . . . They go far back in our lost distance where what we never had stands waiting . . . one would will to die of it too, with two feelings, terror and joy, where a swan (would it be ourselves, or her or him, or a mystery of all) sinks crying" (136). The mystery of the subjection, or abjection, to authority is a mystery of desire, and so the questions of what authorities and norms Robin rejects or, conversely, what forces she merges with are the same question. Subjection to the Leader and the State codifies subjection to the blood and liberates one from rival, trivial powers. Thus, we can understand, in Susan Sontag's phrase, the *fascination* of fascism, a formulation that follows from Georges Bataille's analysis of fascism as the moment when heterogeneities previously situated at social and psychic margins come to the center and assume sovereignty. The heterogeneous, for Bataille, comprises the unproductive, wasteful, exterior-to-logos parts of an economy. The unconscious, the sexually "perverse," the magical, the sacred, violent, excessive, taboo, abject, excremental, animal—all are heterogeneous. Science, writes Bataille, "cannot know heterogeneous elements as such." These elements constitute a field of "*nonexplainable difference*, which supposes the immediate access of the intellect to a body of material prior to any intellectual reduction" (141, emphasis in original). And fascist leaders, Bataille argues, "are incontestably part of heterogeneous existence" (143). In times of peace and prosperity, heterogeneous forces are contained and expressed in art, entertainment, sports, religion, etc.—elements "in a free field, open to all possibilities of effervescence and movement" (158). But in times of crisis, "once the fundamental homogeneity of society . . . has become dissociated because of its internal contradictions," the heterogeneous elements may become active political forces, signifying "a solution to the problem posed by the contradictions of homogeneity" (156). Once the heterogeneous takes power through the fascist leader and accompanying violent force, Bataille continues, it will ultimately reinforce the homogeneous, capitalist regime that it replaces—thus circumventing a Marxian revolution and providing a darker variant on the Weberian routinization of charisma.

Fascism, in Bataille's description, is another—yet another—channeling, de-channeling, and ultimate mischanneling of desire. Bataille's proximity to late Freud—in particular, to *Civilization and its Discontents* and that text's refocusing of the arguments of *Beyond the Pleasure Principle*—is obvious. But *Civilization and its Discontents*, published four years before the publication of "The Psychological Structure of Fascism," separates eros from the death drive more distinctly than do the texts of Bataille and Barnes. Freud more typically wrote of the death drive as unrepresentable in itself, as evident only in its expressions through erotic or other social behaviors. But driven, perhaps, by the portents, visible even in the early 1930s, of political catastrophe unfolding in Europe, Freud simplified the question: "And now, I think, the meaning of the evolution of civilization is no longer obscure to us. It must present the struggle between Eros and Death, between the instinct of life and the instinct of destruction, as it works itself out in the human species" (69). And Freud concluded his text by referring to the augmented power of the destructive instinct in its conjunction with modern technologies, adding a final sentence, as editor James Strachey informs us, in the 1931 edition, "when the menace of Hitler was already beginning to be apparent," which Freud worded thus: "And now it is to be expected that the other of the two 'Heavenly Powers,' eternal Eros, will make an effort to assert himself in the struggle with his equally immortal adversary. But who can foresee with what success and with what result?" (92). Posing the matter in this way, while faced with the growing probabilities of tyranny and global war, Freud neglected his earlier insights on the perpetual intertwining of aggression and libido— insights that also are central to the thinking of his contemporaries Bataille and Barnes. For Bataille, the heterogeneous is a broad assemblage of impulses and behaviors that includes war, aggression, sexual excess, the traumatic, and the sacred, which, as I take it, would subsume the "death drive" so-called, and which forms a hidden, unspeakable economy that underlies and partly motivates the visible, homogeneous economy of production and normative social and psychic life. Perhaps the two concepts are, at deeper levels, synonymous. The death drive for Freud does, in fact, take on at different times most of the features attributed by

Bataille to the heterogeneous. And perhaps the heterogeneous can, in its most fundamental moments, be understood as a biological urge toward nonexistence. Yet, to equate them seems to overcomplicate the one and oversimplify the other. Freud's impulse in conceiving of the death drive is reductive; it is, ultimately, a single thing, a final thing (or, given Freud's understanding of trauma as a threat to organic stability, an originary thing). Bataille's goal in articulating the heterogeneous is expansive; he imagines a clamoring heterocracy linked chiefly by the principle of "non-explainable difference," yet also of a cumulative reality which is "that of a force or a shock" (143). Here may lie the chief theoretical difference. The death drive ultimately negates the traumatic violation of the organism by impelling it back toward an inorganic state. Heterogeneity *is* the traumatic violation; but it is also an auto-traumatization, intrinsic to the psycho-social world of the organism itself. And—or, "and/but"— the heterogeneous instantiates a movement back out from the social toward the nonsymbolic and biological, so that here again the heterogeneous coincides with the death drive.[28]

Robin in *Nightwood* turns us toward the biological and the heterogeneous. "Always she seemed to be listening to the echo of some foray in the blood that had no known setting" (44). As has often been noted, she is consistently linked to animals, both through her physical presence and actions (as with the lion at the circus and the dog at the book's ending) and figuratively, with her unfocused vision likened to "the long unqualified range in the iris of wild beasts who have not tamed the locus down to meet the human eye" (37), and with descriptions of her as "a woman who is a beast turning human" (37), or as "outside the 'human type'— a wild thing caught in a woman's skin" (146). But her characterization as purely organic and exterior to all consciousness extends also to the vegetable world: her smell has "the quality of that earth-flesh, fungi," and "her flesh was the texture of plant life" (34). Robin is the conduit to that other world, but a conduit with no opening. As "beast turning human," she never arrives. She is irreducible; her interiority will never be recorded or deduced or divined. Yet the biological in *Nightwood* is always talking. The book's entire discourse—at least its most compelling discourse, that of Matthew O'Connor— is presented as a *bio-logos*, and there is no cultural or linguistic expression that does not finally emanate from the body. "If one gave birth to a heart on a plate, it would say 'Love' and twitch like the lopped leg of a frog" (26); "for no man can find a greater truth than his kidney will allow" (84); "you beat the liver out of a goose to get a pate; you pound the muscles of a man's cardia to get a philosopher" (87). The biological, the organic—the life of organs—is the basic level of all human emotional and intellectual life. But a process is required—of birth or excretion or violence—either to bring the organic to consciousness or take consciousness back to the organic.

Human life is this continual maieutic, evacuating, violent vacillation, and human culture constructs the document of its inscription. For what is writing in this novel? It is conscious and unconscious, of the day and the night, but these domains are not so clearly separated. On one hand, Nora, in dreams, takes "the body of Robin down with her into it ['the tide of dreams'], as the ground things take the corpse, with minute persistence, down into the earth, leaving a pattern of it on the grass, as if they stitched as they descended" (56). And on the other, as Dr. O'Connor tells Nora,

> "Do you know what has made me the greatest liar this side of the moon, telling my stories to people like you, to take the mortal agony out of their guts, and to stop them from rolling about, and drawing up their feet, and screaming, with their eyes staring over their knuckles with misery which they are trying to keep off, saying, 'Say something, Doctor, for the love of God!' And me talking away like mad. Well, that, and nothing else, has made me the liar that I am." (135)

Representation, the stitching or telling, is a response to loss, suffering, or trauma—partly an indexical tracing of the lost object that resembles symptomatic repetition, partly an improvisatory confabulation in which pleasure makes possible the replacement of inchoate, uncontrollable physical reactions. Again, the bodily, organic realm seems to have the most powerful urge, impelled by the suffering experienced by the conscious subject, to achieve representation. The stitching and narrating of loss seems to be an inevitable current of human life, and to make possible the movement between day and night, "I" and "it," the homogeneous and heterogeneous.

The process, of course, has several hitches. Most obviously, it doesn't work. The misery that impels representation survives it. It may be the case, as Marcus, Scott, and Rohman in different ways argue, that *Night-wood* gives voice to marginalized, silenced groups, or even that it valorizes the radical nonidentity of Robin, but there is no sense that anyone in any human community is actually made happier in any of their physical or mental organs through the process of articulation.[29] This may be owing to the fact that the stitching and impoverished telling that the novel presents ("I have a narrative, but you will be put to it to find it" [97]) is itself a series of hitches and approximations. It is not only that all saying is confined to the ideological and representational areas defined by the "garments of the known," Barnes's equivalent of Conrad's "current words," but that nothing can be said directly even within the verbal drapery. It is obvious that *Nightwood*'s language is almost unintermittently figurative, but what are the forms of the figures, and to what purpose? The predominant tropes are not metaphors or metonyms, though these are used at times. Rather, the novel's characteristic and, I would argue, defining tropes are similes, and similes of a particularly abstract kind: one might call them simply analogies. They take roughly the form, "as x, so y," or "x, as if y." A few examples: "As an amputated hand cannot be disowned because it is experiencing a futurity, of which the victim is its forebear, so Robin was an amputation that Nora could not renounce. As the wrist longs, so her heart longed" (59); "where the virgin blue of the eyeballs curved out the lids as if another medium than that of sight had taken its stand beneath that flesh" (7); "as insupportable a joy as would be the vision of an eland coming down an aisle of trees . . . stepping in the trepidation of flesh that will become myth; as the unicorn is neither man nor beast deprived, but human hunger pressing its breast to its prey" (37). We could also cite the passage quoted earlier telling how Nora took "the body of Robin down with her into it, as the ground things take the corpse, with minute persistence, down into the earth, leaving a pattern of it on the grass, as if they stitched as they descended" (56); or, "We swoon with the thickness of our own tongue when we say, 'I love you,' as in the eye of a child lost a long while will be found the contraction of that distance—a child going small in the claws of a beast, coming furiously up the furlongs of the iris" (83).

These are a few of many instances, and they show a great deal about the novel's representational strategies. First, in keeping with *Nightwood*'s ideological preoccupations, each trope links a physical, biological, or animal element with a discursive element. Second, as I mentioned above, these figures are not so much similes as they are analogies. Barnes herself indicates the importance of the poetics of the analogy on at least two occasions. Introducing the passage describing "taking the body of Robin down," Barnes writes, "love becomes the deposit of the heart, analogous in all degrees to the 'findings' in a tomb" (56). And later we read, "cannot a beastly thing be analogous to a fine thing if both are apprehensions?" (125). These direct uses of the analogy echo the logics of the other "as . . . as . . ." constructions and confirm the sense that analogy is the basis of *Nightwood*'s style, logic, and *bio-logos*. The "beastly"—the biological/animal/unconscious/nocturnal—is analogous to the "fine": the linguistic/conscious/ daytime. Further, we should note that Barnes creates intricate chains of analogy, which include analogies within analogies to generate further analogies. Felix bows to aristocrats "as an animal will turn its head away from a human, as if in mortal shame" (123); or, "as the ground things take the corpse . . . as if they stitched as they descended" (57). But what does this mean? How exactly does it work? Does each successive analogy strengthen or vitiate the connection being made? Why make these links through analogy rather than through more typically poetic tropes, such as simile or metaphor or metonymy?

Barnes's preference for analogy indicates her wish to establish simultaneously relation and distance. There must be no possibility of identity between the two parts of the analogy, which is to say, between the nonspeaking/biological element and the linguistic element. Analogy preserves the maieutic and violent nature of the relation in that it leaves no doubt that the one does not become the other. Barnes's implied distinction between analogy and metaphor, then, resembles Paul de Man's distinction between allegory and symbol. As he writes in "The Rhetoric of Temporality," "Whereas the symbol postulates the possibility of an identity or identification, allegory designates primarily a distance in relation to its own origin, and renouncing the nostalgia and the desire to coincide, it establishes its language in the void of this temporal difference" (207). Analogy, we might say, does not *carry across*, as is the function of metaphor. It leaves each element separate, proximate, but split by their shared, hypothetical "as": and thus marked as, at best, approximate partners in meaning. We should doubt "'everything seen, done, spoken,'" the doctor tells Nora, "'precisely because we have a word for it, and not

its alchemy'" (83). Alchemy, presumably, would be language as communion, as described in the final section of *The Sound and the Fury*, a "face-
to-face" relation "beyond the need for words." It is magic, the genuine
transformation of one element into another, the life of the night brought
fully into the articulated day. Analogy is the trope that most emphatically rejects alchemy and communion, maintaining the separateness of
each word and highlighting the inevitable failure of any precise articulation or reading of the body and every other habitat of the non-linguistic.

In so doing, the analogical *bio-logos* of *Nightwood* also contests the
dominant contemporaneous Darwinian and Lombrosian social-scien-
tific modes of reading the body, whose promise is that the body will be
readable and display consistent signifiers, if not now, then eventually.
And this certain legibility that helps construct the norms of race, gender, class, and acceptable behavior is a crucial part of the totalizing tendencies of modernity discussed earlier in this chapter, for these tendencies would have no basis if not for their claims to biological knowledge.
The body speaks and can be measured, and its utterances and numbers
can be understood, and this understanding will make possible better
social planning. This is the lesson to be learned from Broca, Agassiz,
Lombroso, and Goddard. In retrospect, this intellectual lineage appears
like alchemy: the creation of social others according to the formulae
uttered by their bodies, the empirical-rational carrying across from
body to meaning. On the other hand, we learn from *Nightwood* that
"we were created that the earth might be made sensible of her inhuman
taste; and love that the body might be so dear that even the earth should
roar with it" (83). And how is that to be translated?

Part of the pounding, then, that transforms the cardia into a philosopher comes through the agonized stresses and starts of a rhetoric
of analogy that exposes the gap between the material-biological-non-
linguistic and any form of linguistic articulation. We see in *Nightwood*
the impossibility of a comprehensive, comprehensible *bio-logos*, and
so a turning around of dys-/disarticulation from its marginal locations
back toward the assumed centers of the social-symbolic order. Impairment, defectiveness, degeneration are not where they were supposed
to have been. This reorientation cuts off the projected readings and
meanings of the totalizing social—and biologic—symbolic order, and
this may explain the novel's emphasis on images of amputation, which

always have an indexical quality, pointing across a gap toward the lost object that might complete the picture. The amputated hand to which Dr. O'Connor refers "is experiencing a futurity of which the victim is its forebear" (59). Yet, conversely, the idea of completion is always only a similitude. As the doctor says of Felix, with subsequent reference to Mlle. Basquette who had no legs, "'there's something missing and whole'" about him (26). And of Jenny, the narrator remarks, "only severed could any part of her have been called 'right'" (65).

What could it mean for a human subject to be "missing and whole"? What does it mean to establish the gap between the two sides of the analogy, but then also to cross the gap, to negate identity, but then partly recuperate it, even if ambiguously? To create a complete analogy that would go beyond the failure it intends, to realize the connection between day and night, beast and human, material or biological and linguistic—connections that the analogy will not permit, or will permit . . . only as analogy? *Nightwood* posits, hesitantly, these possibilities.

> And once Father Lucas said to me, "Be simple, Matthew, life is a simple book, and an open book, read and be simple as the beasts in the field; just being miserable isn't enough—you have got to know how." So I got to thinking and I said to myself, "This is a terrible thing that Father Lucas has put on me—be simple like the beasts and yet think and harm nobody." (131)

This pastoral admonition contains, of course, premises that the bulk of *Nightwood* rejects. Life, whether as experience or narrative or *bios*, may be analogized to a book, but it is by no means a simple book and certainly not an open or easily readable book; nor are beasts as we encounter them here particularly simple. But after a small revision, we can say, Live in the night, without linguistic consciousness, like an animal (like Robin), and yet think, and act ethically. An admonition in this form entails both a genuine bio-logos and a bio-ethics: It suggests a recognition of animality as mortal, vulnerable, unstable, with only partial conscious autonomy. It is like an adulthood that does not forget its infancy. And this recognition applies both to the subject and the other. To be an animal and to know that one is an animal, and to think and harm nobody. This is certainly, as Matthew says, "a terrible thing," but it seems to be, more or less, where we find ourselves as human beings. It would be easier to stand only on one side of the relation: with the *logos*, ascribing animality only to others; or fully with the *bios* (which is also the Dionysian, the transgressive, the abject, the heterogenous, the death-drive) and leave the *logos* to its own devices.

And here we find Robin. We noted earlier Robin's relation both to plant and animal life, her standing on the *bio-* side of the biological street, and thus her being "unwilling or unable to give an account of herself" (49). Carrie Rohman writes, quite correctly, that Robin rejects Father Lucas's directive to be an animal and yet think, that she "abandons this goal and almost celebrates the impossibility of attaining it by variously rejecting the symbolic and embracing animality" (78–79). The question then becomes, what does this rejection mean? What does it mean to be where Robin is? Robin seems to be beyond even the reach of analogy. The doctor's and others' descriptions of her try to tell what she *is*, not what she is *like* or *as*. Not entirely, of course. She is, the doctor tells Nora, "outside the 'human type'—a wild thing caught in a woman's skin, monstrously alone, monstrously vain"; but, the doctor continues, "like the paralyzed man in Coney Island" (146), a comparison that then proceeds along an even more bizarre and extended route than most of Barnes's similitudes.[30] But for the most part, characterizations of Robin apply terms to her without mediation—which, given the book's prevalent rhetorical strategy is unexpected. But then, how could Robin be analogized, whose existence works to negate all transfers from *bios* to *logos*, even those qualified and distanced by analogy? She thinks "unpeopled thoughts" (46); she is the "uninhabited angel" (148), the "eternal momentary" (127); she looks "as if the hide of time had been stripped from her, and with it, all transactions with knowledge" (134).[31] As animal, vegetable, angel, child, eternal, momentary, unknowing, Robin is innocent, and, the doctor tells Nora, "'to be utterly innocent would be to be utterly unknown, particularly to oneself'" (138). And what does innocence mean—in this book and at this moment in history?

Robin is a way out, an outside to a totalizing social-symbolic order in the process of moving toward an overtly totalitarian, fascist state which would not just assimilate or redetermine, but would eliminate all alterity. The garments of the known do not fit her; she is unreachable through the current words. She lays down, as Matthew says, "in the Great Bed and her identity is not her own, her 'trust' is not with her, and her 'willingness' is of another permission" (81). The rigidities, the particularly masculinist rigidities, we associate with fascism are absent from her, as are the rigidities of racial identity advanced by social scientists and theorists of degeneration and eugenics. Conrad and Faulkner imagined dys-/disarticulate figures who stood in epistemological and ethical contrast to the totalizing forces of modernity, but their struggles were conceived as failures. Ultimately, Stevie's and Benjy's cognitive impairments and linguistic marginalities rendered them morally central, but practically powerless, and the social-symbolic order destroyed them. Irony and mysticism respectively seem the only ways out of modernity in *The Secret Agent* and *The Sound and the Fury*. Robin, on the other hand, is not destroyed, though her status at the end of the book is ambiguous. Nevertheless, if she is a way out, a figure of transgression and liberation, it seems clear what she is liberated from—from the "human type" as ideologically determined by the social-symbolic order of modernity— but not at all clear what she has liberated herself into.

Robin's situation is complicated by her dual status as an object of care and an object of desire. In *The Secret Agent* and *The Sound and the Fury*, great energy was expended to keep these positions separate, and this separation brought serious consequences. Sexuality and care were, apparently, incompatible, and the dys-/disarticulate figure who required care had to be maintained in a state of asexual innocence. Any mingling whatever of care and sexuality—especially within the family relationships prevailing in these novels—could only be catastrophic. In *Nightwood*, this separation is breached. Nora, Felix, and Jenny in their different ways all care for and sexually desire Robin. And in this mingling, or flooding, of care into desire, we see again the impossibility of either in relation to modernity; or, rather, we see the appropriation of desire into modern relations of power. In his lecture to Nora on the night, Matthew describes the anarchy of desire—"He lies down with his Nelly and drops off into the arms of his Gretchen"—but throughout the novel, desire, even in its animality, expresses itself in the trappings of social hierarchy. Felix's genuflections to aristocracy are like those of an animal turning "its head away from a human, as if in mortal shame" (123). The lion at the circus bows to Robin. All the erotic relationships in the novel are hierarchical, animated by differing positions of power, by the abasement of one lover to the other. As Nora says, "'there's something evil in me that loves evil and degradation—purity's black backside'" (135). And we might say that this need for abasement, or domination, in sexual life is an effect of the hierarchical traumatisms of social life or, as Freud thought, of the Oedipal traumas of early childhood, except that in *Nightwood*, animals experience it too, and so does Robin with her lack of "all transactions with knowledge" (134). At the end of the novel, she and a dog approach each other in a frenzy of mutual subjection:

> Then she began to bark also, crawling after him—barking in a fit of laughter, obscene and touching. The dog began to cry then, running with her, head-on with her head, as if to circumvent her; soft and slow his feet went padding. He went this way and that, low down in his throat crying, and she grinning and crying with him; crying in shorter and shorter spaces, moving head to head, until she gave up, lying out, her hands beside her, her face turned and weeping; and the dog too gave up then, and lay down, his eyes bloodshot, his head flat along her knees. (170)

The stylistic difference we see in this passage, and throughout the final chapter, from the rest of the novel is obvious. There are no analogies, no figures of speech at all. Singularly in the book, here we find only straight narration as Robin and the dog approach their strange communion. If the function of analogy is, as I have described it, to emphasize the gap between matter and language, between biological organism and the speaking subject, and thus to emphasize also the violent, maieutic character of verbal expression, then the purposeful absence of analogy implies the elimination of that gap, or elimination of the need for the gap through the negation of the second term—that is, language and the speaking subject. Robin's transaction with the dog is an approximate illustration of Reverend Shegog's sermon in *The Sound and the Fury*— a "communion beyond the need for words"—but transposed from the spiritual to the animal realm. The gap is eliminated, but the violence is not. So, here we see the convergence of the radical absence of thought and language; innocence; instinct; echoes of the blood; dramas of abasement and domination; a vacating of the social-symbolic order, and its return as a biological force. Liberation from modern totality turns out perhaps to be liberation into totalitarian or fascist structures.

Not that this is clear. It is certainly the case that Robin cannot occupy the places held by Stevie and Benjy as figure of a dys-/dis-articulated premodern, Christian ethics of care. It may be that her transgressive, nomadic modes of desire, which cause such damage to all who desire and care for her, point toward a utopian area of desire unbound from ego structures and their corollary social norms—like a place described by Deleuze and Guattari—and that the hierarchical presentation of desire that suffuses the novel functions as, in effect, sexuality's "current words," an ideology of desire that will eventually be overcome. In that case, the book's ending replays and transforms the end of Forster's *A Passage to India*, when, at Aziz and Fielding's final meeting, all of culture and nature seem to prohibit their friendship: "No, not yet. . . . No, not there" (322). And yet, the ending implies, *someday*, in a different social order, the human basis for their friendship persists. Likewise, *Nightwood* perhaps implies that in a different social order, the unboundedness of desire, the concord and reciprocal genuflection between human and animal, the liberation from all limits of the symbolic will prevail, and a new kind of happiness will be born. For clearly, a new kind of happiness is necessary, particularly given the perspective of political crises of the 1930s. The sense of fundamental incompatibility between the most basic psychic and social energies—the homogeneous and heterogeneous economies, eros and the death drive, *bios* and *logos*—insists that there is no way out of the impasse with only the resources currently available. But it seems a lot to ask that Robin be the purveyor of the new happiness, or to read much utopian inclination into *Nightwood*. The book points down, as several of its chapter titles indicate. It reorients contemporary racist, misogynist, homophobic, xenophobic senses of degeneration, but only to endorse the notion in a way less prudish and middlebrow, yet just as thorough as that of Nordau. To be the "uninhabited angel" thinking "unpeopled thoughts" and hearing "echoes of the blood" is one way to shake out of the "garments of the known" that cause such oppression and misery. But, as I read it, *Nightwood*'s ethics are more akin to Habermas's response to the various critiques of reason in modern western philosophy and social thought: that whatever reason's limits and failures, what we need is more of it, not less.[32] The utopian injunction of *Nightwood* is to be like the animals, "and yet think."

3

Post-Modern Wild Children, Falling Towers,
and the Counter-Linguistic Turn

Most commentaries on the destruction of the Tower of Babel regard it
as a second Fall, a fragmentation of the perfect language of naming that
Adam conceived and so the beginning of the split between word and
thing that brought into the world lying, ambiguity, irony, negation, arti-
fice, the unconscious, ideology, the subject, the Other, and all the various
woes and pleasures we now associate with language. In the Zohar we
read that the biblical phrase "the whole earth was of one language" indicates that "the world was still a unity with one single faith in the Holy
One" (253), and a bit further, that when this language was lost to the
majority of humankind, their prayers became fruitless because angels
only understood the holy tongue (256).[1] One commentary, however, in
the Middrash Rabbah, regards the pre-Babel unity of language in a less
favorable light. "All the earth was of one language of sharp words," it
remarks, and the people were "united in idol worship" (306). This gloss,
I think, can be read in two ways. First, we can take it to mean that what
appeared to be a unified language was, in fact, already divided. It was a
language of disagreement and strife (which we would not expect of the
Adamic language of perfect correspondence). Moreover, the worship
of idols suggests a multiplicity of deities and not a unity. In this view,
the Adamic language was not so perfect after all, was perhaps already
partly fallen—a perspective Walter Benjamin suggested in his essay on
the distinction between human language and what he called "language
as such." But second, we might also take this middrashic disparagement

of language before Babel as an implicit critique of unity, transparency of meaning, and all other purported virtues of the primal, perfect language. If the singleness of Adamic language is a unity in idolatry, then the tower itself, as an affront to the single God of justice, is also a monument to the Adamic singleness of meaning. And if this is so, then God's entrusting Adam with the creation of a single world language was an enormous mistake. All of Adam's undivided significations must, of necessity, have piled together into a single huge signifier whose single aspiration and referent could only be God. And God, then, in a surprising act of good sense and modesty, smashed this natural signifier, this excrescence of Adamic meaning, and henceforth authorized only multiple and divided significations. The broken tower was a sign of liberation, and God was the first polytheist.

Glossed in this way, the fall of Babel can be seen as a figure for the condition of post-modernity as theorized in the 1970s and 1980s. As with the discourses of modernity and modernism we examined in chapter 2, there is in discussions of the post-modern a stress on brokenness, an anxiety regarding the encroachment of totalizing discursive power into all areas of life, and a distrust of language altogether. There is indeed so much continuity in these modernist and post-modern attitudes that we might question the value of the distinction except perhaps as a strictly chronological one that separates, though imprecisely, phenomena of the first half of the twentieth century from those of the second half. There seems though to be a difference in affect, as the post-modern often exhibits an exhilaration rather than a despair at the collapse of governing discourses. The post-modern subject does not "shore fragments" against his "ruin," as Eliot propounded in "The Waste Land." There is not the gnostic sense, so powerful in modernist texts, that world, culture, language—some shattered god-term—might somehow be reassembled (or, in its devastation, redeemed), or, conversely, that a greater, more conclusive catastrophe is soon to come. A modernist sensibility assumes an origin (though shattered) and a telos (though unfulfilled). Modernity, in this view, stands, as Frank Kermode's still-compelling argument asserts, at a moment of crisis in between two temporal points. There is, thus, an assumption regarding the possibility and efficacy of narrative—the depiction of events and motivated actions occurring in time—and of hermeneutic depth, since origins, ends, action, and narrative require interpretation. This is not the case in theorizations of the post-modern. The great explanatory narratives of origins and ends, the psychological theories that inform those narratives' presentations of intention and action, and the hermeneutic methods used to interpret texts and the world as text are all rejected, abandoned, or, ideally, forgotten, in post-modernism.[2]

But the theory necessarily becomes muddled. We see a wish for the end of the symbolic—for a new version of dys-/disarticulation that would enter and, ultimately, dominate a social-political scene so defined by symbolic, and especially economic, relations as to render all of them without depth or meaning. This scene is best encapsulated as the Baudrillardian "matrix," that dystopia of global capital (whose euphemistic name is "the machine") that begs for some experiential "real" to bring its liberation. What saves us from the symbolic can only be the non-symbolic. Or would that be the *narrative* of the non-symbolic, in which amnesia, denial, oppression, and liberation are given their places? A new innocence with no satellites or tributaries of nostalgia is installed, then broken; pastiche reverts or fattens into parody; history resumes. Modern fallenness oscillates with post-modern innocence. The modern degenerate morphs into a post-modern wild child.

This chapter explores some of the consequences of damage to a linguistic-social order, for which the destruction of Babel serves as prototype. First, a society may regard its world as fallen and look back nostalgically to the world before the Fall. In this view, the catastrophe is an event of pre-history that has no active consequences, since the world has been as it is through all historical memory. In this case, catastrophe does not entail trauma. Conversely, people who feel the damage to the symbolic order more acutely and traumatically may try to restore the previous order exactly as it was—to rebuild the tower, to reestablish what was imagined to be a perfect language without ambiguity, the language of Adam. This approach, with its rigidity and its determination to rediscover and impose a set of single, absolute signifiers, I associate with a logic of terror and terrorism. Third, in the wake of perceived damage to the symbolic order, people may try to imagine modes of human life removed from symbolic-linguistic behavior altogether—in other words, try to imagine modes of transcendence. What is at stake in this discussion is the status of language and representation in relation to social trauma. As I have been arguing, portrayals of cognitively and

linguistically impaired people—the dys-/disarticulate—have played crucial roles in helping European and American cultures to come to terms
with social traumas that are perceived to have damaged not just persons
and institutions but ways of thinking, feeling, and living in a world constructed and mediated by symbols, especially language. Indeed, a trajectory of such portrayals of cognitive and linguistic impairment from,
for example, *Billy Budd* through *Forrest Gump* forms a history of self-
scrutiny for European and American cultures. This chapter will examine, in particular, portrayals of neurologically impaired people in the
case studies of Oliver Sacks and in novels of Paul Auster, Jerzy Kosinski,
and Don DeLillo. The cognitively and linguistically impaired figures in
these narratives—whom I call "post-modern wild children"—illustrate
contemporary tendencies toward desires for terror and transcendence in
response to traumatic damage to the symbolic order.[3]

Verses and Reverses: The Language of Turning

A tower falls, and in the rubble numerous post-catastrophic revelations
take shape. One can embrace the fall or deny it, memorialize it or force
it into oblivion, or try to restore the tower just as it was. But in any case,
we encounter a condition of trauma, of living in the wake of a previously unimaginable and still unassimilable disaster that in conscious
and unconscious ways fills our psychic and social spaces. For al Queda,
the Tower was the golden age of Islam, despoiled by Western colonial-
ism and the loss of pure faith. For the administration of George W.
Bush, the twin towers became, in retrospect, embodiments of America's
physical invulnerability, which was adjunct to its moral invulnerability, its absolute innocence. The logic and desire both of terrorism and
of anti-terrorism is to restore the imagined former state of social harmony and perfect correspondence between word and thing—to rebuild
its tower, in no matter how grotesque a form. Every historical catastrophe replays the destruction of Babel, for not only buildings and lives are
lost, but ways of thinking and speaking are transformed.

But in the post-Babel moment, there may also arise a logic and desire
of something else, for whose terminology we must resort to catachresis. It is a turn against the symbolic altogether, a counter-linguistic
turn, an urge to dys-/disarticulate. We might call this a move toward

transcendence if by this word we mean whatever surpasses, or passes below, all conceptual categories and symbolic forms. The divine, the sublime, the abject, the real, as well as the term "transcendent" itself, serve as catachreses for all that is beyond conceptualization but not necessarily beyond experience. The urges both toward terrorism and toward transcendence are post-apocalyptic responses to a catastrophe that is experienced as a disaster of language. Terrorism holds that the original, primal, pre-Babel language must be restored, and that the restoration can be achieved only through violence. The move toward transcendence finds revealed in the catastrophe the idea that language in any form is inadequate. If we can refer for a moment to Plato's "Cratyllus," the desire for transcendence challenges Cratyllus's position that language can, or should, perfectly correspond to the world; on the other hand, it is not satisfied with Hermogenes's conventionalist argument, whose implication, if we follow it through Saussure, Althusser, and the whole twentieth-century linguistic turn, is that we are creatures of language, socialized into language, and that language goes, as they say, all the way down. In the linguistic turn's most dramatic and exuberant form, post-structuralism of the late 1960s and early 1970s, there is a reveling, at times an ecstatic immersion, in the post-Babel, Saussurean condition, which is understood as an epistemological, psychological, and political liberation from the totalizing (yet naive) monologic of some imagined language of correspondence. Yet, in breaking the tyrannical link between signifier and referent, we are then left with only the signifier, whose subsequent determining functions may be no less tyrannical, merely more arbitrary.[4]

In a broad sense, for the variants of the linguistic turn, there is nothing other than language. Meaning, following Saussure, is construed out of differences, which is to say, out of minor or local alterities—alterities within the language system—but there is nothing (or, at any rate, nothing in any way intelligible) other than language. Even apparently non-linguistic entities—the unconscious, the body, nature, sexuality—attain all that they can attain of identity and ontological and social standing insofar as they are signifiers. The linguistic turn in all its forms conceives of itself as de-mystifying and secular. It is iconoclastic in that it sets out to destroy or discredit any forms of representation that claim to be mimetic. At the same time, it is deeply iconophilic in that, however critically, its focus remains always on the representation. The sign is both nothing and everything.

Variations on the linguistic turn have provided the theoretical bases for the humanities and some of the social sciences for much of the twentieth century.[5] Concurrently, however, and with increasing influence over the past fifteen or twenty years, we can see in the academic humanities, in some literary fiction, and in areas of popular culture, varieties of what we might call a "counter-linguistic turn." In its academic forms, the counter-linguistic turn is not a direct repudiation of the linguistic turn; in particular, it draws much of its impetus from post-structuralism's concern with questions of difference and alterity. But the forms of thinking I'm calling "counter-linguistic" do not focus only on the local alterities that create meaning in Saussurean terms. Rather, their central claim is that there *is* an other of language, whether or not this other can be conceptualized, and that language does not go "all the way down."[6]

Here are a few examples: 1) Early in the twentieth century, the mystical tendency in one of the foundational texts of the linguistic turn, Wittgenstein's *Tractatus*, with its suggestion that ultimately what cannot be said is of more value than what can be said; a bit later, Bataille's discussions of heterogeneity and waste as the true bases of culture; and in the 1950s, Levinas's thinking on the Other that cannot be thematized. 2) The "ethical turn" in post-structuralism (e.g., in Lyotard and Derrida) which focuses largely on social relations and historical and social knowledges that are not commensurable with existing (linguistic) conceptualizations. Related to this ethical turn is a renewed interest in religion on the part of post-structuralist and psychoanalytic thinkers (for instance, Derrida, Slavoj Zizek, Eric Santner).[7] 3) The shift in Lacanian theory from a focus on the symbolic, and on subjectivity as interpellation, to a focus on the real—that is, on the unsymbolizable gaps in the symbolic (the shift from Althusser to Zizek).[8] 4) An interest among literary scholars in developments in cognitive science and evolutionary psychology and linguistics, which suggest forms of consciousness and thought not based in language. 5) The growing importance of the concept of trauma in literary studies, where trauma is understood not just as a grievous injury and its symptomatic aftermaths, but as a fundamental shock to, and even negation of, the whole process of conceptualization and representation. 6) The emergence of animal studies whose interest is the semiotic and ethical status of the non-human, non-linguistic animal.[9]

7) Studies across several fields that stress materiality or physicality. This work often focuses on the body, which serves as a crucial and contested boundary marker for the limits of language. Debates surrounding the discursive status of the body illustrate the ongoing tensions and interrelations between linguistic and counter-linguistic tendencies in contemporary theory. Judith Butler, for instance, has made compelling arguments that the body is itself a discursive, performative formation. "The matter of bodies," she writes, "will be indissociable from the regulatory norms that govern their materialization and the signification of those material effects" (2), and what one may refer to as "extra-discursive" is "formed by the very discourse from which it seeks to free itself" (11). Butler disclaims a naive constructivism in which "the materiality of bodies is simply and only a linguistic effect" (30), but clearly she hedges her bets on the side of the linguistic, which she regards as "the very condition under which matter may be said to appear" (31). In contrast, Elizabeth Bronfen, while describing the relations between the body and language in terms similar to those used by Butler, argues a more counter-linguistic position that emphasizes the persistent presence and effect of what language cannot encompass:

> This primacy of the body as object of negotiation and representation . . . also readily calls forth the question whether there is a body outside language or whether our knowledge of the body depends on the highly diverse and differentiated images of it that come to be constructed in accordance with particular social contexts and questions of normalcy relevant at specific historical moments. Is the body always already cultured or does the body pose as the measure and demarcation point of culture, as the site of truth, authenticity and inevitability? Is the body perhaps such a privileged object of our cultural image repertoire as well as such a pressing category in cultural criticism precisely because it quite literally embodies the fact that the incommensurability between the real and its representations can never fully be resolved? (112–13)

8) Most prominent, and perhaps encompassing these other tendencies, is the pervasive concern across a number of disciplines with alterity and the "other" as categories that by definition escape whatever concepts we might apply to them.

It is important to state again that these forms of the counter-linguistic turn tend to be not so much repudiations of the linguistic turn as developments of its terms and assumptions. Theorizations of alterity, for example, can be seen as elaborations of Saussurean descriptions of differentiation. Rather than showing how meaning is created through distinctions between signs in a semiotic system, theories of alterity try to explain how the system itself acquires meaning through its relation with what is posited as outside it. Categories elaborated in post-structuralism are especially important in this regard, as often the secondary term of a binary structure returns as the supplement that simultaneously reveals and heals the lack in a symbolic network. Thus, the "queer" and the "crip" (in queer and disability studies, respectively) reemerge as banished "others" that both destabilize and enable norms of gender and physical ability. As has often been pointed out, much of the formative work of the New Historicism criticized what it took to be the ahistorical, apolitical, non-materialist approaches of post-structuralism while using post-structuralist techniques of textual analysis. More broadly, Levinas's transcendent, unthematizable other makes possible an ethics; Gayatri Spivak's silent subaltern demands a politics. In Zizek, the traumatic real is both the "rock on which every formalization stumbles" (*Sublime Object* 172) and the fissure or wound or threatening alterity in every symbolic order, and simultaneously it is that which generates further symbolization in the effort to cover over or deny the fissure.[10]

The two recurring and often intertwined motifs of the counter-linguistic turn are trauma and transcendence. Language is not enough; language is broken. And something has broken it. The damage to the symbolic order is not just structural, as it sometimes appears in Zizek, but is historical. Events have happened which have had lasting and symptomatic effects on modes of representation and communication.[11] Trauma theory as it has developed in literary studies consistently returns to the Holocaust as the singular obliterating event that shows how historical trauma works: how a morally and conceptually unassimilable crime both generates and stymies efforts to understand and represent it, and how societies can compulsively, symptomatically repeat it. At the same time as it provides a paradigm for trauma, however, the Holocaust has become venerated as a sacred object. Its presumed status outside of language allows it to be both at once—for the traumatic and the sacred are equally unrepresentable, and so the same inadequate terms may be used indistinguishably for both. The witness and survivor take on a sacred status as having returned from beyond the boundary of all previous moral imaginings, and their language can be seen as an awful, almost non-linguistic mix of metaphor, literal repetition, and indexical pointing which in some sense conveys the traumatic event without being able to represent it. The survivor is Daniel, is Jonah, but a Daniel whose language has been devoured, a Jonah whose language has been drowned.[12]

All these forms of the counter-linguistic turn begin from some version of a post-Babel condition. Language is broken—has been traumatically broken—yet remains nevertheless ideologically imprisoning. There *is* some other of language (whether divine, traumatic, or neurological), but we have only our existing broken language with which to summon and encounter it. Thus, the transcendent can be expressed or addressed only in terms of the traumatic. What is whole can be represented only in terms of what is broken. At the same time, what is broken also can be represented only by what is broken. The relation of this paradox and this tautology is a persistent, irreducible fact and motive in modern representation. The most bereft and abject circumstance finds available to it only those same tropes that are available to ideas of the divine or transcendent. In the post-Babel condition that has been so widely depicted in Europe and America at least since World War I, the abject, the traumatic, and the transcendent have been linguistically indistinguishable.

In this context of a modern tension between language and its traumatic-transcendent other, the older, Enlightenment figure of the "wild child" has returned in new forms. The wild child of the Enlightenment was seen as occupying a boundary between nature and culture, as a biologically human being who had not been socialized and did not possess language. As such, the real or purported feral children who became well known in the eighteenth and early nineteenth centuries fascinated Enlightenment thinkers who used them as occasions for contemplating what human qualities, especially moral or spiritual qualities, were innate or natural and what were products of society and language. The wild child provided an apparent test of human nature, though with ambiguous results. The affectionate and generous Kaspar Hauser seemed to confirm a Rousseauean view of natural goodness— "a living refutation of the doctrine of original sin," one witness described him (Masson 44)—while Victor of Averyon inspired an observer to remark that "nature . . . is a state of nullity and barbarism" and "that moral superiority said to be *natural* to man is only the result of civilization" (Lane 129). The Enlightenment wild child functioned as a thought experiment that permitted the social-linguistic person to be separated from some more primal existence—as noble or ignoble savage, as animal or divinity. He would be the case in point that might illustrate, if not determine, the most important and troubling questions about human subjectivity, language, moral development, and social organization. If only he could be taught to speak, the wild child would tell for the first time of human existence outside of language; he would give testimony of Eden, just before Adam named the world and before he learned transgression.

What I am calling the post-modern wild child differs in significant ways from its Enlightenment predecessors. In the Enlightenment myth, the child isolated from society and language might unveil essential human truths. The crucial prerequisite was that the child enter society from outside, that his "wildness" derive from an unsocialized life in nature. For the post-modern wild child, this clear distinction between society and nature is problematized. The "wildness" in question emerges from within the social or as a hybrid of social-symbolic, natural (in the traditional sense of non- or pre-social—the "state of nature"), and biological (that is, genetic and neurological). Thus, in Paul Auster's novel *City of Glass*, Peter Stillman, Jr., achieves his wild child, dys/disarticulate status through a horrible instance of paternal abuse— a descendent of the "forbidden experiments" chronicled by Roger Shattuck and repeated with unspeakably tragic results in the more recent case of "Genie."[13] In Don DeLillo's *White Noise*, Wilder seems to have some unstated genetic developmental disability, but also appears to derive some of his "wildness" through an unmediated relation to technology. Jerzy Kosinski's Chance, in *Being There*, reaches his peculiar state of innocence through his simultaneous immersions in gardening and television. Or, in case studies of Oliver Sacks that might serve as clinical counterpoints to these novels, the wild child is a neurological other, a construction of scientific discourses that, in Sacks's presentation, retains many of the older, Enlightenment features of the wild child.

Contemporary portrayals of such individuals focus less on innate ideas and moral qualities, and more on the nature of consciousness as a physical or spiritual condition and on the nature of the boundary between a non-linguistic alterity and the social-symbolic order. Thus, these figures of neurological/linguistic impairment are of enormous value in understanding contemporary thought and culture, and an interest in linguistically, cognitively, or neurologically impaired versions of wild children extends through recent fiction, popular films, and popularizations of science and medicine. Not in all cases, but in general, linguistic and cognitive impairment in these works is a figure for impairments of language and cognition more broadly, and the linguistically impaired person is a site both of social-linguistic trauma and of some kind of redemption of that trauma that reaches beyond language.

As with the Enlightenment wild child, the post-modern wild child, standing just outside the social-symbolic order, tests the capacities of that order. He or she is also, however, an index or symptom pointing to the damage that language has suffered. The Enlightenment wild child stood as a potential answer to important philosophical questions; he pointed toward origins. The post-modern wild child plays, if anything, a weightier imaginative role, for he points toward ends, toward redemption. Cut off from language through neurological impairment, or, as in Auster's novel, paternal abuse, the contemporary wild child, as presented in the texts I will examine, embodies the full traumatic-transcendent possibilities of human existence outside of language. This is an enormous burden for any representation to bear—even more so since contemporary wild children are encountered in ostensibly secular aesthetic and clinical contexts. The question that is at stake here is how these linguistically damaged figures are responses to modern social trauma in which language—the chief vehicle and transmitter of the social—is itself seen as damaged.[14]

City of Glass: The Opacity of the Broken Thing

Paul Auster's *City of Glass* appears to be a paradigmatic post-modern text. Intensely concerned with its status as text, it abounds in meta-textual devices. There are multiple identities, shared and diverging names, characters who split into two, characters who diminish into nothing.

The name of the author, "Paul Auster," appears as the name of a character who strongly resembles the actual Paul Auster and also as the name of a private detective who never appears in the book but which is appropriated by the book's protagonist, Daniel Quinn. The book is full of theories—of authorship, of language, of the status of fictional characters, of the verisimilitude of a fictional text. Paul Auster (the character) speculates on the authorship of *Don Quixote*, but Daniel Quinn may be a version of that questing knight—at any rate, he shares his initials. "Henry Dark," an invented creation of the mad religion professor, Peter Stillman, postulates Miltonic theories of fallen language and shares initials with another fictional philosopher of language, Humpty Dumpty. Peter Stillman, and his son, Peter Stillman, Jr., who was deprived of language by his father in order that he might spontaneously reveal the original, divine, Adamic language, have the initials "P.S."—post-script. There are, furthermore, two versions of Peter Stillman, Sr., who step off the train at Grand Central Station, and Quinn must decide which one to follow. Quinn's son, who died in a car accident with Quinn's wife, was also named Peter. The novel, having been narrated by an omniscient, third-person voice for 134 pages, suddenly acquires an "author" on page 135, who, now in the first person, tells the rest of the story. This author, we learn at the end, harbors great hostility toward "Paul Auster" and sympathy toward the unfortunate Daniel Quinn. (And yet, according to "Auster's" theory of authorship, the true author of this text may be Quinn himself!). Quinn, even at the start of the narrative, is divided into three entities—the person Quinn, the pseudonym under which he writes mystery novels (William Wilson), and the detective-hero of these novels (Max Work). William Wilson many readers might recognize as a character from Edgar Allen Poe who possesses a malevolent *doppelganger*; and well-informed fans of the New York Mets baseball team might recall, and as we learn later in the novel, that this is also the true name of the Mets' excellent center-fielder from the late 1970s through the late 1980s, better known as "Mookie." When Quinn begins his work (modeled on "Max Work") as an ersatz detective named Paul Auster (trying to protect Peter Stillman, Jr., from his father who has just been released from prison), he buys a red notebook in which to record his notes on his case. When the red notebook runs out of pages, Quinn's existence ceases.

The novel plays with realism and verisimilitude. In the first few pages, Quinn is reading a passage from *The Travels* of Marco Polo, which promises that "'we will set down things seen as seen, things heard as heard, so that our book may be an accurate record, free from any sort of fabrication'" (7). This book is well known as a compendium of fact and fantasy, and Polo's stated commitment to reality in the midst of such fabulous textuality is a consistent feature of Auster's text as well. The mysterious "author" who enters the text belatedly concludes that "I have followed the red notebook as closely as I could, and any inaccuracies in the story should be blamed on me. There were moments when the text was difficult to decipher, but I have done my best with it and have refrained from any interpretation. The red notebook, of course, is only half the story, as any sensitive reader will understand" (158). This gambit of grounding the fictional, or fantastical, in a generic shape of verisimilitude is Roland Barthes's notion of the "reality effect." For Barthes, it is primarily a function of ideology. The accumulation of mundane detail and presumed psychological depth produces a woven surface seemingly free of ideological presence. It is reality; there is no arguing with it. *City of Glass*'s most notable triumph of verisimilitude comes in chapter 5 when Quinn visits the "Heights Luncheonette" on Broadway and 112th Street. The text describes in wonderful detail this dingy establishment selling stationery and magazines, with a small lunch counter, a Puerto Rican cook who talks about the New York Mets, the elderly proprietor at the cash register with a concentration camp tattoo on his forearm. It is a marvelous textual creation. And, as anyone who lived in Morningside Heights in the 1970s or early 1980s can testify, it is entirely accurate. This is none other than the Mill Luncheonette on Broadway and 112th Street, with its egg creams, terrible hamburgers, assorted school supplies, pornographic magazines, the tall Puerto Rican cook, whose name was Benny Alicea, the old Holocaust survivor, Morris Drogin, who owned the store and always worked the register. As a former patron of the Mill myself, I am amazed each time I read this scene and see this little dive depicted with such accuracy and, I would venture, love. Wonderful also is Auster's depiction of the conversation between two forlorn New York Mets fans. The players mentioned (Dave Kingman, George Foster, Hubie Brooks, Mookie Wilson, John Stearns, and Randy Jones) appear to place the scene in 1982; I regret that I was unable to find in the archives any notice of a 3–2 Pirates victory with Randy Jones the losing pitcher and Kingman hitting two home runs and committing a ninth-inning error. Auster's perfect construction of a typical Mets defeat from that era is imaginary—like much of Marco Polo's recorded travels and like most of Auster's novel.[15]

At the same time, Auster's reconstruction of a post-Babel, Cratyllic desire for a perfect, Adamic language of correspondence between word and thing—a language of God—is exactly on target. There is a strange tension here. Many of the novel's textual mechanisms seem to partake in Peter Stillman's quest for a new, divine language of genuine representation that would rectify the duplications and misnamings characteristic of the post-Babel, and post-modern, condition. Redemptive linguistic purity, semiotic transparency in some "city of glass," is the novel's motive from beginning to end, from the "wrong number" that "started it" (3) to the disappearance of Quinn into the indecipherable red notebook. But to what end is all this game-playing? What are the aims of these doublings, of the delights of verisimilitude that end in a box-score that can never be found, of the exuberant play of theories of language? "Paul Auster," writer and aspiring authority on authorship, provides one answer—one we might call typically post-modern: a text—that is, a meta-textual text like *Don Quixote* or *City of Glass*—is a kind of experiment to test the plausibility of the impossible; to see whether one might "stand up before the world and with the utmost conviction spew out lies and nonsense" and have people believe it. The answer, for Auster, is a resounding yes. "'To what extent would people tolerate blasphemies if they gave them amusement? The answer is obvious, isn't it? To any extent. For the proof is that we still read the book. It remains highly amusing to us. And that's finally all anyone wants out of a book—to be amused'" (120).

This answer is unsatisfying to Quinn, and probably to most readers. It renders the project—of fiction, of making meaning—trivial, and we recognize that *this* Paul Auster could not possibly be the author of this book. It is some other Paul Auster, and that is not his real name. The "author," at this point becomes increasingly cruel to Daniel Quinn. The scene with "Auster" is shattering, rubbing in Quinn's face the images of the wife and son he has lost. "Auster"'s" complacency exacerbates Quinn's losses—he has by this time lost the Stillmans as well. Yes, it is fun to play, and textual-authorial instability is certainly as amusing as "Auster" says it is. It would seem to be the reverse of any dys/dis-articulation. Its virtuosity is a hyper-articulation. Anything is possible, from precise realism to oblivion. Problematics of representation are another theme in a symbolic system whose every door opens into another genre. The Fall is a myth, a trope, with countless historical variants. I play with it myself, perhaps resembling the post-modern "Auster," "obviously enjoying [myself], but the precise nature of that pleasure" remaining elusive. There is a grid, a system of losses until the text swallows its tale and ends with a last recrimination.

Part of the amusement in this text comes through the two experiments in Peter Stillman, Sr.'s "search for a perfect language," in Umberto Eco's phrase. In the first, he locked his small, not-yet-speaking son in a dark room for nine years, depriving him of all contact with language. The father's goal was that, without knowledge of any fallen, post-Babel language, the child might spontaneously apprehend the original, divine language given by God to Adam. The child emerged, of course, horribly damaged. When Quinn encounters him thirteen later, after extensive language therapy (and having, for obscure reasons, been married to his speech therapist), he tells his story to the false detective in a remarkable *coup de theatre*, or *coup de roman*. Peter, who is dressed all in white, appears "machine-like, fitful, alternating between slow and rapid gestures, rigid and yet expressive, as if the operation were out of control, not quite corresponding to the will that lay behind it" (17), and this description could apply to his language as well. That language, which we hear as a monologue that Peter insists not be interrupted, is composed of repetitions, rhymes, urgent declamations ("'There is the dark then. I am telling you. There was food in the dark, yes, mush food in the hush dark room'" [19]), gestures toward humor ("'As for me, I think that Peter could not think. Did he blink? Did he drink? Did he stink? Ha ha ha. Excuse me. Sometimes I am so funny'" [20]), cliches ("'hit the nail on the head,'" "'you bet your bottom dollar'" [22]), and nonsense ("'wimble click crumblechaw beloo. Clack clack bedrack. Numb noise, flacklemuch, chewmanna'" [20]). Peter, who in his peculiar way describes his isolation and his father's theo-linguistic theory, in fact believes that the father's experiment succeeded and that his nonsense utterances are a divine poetry or glossolalia. "'Peter can talk like people now,'" he tells Quinn. "'But he still has the other words in his head. They are God's language, and no one else can speak them. They cannot be translated. That is why Peter lives so close to God. That is why he is a famous poet'" (24). The text provides no interpretive level at which this claim is credible. Peter is heir to the whole dys-/disarticulate legacy of sacred fools, wild children, and modernist savants, but this text refuses even an agnosticism regarding his claims.[16] Through his social-symbolic deprivation, Peter is damaged, that is the end of it—he does not chew on manna—and Quinn is determined to protect him from further harm.

Stillman, Sr.'s second experiment is a non-abusive extension to his first, another attempt to rebuild Babel and recreate an Adamic language of correspondence between word and thing. Since the world, as Stillman tells Quinn, has broken into fragments, it is necessary to invent a language that will be adequate to the new reality (93). Stillman appears to have forgotten that human language, according to the Babel story that forms the basis of his theology, is already a broken language. His experiment with Peter is an effort to reach back before the linguistic Fall. Now, substituting Humpty Dumpty for Henry Dark (his academic fiction who inspired the first experiment), Stillman appears more pragmatic. There will be no more monumental forays toward Eden, only the quiet, painstaking work of archiving the world's brokenness and giving each broken thing its true name—since an object, once broken (Stillman's example is an umbrella, and there is a wealth of broken umbrellas in Manhattan) cannot in truth retain its unbroken name. Evidently, the modern, urban world is the scene of a new geography of damage. As Babel was a second Fall, modernity appears to be a third, and the languages that emerged from the ruins of Babel do not fragment fast enough to keep up with the accelerating descent of the modern city. Thus, the aged Stillman takes on the vocation of inventing a word for each increasingly broken thing. Though he does not say it, the task of creating language in a *falling* not a *fallen* world would have to be a kind of calculus, a plotting of trajectories and velocities of damage.

The scenes with Stillman, Sr., are delightful, and it is wonderful to engage with this Cratyllic hunger at the center of the novel's post-modern Hermogeneity, just as it is wonderful to witness the virtuoso presentation of the dys-/disarticulate Peter Stillman, Jr., the other symptom of the failed desire to achieve a language beyond duplicity. To those of a certain intellectual bent, say, the "Paul Austers" among us—and we are a small but vigorous demographic—the amusement contained in these dramas of representation and myth is sufficient. It is another game. Books in the mystery genre often carry these cute cerebral-historical backstories—as in Eco's *Romance of the Rose* or Brown's *The DaVinci Codes*, to pick two disparate but overlapping examples.

Aside from the meta-textual thematics, or theatrics, it is necessary now to attend to the level of plot. By the end of chapter 10, in which Quinn meets "Paul Auster" (theorist of authorship of D.Q., a writer not a detective; and the wife and son who are lacerating doubles of the family Quinn has lost), the game is over. Quinn will never find Stillman, and we soon learn that Virginia Stillman and Peter, Jr., have disappeared as well. Chapter 11 begins:

> Quinn was nowhere now. He had nothing, he knew nothing, he knew that he knew nothing. Not only had he been sent back to the beginning, he was now before the beginning, and so far before the beginning that it was worse than any end he could imagine. (124)

This is the start of Quinn's final negation, and it is presented as a move toward some primal state "before the beginning." He will end up in the Stillman apartment, without light, naked, having food brought to him—repersonifying Peter Stillman, Jr. The book ends with Quinn as dys-/disarticulate wild child, revealed, as we have seen, as a fantasy of textuality, a "P.S.," a post-script and primal-script contained in a red notebook.

But when Quinn begins his negation, he sets off on a long walk from the Upper West Side down to the tip of Manhattan—another descent. Later in the day, he writes down what he has seen in the notebook, the first time he has recorded there anything not related to the Stillman case. What he has seen on his walk and written down is unmitigated suffering, despair, madness, and trauma—people ranging from "the merely destitute to the wretchedly broken" (129). He writes of beggars of all kinds, homeless performers, "drunks—but that term does not do justice to the devastation they embody," people destined to die of starvation, exposure, beatings, burning, or torture (130). These are the disarticulates, amputated from the social fabric; and they are dysarticulate as well. "They are the ones who talk to themselves, who mutter, who scream, who curse, who groan, who tell themselves stories as if to someone else" (131). There is even an echo of Bartleby, as one woman shouts "at an invisible companion: 'And what if I don't want to! What if I just fucking don't want to!'" (131). The day's journey ends with Quinn inhabiting an alley behind the Stillman building, abandoning his former life and work (Quinn, Wilson, Max Work) on the articulate surface of things and taking on the awesome and hopeless responsibility of finding the lost and restoring the broken from a position of absolute vigilance, silent and still.

This geographical, sociological and, finally, personal fall takes Quinn into the world of trauma that underlies the novel from the beginning. It is obvious; no one who reads *City of Glass* overlooks it. But somehow the novel's formal and meta-textual features overtake the narrative's continual emphasis on suffering and loss. The interlocked meta-textual devices we have discussed are analogous, or palimpsestic, to the novel's interlocked traumatic figures. The plot's realistic disasters—the death of Quinn's wife and son, the devastating mistreatment of Peter Stillman, Jr., the death (perhaps murder) of his mother, the social ruin that forms the lower level of the post-modern city, and Quinn's final descent and disappearance—are figuratively connected to the more mythic losses and falls of Babel, Humpty Dumpty, the NY Mets. There is a formal fabric of loss that tempts the sophisticated reader to forget that loss and suffering are real, and, I would argue, are the real sources of dys-/disarticulation in this novel, and in post-modern theory more generally.[17]

To write a book, one must first imagine a writer capable of writing that book. In the case of *City of Glass*, it is Paul Auster. But Paul Auster realizes that *he* is incapable of writing this book. He is too clever, too preoccupied with theories and meta-textualities. The author, then, must be someone deeply antagonistic to him, who feels the characters' losses and agonies, and who blames Auster—his own creator, the text's god or demiurge (though not its author)—for inflicting needless suffering on his creatures. "Auster" creates the meta-textual universe in which the "author" constructs this text. Peter Stillman, Jr., the dys-/disarticulate post-modern wild child, emerges from the crack between meta-text and narrative pain, or between structure and trauma, structure and history. In this self-consciously post-modern text, the two principal dys-/disarticulations—the babbling of Peter Stillman, Jr., and the silence of Quinn P.S. (after writing)—both stand as places of convergence of meta-textual play and the consequences of traumatic events.

City of Glass, then, is a book about trauma and loss, and not, to use LaCapra's oppositions, about "absence." It is a book about falling not about fallenness, or about fallenness as an active, ongoing condition with shocks continuing to produce symptomatic effects. But then, from this perspective, another question emerges. It is easy to see the pervasiveness of suffering, the ease of disintegration. How can we explain the durability of pleasure, of integration, of love, or of what "Paul Auster" calls "amusement"? We are equipped, biologically and culturally, to enjoy the world. Art is unique among human creations in its capacity to comprehend the very close formal relation, the thin distinction, between loss and plenitude. Plots of comedies and tragedies, after all, are nearly identical. At almost any point, a comic plot might darken and its characters plunge into suffering and death. They are saved only by their placement in the genre. This is especially clear in Shakespeare's comedies, the plots of which always point toward disaster. The disasters are thwarted, but are the same disasters that, when they occur, define tragedies. Or think of the silent film comedians: Charlie Chaplin roller-skating blindfolded on the department store balcony with the missing railing as Paulette Godard, who cannot skate, looks on in horror. He is the comic character, she the tragic; she always sees the precipice and knows the height of the fall. Or recall Buster Keaton's exploits in any of his roles; he climbs, swings, falls, and can never be damaged. The comic character lives in a world whose laws of biology and physics declare he cannot die. But if he could, he would.

How is it that one character's exile is into Arden while another's is onto a blasted heath? Why does Quinn follow the decrepit Stillman, Sr., rather than the prosperous one as they get off the same train at Grand Central Station? An arbitrary choice in a world that denies arbitrary choices, with a decision chain that goes from character to "author" to demiurge—a decision of genre, of the type of world the characters are to inhabit. Don Quixote in a single body inhabits several worlds, that is, several genres. In *City of Glass*, characters are divided, spinning off into different worlds. In one, "Paul Auster" makes omelettes. In another, another author imagines a world in which "Paul Auster" makes omelettes while Quinn is broken like an egg. And from the egg, or from the interstice between the genres, comes a post-modern wild child, dys-/disarticulate, infectious carrier of catachresis.

I make up all the words myself, just like when I lived in the dark. I begin
to remember things that way, to pretend that I am back in the dark again. I
am the only one who knows what the words mean. They cannot be translated. These poems will make me famous. Hit the nail on the head. (22)

The wild child here stands for the fallen and irreparable. But he is the
product of his father's search for prelapsarian innocence in the midst of
fallenness and trauma. And to this search, we might add another also
characteristic of post–World War II America, the search for a state of
nature in the midst of overwhelming social-administrative-technolog-
ical processes. If for modernist writers, dys-/disarticulation was a tool
for contending with ideologies of eugenics and degeneration, for writers in the post-modern moment in the wake of the 1960s, dys-/disar-
ticulation became a foil in relation to a revival of ideas of innocence
and nature—with both these conceptual struggles taking place in the
context of the perceived totalizing powers of modernity/post-moder-
nity. The post-modern wild child as he appears in Auster, Kosinski, and
DeLillo is a double foil. As innocent or natural, he serves as critique
of the prevailing social-symbolic order; but the failure or impossibility of innocence and nature in these texts undermines these ideas as
well, along with the utopian possibilities they gesture toward. Thus, as
in the modernist fictions we examined, the post-modern dys-/disartic-
ulate figures a political impasse. But while such an impasse is in keeping with prevailing political-emotional tendencies of the first half of the
twentieth century—the apocalyptic anomie of a world lurching toward
catastrophe—the post-modern version of this impasse is a pessimistic
reaction against the utopian energies of the 1960s in which nature and
innocence were prominent topoi.

Wild Children, Salvation, and the Gardens of Capital

There are, of course, many ways to analyze the 1960s. One must look at
the histories of the civil rights movement, the New Left and the anti-
war movement, the renewal and expansion of feminism, the social and
political transformations brought on by Great Society legislation, the
beginnings of the rise of modern conservatism and the decline of liberalism. As Alexander Bloom writes, "we are living with a number of

competing (and, sometimes, contradictory) popular meanings [of the 1960s]—not one consensus but several. We have a divided—perhaps schizophrenic—legacy from this era" (4). Among these was the quest to redefine some "state of nature" which would stand in opposition to the combined social forces of post-war American capitalism, administration, and technocracy. Paul Goodman noted in 1960 that contemporary social science, in its focus on the broad adaptability or amenability to social conditioning of human subjects, had come to see "human nature" as an obsolete, archaic category. This attitude, Goodman argued, entailed abandoning any notion of genuine social change. In contrast, Goodman urged a recognition of people's "developing potentiality *not* yet cultured, and yet not blank," with needs and desires that society should be designed to satisfy (9). Similarly, Theodore Roszak in his depiction of 1960s counterculture praised hippies' "radical disaffiliation" from corporate America "in a form that captures the need of the young for unrestricted joy" (40). In these counter-cultural views, the child, unsocialized or rejecting socialization, closer to nature and to natural rhythms (e.g., those of folk music, rock and roll, or African American popular forms), stood for a range of inchoate utopian possibilities. Morris Dickstein located the countercultural energies of the 60s in the poetic tradition of Blake, Whitman, and Ginsberg, whose visions directed readers "to see with an innocent eye" (19).[18]

This is part of the cultural stage Chance enters when he leaves his garden. He does not know his father (though this figure is probably "the old man" whose suits fit Chance so admirably). He has had no education and cannot read or write. His spoken language is simple and literal. As we learn from his interview with the estate's lawyer, Chance has no formal identification, has filed no tax returns, has no medical history, no legal records of any kind. He knows how to work in the garden and thus knows the rhythms of vegetable growth and decay. Chance emerges from a state of nature, and he is the wild child, the new Adam, the consciousness outside of and prior to symbolization. When he enters the world, the human essence will be understood and all social relations will be transformed.

But the state of nature, as even Rousseau understood, is a place of hypothesis and projection. What Hobbes took to be a state of nature, Rousseau asserted, was merely Hobbes's view of his own world dressed in primitive costumes. The primal man, the savage, the wild child reflects back to us whatever fantasies of philosophy, science, or sex that we place on it.[19] And so it is with Chance. When he bumbles from his garden dressed in an expensive, perfectly fitting suit of the now deceased "old man," Chance is mistaken for a financier. He awes the Wall Street and Washington giant Benjamin Rand, his wife E.E. (Elizabeth Eve, perhaps a refugee from another garden), the president of the United States, the mass media, the international diplomatic corps, indeed the whole world, as a reticent, modest man of incomparable depth and wisdom. As Chance tells the president, "'in a garden, growth has its season. There are spring and summer, but there are also fall and winter. And then spring and summer again. As long as the roots are not severed, all is well and all will be well'" (54). The president agrees with Chance's homely yet brilliant analogy of the natural order to the economic, just as earlier, Benjamin Rand had felt the cogency of Chance's metaphor of the businessman as gardener. Chance's remarks articulate for these leaders a sense of themselves as nurturing tenders of a difficult economy that will improve if left to its natural harmonies. His invocation of the garden validates their idealized vision of the market. Similarly, the Soviet ambassador sees in Chance a cosmopolitan intellectual, steeped in Russian literature, able to see past the platitudes animating both sides of the cold war, and thus able to employ and respond to power with skill and maturity—in other words, he sees in Chance a perfected image of himself. E.E. sees Chance as a perfect man and perfect lover who allows her to complete her own desires, to achieve a freedom to desire *as* herself. "'You uncoil my wants,'" she tells him. "'Desire flows within me, and when you watch me my passion dissolves it. You make me free. I reveal myself to myself and I am drenched and purged'" (116).

E.E.'s response to Chance is, of course, in light of Chance's lack of any sexual desire or response whatever. The novel suggests that Chance's inability to function sexually is the result of the prudish television mores of the time. In the pre-cable era, sexual scenes would end in the midst of a kiss between actors still wearing their clothes, and so Chance, who learned human social relations through watching television, had no knowledge of sex. This explanation seems obviously incomplete, for it ignores what appears to be a psycho-biological incapacity to be sexually aroused at all. The answer, rather, is to be found in Chance's broader dys-/disarticulation. If Chance is a wild child, exiled from his garden state of nature, while able, oddly though convincingly, to mimic social codes, his complete sexual indifference suggests that human sexuality cannot exist in a state of nature. To be dys-/disarticulated from the symbolic is to be removed from human sexuality as well. Sex among human beings, the novel suggests, is entirely social and symbolic in all its physical and mental properties, its actions, feelings, and fantasies. Thus, Chance's formation outside the social-symbolic world makes him incapable of sex; but, as with the economic and political fantasy projections of Rand and others, Chance presents a receptive space for sexual fantasy. In both cases, in effect, he makes it possible for his interlocutor to masturbate.

Chance's dys-/disarticulate sexuality, in fact, exactly parallels his linguistic incapacity. We have seen that Chance's earnest observations on the natural cycles of the garden are taken by his new acquaintances in business and government to be trenchant metaphors for the capitalist marketplace. But we know that Chance is speaking entirely literally. His discourses on gardens pertain to gardens alone and to nothing beyond them. Chance is as incapable of metaphor as he is of sex. And without metaphor—that is, without the multivalent character of signs—there can be no language. As he mimics behaviors and verbal patterns he has seen on television, Chance, we might say, is speaking, but he is not speaking a language.

The innocence of a state of nature here is twice turned on its head. There is neither innocence—but only a blank dys-/disarticulate site of projection—nor nature. Growing up both in the garden and in front of a television, Chance is outside the symbolic, yet still mediated. His mimicking blankness does not oppose the prevailing order, as 1960s utopian ideologies would assert of the wild child, but reinforces it. Chance's pseudo-profundities which so captivate the ruling elite and their media are ideological in the purest sense in that they equate a particular social system—capitalism—with the natural order and thus render it inevitable. This wild child in his inherited custom-made suit tells the capitalist elite that "all is well and all will be well." He is unaware of the Vietnam War except as a set of vague televised images. He is unaware of race except in the person of Louisa, the West Indian maid, now dead, who brought him his meals. In *Being There*, we see no questions of gender or social class. There is no social protest, anti-war movement, civil rights movement, no critique of the political-economic status quo. There are no alternatives suggested to the powers of capital and militarism. Nature, innocence, the wild child in the world of *Being There* can appear only as parodic—the legitimating fantasies of a ruling class. The garden—that presumed site of utopian projection—opens directly into the portals of capital.

There are, of course, cultural products where the redeeming power of the wild child still is depicted unambivalently. In popular film in particular, we see examples of cognitively or linguistically impaired characters who reveal the goodness of the human soul and the possibility of social reclamation. *Forrest Gump* is the most striking example, and we can cite as well the lead characters in *Nell, Sling Blade, What's Eating Gilbert Grape, Rain Man, I Am Sam, Shine*, and indeed in the film version of *Being There*.[20] But I would like to discuss now what seems to me a set of striking and in some ways anomalous examples of late twentieth-century wild children in the work of Oliver Sacks.

Oliver Sacks is a clinical neurologist, but in his popular case studies he has become, in effect, a theologian for a class of secular, educated readers—the house theologian for the *New York Review of Books*, we might say.[21] Sacks introduces his readers to neurologically impaired "others," whom he describes as being in some, not especially clearly defined, sense outside of language and culture. The alterity of these subjects, to which Sacks refers at least partly in religious terms, is eventually revealed to be what is for all of us most familiar, but often most neglected: the feeling of being at home in our own bodies, a kinesthetic rather than a linguistic sense of being human. Normative professional neurology, for Sacks, does not recognize this sense, and so neglects what is most deeply human, which in turn corresponds (again, for Sacks) to whatever can be known about the sacred.

In a brief discussion, a good place to start is with Sacks' narrative of his own injury (in *A Leg to Stand On*), which did not involve language directly but which set the terms for his subsequent case studies. Sacks seriously injured his leg climbing a mountain alone in a remote area of Norway, and was lucky to be found and brought to safety before he froze to death. He immediately returned to England and had an operation to repair the extensive damage to his ligaments and knee. The operation was apparently successful, but then his real problems began, for he found that he had no feeling and no power of movement in the injured leg. He had suffered some undiagnosed neurological damage, and, to make matters worse, none of his doctors would acknowledge that anything was wrong. From their perspective, the operation had been successful, and he should proceed with rehabilitation and not bother them any further.

Sacks describes his experience of his non-working leg as more than simply disturbing and frightening. It is uncanny, a source of absolute horror, and it triggers a crisis that is more spiritual than medical. The leg becomes to him "alien and incomprehensible" (70), "absolutely not-me" (72), a "foreign inconceivable *thing*" (74). There was, Sacks writes, "a gap—an absolute gap—between then and now; and in that gap, into that void . . . the reality and possibilities of the leg had passed" (86). Sacks invokes the medical term "scotoma," which usually refers to a gap in the visual field often brought on by migraines, to help him conceptualize what had happened to his leg, but giving his condition a name—a "scotoma of the leg"—is small relief to him, for his diagnosis is ignored by his doctors, and he realizes that "all the cognitive and intellectual and imaginative powers" he had previously used were "wholly useless. I had fallen off the map, the world, of the knowable" (110). Sacks even has an apocalyptic dream in which an enemy has developed a "Derealization Bomb" with the power to "blow a hole in reality." This bomb did not destroy physical objects, but rather, it "destroyed thought and thought-space itself" (96).

In order for Sacks to regain physical and symbolic wholeness, to mend the hole in reality, he must make contact with some part of reality that is deeper than language. For Sacks, this deeper level is reached through music and physical movement. Listening to a tape of a Mendelssohn violin concerto, Sacks begins to feel that his leg, and the world, was beginning to be reintegrated, and this sense of reintegration was part of a greater revelation that "life itself was music, or consubstantial with music; that our living moving flesh itself was 'solid' music"(118). Later, during his physical therapy, the music again comes into his mind and suddenly, miraculously, what he calls his "kinetic melody" (144) reconnects his mind and his body, and his leg returns to him. He is able to walk almost normally and, as he writes, "all of me, body and soul, became music in that moment" (148). There are further setbacks, but his true recovery has begun. Sacks now knows what it is to be balanced, to be at home in his body. He uses the term "grace," in both its physical and religious senses, to describe his new condition.

And this is, Sacks makes clear, a *new* condition, not merely a recovery of what he had lost. Before his injury and impairment, Sacks could not be whole or grace-ful, for he regarded his body according to a mechanical, medical terminology. The traumatic impairment forced him to understand the body in a new way, as a kinetic, musical, spiritual entity; further, it impelled him to rethink his relation to his profession and begin to imagine what he calls a "neurology of the soul" which would discover and evoke "a living personal center, an 'I,' amid the debris of neurological devastation" (219).

After making these discoveries through his own experience, Sacks goes on to rediscover and refine them in his work with people with severe amnesia, autism, mental retardation, Tourette's Syndrome, and other neurological conditions. In each case, Sacks describes his contact with a person in some degree outside of language or the normal use of symbols; and in each case, Sacks is able to find a moment when this person achieves a form of wholeness, grace, or at-homeness which is beyond or deeper than language. In the character's apparent alterity, Sacks identifies a deeper humanity. To be "at home" in this sense is, for Sacks, the most profoundly human state, and each of Sacks's case studies is, in effect, a test case of the human. Sacks's subjects appear to achieve the state of "being there" that Kosinski parodies. Each patient is a kind of clinical "wild child," an other encountered outside the symbolic who reveals how much of what we think is essential can be stripped away before a core of humanity, which is not linguistic, becomes visible. The patients' separation from language, and from the personal, social and historical coherence that language makes possible, is in every case debilitating, and most often terribly sad. But it is only through this traumatic lack or loss of language that the kinethestic, emotional, and spiritual foundation of the human can shine forth unimpeded. The strangeness, the alterity, of the other is ultimately, in Sacks's accounts, not other at all; it is what is most human, possessed by everyone, but not recognized.

Through the study of neurological damage, Sacks encounters both alterity and shared humanity. But these moments of encounter when non-linguistic, human transcendence is revealed often occur with his patients, as happened with him, during aesthetic, most often musical, experiences. With retarded people, he writes, "their uncouth movements may disappear in a moment with music and dancing," for music has the power to hold together a coherent self "when abstract or schematic forms of organization fail" (*Hat* 185–86). Regarding an autistic person, Sacks also notes that when making music, "his entire autistic persona . . . had totally vanished, replaced by movements that were free, graceful, with emotional appropriateness and range" *(Mars* 239). A drummer with Tourette's syndrome finds he must stop taking medication in order to drum most inventively; without his tics, he lost also his "wild and creative urges" (*Hat* 100–101). An amnesiac, who for twenty years had been able to retain no memory for longer than five minutes, seemed transformed when Sacks took him to a Grateful Dead concert. Sacks writes of his "rare and wonderful continuity of attention, everything orienting him, holding him together. . . . I could see no trace of his amnesia, his frontal lobe syndrome—he seemed at this moment completely normal, as if the music was infusing him with its own strength, its coherence, its spirit" (*Mars* 75).[22]

Sacks's accounts of neurological impairment and of the non-linguistic selfhood that can be discovered by means of, but deeper than, the impairment are paradoxical. His impaired subjects are presented as versions of wild children, outside the symbolic loop, products of nature not of culture. This obviously cannot be true in any strict sense, since the people he writes about were not raised in isolation, but grew up in families, had contact with institutions, and were in varying degrees able to use language. But, as Sacks writes of the mentally retarded, they "have never known, been seduced by the abstract, but have always experienced reality direct and unmediated, with an elemental and at times overwhelming intensity" (*Hat* 175). Similarly, for Sacks, autism reveals an intelligence "scarcely touched by tradition and culture— unconventional, unorthodox, strangely 'pure' and original, akin to the intelligence of true creativity" (*Mars* 253). Sacks intends that by showing us what we socialized, symbol-using beings are not, these neurological wild children show us more deeply what we are.

But even more paradoxical, this alterity outside of culture is manifested most strongly during experiences of highly structured, sophisticated, in every sense *acculturated* aesthetic events. The immediacy that characterizes the non-linguistic human core emerges through immersion in the most highly mediated cultural products. Most often, the music is classical—Bach, Mendelssohn, Schumann. Even poetry can reveal the non-linguistic, as Sacks tells how a mentally retarded woman was "at home with poetic language," a kind of "primitive, natural poet" who could "follow the metaphors and symbols of even quite deep poems, in striking contrast to her incapacity with simple propositions and instructions" (*Hat* 179). Sacks's sense of alterity, of the non-linguistic, of transcendence seems to rely on an implicit theory of art, which is something like the following.

The deepest experience of living as a human animal, the most basic form of consciousness, is not symbolic or linguistic. It is bodily, a sense of at-homeness in the body, or what Sacks calls "proprioception," the sense of one's body as one's own.[23] Forms of art are conduits to the non-linguistic insofar as they are experienced through the body. The organized, felt rhythms of art, most vividly of music, as Sacks presents it, correspond to the deepest sensations of embodied life. With this view of art, Sacks can both posit a kind of selfhood that is not a product of language and culture and at the same time provide a cultural means through which we can approach and retrieve it. Art then, for Sacks, is essentially kinesthetic. No matter how sophisticated or esoteric, it remains an elaboration of the body itself: a form, or expression, or experience that is both symbolic and physical. Thus, fortuitously, we possess, on the one hand, forms of selfhood that are not determined by our social-symbolic orders, that transcend the symbolic, that are, in some way of speaking, sacred; yet, on the other hand, we possess particular cultural media—the products and processes of artistic creation—that appear as direct, though stylized, kinesthetic outcroppings of the transcendent. In its art, culture contains the path to its own alterity; but the alterity is there, in everyone, seen most clearly in the neurologically impaired, and in them most particularly in their moments of immersion in art. We are not, then, alienated from our culture; but we are connected to it not through our language but through our bodies, and not through the conceptual, but through the kinesthetic qualities of art.[24]

Sacks's seemingly uncritical faith in the redemptive powers of the impaired wild child puts him in company with popular culture products like the films *Nell*, *Rain Man*, *Shine*, the film adaptation of his book *Awakenings*, or with popular understandings of the life of Helen Keller.[25]

Yet while there is something uncomfortably comforting about Sacks's encounters with the Other, there is also, I think, a danger in dismissing him too easily. He is uncritical about his biases toward high, classical art, but if we broaden the aesthetic boundaries, we arrive at positions resembling those of Kristeva, Heller-Roazen, Blasing, and Ricoeur in which a non-linguistic alterity is structured into aesthetic, even narrative, products.[26] These theoretical stances parallel recent work in evolutionary neurology and linguistics carried out by Terrence Deacon, Gerald Edelman, Antonio Damasio, Steven Pinker, and others, theorizing how symbol use and brain physiology co-evolved, with advances in one provoking advances in the other, while a core, non-symbolic, emotional, and kinesthetic layer of consciousness remained intact. The problem with Sacks's writing is not necessarily that he is wrong either about human consciousness or about art. I think, on the whole, he is right. My reservations concerning Sacks's work lie in my sense that he ignores the role of desire in the relations between cognitive and linguistic impairment and culture. That is, Sacks never questions either his own or the broader culture's wish to see these neurological wild children function as redeemers of human consciousness and culture; nor does he examine the general traumatic condition that would call for this redemption.

What would it mean, then, to employ the neurological wild child in order to consider more thoroughly the contemporary desire for transcendence in the wake of trauma, and to consider also the possibility of terror as another symptomatic response to the "fall" of language? Don DeLillo has spent much of his career writing as a kind of refugee from Babel, investigating ways that ruined, traumatized language can be reassembled. His novels of the 1980s focus on wild child characters, neurological impairments, and especially on the desire to imagine wild children with the power to redeem us and pull us with them outside the symbolic order. In addition, DeLillo places this ineffable, wild, or innocent, uttering or muttering of transcendence in relation to the logic of terror. In *White Noise*, both the transcendent wild child, Wilder, and the terroristic reunion of word and thing made possible by the drug dylar are made objects of desire and of parody. Escape from the symbolic is impossible, yet the desire for and imagining of escape is continual. In the preceding novel, *The Names*, both transcendence and terror seem more attainable. A terrorist cult seems to mirror the symbolic manipulations of the CIA. And, somewhat as in Sacks, aesthetic production—a chapter from the novel written by Tap, the quasi-wild-child character—appears to point toward or echo the transcendent. But, unlike Sacks, and recent popular cinematic portrayals of wild children, DeLillo commits himself to portraying the traumatic burden of a damaged symbolic order and the desperate desire to escape from it—which can take political, artistic, sexual, and simply violent forms.[27]

"'I don't want him to talk,'" his mother says of Wilder, whose vocabulary is "stalled at about twenty-five words" (35). "'The less he talks, the better. . . . Talk is radio'" (264). Wilder represents to the other characters a transcendent place outside of symbols and mediation. He is the personified desire for that place. Wilder resembles one of his impaired wild child precursors, Faulkner's Benjy, but with two crucial differences. First, Faulkner portrays Benjy's non-temporal, non-linguistic consciousness—in exquisite language—and reveals it as a site of continual, unforgotten trauma. Benjy lives forever at the precise moment of greatest loss, while Wilder is regarded as the redemption of all loss. Secondly, Wilder is explicitly an object of desire while Benjy lives in a state of perpetual desire. Indeed, Benjy's longing for his lost sister can be seen as the energy that motivates the entire novel. It is important to Faulkner's novel that the reader understand the source of Benjy's lamentation, and that his consciousness, though difficult to approach, and though depicted explicitly as damaged, nevertheless be accessible. It is equally important to DeLillo's novel that its damaged child not be accessible, that he be fully other with regard to language. Benjy's prose consciousness provides a set of interpretive puzzles and, ultimately, a set of understandings of damage and loss that have individual and social resonances. Our lack of linguistic access to Wilder's consciousness, his status as nearly wholly other, encourages his fellow characters and, perhaps, also readers to grasp at interpretations that partake more of transcendence.

The scene late in *The Sound and the Fury*, when we see Benjy for the first time from an external perspective, affords particular insight into DeLillo's depiction of Wilder. No longer inside Benjy's consciousness, we see Benjy's incomprehensible moaning described as "hopeless and prolonged. . . . [It was] was nothing. Just sound. It might have been all time and injustice and sorrow become vocal for an instant" (288). Experienced now externally, as producer of "just sound," an other of language, Benjy is immediately open to theological or transcendent interpretations that would have been more tenuous (though not impossible) when his consciousness was rendered in language. In relation to the rest of the novel, the absence of a personal narrative perspective in this final section is uncanny. Whose desire is portrayed at this point? For someone, evidently, wishes to see Benjy's non-linguistic sorrow figured now in cosmic terms that had not previously been introduced. And at this moment, Benjy most resembles Wilder. Wilder's similar moment, what we might call his "Benjy moment," comes when he cries for seven hours straight. In an echo of Faulkner, this crying is described as an existential and spiritual event. This description comes, however, not from an external narrator as in Faulkner, but from Jack Gladney, Wilder's stepfather, the character most invested in Wilder's transcendent, redemptive position. Jack regards Wilder "as though he'd just returned from a period of wandering in some remote and holy place" (79), uttering "a sound so large and pure . . . saying nameless things . . . an ancient dirge all the more impressive for its resolute monotony" (78). This may or may not be true; all we know is that it is Jack's wish.

For Jack and his wife, Wilder lives in an extended and unmediated present moment, without knowledge of time or death. Wilder's transcendent obliviousness to death becomes clearest in a parodically triumphal moment near the end of the novel when Wilder resolutely and inexplicably rides his tricycle across a six lane highway. His pedaling, reports Jack, is "mystically charged" (322) and is incomprehensible to the drivers who swerve to avoid him. But, miraculously, he reaches the other side, "a cloud of unknowing, an omnipotent little person" (289), as he was described earlier.[28] Why did the wild child cross the highway? To show his imperviousness to every medium of symbolic exchange. He emerges unharmed, triumphant, transcendent; and yet, of course, the scene is ludicrous. It does not so much support Jack's evaluation as expose its hopelessness. Indeed, at the end of his ride, safely across the highway, Wilder falls into a ditch and again begins crying.[29]

Wilder is one possible, though insufficient, way out of the symbolic and its accompanying knowledge of death.[30] The other is the drug dylar, a sophisticated neural inhibitor. But dylar's chief side effect is to cure language of its ambiguities. Under the influence of dylar, a person cannot distinguish between word and thing, and so language is imagined to return to its pre-Babel, Adamic or Cratyllic condition. When Jack Gladney confronts Willie Mink, the inventor, and addictive user, of dylar, he need only say, "hail of bullets," and Mink falls to the floor and tries to avoid them. Every sign becomes latched to its proper referent in an unveiling of true significance. As Jack says, "I knew who I was in the network of meanings. . . . I saw things new." And a moment later, as he fires the actual gun, "I saw beyond words. I knew what red was, saw it in terms of dominant wavelength, luminance, purity" (312). This Adamic restoration of language to perfect correspondence also aims at transcendence, but its method is one of terror. The problem of death and the problem of symbolization are united, and murder seems to solve them both. But again, as with Wilder's triumphal tricycle ride, this dylar scene is silly. As usual, Jack's inflated language denies it credibility beyond the ratio of his desire. He *wants* his impaired son to be transcendent; he *wants* this drug to unite word and thing and eliminate the fear of death.[31]

Terror is the primary response to the problem of sliding signification in DeLillo's previous novel, *The Names*. A cult called "The Names," operating in Greece and the Middle East, has as its central practice a ritual murder based on the alphabet. When a person enters a village that has the same initials as those of the person's name (e.g., when Michaelis Kalliambetsos enters Mikro Kamini), the cult kills him. The link between the names, and between the names and the act of murder, is merely alphabetic, entirely arbitrary, and utterly without meaning. The cult, rebelling against the arbitrariness of linguistic signification, imposes an ultimate meaning on linguistic chance. Through their act, the name one has *will* mean something; no further sliding of signification will be possible.

The cult's rebellion against the shifting Sausurrean system of language takes place in the context of shifting and ambiguous economic, political, and military power relations. The novel's protagonist, James Axton, works in Athens for a company that does "risk assessment" to determine insurance rates for companies doing business in the Middle East. Only near the end of the novel does he discover that his company is a front for the CIA, and then he realizes that his efforts to determine an economic order in the region's social chaos serve also as a means to impose a new political order. What was ambiguous, shifting, uncontrollable will now be constructed and manipulated with certainty. Axton's and the CIA's creation of empire seems to be corollary to the cult's violent conquest of the alphabet. And Axton, in his sexual life, shows a corresponding wish that signs never depart from their referents. He partly seduces, partly rapes an American amateur belly dancer in Athens because her dancing is for her just a set of gestures she has learned and is practicing; it is a system of signs without fixed meanings. She tells him, "'the dancing isn't sexy to me,'" and he replies that this is "'the reason I want you so badly'" (227). "'Your voice,'" he continues, is "'outside your body. . . . There's a lack of connection between your words and the physical action they describe, the parts of the body they describe. That's what draws me to you so intensely. I want to put your voice back inside your body, where it belongs'" (228).

Terror means the forcing of signification into a singleness of meaning, and its semantic territory can be sexual, political, and economic. Once signification has been forced into obedience, material conditions and relations will follow.[32]

But the other response to the sliding signifier—the desire to transcend language, and the figure of the wild child—is also present in *The Names*. James Axton's ten-year-old son is called Tap, which is an acronym of his initials and thus an arbitrary name (unlike Wilder, whose name signifies what he is). But Tap too is a kind of wild child on the borders of language who, in fact, taps the roots of signification and who, in his writing, is a tap from which flows a spontaneous, almost primal pouring of words. As with the alphabet terrorist cult, the arbitrariness of signification, pushed to its limit, creates significance.

What we see of Tap's novel focuses on a scene in a midwestern pentacostal church in which a young boy, based on an archaeologist friend of the Axtons (who becomes fascinated with the alphabet cult), tries, and is unable, to speak in tongues. Through glossolalia, one hopes, presumably, to transcend the semantic and mediating aspects of language and apprehend the divine in a relation of immediacy, "face to face." Tap's scene depicts a failure of glossolalia, a failure to escape from language, but in doing so, it translates glossolalia into aesthetic form, which resembles a kind of Joycean, or Kristevan, modernist word play. His mother says that his writing "absolutely collides with the language" (32). His father finds the "mangled words exhilarating. He'd made them new again, made me see how they worked, what they really were. They were ancient things, secret, reshapable," and his misspellings "seemed to contain curious perceptions about the words themselves, second and deeper meanings, original meanings" (313).[33]

The chapter from Tap's novel ends the book:

> Why couldn't he understand and speak? There was no answer that the living could give. Tongue tied! His fait was signed. He ran into the rainy distance, smaller and smaller. This was worse than a retched nightmare. It was the nightmare of real things, the fallen wonder of the world. (339)

Genuine immediacy, genuine face-to-face contact with alterity, which here is the real and the traumatic, DeLillo takes to be impossible; but as a substitute, he presents the art of the quasi-wild child as conduit to the traumatic-real-transcendent-other. The way out of language, glossolalia, becomes, in its failure and impossibility, the means for a renovation of language.[34] The trauma of failed escape, the fact, the "fait," of life in a world of signs and "fallen wonder," generates new signs, new wonders. Trauma functions here, as I believe it does in the literary versions of trauma theory, as the originary moment of a poetics—an obliterating moment in which new possibilities of language are revealed. Trauma theory explains how novelty is possible and, even more basically, how the non-linguistic, "the nightmare of real" things, can take linguistic form, and how a mediation can bear the imprint of lost immediacy.[35]

* * *

In this chapter, I've described a set of conditions that apply after the fall of a mythical tower, which, I've argued, seem to have been in effect since the origins of narrative, since Gilgamesh's companion Enkidu learned language and then could no longer run with the animals. Contemporary political culture still seems immersed in a logic of terror that seeks to impose absolute, reductive, and imprisoning meanings on our most important words, and still hangs traumatically from the fallen signifiers of the World Trade Center. This Cratyllic, Adamic impulse to restore language from a fallen, ambiguous condition to one of certainty has always been a traumatized, or opportunistic, attempt to destroy language as an instrument of thought. On the other hand, the various counter-linguistic turns toward forms of unrepresentable alterity have a great appeal. The concept of the inconceivable, of the other that is wholly other—whether in Levinas, or as the "event" in Badiou, or the Lacanian real—can have genuine social and political value, for it urges us never to be satisfied with the prevailing codifications of justice and ethics. As Derrida insists, most pointedly in "The Force of Law," there is always an incommensurability between justice or ethics and established law. Justice, and its utopian impulse, begins with negation.[36]

But negation, and the notions of alterity that it makes possible, is the quintessential product of language, is impossible without language. Without language, we have a world in which what is, is. This is the world of animals, angels, mystics, and wild children—the world that Oliver Sacks and Don DeLillo tried to imagine. But with language, we live in a world in which what is *not*, also is. The other, justice, the possibilities of yet unformed aesthetic forms are not so inaccessible. "It is not in heaven," as a famous Talmudic commentary proclaims.[37] That is, our relation with alterity comes not by means of supernatural revelation, but through human dialogue. And yet, all our dialogues will also be symptomatic of histories of damage and crime, including the dialogues and narratives we create in trying to address our traumatic histories. The most intractable political problems—in the Middle East, for example—generally involve the intersection and concussion of different traumatic histories. Perhaps Freud's speculative anthropologies in *Totem and Taboo* and *Moses and Monotheism* are not so far off the mark after all. Each historical trauma is the latest in an interlocking series that may be infinite. Though there was no fall of any historical Babel, nor any primal father to be murdered, such a sequence of trauma is the ongoing post-Babel condition. (And this is my best gloss of Cathy Caruth's evocative and elusive comment that "history, like trauma, is never one's own, that history is precisely the way we are implicated in each other's traumas" [24]).

In this context, the distinctions between the tendencies of the linguistic and counter-linguistic turns, which were always tentative, appear even less distinct. Taking trauma, and its linguistic ur-site, Babel, as principal terms, language stands between two permeable boundaries. It emerges out of, or together with, material sources: the development of human physiology and neurology; the concomitant development of social relations, economies, and institutions; the almost unbearable emotional pressures that creatures with such complex nervous systems experience simply by living. And language then gestures back toward the non-linguistic, rendering the material world symbolic, and regarding the symbolic as insufficient. Especially in the wake of trauma, part of whose power is to overwhelm symbolic capacities, language is a middle realm, never fully itself, always in creative and agonized relation with what it is not.

4

Dys-/Disarticulation and Disability

There would seem to be a gap in my thinking that now it is time to try to discuss. My notion of the dys-/disarticulate appears to fall under the broad category of "disability" as it has been delineated over the past twenty years in the field of disability studies. I have referred to some of this work in preceding chapters, but have not yet addressed directly the question of this project's relation to the field. The study of dys-/disarticulation is in part a study of the uses and changes in terminologies for people with varieties of cognitive impairment—idiot, feeble-minded, degenerate, etc.—and of the ideological values associated with these terms. I have tried to show how literary texts have been invested in these ideologies, but have, at the same time, used dys-/disarticulate figures as points of opposition or negation. In the dys-/disarticulate figure, aesthetic, political, scientific, ethical, and spiritual discourses have converged, and in the tensions of these convergences have emerged critiques of the totalizing forces associated with modernity—forces that would explain, assimilate, and exclude the cognitively impaired people whom the dys-/disarticulate figures present. My analyses, then, have, in the terms of disability studies, served to reveal ideologies and social mechanisms that have consistently stigmatized disabled people and furthered the construction of norms of physical and mental ability. Characters like Verloc and Ossipon, Jason Compson, Jenny Petherbridge, or even Nora Flood desperately try to occupy the place defined by Rosemary Garland-Thomson as the "normate," an evocative neologism

intended to underscore the artificiality and impossibility of all norms—
they are, of course, unsuccessful.[1] My readings of the dys-/disarticulate
figures of modernism closely parallel disability studies approaches to
revealing and critiquing the workings of "ableist" ideologies in literary
texts and their contemporaneous historical contexts. One might say, at
least in a broad sense, that my discussions extend the analytical lines set
out by David Mitchell and Sharon Snyder in their writing on "narrative
prosthesis." This is the sense that the physical and mental differences
construed as "disability" have served as essential tropes through which
historical tensions and anxieties have been portrayed, or, as Mitchell and Snyder put it, that "disabled bodies and lives have historically
served as the crutch upon which artistic discourses and cultural narratives have leaned" (13). *The Disarticulate*, then, is an intervention in the
field of disability studies. At the same time, though, my sense of dys-/
disarticulation stands in a somewhat uncomfortable relation to disability studies, particularly with regard to metaphor, trauma, and care.
I hope in this chapter I can clarify my sense of that field and where I
stand in relation to it.[2]

Philoctetes and the Troubles of Definition

In Sophocles' *Philoctetes*, the eponymous hero, or victim, suffers from
a festering wound on his foot as the result of a snake bite while stopping with his shipmates on an island on their way to the Trojan War.
The hideousness and smell of the wound and Philoctetes' incessant
howls of pain cause his companions to maroon him on the uninhabited
island. Philoctetes, able to crawl or limp, makes a home for himself in
a cave. Fortunately, he is able to hunt for food with a magic bow and
arrows given to him by Herakles—the arrows "never miss and always
kill." Nearly ten years into the war, the Greeks receive a prophecy that
they will capture Troy only with the aid of Philoctetes and his bow.
Odysseus—the same commander who abandoned Philoctetes—is now
assigned to bring him to Troy. Accompanying Odysseus is young Neoptolemos, the son of the late Achilles, who joined the war only after his
father's death and so is unknown to Philoctetes. Anticipating a hostile
response, the ever-resourceful Odysseus concocts a scheme whereby
Neoptolemos will pretend to sympathize with the wounded man, will

even profess a shared hostility toward the Greek leadership, and Odysseus in particular. Having gained Philoctetes' confidence, Neoptolemos will persuade him to trust him with the bow and will guide Philoctetes to the ship where he will be held and transported to Troy.

This has some qualities of a standard disability tale as described in disability studies scholarship. Odysseus represents the social order and the state. He initially stigmatizes, marginalizes, and abandons Philoctetes because he disrupts social stability. The painful physical difference that Philoctetes embodies is unendurable to his able-bodied comrades, and whatever initial sympathy they had for him is gradually lost when he fails to recover and return to health, normality, and docility. And Philoctetes, the disabled subject, is precisely what most disrupts the able-ist social hegemony: the spectacle of a physical difference perceived as repulsive, the intimation of the universal vulnerability and mortality of embodied life, an understanding of the body that the social order must repress and reject, must maroon on an island to fend for itself. And this response is especially significant in that the social body that rejects Philoctetes is composed of soldiers who are familiar with wounded bodies. On the battlefield, Philoctetes would be rescued and treated; but away from war, on a ship in passage, he is abandoned. (And we see this strange dichotomy today as well in the contrasting social responses to wounded war veterans and to soldiers.) Thus, we see the social character of disability. The nature and severity of a disability is a function of its social context— of the social response to it— not of the physical condition itself. And yet, in the terms the narrative presents, the problem lies entirely with the disabled person. He—and his impairment—not the social order, is the object of attention. He must be separated, distinguished from others; he must be cured or permanently banished. The social character of disability is obvious, but never acknowledged.

This recital could provide the basis for a disability studies reading along the lines set out by Rosemarie Garland-Thomson or David Mitchell and Sharon Snyder. The normative social order imagines and sustains itself through the construction and consequent exclusion of a disabled other. The disabled subject becomes then the "material metaphor," as Mitchell and Snyder put it, for all forms of corporeality that are unacceptable to the idealized embodiments of the normative. Moreover, the story is not merely a representation of typical social processes, but is ideologically integral to those processes. Narratives of disability, as Mitchell and Snyder argue, have a prosthetic quality in that a dominant social order depends on these narratives of brokenness in order to achieve their (illusory) self-images of wholeness and coherence. "Disabled lives and bodies," they write, "have historically served as the crutch upon which artistic discourses and cultural narratives have leaned " (*Narrative Prosthesis* 13). In the case of Philoctetes, one might argue that his portrayal is the prosthetic through which Sophocles explores the relation of political necessity to personal ethics (as he did by other means in *Antigone*) and note that with divine intervention Philoctetes is indeed reintegrated into the normative world through the promise of magical cure. Thus, as Mitchell and Snyder's thesis would suggest, Philoctetes' condition in and of itself is subordinated in the narrative to its function in support of the ethical tensions under investigation—it is primarily metaphorical. And, while initially disruptive and casting doubt on the ethics of social normativity, Philoctetes ultimately is reassimilated to the social order. Disability disappears, and social coherence can be achieved only at the moment of its disappearance. As Garland-Thomson writes, "corporeal departures from dominant expectations never go uninterpreted or unpunished, and conformities are almost always rewarded" (7).

Such a reading is possible, but it makes too clear what the text presents as confusion. The problem with this reading is not primarily that it is anachronistic. As Martha Rose has observed in her study of disability in ancient Greece, the relevant category covering congenital physical abnormalities, injuries, and lingering or degenerative illness was not a notion of disability as understood by activists and scholars of our time (and even less as understood by the perjorative or patronizing views opposed by activists and scholars), but a notion conveyed by the term *adunatos*, which means, roughly, "unable." In Athens, during the fifth through the third centuries BCE, the term signified the inability to function fully as a citizen—that is, to take the role in public, civic life that was expected of a free adult male. As Rose points out, people with physical impairments participated in public and economic life in ancient Greece, even in military service. "A physically handicapped person earning a living," Rose notes, "would not have been a remarkable sight" (39), and people with a wide variety of congenital and acquired impairments would have been more common in antiquity than today, owing to less developed medical treatments. To be genuinely *adunatos* meant to be unable to survive economically (one further consequence of which would be restricted citizenship status). In fourth-century Athens, the *adunatoi* were given small pensions, and Rose cites a legal case argued by the orator Lysias in which a man with a damaged leg was denied this pension because he had an income and wealthy friends and participated in civic life: thus, he was not legally *adunatos* (95–98). Sophocles' representations of physical impairments in the *Philoctetes* and the Oedipus plays, then, in stressing the traumatic and portentous nature of Philoctetes' and Oedipus's injuries, are not in harmony with Rose's depiction of how impairment functioned in Athenian society of the time. Philoctetes could certainly have participated in the war in some way. Given the power of his bow/prosthesis, he could have fought; and the Greeks, at last, needed him in the fighting. He is by no means *adunatos*.

It appears that Philoctetes provided Sophocles with a limit-case of the social, a figure at the boundary of disarticulation who would issue a critique of the social world as defined by its Odysseuses. The aesthetic product here is not directly congruent with the dominant ideologies and social practices concerning physical impairment. Philoctetes works as a metaphor, as a figure for broad political-ethical concerns, but not, apparently, for existing, dominant attitudes toward impairment which, as Rose presents them, were far more mundane. I would argue then that yes, Philoctetes is a metaphor, but not a metaphor *for* some clearly identifiable object or idea or set of social relations. He is *disruptive*—a quality often cited by disability studies scholars as characteristic of representations of disability. But what is he disrupting?

When we first encounter Philoctetes, he is thoroughly disarticulated. Neoptolemos and the Chorus hear his cries of pain offstage—inarticulate "squeals and laments," and compared to the sounds of an animal, "howling wild like a wolf" (13). Outside of language, he is outside of the human. But then Philoctetes enters, and what he desires most is simply speech. "'I need to hear your voices,'" he says. "'Do the friendly human thing and speak'" (15). But speech,of course, is double, or, rather, triple. Neoptolemos lies to Philoctetes, just as Odysseus had instructed. And yet, in the act and process of verbal deception, Neoptolemus establishes a genuine relation of sympathy with Philoctetes—indeed, a mutual relation, even though the ills and insults that Neoptolemus tells of are fictitious. They speak of mutual friends and family who died in the war: Achilles, Ajax, Patrochlus. "'Life is shaky,'" Philoctetes tells the younger man. "'Never forget, son, how risky and slippy things are in this world. . . . Count your blessings and always be ready to pity other people'" (27). Soon, Neoptolemus resolves to help Philoctetes, to bring him home instead of to Troy. There is, he posits, "'a whole economy of kindness possible in the world. Befriend a friend and the chance of it's increased and multiplied'" (37). This economy of kindness is in contrast to the realpolitik practiced by Odysseus, in which acts are evaluated only for their efficacy in furthering the interests of the polity. As Odysseus insists, "'we're Greeks with a job to do,'" and personal honor or virtue or any ethical relation not sanctioned by state policy must be subordinated. Sympathy of the sort that Neoptolemus extends to Philoctetes is excluded. That the state policy in question—the war against Troy—is nothing but a personal vendetta of the ruling elite is, of course, implicit in all the play's action. But the myth cannot be wholly rewritten. Troy must fall, and so Philoctetes must be reintegrated, rearticulated. In fact, he must be cured. And his rearticulation is not the result of Neoptolemus's economy of kindness, but of divine, or state, necessity.

And here Philoctetes rebels. Resisting persuasion, force, and prophecy, Philoctetes will not give up his rage and his wish for vengeance on the established order. He shouts at Odysseus, "'I'd give the whole agony of my life just to see you cut down in the end, and your tongue ripped out of you like a bleeding ox-tongue'" (57). That is, he wishes to see Odysseus rendered as disarticulate as himself, wounded, cut off from speech, transformed into an animal. At this point, the Chorus and Neoptolemus turn against him. "'Don't contradict a god,'" the Chorus tells him. "'Your wound is what you feed on, Philoctetes. I say it again in friendship. . . . Stop eating yourself up with hate and come with us'" (60–61). And Neoptolemus adds, "'You know human beings have to bear up and face whatever's meant to be. There's a courage and dignity in ordinary people that can be breathtaking. But you're the opposite. Your courage has gone wild, you're like a brute that can only foam at the mouth. . . . Anybody that ever tries to help you just gets savaged. You're a wounded man in terrible need of healing'" (72).

Philoctetes can be healed, Neoptolemus tells him; the gods have declared it. Philoctetes must acknowledge his wounds—both physical and spiritual—and his need for healing. Philoctetes, however, refuses to compromise or be placated. The drama is at an impasse. The wounded and newly disarticulated subject ("like a brute that can only foam at the mouth") stands absolutely at odds with state power; the economy of kindness is unable to mediate.

And so a god must intervene. The newly apotheosized Herakles, who had given Philoctetes the sacred bow, appears and directs Philoctetes to "'go and be cured and capture Troy. Asclepius [the physician of the Greek army, later himself transformed into a deity] will make you whole, relieve your body and your soul'" (79). And so the impasse is resolved, miraculously. As the god steps out of the narrative's mechansim, Philoctetes has no choice but to be rearticulated in the social order. But his cure appears as much a cost as a reward.

So much is contained in this text, with its pointed emphases on the tensions between the ostracized, disarticulated subject and the interests of the state or community; on the status of the wound, or trauma, or inarticulable suffering; on care (the economy of kindness) as an ethical imperative that claims to supercede political authority; on disability or disarticulation as a transgressive stance; on the status of the cure and healing; on the relation between a literary text and the larger social-political-ideological order. And in raising but not resolving these issues, Sophocles' play points toward tensions in contemporary disability studies.

Disability and Metaphor

As we have seen, Philoctetes' experience in this drama does not much correspond to the lived experience of people with physical impairments in ancient Greece. Sophocles wished rather to position the wounded, ostracized character in an ethical-political dialogue. He stands for something else, other than what he *is*. We might ask, What is he? Why might a character in a drama *not* be a position in a dialogue? And what is he to represent? Ought he to represent exclusively people with impairments of mobility, or people with chronic pain, or people who have been betrayed by their compatriots? If we take Philoctetes, or any fictional character, to be *disabled*, then must he represent disabled people—and represent them accurately, according to their actual lived experience, and not, therefore, metaphorically or figuratively, as standing in for some other set of persons or ideas? The problem of the figurative representation of disability was, I think we can say, the core problem for a certain moment of disability studies. For Garland-Thomson, "because disability is so strongly stigmatized and is countered by so few mitigating narratives, the literary traffic in metaphors often misrepresents or flattens the experience real people have" (10). Mitchell and Snyder describe the metaphorical use of disability as a "narrative prosthetic," a "crutch upon which literary narratives lean for their representative power, disruptive potential, and analytical insight"(490); but, while relying on "the potency of disability as a symbolic figure" these narratives "rarely take up disability as an experience of social or political dimensions" (48). In a similar vein, Tobin Siebers argues that disability is the other that helps make otherness imaginable. Throughout history, it has been attached to other representations of otherness to grant them supplementary meaning, sharper focus, and additional weight. In providing this service, however,

> disability has lost the power of its own symbolism, and it is now time for disability activists to recapture it. . . . The political cannot exist in the absence of such symbolism because it describes the dynamic by which individuals are recognized by others and gather into communities. Disability has provided the public imagination with one of its most powerful symbols for the understanding of individuality, but it always symbolizes something other than itself. Now disabled people need to introduce the reality of disability into the public imagination. (48)

Michael Davidson effectively summarizes this line of thought in writing that

> a common recent criticism among disability scholars is that metaphoric treatments of impairment seldom confront the material conditions of actual disabled persons, permitting dominant social norms to be written on the body of a person who is politely asked to step offstage once the metaphoric exchange is made. (1)[3]

There seem to me several problems with critiques of metaphor such as these. First, they seem to rely on a misleading, roughly Aristotelian, view of metaphor in which one term (the metaphorical, and therefore false term) substitutes for another (the actual, true term). This position assumes that one can unequivocally know what is the true term—the term that would portray the lived experience or material conditions of disability; and it assumes that this true term itself contains no metaphorical implications. Metaphor, as I argue in this book, does not work by means of simple substitutions. Its mechanism is closer to that of catachresis, in which a word is reconfigured to denote some entity that has not yet been adequately conceptualized and that has, at present, no word that signifies it. Metaphor as catachresis is a creative and maieutic, not simply a manipulative, act; it brings something new into the world. How can language be used, as Siebers suggests, to permit something to symbolize only itself, without remainder? How can there possibly be signification with no residue of meaning—no connotation, ambiguity, no unconscious or ideological upswellings, no imperatives of genre? Poetics as catachresis as I have tried to describe it makes possible new perspectives and thus new knowledge. This knowledge, of course, can be evaluated and critiqued. It may be determined that it is ethically untenable, or so incompatible with other, prior knowledge that it ought to be rejected—deemed to be not knowledge at all, but a fantasy deriving from ideological or other unconscious forces that ought to be exposed and condemned. That process is certainly within the purview of disability studies, but does not involve a critique of the practice of metaphor per se—which, as the work of thinkers as disparate as Derrida, Lakoff and Johnson, Ricoeur, and Black demonstrates, is an essential, if not the essential, element in human thought.

And writers as sophisticated as Garland-Thomson, Mitchell and Snyder, and Siebers know this too. The intimation of a radical iconoclasm—the "censorious literalism"("Disability and Narrative" 570) that Michael Bérubé refers to—is clearly hyperbolic, the theoretical outcropping of an emotional-political geology. The critique of disability metaphor derives, I think, from the political struggle over the ownership of disability, whose most common political form has been the struggle against the medical model. The disability studies critique of writers is another form of the disability rights movement's critique of doctors. The question in both cases is, who is to define and speak for the community of disabled people—a community that comes into being as these questions of definition and representation are debated and resolved. The hyperbolic quality one detects in the critiques of disability metaphor arises first from the strained sense of metaphor it employs, its sense of the possibility of a fully literal depiction in which disability can symbolize "only itself." It arises second from the instability of the term disability—the "itself" to which Siebers refers, that which is to be depicted, and who would be included in it. On the one hand, disability is universal: All of us enter the world, as it were, disabled, as infants; throughout our lives all of us encounter illnesses and injuries that impair some of our capacities; as we age, our incapacities increase until, finally, all of us die. This is a commonplace, and observed by many disability scholars. But, alongside this universal sense, there is a particular sense of disability as a kind of ethnicity: a status construed to be in contrast to the norms of adult physical and mental abilities, occupied at any given moment only by a minority of people whose autonomy then is restricted by socially constructed barriers that fail to account for their impairments and who frequently are stigmatized and excluded from civic and economic life. Rhetorical appeals are often made regarding the first sense of disability, but the primary political and polemical thrust of disability studies is toward the latter.[4] The broader critique of metaphor, the consequence of which is a radical and impossible iconoclasm, is presented in the service of more specific criticisms of representations of disability.

In Philip Roth's novel *The Ghost Writer*, a young Jewish writer, Nathan Zuckerman, is castigated by his father for publishing stories that seemed to him to cast Jews in an unfavorable light. "'Nathan,'" his father pleads,

> your story, as far as Gentiles are concerned, is about one thing and one thing only. . . . It is about kikes. Kikes and their love of money. That is all our good Christian friends will see, I guarantee you. It is not about the scientists and teachers and lawyers they become and the things such people accomplish for others. It is not about the immigrants like Chaya who worked and saved and sacrificed to get a decent footing in America. . . . No, it's about Essie and her hammer, and Sidney and his chorus girls, and that shyster of Essie's and his filthy mouth, and, as best as I can see, about what a jerk I was begging them to reach a decent compromise before the whole family had to be dragged up in front of a *goyisher* judge." (94)

Later, a friend of the family, Judge Wachter, poses questions to Nathan such as, "If you had been living in Nazi Germany in the thirties, would you have written such a story?" and "Do you believe Shakespeare's Shy-lock and Dickens' Fagin have been of no use to anti-Semites?" and "Can you honestly say that there is anything in your story that would not warm the heart of a Julius Streicher or a Joseph Goebbels?" (102–104).

The problem for both men is that of judgment of the vulnerable minority in the eyes of a hostile majority. Jews, for Nathan's father, are always, in effect, in a state of being dragged up before the *goyisher* judge. And, to give his point authority, he summons the Jewish judge who again points to how Nathan's autobiographically based fiction will be read by people already predisposed to anti-Jewish feeling. Literature that appears to invoke pejorative stereotypes, for whatever reason, will reinforce those sterotypes. Satire, parody, irony, over-the-top humor—all that will be lost. The story will be about "one thing and one thing only." All reading of stigmatized minorities (and stigmatized minorities are always being read) will be reductive. And so the only relevant ques-tion regarding Jewish literature, as Dr. Zuckerman and Judge Wachter see it, is, Is it good for the Jews?

This attitude has been prevalent in disability studies as well. The radi-cal critique of metaphor per se—of a portrayal of disability representing "something other than itself'—quickly breaks down and reveals itself to be, in fact, a criticism of particular, reductive or stereotypical representa-tions of disability, often with the related argument that all or most rep-resentations of disability fall into this category. The question of whether a given portrayal is good for, or fair to, the disabled is not unreasonable. Indeed, as Roth presents it, Nathan's father is not a fool (though Judge Wachter appears as something of a buffoon), and his interrogation of his son seems fair. Why should Jews, or the disabled or any other stigma-tized group, be portrayed in ways that seem to mock them and play into stereotypes that already confine them? Our first answer should be, obvi-ously, they should not be so portrayed. There is a legitimate place for a moralizing criticism that calls out oppressive ideologies as they appear in aesthetic representation. But, this may not be so easy to determine. The subtleties that Nathan's father wanted to dismiss in his claim that readers will see "one thing and one thing only" ultimately must play their part in a reading; otherwise, Michael Bérubé's fear that disability studies is incompatible with literary studies will be confirmed, and I do not believe that this is the case.[5] Garland-Thomson, I would argue, surely is wrong in her claims that disabled characters "usually remain on the margins of fiction as uncomplicated figures or exotic aliens" (10), that disability in a character "cancels out other qualities, reducing the complex person to a single attribute" (12), or that "the disabled body is almost always a freakish spectacle presented by the mediated narrative voice" (10). I would contest further Lennard Davis's argument that modern novels serve chiefly to "promulgate and disburse notions of normalcy. . . . From the typicality of the central character to the normalizing devices of plot to bring deviant characters back into the norms of society, to the normalizing codas of ends, the nineteenth- and twentieth-century novel promulgates and disburses notions of normalcy and by extension makes of physical differences ideological differences" (*Enforcing Normalcy* 49). Mitchell and Snyder's position that narrative's primary function is to resolve deviance back into a dominant ideology is also questionable. According to the analyses I have undertaken in this work, the portrayals of dys-/disarticulate characters and the ideological directions of the texts overall are far more multivalent than straightforward disability analyses would seem to allow. Billy Budd, Stevie, Benjy, and Robin are indeed disarticulated, torn from the social fabric, even torn to pieces, but less dys-/disarticulate characters are not commensurately rewarded for their purported normality. Indeed, these modernist texts use dys-/disarticulation as a means of critique, not of ideological affirmation. Nor, I would argue, are the cognitively impaired characters defined by their impairments any more than other characters are defined by their moral or perceptual characteristics.[6]

Disability, Disruption, and Transgression

On the obverse side of disability studies' concerns with adequate representation (in which politics and aesthetics converge) stand a set of descriptions in which disability is the antithesis of representation. There are two broad stances here: one from the perspective of the social-symbolic order in its encounter with disability; the other from the perspective of a disabled subject deliberately working to disrupt that order. In the first stance, we see disability under the categories of the freakish, the sublime, and the Lacanian real. In the second, disability assumes the role of the defamiliarizing (in the sense put forward by Russian formalism) or, in a stronger way, the transgressive. As disability scholar and activist Simi Linton points out, and as the analyses of chapter 2 confirm, modern medical-scientific-administrative understandings of disability "cast human variation as deviance from the norm, as pathological condition, as deficit, and, significantly, as an individual burden and personal tragedy" (*Claiming Disability* 11), thus evading, from a disability perspective, analysis of the ideological and physical obstacles that prevent full participatory citizenship for disabled people. Corollary to this insight regarding the pathologizing and stigmatizing force of ableist, normative ideology, disability studies have, in several ways, turned this insight on its head and placed in the foreground the power of disability to disrupt or transgress dominant ideology and its practices and institutions. Disruption, transgression, and the refusal to be normalized are, indeed, key moves in much disability theory. Disability then becomes not merely a marginalized, stigmatized position, but a position of critique and potential liberation.

"Disability is the unorthodox made flesh," writes Rosemarie Garland-Thomson, "refusing to be normalized, neutralized, or homogenized" (24). Not only is disability, in this sense, intrinsically at odds with social norms—that "other that makes otherness imaginable," as Siebers put it; or "an interrupting force that confronts cultural truisms," in Mitchell and Snyder's words—but it *refuses* to be normalized. The normative, ableist social order responds with shock and horror to the presence of disablity. Alluding to Zizek's reading of Lacan, Mitchell and Snyder argue that "disability serves as the 'hard kernel' or recalcitrant corporeal matter that cannot be deconstructed away. . . . Representations of disability allow an interrogation of static beliefs about the body while also erupting as the unseemly matter of narrative that cannot be textually contained" (*Narrative Prosthesis* 17). This is the gist also of Ato Quayson's analysis of disability texts as rewritings of the sublime. What Quayson calls an "aesthetic nervousness" occurs when, in attempting to represent disability, "the dominant protocols of representation within the literary text are shortcircuited" (15). As Quayson shows in analyses of texts by Beckett, Coetzee, and Morrison, the text must accommodate itself to the disabled figure through the impairment of its own form. The result of this formal anxiety in the face of disability resembles the sublime in its production of "a contradictory semiotics of inarticulacy and articulation" (23). But this formal impairment, Quayson argues, is complicated by its being "specifically tied to forms of social hierarchization" (23). Formal dislocations are brought on not merely by interactions with other forms, or with the natural world or some other phenomenon that overwhelms the mind's ability to give it shape, or category, or syntax. Rather, the interaction of the literary text with disability is with the entire social-political-symbolic location in which disability is construed. In this way, for Quayson, "disability returns the aesthetic domain to an active ethical core" (19), and so reading the nervous-sublime (disabled) text requires also an encounter with social hierarchy and stigmatization—and an encounter with one's own nervousness and incapacity as one approaches disability both in literature and society. Quayson's ethics seem to imply a universalism. Disability disrupts aesthetic representation because it is itself unrepresented socially and politically. Presumably, once disability attains social-political recognition, its unsettling effects on aesthetic representation will diminish, and this, presumably, is to be desired. If ethical imbalance produces aesthetic deformation, then ethical transformation will find its aesthetic equivalent as well.[7]

In contrast to this ethically centered, ultimately normalizing view of the disruption occasioned by disability is the view of disability as transgression. This view is expressed most powerfully by Robert McRuer in his work on the "crip," who is precisely the disabled subject who, in Garland-Thomson's words cited above, "refuses to be normalized, neutralized, or homogenized." The crip stands to the good disabled citizen as the queer stands to the domesticated gay subject. The crip, as McRuer descibes him, does not just oppose any particular social norms that exclude him, or others. The crip is opposed to the norm as such, and to the processes of normalization. Just as the queer has no use for "gay marriage"—the problem being marriage itself, not who is permitted to engage in it—so the crip wants a full reimagining of what an "accessible" society would mean. In art, public policy, and education, McRuer critiques all aesthetic and political norms. The crip would constitute a permanent political and aesthetic avant-garde, a never-ending pressure on society to break open all enclosures, to transgress anew each new boundary, including the demolition of the empty vessel of "identity." For McRuer, a truly *accessible* society is not simply a society equipped with sufficient ramps, braille postings, ASL translators, and professional care attendants, "but one in which our ways of relating to, and depending on, each other have been reconfigured" (94). McRuer's is a utopian project "of resisting closure or containment and accessing other possibilities" (159) to be achieved by the transgressive means made available through crip/queer activism and cultural representation.[8]

There is necessarily an uneasy relation between the utopian and the transgressive. Utopian thought requires the imaginative negation of the world as it is, and transgression is a category of negation, a bursting of whatever limits define a status quo. But transgression has two sides. On one hand, it can never stop, or can never stop and still remain transgressive. Having burst through one set of limits, it will encounter another and must burst through them as well, and not for the sake of any positive outcome. If a utopian goal should somehow be achieved, the transgressive impulse will not, for that reason, moderate itself; it must burst the utopia as well. But at the same time, as McRuer recognizes, modes of transgression are always encountering, and frequently succumbing to, forces of routinization—a process outlined a century ago by Max Weber in his writing on charisma. The other must remain other, but how can it retain its alterity when it is covered with the language of the same and can only speak—insofar as it speaks—in that language? The problem of the crip, in this sense, is the same as the problem of the dys-/disarticulate. It must, to cite again Joseph Conrad, use "the current words" yet remain "unaccountable." And current words multiply. What was unaccountable last week is now on everyone's tongue.

In order to withstand these continual normalizing processes—which are augmented through consumer capitalism—a crip identity must continually be reaffirmed. One must "come out" as crip, McRuer argues, in order to reveal repeatedly and with new force the injustice inherent in all manner of norms. To be avowedly and actively crip means to occupy the most radical and transgressive position possible in relation to normativity—to discover, as it were, and manipulate the unaccountability in all the current words. This may be, and yet I find McRuer's most striking instance of crip politics problematic. This is the case of Bob Flanagan, a performance artist who has cystic fibrosis and is a "self-proclaimed 'supermasochist,'"who has created works of performance art (shown, among other locations, at the Santa Monica Museum of Art and the Museum of Modern Art in New York) that display acts of sado-masochism with his partner and "mistress" which included "a beating characteristic of their erotic and sexual practices together" (181–82). Flanagan is also "famous," as McRuer reports, "for pounding a nail through his penis" (181). For my own part, I'm entirely able to be shocked or discomforted by such a performance, even by a report of it. But shock and discomfort are transient, and I'm left finally not certain what is the true location of the shock. McRuer cites Linda Kauffman's judgement that Flanagan "deals with fantasies that have not been coopted by consumer culture" (193), but this seems to me dubious. What could be more commodifiable than S/M? It has become a classic gesture of transgression, as Susan Sontag observed back in 1974. It is an industry, and Flanagan, whatever else his accomplishments, is part of it. And to perform in high-prestige museums and performance spaces moves his creation into another area of consumer culture. Nevertheless, McRuer is right that there is still something deep and powerful in Flanagan's performance, even having accounted for the S/M stylistics. The style may be a commodity, but it also points toward genuine pain and toward something genuinely shocking. But the shock, it seems to me, lies not in the transgressive cripping against normativity, but rather in Flanagan's revelation of his own relation to the deterioration of his body, to his physical pain, to the humiliations that deterioration and pain inflict on him, and to the knowledge and claim of his mortality. There is in Flanagan's work a sense of "signaling through the flames" (13), as Artaud described it. It is hard not to read the nail through the penis as a violent condemnation of all the processes of biological generation, a sardonic, outraged parody of death. It is an act in which symptom merges with symbol. The transgressive quality in Flanagan's work, I would argue, is connected with the artist's own traumatization—the universal trauma of the expiring body in his case condensed and accelerated. And trauma, as I will argue shortly, is a factor seldom acknowledged in disability studies and not acknowledged here by Flanagan or McRuer.

But the crucial political question McRuer poses is what possibilities are opened in those moments when the limit has been jumped or punctured, the moment of "signaling through the flames," just before the bubble of the norm reshapes itself? Something opens, and to go through the opening is to jump past the existing conceptual, symbolic limits—or, to put it more accurately, to conceive of a symbolic gesture that indicates a point beyond those limits and that, thereby, shows a new vision of the shape of those limits and brings to life a new possibility of critique and opposition. The transgressive, counter-normative politics that McRuer proposes is a politically more active version of what this book has been calling the dys-/disarticulate. Dys-/disarticulation principally describes the *problem* of how to imagine an outside to a social-symbolic order conceived as total and totalizing. McRuer, in effect, tries to imagine an active politics that might follow from dys-/disarticulation, that would blast its way past the social-symbolic boundary and then return—with what is not clear. McRuer hearkens, as do many others at the present moment, to Walter Benjamin's encouragement that we "seize hold of a memory as it flashes up at a moment of danger," from which emerge the "chips of messianic time" that activate the "jetztzeit"—that "time of the now" in which the present becomes truly present because infused with failed utopian impulses of the past ("Theses on the Philosophy of History"). These failures are continually and traumatically repeated, and McRuer's active, transgressive politics, I would argue, responds both to the utopian content and to the traumas of their failures. The crip, however, is not Benjamin's angel of history, hurled in a state of stunned, pure traumatization (and dys-/disarticulation) into the future. The crip is in the trenches, reopening closures, changing curricula, joining and transforming the struggles against global capital.

This is just practical, counter-hegemonic politics. There remains, though, in McRuer's vision something of the traumatic-esctatic self-dissolution of Benjamin's angel, or of Bob Flanagan immersing himself performatively in catastrophe. To get from one to the other, to move from the economy of trauma and symptom, from the *jouissance* of transgression toward political action one must, returning to Benjamin's dictum, "seize hold" of the political occasion—that is, make a conscious choice that one's status as disabled be the occasion not simply for particular local interventions but also for the fundamental, counter-normative critique that McRuer calls for. As McRuer puts it, one must "come out" as crip. This coming out indicates neither the biological status defined by the medical model of disability nor quite the identity in relation to social barriers as posited by the social model. It is intended, I think, as a revolutionary gesture whose origins lie in the particular differences and oppressions located in more standard, liberal disability politics, but which turns the disruptive force of the disabled body (though not, we must add, the disabled mind) toward a critique of all hierarchies and norms.

Two questions occur to me here. First, who is eligible to come out as crip? And second, how radical is such a coming out? McRuer argues convincingly that issues of disability are entirely consonant with progressive politics overall, and that progressive activists should be obliged to come out crip—to disavow the stance that disability issues pertain only to the obviously disabled, and to recognize that their new crip status signifies opposition to (and determination to transgress) all oppressive normativities. McRuer himself, for instance, tells of "coming out" at a conference talk as HIV positive, although he is not, in fact, HIV positive, in order to support movements struggling not only to combat the epidemic, but "against the global structures that sustain the epidemic by capitalizing on those most affected by it" (57). McRuer acknowledges the strategic and problematic character of (mis)identifications such as the one he made, and that "coming out crip at times involves embracing and at times disidentifying with the most familiar kinds of identity politics" (57). It is important, and McRuer is certainly correct on this point, that progressives recognize that disability issues are an essential part of any progressive politics, and cannot simply be afterthoughts. But this is liberalism, diversity, accretion, "we are the world"—as McRuer recognizes. McRuer's real goal in this book is to imagine a genuine opposition to global capitalism—a difficult task given capitalism's material and ideological power and, after the "death of communism" and the end of the Cold War, the apparent lack of any coherent alternative. What would be a genuinely transgressive, shocking, liberating "coming out" in this political context—at a moment when global capital seems capable of appropriating instantly any transgressive gesture, when its ideologically totalizing power seems secure even at a time of economic crisis?

If we want to get under the skin of capital, to truly "seize hold of the past in a moment of danger," why not follow Slavoj Zizek's example and "come out" as a communist, whether or not one is for real? It is unclear, of course, what exactly it means at this moment to "be a communist." But what is in fact more repulsive and shocking to normative ideology right now—to be paralyzed and in a wheelchair, or to be blind, or to have, say, cerebral palsy and have difficulty speaking clearly, or to have a cognitive impairment, or be unable to control one's bowels, or to be

HIV positive, or dying of cancer . . . or . . . to be a communist? It seems to me that in the United States at this time—even at this time, so many years after McCarthy, and with capitalism in a state of panic—the communist is more shocking and transgressive and counternormative than the crip. Communism: a "lame" idea, historically "crippled," repulsive, foreign, obscurantist, anachronistic. And, I would add, exceedingly difficult to commodify, though nothing is impossible.[9]

But there we are again—to ironically disparage communism as seen by global neoliberalism, I resorted to parodic references to disability. When will I stop leaning and stand on my own two feet? When will I hang from my own tale? McRuer's project is as dys-/disarticulated as mine. It gestures toward utopian alterities that would destabilize the social-symbolic order. But it appeals to existing counter-hegemonic movements and urges them to move toward a more radically counter-hegemonic position, one that insists on disability as a central, universal, and, I would have to add, *normative* category. In the end, McRuer calls for "a postidentity politics that allows us to work together, one that acknowledges the complex and contradictory histories of our various movements, drawing on and learning from those histories rather than transcending them. We can't afford to position any body of thought, not even disability studies, as global in the sense of offering *the* subject position, *the* key" (202, emphasis in original). Transgression in *Crip Theory* is, at last, a rhetorical hyperbole, a device for imagining the radical erasure of oppressive norms so as to imagine a world without them, and then organize a politics that might get there. In this moment of danger, he reaches back to seize some ideal of justice in which human abilities and dependencies can be reimagined; and he seeks to reach out, past the limits of normative subjecthood, into an ecstatic dissolution, but from which one returns a better, more humane and more cripped political subject, though one should not expect from him wedding invitations.[10]

Disability, Pain, and Impairment

But something still is missing.

Disability differs; disability disrupts; disability is prosthetic; disability may at certain valences transgress. But there seems to be no negative. Aside from social barriers, there would appear to be no down side to disability. One can say truly that, apart from social attitudes and policies, there is no intrinsic negative to being African American or Jewish or Latino or a woman. But with disability, while there certainly are social impediments, there are also biological impairments, there may be pain, there may be or may have been trauma. It seems a mistake to regard these as inconsequential, however much one works to reform social attitudes and policies. It was of great political importance that disability rights activists wrested exclusive control of the understanding of disability away from medicine and toward a broader social conceptualization. As Simi Linton urges, it is wrong to discuss disability "exclusively in terms of pathology, deficits, and abnormality" (*Claiming Disability* 85). And Rosemarie Garland-Thomson makes a powerful point—one often made in disability studies—that disability is "not so much a property of bodies as a product of cultural rules about what bodies should be or do" and that the meanings attributed to disability "reside not in inherent physical flaws, but in social relationships" based on ideologies of bodily types (6–7). But an exclusive reliance on a social model of disability that denies any biological or even emotional component is also untenable.

Disability studies has not yet conceived a way of thinking the negative. One need not say "deficit" or "pathology" or any other medical term. But it seems necessary to theorize the experiences of disability that are not directly socially induced—that involve sensation, emotion, and physical or mental limitations that social reform will not completely alleviate, and that will have further social consequences. Linton has acknowledged this problem. "We have been hesitant," she writes,

> to go in a particular direction in the development of theory—that is, toward the issue of impairment itself. As we talk about it among ourselves, we've acknowledged that we have been reluctant to theorize about the actual pain and limitations that we experience. It may be the manifestation in theory of a personal denial of the impact and consequences of impairment. Yet it may also be the tremendous difficulty in articulating impairment in ways that do not essentialize disability or reduce it to an individual problem. (138)

Linton published that comment in 1998. In 2010, Claire Barker could still accurately report that pain is "a topic that tends to cause an impasse within Disability Studies" (106). The problem is, indeed, considerable, for the political and theoretical stakes are large. To acknowledge pain and incapacity would be to risk the image of autonomy that political participation traditionally has required, and it would risk severing disability studies from disability rights, a move most disability scholars are unwilling to contemplate. Disability studies nevertheless has begun to address this dilemma in two ways. First, following Linton's suggestion, there have been tentative steps toward thinking about pain and intrinsic limitation. And second, as I will discuss later in this chapter, disability theory has begun to pursue directions indicated by thinkers like Martha Nussbaum and Eva Kittay, who criticize the hypostatization of autonomy and rationality as sole criteria of ethical subjecthood.

Tobin Siebers has set out both to make pain a legitimate topic of disability discourse and at the same time to direct the discussion of pain back into the kind of disability-as-identity politics that has always been averse to discussion of pain. As he writes, "the greatest stake in disability studies at the present moment is to find ways to represent pain and to resist models of the body that blunt the political effectiveness of these representations" (*Disability Theory* 61). For Siebers, the target of critique is not disability's social model that transfers all negativity into social barriers, but rather the constructivist thinking of post-structuralist thinkers, particularly Judith Butler and Donna Haraway, in which the body is in all respects an ideological-textual product, and pain is associated with transgressive *jouissance* or, for Haraway, the semiotic prosthesis of the cyborg. "Rare is the theoretical account," Siebers concludes, "where physical suffering remains harmful for very long. The ideology of ability requires that any sign of disability be viewed exclusively as awakening new and magical opportunities for ability" (63). It is important to note here that Siebers's critique applies not only to Butler and Haraway, but to disability studies work as well, though Siebers does not say so. He seeks to break through the impasse cited by Barker (in the context, by the way, of a quite favorable review of Siebers's book) by transferring its location elsewhere. Siebers does indeed break new ground in disability studies simply by emphasizing pain in the way he does. His discussion of the "blunt, crude realities" of the disabled body—and, as he adds, of all bodies ("the disabled body is no more real than the able body—and no less real" [67])—is a welcome intervention. But it would be helpful if he would acknowledge that his polemic reaches targets within the field of disability studies, not just those beyond it.

Tom Shakespeare's recent work is more forthright. One of the early formulators of the social model of disability in the United Kingdom, Shakespeare now criticizes directly both the model and his old collaborators and so has aroused considerable antagonism among some disability scholars—a fate that Siebers, with his more indirect critiques, has avoided.[11] Disability studies' central theoretical drawback, Shakespeare asserts, is the disregard, even to the point of denial, of impairment. Shakespeare first contests the distinction between impairment (understood as a biological condition with no particular, necessarily negative consequences) and disability (understood as the stigmatizing social barriers erected against people with certain, though not all, impairments). Impairment frequently is imbricated with social factors—malnutrition, for instance, or working conditions; and a disability, he argues, cannot be understood as distinct from the biological condition attached to it. This first point is rapidly gaining currency, especially as disability is being investigated in global contexts which necessarily entail thinking about class difference and poverty. Robert McRuer and Michael Davidson have written powerfully on this topic. The second point is more difficult. Siebers's thinking toward a "new realism of the body" (53) provides a good entry, but on the whole, disability studies' approach to impairment and its vicissitudes remains, as Barker put it, at an impasse. As Shakespeare notes, the social model which isolates impairment from disability and regards it as a neutral factor was conceived originally as part of a political strategy, not as an overall social theory. It was meant to absolve disabled people from feelings of guilt, to free them from perceiving their lives as tragic, and to create a sense of political solidarity that extended across barriers of class, race, gender, and particular impairments and medical conditions. In this, it succeeded imperfectly—there is still much to be achieved in improving the social-political status of the disabled—but fairly well, with genuine political accomplishments. But the strong sense of political identity which the social model helped to foster has become, Shakespeare argues, "an end in itself," rather than a means to an end, and so has inhibited a full understanding of the range of disability experiences. The disregard of the reality of impairment has become a dogma which "enables disabled people to deny the relevance of their impaired bodies or brains" (80). For Shakespeare, "people are disabled by society and by their bodies" (56). "Even in the absence of social barriers or oppression," he writes, "it would still be problematic to have an impairment, because many impairments are limiting or difficult, not neutral," and a disabled person suffers "both the intrinsic limitations of impairment and the externally imposed social discrimination" (41).

So, what is disability for Shakespeare? He agrees with most disability writers that it is not a tragedy, or certainly not necessarily one. It should neither be a stigmatizing label (e.g., the "cripple," the "retard") nor a celebratory badge (e.g., McRuer's transgressive "crip"). Disability—that "complex interaction of biological, psychological, cultural and socio-political factors which cannot be extricated except with imprecision" (38)—is, for Shakespeare, a "predicament," and a predicament, as he observes, citing *The Concise Oxford Dictionary*, is "'an unpleasant, trying or dangerous situation.'" Thus, for Shakespeare, a predicament,

> although still negative . . . , does not have the inescapable emphasis of "tragedy." The added burdens of social oppression and social exclusion, which turn impairment into disadvantage, need to be removed. . . . Everything possible needs to be provided to make coping with impairment easier. But even with the removal of barriers and the provision of support, impairment will remain problematic for many people. (63)

Disability and Trauma: A Disciplinary Divide

There is a further category of disruption that disability studies has avoided almost entirely, and that is trauma. Though not all instances of physical or mental impairment involve trauma, many do, and one might expect the field to acknowledge a traumatic component to disability and theorize its role. One might expect also that disability studies might engage with trauma studies, a field that emerged in the humanities at roughly the same time as did disability studies.[12] Conversely, one might think that work in trauma studies would engage with disability studies, since trauma necessarily implies some kind of impairment or disabling of the individual or society. Such assumptions would be mistaken. Disability studies has been silent on the topic of trauma, and the contemporaneous fields of trauma studies and disability studies have remained deeply separate. Indexes and bibliographies of the significant works in each field indicate almost no familiarity with work in the other.[13]

I would suggest two broad factors in explaining this separation. First, disability studies and trauma studies differ on the status of the event. The trauma is, above all, a thing that happens; it is an event with consequences. The consequences may not appear directly related to the event. They may take the forms of symptoms, and memory of the event may be obscured or even obliterated. But the crucial fact of trauma is the event that destabilizes an individual or social entity and that continues to destabilize as recurring symptom. The repression or denial of the trauma as a thing that happened and that has ongoing consequences brings on further symptomatic consequences. In social terms, traumatic symptoms may take the form of political tendencies, historical narratives, and a broad range of cultural representations. Memorialization, distortion, reaction, gestures toward healing, toward panic, toward a normalization that cannot be achieved, toward a more effective coming to terms with the event and its aftermaths—all are parts of the cultural apparatus of responding to a traumatic event over time. As Dominick LaCapra has pointed out, responses to trauma necessarily involve components both of working through and of acting out. One is seldom doing exclusively one or the other, for response to trauma cannot help but be affective; we cannot step outside an emotional relation to the event and symptoms in question. A discursive working through will sometimes swerve into symptomatic forms, but these swerves may be necessary to create a more genuinely healing relation to the trauma.[14]

These concerns are not particularly germane to disability studies. How a person acquired an impairment, whether it is congenital or the result of illness, age, or injury, is not important. A traumatically induced impairment is not different than a congenital impairment from the perspective of disability studies because the disability itself (as distinct from the impairment) results from the physical and ideological barriers created by "normate" society. The focus of disability studies returns to the political goal of access and the ideological goal of the removal of stigmas. What is destabilized in theories of disability is not the disabled subject, but normative society in the presence of disability. The stigmatization and the consequent ignoring of the legitimate civic needs and rights of the disabled amount to a collective denial of vulnerability, interdependence, and mortality. Thus, the continued presence of disabled people constitutes a return of the repressed. If the disabled exist, then the normate project of physical perfection and immortality is doomed. Thus, if trauma is, at all or implicitly, a factor in disability studies, the trauma is an ongoing or structural presence in the norm itself—a rupture in its self-perception—but not a concrete historical occurrence. As there is no crying in baseball, as Tom Hanks tells us, there is no trauma in disability. Nothing happened. Trauma is on the other side. If indeed, disability constitutes a trauma for the norm, then it is the norm that must come to terms with it, as it must with all varieties of difference.

The second area around which disability studies and trauma studies have distinctly different emphases is metaphor. As I argued earlier, disability studies displays a suspicion of metaphor that amounts almost to iconoclasm. It seems at times that the only theoretically viable representation of disability would be the most literal representation possible and one created by a disabled person him/herself. It would be difficult to conceive of a metaphorical representation of disability that would not constitute an illegitimate appropriation and distortion of the reality of the experience of disability, whether as a continuation of the general stigmatization of the disabled (as in Garland-Thomson) or as prosthesis supporting other philosophical or aesthetic agendas (as in Mitchell and Snyder) or as an instance of the sublime (as in Quayson). The entire process of metaphor, it would seem, is antithetical to the political goals of disability studies. Conversely, trauma theory, I would argue, is fundamentally a theory of poesis—of making, of metaphor.

To study trauma is to focus on an idea of direct experience. An event occurs; one passes through it, or undergoes it; one *suffers* it. The event is real, is overwhelming, and the psyche (or the culture) is, in some sense, shattered. But the direct experience of trauma is mediated in two ways, as trauma theory conceives it. First, the traumatic event is defined as being so overwhelming that it cannot consciously be apprehended as it occurs; it can only be reconstructed in retrospect, is always belated, at a distance. Second, and following from this, the apprehension of trauma involves always a study of symptoms, and so the central focus of trauma studies is not an attempt magically to reconstitute a direct experience of trauma, which must always be inaccessible even to its subject, but rather is on acts of interpretation of traumatic symptoms. Trauma studies is primarily a hermeneutics whose goal is to read traumatic-symptomatic texts.

Insofar as trauma studies aims toward the interpretation of symptomatic texts separated in time from the events they refer to, it is a study also of historical transmission. We can understand a present situation only in relation to some past event; yet, because this past event has, through its overwhelming violence and horror, obliterated itself, it can be encountered only by means of its effects in the present. And these effects are not direct: transmission is achieved through transformation and metamorphosis. Furthermore, the nature of these changes, as Zizek describes in the greatest detail, is in part determined by ideology, which, in Zizek's view, is a kind of fantasy in which all traumatic damage is repaired. Yet ideology is itself a symptom, and contributes to further damage even as it helps maintain a semblance of social stability.[15]

An event occurs, so destructive, so obliterating that it seems to wipe out even the symbolic means of its own representation. Jean-François Lyotard compared the Holocaust to an earthquake so powerful that it destroyed the seismographs that would have measured it (56). This claim is of course hyperbolic, for few crimes of this magnitude have been so amply documented. But hyperbole is part of the rhetoric of trauma studies, and indeed, in moral, rather than empirical, terms, Lyotard's claim is both evocative and valid.[16] And yet, after this negation—figured, often hyperbolically, as absolute and definitive— comes . . . something. Trauma theory posits transmission, but it posits also the impossibility of transmission. Trauma signifies the collapse of signification. The post-traumatic world is an emergence of *something* from *nothing*. It is not transmission; it is something else. At least this is what the language of trauma studies suggests.[17]

Trauma studies articulates a poetics, a theory of making. Traces (we might say, ruins) from the destroyed world, consciousness, or society survive, and from these traces, or ruins, and from the somatic/symbolic symptoms that grow in them, new discourses take shape. Trauma studies focuses on how these post-traumatic discourses come into being. Its emphases on transmission, transformation, the creation of language and thought from a condition before a traumatic event to a condition after suggest an overarching, if implicit, concern with metaphor. Trauma theory describes the carrying-across, the *meta-pherein*, of subjectivity or culture across or through a traumatic crucible into a new linguistic, social, somatic world of symptoms, ruins, ideological constructs and fantasies—all of which are indirect, symbolic, metaphoric figures for what occurred during the missing, obliterated, time of trauma. Trauma studies is always concerned with objects that signify, that exist materially, but are more than what they are. The post-traumatic world is full of signifiers, but emptied of signifieds and referents, for these have been destroyed or transformed past recognition. And yet, a world remains and continues to take shape. Rupture and continuity coexist, and this coexistence may be both the precondition and the effective mechanism for metaphor. Something is not, but is; something is, but is something else. As I argued in chapter 1, metaphor should be considered a category of catachresis. Thus, in sometimes problematic ways, trauma studies merges with discourses of the sublime, the sacred, the abject, and the apocalyptic. It is understandable that such mergers take place, for discourses which posit absent referents may well tend to have overlapping vocabularies since no point of reference is there to distinguish them. This is a problem that has particularly beset areas of Holocaust studies.[18]

It should be evident at this point that the study of the dys-/disarticulate is also, in part, a study of trauma. As we have seen, the dys-/disarticulate finds representation at those places where the social-symbolic order is threatened, where it perceives (and represents) alterity in traumatic forms. Dys-/disarticulation and social trauma are almost invariably linked. At the same time, the dys-/disarticulate figure is also a figure of actual cognitive or linguistic impairment, and so, as Quayson observes so effectively, the impaired figure serves as a marker for where a disrupted aesthetic form encounters an ethical perspective. But I would add that ethics—and the political, philosophical, scientific, and medical discourses in which ethics is immersed—was present in the dys-/disarticulate representation from the beginning; and that what Quayson reads as sublime is the traumatic impasse of these relations. It may be, then, that the dys-/disarticulate is the vehicle that can link trauma studies with disability studies. And this link brings in also the somewhat vexed—in both fields—question of healing. Trauma studies warns consistently against forms of healing or closure that are merely ideological coverings over wounds that, in reality, are far from healed and still producing symptoms. As I will discuss a bit later, disability studies is often hostile to the notion of healing or rehabilitation per se, at least as these pertain to individuals confronted with the medical establishment. Trauma studies does admit the possibility of healing, but only insofar as it involves genuine social reformation, and here, I think, disability studies would be in accord. The social-historical possibilities of healing according to trauma studies are best seen, I think, in Adorno's admonition that "we will not have come to terms with [*aufarbeiten*: literally, to work through] the past until the causes of what happened then are no longer active. Only because these causes live on does the spell of the past remain, to this very day, unbroken" ("What Does 'Coming to Terms with the Past' Mean?" 129).

For trauma studies, the world is seen as broken, shattered, wounded, even as fallen. There is something cabalistic, certainly Benjaminian, in its perspective. The world is described as obliterated. But the world is never described as *disabled*. Trauma studies describes a condition—of disintegration and negation, revealed and obscured by symptoms—but it does not describe this condition in terms of its possible agency or abilities, or in terms of abilities which might have been lost. Such terminology is not within the field's metaphorical range. And yet, this set of metaphors surely could be invoked. The earth, or some part of it (a given society), could be described as having the ability to create and sustain life, the ability to provide food, shelter, medical care, education, the ability to sustain a people spiritually, intellectually, economically, and aesthetically. And having posited these abilities, trauma could be described as an event in which a world or society becomes impaired or disabled. In spite of its extensive use of metaphor of damage and recuperation, and of its function as a theory of metaphor, trauma studies does not employ figures suggesting disability. In this regard, trauma studies is actually more apocalyptic in attitude than it might like to admit. Its concern is with absolute catastrophe, obliteration, absolute transformation, total alterity. Disability studies, on the other hand, since it has developed together with movements for disability rights, is necessarily more mundane and anti-apocalyptic. It is concerned with particularities of physical difference rather than with radical, incommensurable otherness.

But what about trauma in its more mundane, less theological sense of a catastrophic event that happens and has consequences? Does this sense of trauma have any place in disability studies? Let me examine one significant instance of trauma and disability emerging in conflict in a critical text: Mitchell and Snyder's analysis of Melville's presentation of Captain Ahab in *Moby Dick*. Mitchell and Snyder begin by observing the obvious point that critics tend to acknowledge and then ignore: that the novel's central figure, Ahab, is disabled and walks with the aid of a prosthetic leg, and that whatever is at stake in an interpretation of the novel must return to the fact of Ahab's disability. Mitchell and Snyder observe that while the novel presents a world of demographic and semantic fluidity, without stable or ultimate meanings, in which all signs are infinitely interpretable, Ahab, the one disabled character, is static, locked in his monomania regarding the white whale. And, moreover, Ahab's imprisonment in a singleness of interpretation, Mitchell and Snyder argue, is a direct consequence, indeed almost an emanation, of his disability. This crucial distinction in semantic status between Ahab and all other characters indicates the novel's bias toward a physiological determinism of which the disabled character is emblem, since, for Mitchell and Snyder, all of Ahab's character and all his actions are functions of his physical condition. "The significance of disability as a prescription for Ahab's mysterious behavior," Mitchell and Snyder write, "suggests that people with disabilities can be reduced to the physical evidence of their bodily differences" (*Narrative Prosthesis* 123), and so "physical disability becomes synonymous in the text with the tragedy of a deterministic fate" (138). Mitchell and Snyder propose a specific allegorical, or prosthetic, function for Ahab and his search for a fixed, stable meaning embodied in the whale who injured him.

> To seek "knowledge" in the postlapsarian world of sliding signifiers means to enter into the insufficiency and discomfort of a prosthetic relation. Disabilities bear the stigma of a reminder that the body proves no less mutable or unpredictable than the chaos of nature itself. Ahab's character becomes the tragic embodiment of this linguistic equivalent to original sin, and his prostheticized limb serves as the visual evidence of his metaphorical plight. (126)

This insightful passage suggests that Ahab's pursuit of the whale is an effort, in effect, to rebuild the Tower of Babel and rediscover the primal language of Adam in which each name stood truly and stably for its object. And yet, this effort to rediscover the Word requires violence: One must "strike through the mask" and destroy the enormous, inscrutable manifestation of ambiguity. Ahab, in this description, becomes a kind of terrorist: For him, there is only one direction, one truth, and it can only be achieved through acts of revelatory, quasi-apocalyptic violence—a process similar to that pursued by the terrorists in DeLillo's *The Names*, discussed in chapter 4.

I agree with this description of Ahab as semantic terrorist, but am not convinced by Mitchell and Snyder's argument that his status is entirely a function of his disability. Missing from their analysis are crucial roles for trauma and loss. Mitchell and Snyder acknowledge, but do not emphasize, that Ahab's monomania is linked not to his present prosthetic condition, his disability, but to the event of his dismembering. His thinking returns always to that moment of injury—of pain, violation, humiliation, helplessness, in short, of trauma. Indeed, in a manner strikingly in accord with psychoanalytic theory, Ahab seeks compulsively to *repeat* the moment of trauma. His disability in itself is not what concerns or motivates him. Ahab lives and works quite well with his prosthetic leg and the various technologies he has installed to help him move around his ship. When he finds himself beyond the reach of his technologies, as when he boards the *Samuel Enderby*, Ahab negotiates a potentially humiliating situation with relatively good humor. Yet Ahab is still tormented, so it would seem that his singleness of purpose and his compulsion to re-encounter the white whale stem not from his condition of having one leg but rather from the trauma of the loss of the other.

It is striking, and I believe emblematic, that Mitchell and Snyder cannot acknowledge Ahab's condition as a condition of *loss*. Their single use of the word is in quotation marks: "Ahab desires nothing short of a denial of this prosthetic relation and, in doing so, situates his 'loss' as an insult to an originary whole that he longs to reinstate" (125). It is unclear to me why the fact of this loss cannot be admitted directly into the discourse. In the novel, certainly, it is real, its circumstances violent, and its effects traumatic. Indeed, if, as Mitchell and Snyder surmise, Ahab's goal is to instate a condition of fixed meanings, the traumatic loss of meaning (which must be apocalyptically reinscribed) is a function, for Ahab, of his personal traumatic loss. As trauma theory in all its forms argues, trauma disrupts meaning. And in working through trauma, one strives not for some rigid Babel of certainty—that is, some fetish or ideological fantasy of wholeness; one seeks rather to come to terms with contingency, to remember and tell one's story with new understanding, to mourn one's loss and eventually be able to live beyond mourning. But in order to do so, one must not put one's loss in quotation marks, as if it were not really loss.

Striking also is Mitchell and Snyder's elision of Ahab's conversation with Captain Boomer of the *Samuel Enderby*, who lost his arm in an encounter with Moby Dick. This encounter between the two disabled captains suggests a different, less deterministic presentation of disability than the one Mitchell and Snyder claim informs the novel. Far from being monomaniacally obsessed with destroying the white whale, Captain Boomer seems far more engaged in humorous banter with his ship's doctor. And rather than seeking to reinstate fixed meanings, Captain Boomer's interchanges with Dr. Bunger serve as small paradigms of undecidability, as Boomer continually accuses the doctor of drunkenness while Bunger insists that he never touches alcohol. Captain Boomer's injury did not leave the psychic scars that Ahab's did, perhaps because it seemed to be more inadvertent, not the result of an apparently deliberate and malicious attack as was the case with Ahab. Boomer then recovered from his injury, both physically and emotionally, and—again unlike Ahab—does not hope to meet Moby Dick again. He is not caught in a cycle of traumatic repetition. "'He's welcome to the arm he has,'" Boomer tells Ahab, "'since I can't help it, and didn't know him then; but not to another one. No more White Whales for me; I've lowered for him once, and that has satisfied me'" (533). It would seem then, contrary to Mitchell and Snyder's claim, that it is not disability in itself that determines character in *Moby Dick*. We must look not to a character's physical condition, but rather to his response to the traumatic event, the moment of loss, that caused the physical condition.

Melville's text suggests as well that the traumatic moment, while negating a prevailing symbolic system, generates others. From Ahab's trauma comes a central metaphor, a metaphysics, and even a politics, for Ahab cannot act on his new world view without enlisting the support of his crew. Symptoms of past trauma become the symbols that structure the post-traumatic world. A similar process occurs with Pip, the young deck hand who is traumatized into madness through his abandonment on the ocean after he jumps from a boat during the pursuit of a whale. According to Ishmael's narration, the abyssal isolation Pip experiences has "drowned the infinite of his soul." But out of this negation, a new and extraordinary imaginative world emerges. Revealed to Pip are "wondrous depths, where strange shapes of the unwarped primal world glided to and fro" and "joyous, heartless, everjuvenile eternities. . . . He saw God's foot upon the treadle of the loom, and spoke to it; and therefore his shipmates called him mad" (525). As with Ahab, an overwhelming, unassimilable experience of pain and loss generates a totalizing vision that excessively compensates the failure of previous modes of understanding. In this episode, we see vividly once again that a theory of trauma is a theory of metaphor, of the generation of new forms out of failure and obliteration.

At the same time, however, if we accept this claim that metaphors and other new symbolic forms are, at bottom, elaborations of traumatic symptoms, then we must acknowledge also that the particular forms the emerging metaphors take will be especially malleable to pressures of ideology—itself, in effect, the master symptom and metaphor. Thus, while I have criticized Mitchell and Snyder for eliding any mention of trauma or loss in connection with Ahab's disability, it remains the case that Melville chose a physically disabled character to embody the traumatized, totalizing, apocalyptic vision that dooms the world as represented by the *Pequod*—and chose a diminutive African American, Pip, as the other principle victim of trauma. It would seem that disability (or racial difference) in *Moby Dick* is the sign—the "material metaphor," in Mitchell and Snyder's terminology—of trauma, an omen, in effect, of some imminent apocalyptic breakdown. Even after we account for trauma, then, as a generator of metaphor, it seems we must return to disability studies' critiques of metaphor and ask why it is that Melville needed a physical injury and disability to represent what is essentially a spiritual or metaphysical condition—thus both drawing on and reinforcing social stigmas attached to physical disability.

The foregoing indicates to me that, at least in some of their more prevalent directions, trauma studies reveals certain theoretical inadequacies in disability studies, while disability studies suggests political inadequacies in trauma studies. The theoretical problem is the denial of trauma and loss, a denial that suggests also disability studies' hostility toward metaphor. The political inadequacy is a certain universalizing of trauma that inhibits attention to particular present injustices and ideological distortions. Might we propose, then, that disability studies is marked by an inability to mourn, and trauma studies by an inability to *stop* mourning?

A theory of the dys-/disarticulate would be the critical link between these two incapacities.[19]

Disability, Autonomy, and Care

The discussion of trauma points toward a final problematic area for disability studies. Trauma is a fundamentally destabilizing event. It puts in jeopardy any sense of the integrity, transparent self-knowledge, or autonomy of a self. For this reason, the notion of trauma is difficult for a field that places so much emphasis on the autonomy and conscious voice of the disabled subject. For the activists and scholars determined to improve the lives of the disabled, independent living and clear, directed political presence have been imperatives. As we have seen, disability studies scholars have often portrayed disability as disruptive, destabilizing, even, in effect, traumatic (though that term is seldom used), but the destabilizing effects are exerted by disability against the normative social-symbolic order. In disability studies accounts, the normate is continually traumatized by the spectacle of disability—and so must reintegrate itself through further acts of stigmatization of the disabled other—but the subjectivities of the disabled remain undisrupted, except insofar as they suffer the effects of social oppression. Disability destabilizes the normate social order by presenting it with the palpable reality of physical vulnerability, mutability, and mortality. The illusions of physical perfection and immortality—with the corollary sense of the obscenity of illness, deformity, death, and decay—crash against the barrier of a man or woman in a wheelchair.

But if the normate, ableist subject is divided, susceptible to symptomatic responses to unassimilable difference, repressing his or her own vulnerability and mortality, it seems dubious to assert that the disabled subject can be unified, autonomous, and clear-speaking. The fetishizing of autonomy attributed by disability scholars to the normate is certainly the case, but it is at the same time a projection. In minimizing the

significance of impairment, pain, and trauma—and attributing instability, traumatization, and unconscious response only to the oppressive
normative order—disability studies has constructed a picture of a rigid
disability subjectivity that is a parodic echo of the normative subject it
critiques. This subject says, in effect—echoing the normate—"There is
in me neither physical flaw nor conceptual impasse: all real impairment
resides in the other."[20]

Disability studies scholars have tended to be highly critical of ideas
of cure, healing, and rehabilitation, seeing these as extensions of the
power of the medical professions to define disability exclusively as a
medical condition detached from social practice and political policy.
The point of disability as a political movement has been to fight for
rights and agency for the disabled *as* disabled, to remove their disablity
in terms of social barriers, and to be suspicious of medical approaches
that regard disability in biological terms and see individual impairment as the central problem. Thus, in historian Henri Stikker's influential account, "rehabilitation marks the appearance of a culture that
attempts to complete the act of identification, making identical. This act
will cause the disabled to disappear and with them all that is lacking,
in order to assimilate them, drown them, dissolve them in the greater
and single social whole" (128). If rehabilitation is to be applied at all,
Stikker writes, it "must be to society as society is presently constituted"
(135). The latter point is certainly true, but I cannot see how it precludes
efforts at rehabilitation to achieve a greater range of physical or mental
abilities for disabled individuals as well. Stikker, in effect, positions the
entire disability community as disarticulated and determined to remain
so until society reconstitutes itself around new axes of otherness. There
is an admirable utopian sensibility in this position, as there is in McRuer's transgressive crip politics.[21]

But how, in this state, is one to account for care? As Richard Wood,
former director of the British Council of Organizations of Disabled
People exclaimed, "'Let us state what disabled people do want by stat-
ing first what we don't want: WE DON'T WANT CARE!'" (q. in Shakespeare 139). There is, of course, a philosophical-theoretical literature
critiquing care and compassion, viewing these as akin to pity, and thus
expressing a hierarchical relation in which the one caring or expressing
compassion is necessarily in a position of power over the one receiving

care. As Marjorie Garber writes, compassion moves "in effect, from high to low: shown towards a person in distress by one who is free of it, who is, in this respect, his superior." Thus, compassion stands "between charity and condescension," and even resembles sadism in that "the pain of someone else provides an access of pleasure for the compassionate one" (20). Martha Nussbaum argues that contemporary critiques of care and compassion derive from older stoic arguments in which autonomy is the principle human good. The goal of the stoic was to be spiritually impervious to all the turns and blows of fortune, to be at last free of all dependency. Compassion, for the stoics, as Nussbaum puts it, "has a false cognitive evaluative structure"—that is, it misevaluates what is actually important in human life, placing material suffering over spiritual independence—and thus "insults the dignity of the person who suffers" (*Upheavals of Thought* 357). As Nussbaum quotes Nietzsche's Zarathustra, "to offer pity is as good as to offer contempt" (357).

This problematic of care has shown itself in practical terms in the sometimes vexed relations between disabled people and the workers who care for them. As the terminology for this relation developed in the disability rights movement, the workers were not care-workers or care-givers, but personal attendants, and the disabled individuals were clients or employers. The attendant's job was to help the client achieve access to services and activities which he had been denied by social barriers. This relation was well suited to the interests and needs of those who designed it—young, mostly male wheelchair users who, aside from their impaired mobility, had no notable medical conditions. As Eileen Boris and Jennifer Klein have shown in their recent study of the history of home health care work, the early disability rights movement in California in the mid- to late 1960s brought together relatively affluent, educated paraplegic male clients and far less educated, mostly female care-workers in a relation in which both parties were seeking independence, but in quite different senses. The workers were often channeled into home care work through the social welfare system, moving out of welfare into the labor market but still being paid through publicly funded programs. The money for home assistance was paid by the state or county to the disabled clients who then contracted the work of the attendants, either directly or through private agencies. The relations between client and attendant were often deeply unequal. It has been common for disabled people to complain that their attendants were unskilled, unprofessional, and lacking in understanding of their needs. Dissatisfaction, however, went both ways, as workers could find their clients/employers condescending and impatient. Tom Shakespeare has likened the relation to that of master and servant, in which the employee is intimately involved in the employer's life, but is never regarded as an equal. Initially, as well, it appeared that the disabled and their attendants had opposing economic interests, as the employer tried to stretch his state funding for care as far as it would go, to the detriment of the employee's hourly pay and working conditions. And it should be noted that federal labor laws concerning minimum wage and social security coverage do not apply to home care attendants; in 2007, the Supreme Court once again upheld their exclusion from the nation's laws regulating wages and hours worked. The position of home care attendant has been, we might say, purposefully constructed as exploitative.

Only gradually has the disability rights movement come to a more egalitarian understanding of the relation between the disabled subject and his home (care) attendant. This was so especially as it became clear that the economic interests of the disabled and their attendants were, in fact, closely aligned. Both were dependent on continued generous government funding for home care, and disabled clients came to support the efforts of their attendants to form unions, since union power provided more leverage on state legislatures for appropriations. Thus, the status of funding for care often was contingent on the relative strength of organized labor.[22]

But what of the broader question of care per se? Here too disability studies is shifting its attitudes. And, in fact, regarding the critiques of care and compassion that I mentioned earlier, disability studies already supplies the counter-argument which it subsequently has often rejected. When discussing the rigidities of dominant ideologies, disability theorists effectively critique ableist/normate pretenses to unlimited autonomy, agency, and invulnerability. As Garland-Thomson puts it, the "disabled body becomes a repository for social anxieties about such troubling concerns as vulnerability, control, and identity" (6). The argument, of course, is that human finitude and vulnerability are universals, and yet Garland-Thomson, Mitchell and Snyder, and othersthen draw back from this conclusion when discussing the status of the disabled, whose goal (if not their actual status) is precisely the autonomy and agency that had been critiqued. More recent thinking extends this universalist argument to the disabled as well. This is the point of Siebers's "realism of the body," in which pain and other "blunt, crude realities" are addressed as parts of the experience and political capital of disability. Lennard Davis more explicitly describes "a new kind of universalism and cosmopolitanism" centered on interdependence and vulnerability (*Bending* 26). "Impairment," he writes, "is the rule and normalcy the fantasy. Dependence is the reality and independence grandiose thinking" (31). If this is the case, then the hierarchical character of care and compassion cited by Berlant, Edelman, and others is not a necessary condition but a distortion, a reaction whose goal is to contain the dominant order's panic in the face of the actual universality of dependency.[23]

Of the greatest importance for this rethinking of care in disability studies has been the work of the philosophers Martha Nussbaum and Eva Kittay. Both Nussbaum and Kittay direct their arguments against the liberal, social-contract oriented thinking of John Rawls, especially insofar as Rawls's approach requires an autonomous subject who is capable of entering into contracts. Those incapable of this social standing are excluded as full citizens and ethical subjects. They ought to be cared for, in Rawls's view, but this care is indeed hierarchical, an obligation and benefit bestowed upon them by their social superiors. Rawls argues that society ought to organize itself on the basis of what he calls the "original position," in which each person judges social policy as if he were in the position of least privilege in the society. This thought-experiment is designed to separate people from class and other factional interests and thus to incorporate a powerful egalitarian and universalist element into social decision-making. Nussbaum and Kittay both are sympathetic toward the "original position" argument, except in that it excludes people in positions of extreme dependence who are not capable of entering into it, who must be spoken *for*. Autonomy—in effect, invulnerability—cannot, in Nussbaum's and Kittay's views, be the basis for social standing. There must, rather, be a way to articulate social-ethical status that does not derive from the contract and that takes account of the full nature of human interdependency, vulnerability, and finitude.

In *Frontiers of Justice*, Nussbaum argues that justice ought to be based not on rights but on a sense of human capabilities, seen as "an account

of minimum core social entitlements" (75). These include such functions as life, health, and bodily integrity; the use of the senses, imagination, and reason; the exercise of emotion; the forming of relationships;
enjoyment, play, and leisure; and control over one's environment, which
would include political participation. These capabilities, Nussbaum
judges, are what give human life value and dignity. And in order for as
many people as possible to use as many of these capabilities as possible,
care must be included as "a primary social entitlement" (178). Not all the
things people can do are worthy of value—for instance, cruelty. And no
individual is obligated to enact any particular capability—for instance,
participation in politics. But, taken loosely and in sum, these capabilities
constitute, for Nussbaum, a kind of "species norm." Not all people, of
course, are capable of exercising all these capabilities. People with severe
cognitive impairments are, for Nussbaum, the test case of the theory,
and here Nussbaum argues against positions put forth by some animal
rights theorists that there should be no ethical distinction made between
animals and cognitively impaired people. The capabilities of animals are
different from those of people, and ethical obligation toward an individual should be based on a species norm derived from these capabilities,
not from an estimate of the relative intelligence of a mentally disabled
person and, say, a dog or chimpanzee. Thus, an ancephalic child or person in a persistent vegetative condition is not human in the sense that
Nussbam intends, in that such a person can exercise nearly none of the
capabilities that would define a person as an ethical and political subject.
Conversely, even a severely impaired person like Kittay's daughter Sesha
(now a frequently cited figure in these discussions) has, as Nussbaum
observes, "the ability to love and relate to others, perception, delight in
movement and play. In this sense," Nussbaum adds, "the fact that she is
the child of human parents matters: her life is bound up in a network
of human relations, and she is able to participate actively in many of
those relations, albeit not in all" (188). Disability of this sort, then, in
Nussbaum's view, does not make someone less human, less a valid subject for ethical treatment. But it does place in the foreground the reality of dependence and the need for care.[24] Care, from this perspective,
"becomes not a matter of dealing with the 'incompetence' of a person,
but a way of facilitating that person's access to all the central capabilities"
(199), and so is a matter of fundamental ethical and political importance.

This depiction of care and capability derives, I think, from Nussbaum's thinking on compassion in her earlier book, *Upheavals of Thought*. Nussbaum describes compassion not as an irrational emotion, but as a form of cognition—an evaluation of a state of affairs in which another person is subject to an "undeserved misfortune" (301). What would constitute a misfortune depends on an overall "conception of human flourishing and the major predicaments of life," and the strong ethical sense that one's own flourishing is bound up with the flourishing of others. "Compassion itself," she adds, "is the eye through which people see the good and ill of others, and its full meaning. Without it, the abstract sight of the calculating intellect is value-blind" (392). Would disability necessarily constitute a "misfortune"? No, not if the flourishing of the disabled person were unimpaired. But if the flourishing were impaired, then compassion would be an appropriate response. And this would not, for Nussbaum, be a form of condescension, for, as she puts it, "agency and victimhood" (or, to use her milder term, "misfortune") "are not incompatible" (406). A full understanding of human dignity must include a sense of human vulnerability. But this cognitive-emotional-evaluative response would be only a starting point. Compassion must be active, and not only in an individual but in a social-structural sense. Nussbaum's theory of compassion is determined to answer the objection thrown at us by the cynical narrator of *The Secret Agent*, that compassion might be "the supreme remedy" for injustice, but suffers "the only one disadvantage of being difficult of application on a large scale."[25]

To be applied on a large scale, a politics of compassion must take seriously its premises. Suffering and injustice are real, and anyone at some point in life can be subject to them. If human beings were, in fact, autonomous and invulnerable, there could be neither suffering nor injustice. For how can autonomy be denied a being who is intrinsically autonomous, and how can one suffer who is without vulnerability? But this is not the case, and Nussbaum agrees with disability theorists that pretenses to absolute autonomy and invulnerability are pathologies, reaction formations to the repressed knowledge that each of us shares in the universal human, biological finitude. This denial and its corollary fantasy of omnipotence, Nussbaum argues, arise from projections of shame and disgust, from "the intolerance of humanity in oneself" (350). Compassion is a response to suffering and injustice, vulnerability and dependence that is both emotional and cognitive; it is a recognition and sensation of one's similar status.[26] What this entails for Nussbaum is not individual charity, but a continual reordering of society in the effort to ensure that all human beings are able to live in the human, social world and to achieve their potential as human beings as fully as possible. While this mutual recognition that is compassion, or of which compassion is a critical part, is universal (though it is not universally exercised), Nussbaum stresses that "social institutions construct the shape compassion will take" (343). Institutions and social policies must make compassion practicable and effective. And this means that providing care or assistance for people not otherwise able to live lives expressing their full range of human possibility should be a valued form of labor and not work situated at the bottom of the socio-economic scale. Eva Kittay makes this point memorably in her concept of social doulia. A doulia, Kittay explains, is someone who gives care to a new mother. The mother, of course, provides care for the newborn child, but in order to do this job as well as is required, someone must provide also for the mother's, the primary care-giver's, needs. This caring for care-givers, Kittay argues, ought to apply generally for all applications of care and comprise a social, institutional, policy-based doulia. The purposeful denigration of care work that Boris and Klein have documented is a precise register of our society's ideological fantasy of omnipotence and its denial of mutual interdependence, vulnerability, and mortality. The rich purchase cosmetic surgery while the poor perform care work and are themselves denied care. Thus, I would say in response to Henri Stiker's remark that rehabilitation "must be to society as society is presently constructed" (135), yes, this so; but the result of this social reformation will be better care, or rehabilitation (or *transhabilitation? alterhabilitation?*) for everyone.[27]

The test case for these theories of a political-economy of care is that of severe cognitive impairment, for it is here that a position based on agency and articulate voice will be most compromised; and a number of writers on disability have noted that disability studies has failed to come to terms with intellectual/developmental disabilities. Mark Osteen notes that "disability scholarship has ignored cognitive, intellectual, or neurological disabilities, thereby excluding the intellectually disabled just as mainstream society has done" (*Autism and Representation* 2).[28]

There is a tendency in disability studies even to deny the existence of cognitive impairment. Anna Stubblefield, for example, in an otherwise fascinating historical account of the use of intelligence testing to restrict African American children's access to education by placing them inordinately into special education classes, finds it necessary to argue as well that the whole modern notion of intellect or intelligence "was constructed by white elites to provide a scientific justification for racism" (540). In support of this claim, she also cites various occasions on which people with cerebral palsy were misdiagnosed as being mentally retarded. I would point also to Ralph Savarese's story of rescuing from silence and the presumption of mental retardation his adoptive son, DJ, an autistic boy who could not speak, by teaching him to use a keyboard. I find the story entirely credible, and Savarese and DJ's work admirable and impressive almost beyond my ability to express it. But the implication of Savarese's book, I think, is that such reclamations of the lost, articulate subject and agent (it is crucial that DJ authors the book's final chapter) are possible in all or nearly all cases—that genuine cognitive impairment (particularly in conjunction with autism) is, in effect, a myth that can be dispelled with enough dedication and work.

But this isn't true, and nor are Stubblefield's larger claims. It is true that the abilities of many people with cognitive disabilities are greater than used to be imagined; that in an environment of encouragement, love, social engagement, and creative activity, people with Down Syndrome, autism, and other conditions can reach wonderful levels of achievement and independence. Michael Bérubé's writing about his son Jamie provides eloquent evidence of these newly discovered possibilities. But at the same time, the limited independence, agency, and voice of people with cognitive impairments remain a reality. There is a population that must be spoken for and scrupulously cared for. Eva Kittay's writing about her daughter Sesha provides eloquent evidence of this set of facts. The attempt to attribute articulation and full agency to every apparently cognitively disabled person seems another effort—misdirected, unnecessary, and contrary to disability studies' real principles—to deny the facts of dependence and vulnerability per se.[29]

5

Alterity Is Relative

Impairment, Narrative, and Care in an Age of Neuroscience

A Defense of Narrative?

In chapter 2, I discussed how characters with cognitive and linguistic impairments in modernist fiction served as figures of radical alterity—both dys- and disarticulate—in relation to a modernity characterized as a totalizing social-symbolic system. Alternate, less extreme ways of thinking about language and social organization were available (e.g., James's pluralism, Bahktin's and Voloshinov's analyses of language as a dialogic enactment of multiple social tensions), but we can speculate that the rapid, violent, traumatic character of social change—and, indeed, of many of the significant events of the twentieth century—and the extreme claims made by positivist thinkers in philosophy, government, and science led other philosophers and artists to conclude that the emerging social-symbolic order could be opposed only by gestures and figures entirely outside it. That such gestures and figures were self-evidently impossible helped produce the powerful paradoxes that animated much modernist art and thought. These intellectual, political, and aesthetic tensions intersected in the early twentieth century with new scientific discourses and social anxieties surrounding cognitive impairment, in particular the medical and social status of people labeled as "mentally defective" or "feeble-minded." Through these convergences, dys-/disarticulate figures like Conrad's Stevie, Faulkner's Benjy, and Barnes's Robin—situated at the boundaries of language, serving as focal points of an oppositional ethics of care, and then violently removed from the social-symbolic order—provide occasions for analyzing modernity's fundamental tendencies and conflicts.

Fiction from after the World War II, as I discussed in chapter 4, continued to portray figures with cognitive or linguistic impairments as radical others to the social-symbolic order. The work of DeLillo, Auster, and Kosinski, generally labeled "post-modern," is not significantly different conceptually from earlier modernist representations. The chief distinctions in these writers' portrayals are that they employ more irony with regard to the dys-/disarticulate's links to alterity and that they revive the trope of the wild child. Perhaps as a response to the liberatory politics of the 1960s, the earlier focus on the supposed degeneracy of the dys-/disarticulate was replaced by an ironized focus on Rousseauian innocence. The fundamental problem, however, remained how to find the exit to a totalizing social-symbolic order.

In recent years, the influence of neuroscience, both as science and as ideology, has changed the way writers have depicted characters with cognitive and linguistic impairments. We should note first a change in strategies of representation. The high-functioning autism in Mark Haddon's *Curious Incident*, Tourette's Syndrome in Jonathan Lethem's *Motherless Brooklyn*, Capgras Syndrome in Richard Powers's *The Echo Maker*, and Huntington's Disease in Ian McEwan's *Saturday* are all portrayed in clinical detail far more precise than was presented in earlier modernist and post-modern fictions. The particular neurological conditions of Stevie, Benjy, Robin, Wilder, or Chance were not of concern in their respective texts. Stevie and Benjy were "mentally defective"— probably a "moron" in Stevie's case, an "idiot" in Benjy's. No more exact diagnosis was either available or necessary. Categories for Wilder and Chance were even more amorphous. As for Robin, Barnes consistently portrayed her as standing at the limit of any type of human being. With the revolution in neuroscience, more precise clinical categories of neural impairment became available, and thus the precise significance of particular cognitive impairments, now seen as neurologically based, became important to writers.

More broadly, though, the rapid advances of neuroscience have reoriented the entire discussion of dys-/disarticulation and alterity presented in the previous chapters. On the one hand, neuroscience can be regarded as the latest of modern totalizing ideologies. Insofar as neuroscience "secularizes" the mind, as neuroscientist Jean-Pierre Changeux put it, and entirely identifies mind with the physical processes of the brain, it implicitly promises to provide true knowledge of all mental products—that is, of all thought, emotion, symbolization, and culture. As I will argue, it is crucial to distinguish between the actual practice of neuroscience and the functioning of neuroscience as ideology, but it is ideology that often has the more immediate effects on popular thinking. This sense of neuroscience providing final, irrefutable understanding of the mind has gained wide credence. At the same time, however, neuroscience (in both its scientific and ideological roles) introduces the notion of the spectrum. In placing all subjectivity and all the subject's impairments on a variety of neurological spectrums, neuroscience removes from cognitive and linguistic impairment the dys-/disarticulate aura of radical otherness that served such a crucial, though futile, oppositional function in modernist and post-modern writing.[1] Furthermore, the relation of care must be rethought in the light of neuroscience. It appears not as a pre-modern or Christian atavism with a private, familial character that makes it an ineffectual antithesis to the modern or post-modern administered, mediated world. Rather, care can be regarded as a constitutive feature of biological and social life, both deep and problematic, for despite its universality, it continues in these novels to be portrayed as private. As a character in Powers's *The Echo Maker* puts it, "Of all the alien, damaged brain states . . . none was as strange as care" (94).

The actual accomplishments of neuroscience are, of course, astonishing, barely credible to a lay person. Emily Dickinson's poem "The brain is wider — than the sky" has been revealed to be not a metaphor, but literal truth. The human brain contains approximately one hundred billion neurons. The cerebral cortex has something on the order of sixty trillion synapses. The total length of myelinated neuron fibers is 150,000 to 180,000 kilometers. Through advanced technologies of brain scanning, neuroscientists can study with more precision than previously imaginable the mental mechanics of perception, cognition, and emotion. As neuroscientist Joseph LeDoux argues, our synapses are who we are, neither more nor less. The self is a synaptic self. And with this avalanche of knowledge over the past twenty to thirty years have come significant consequences, both practical and theoretical. Contemporary neuroscience has fundamentally transformed clinical practice in psychiatry. As Hyman and Nestler wrote in their 1993 textbook, the use of purely psychological methods has "reached roadblocks" in the "ability to treat severely disabled patients" (xi), and while "all illnesses have biological, psychological, and social dimensions . . . ultimately, it is the biological understanding of a disease, an understanding of its pathophysiology, that leads to definitive treatment and prevention" (xii). In the late 1980s through the early 1990s, in particular, there was a widespread sense among clinicians and the public that traditional "talk therapy" was obsolete—that mood, consciousness, self-knowledge were governed by specific neurotransmitters and receptors in particular areas of the brain, and that complete knowledge of these processes had nearly been achieved. Thus, as Peter Kramer wrote in his best-selling book on the prevalence of pharmaceutical therapies, *Listening to Prozac*, "we are edging toward what might be called the 'medicalization of personality'" (37).

It is important to note that leading neuroscientists do not share these totalizing impulses. The brain's very complexity prevents the full understanding and possibility of accurate prediction that a totalizing methodology requires. Researchers in the field appear to agree that total knowledge of the brain/mind is not even a theoretical possibility for neuroscience. Nevertheless, as an ideology, neuroscience makes these totalizing claims. The ideology of neuroscience represents a composite of mystified specialized knowledge, a conventional wisdom that values precision and finality, powerful economic interests with expensive and lucrative research agendas, and political biases dedicated to maintaining a status quo and suppressing fundamental dissent. Roughly speaking, the ideology of neurology links the extraordinary progress in research on brain function with the financial interests of pharmaceutical companies, the insurance industry, and research universities, and with political and economic institutions that legitimate themselves through a fetishizing of scientific and scientistic disciplines that rely on quantitative methods.[2]

Methodologically, the victor in this dominance of neuroscience (as well as of economics and the biological determinism that has accompanied the progress of contemporary genetics) is the *model*. The loser has been narrative—or even, more broadly, language itself. A model is the static representation of a fluid state, which, by accounting for relevant variables, claims to provide a picture of the reality of that state and to be able to predict future states. The model is valued by clinicians and policy-makers, by the industries that provide their instruments and ideas, and by the interests and media that legitimate them. The predictive accuracy of models in practice, however, is dubious. Psychopharmaceuticals have not proved to be the miracle cures for all ailments of the soul, as had been thought and hoped. They have helped, of course, especially in the most severe cases, but depression, bipolar conditions, psychoses, and other diseases often resist them stubbornly. And economic predictions have proven, as we learned emphatically in the 2008 financial crisis and continuing recession, to be not only dismally inaccurate, but misguided in their basic assumptions regarding value, productivity, and motivation.[3]

The ideological triumph of the model has put narrative on the defensive. Since the earliest written documents, many of which transcribe and redact much older oral texts, the profoundest knowledge of the psyche, social behavior, social relations and institutions—the knowledge of humanity in its interiority and social being—has come through forms of narrative: in myth, epic, and subsequent forms of literature; and in philosophy, psychology, psychoanalysis, and narrative aspects of the social sciences. The achievements and potentials of neuroscience would seem to put all these forms in doubt. If we can, indeed, know, or are on the verge of knowing, how the mind really, invariably, necessarily works, then the humanities can do no more than add colorful examples to our true knowlege; they cannot constitute knowledge in themselves. In a parodic description of a dubious physician dispensing psychopharmaceuticals on a cruise ship, Jonathan Franzen, in *The Corrections*, encapsulates the ideology of neurology. As the doctor tells an elderly woman who feels depressed and ashamed over her difficulties caring for her ailing husband, "the fear of humiliation and the craving for humiliation are closely linked: psychologists know it, Russian novelists know it. And this turns out to be not only 'true' but really *true*. True at the molecular level" (318). The remedy, of course, is the purchase and ingestion of a drug that will regulate the patient's serotonin levels. The epistemological premise has consequences in economics, subjectivity, and social relations.[4]

The ascendence of this ideology of neuroscience, which continues the work of earlier totalizing ideologies of system and model, puts in question traditional forms of understanding the self and social relations:

narrative, metaphor, and language per se. What would be narrative's defense against these claims of biologically based models? It depends, of course, on how one regards narrative. If, with Hayden White and Roland Barthes, we describe narrative as an ideological product whose most salient feature is closure—i.e., the inevitable emplotment toward a telos inscribed in its premises—then narrative is simply another implement of the rationalizing, systematizing tendencies that can be opposed only by a radical other.[5] But as I argued earlier, while there are reasons for holding this view of narrative and, indeed, of language—the totalizing tyranny of the "current words"—and while the most obvious of these reasons is the apparent imperviousness of the dominant status quo to any real transformation, the problem may not lie in language and narrative themselves as monologic agents of ideological control. It seems more plausible to regard language and narrative as possessing, as Valentin Voloshinov wrote, an"inherent semantic openness, corresponding to a still active social process, from which new meanings and possible meanings can be generated" (q. in Raymond Williams 75). The defense of narrative as a form of knowledge would be, more specifically, a defense of narrative that foregrounds these capacities for openness. Paul Ricoeur, Louis Mink, David Carr, and Gary Saul Morson have all contributed to exploring the epistemology of narrative. To conjoin and abbreviate these writers' views, we can say that narrative is a form of knowledge specific to understanding events in time, that it articulates the subjective and social experiences of time in language, and that it thus provides a knowledge of contingency and ambiguity.[6] As Morson writes, "one needs story because the world is imperfect. One needs story because there is no goal. And one needs story because things do not fit" (66). Conversely, "thinkers who seek to overcome narrative typically insist on the complete orderliness of the world. Though things may look messy, order lurks beneath, and the task of science or philosophy is to discover the order that will make the mess, and along with it the need for narrative, disappear" (66). Narrative's gift is to show not only the genealogy of events and of their meanings, but that events could be other than what they are and can have meanings other than those we have ascribed to them. Unverifiable and lacking predictive powers, narrative is the mode best suited to depicting the lived experience of people and groups, and it does so in the languages and dialects in which life is, in fact, experienced. Unlike the model, it proposes no metalanguage that would step outside of lived experience. Yet, at the same time, as narrative contains numerous languages in dialogue and conflict, it is always a meta-language that provokes further dialogue. Narrative travels at the speed of time, it wears winged sandals; but it splits its reader, throwing half of him or her outside of time and holding the other half within. One experiences the narrated events and pauses to interpret them, sometimes sequentially, sometimes simultaneously. But narrative as a form of knowledge is not part of any rationalized, scientific, econometric understanding of the mind or society. Thus, neither novelists nor poets nor even historians advise political leaders on policy or are asked by media for their commentary.

A novelist who takes seriously the claims of neuroscience and its ideology is in something of the position of the poet in early modernity—of a Sidney or Shelley—who felt impelled to defend the social and epistemological efficacy of poetry against the claims of history, philosophy, and the discourses of practical politics. The novel becomes a defense of the novel, a defense of narrative, or, most broadly, of language itself. In recent work like Rick Moody's *Purple America*, Ian McEwan's *Saturday*, Jonathan Haddon's *A Curious Incident of a Dog in the Night-Time*, Jonathan Lethem's *Motherless Brooklyn*, Jonathan Franzen's *The Corrections*, and Richard Powers's *The Echo Maker*, we see, first, a heightened attention to clinical descriptions of cognitive or linguistic impairments based on insights from neuroscience. This attention is in contrast to depictions in modernist and post-modern fiction—e.g. *The Sound and the Fury*, *The Secret Agent*, *Nightwood*, *White Noise*, *Being There*, *City of Glass*—which show little interest in clinical accuracy and whose intentions are, from the outset, metaphorical. Or, it would be more accurate to say that the modernist texts presented their impaired characters in the contexts of contemporaneous medical and sociological discourses, but in overtly antagonistic ways, and that the post-modern texts tend to ignore medical and scientific discourses on impairment entirely in favor of philosophical and meta-fictional concerns. Second, we see in these recent fictions explorations of possible consequences for narrative of a neurological perspective on mind and impairment. The first practice—the concern with clinical, neurological accuracy premised on some knowledge of and respect for contemporary neuroscience—entails the second, which involves the defense of narrative and questioning of the totalizing claims of neuroscience as ideology.[7]

Such defenses of narrative conducted in uneasy alignment with neuroscientific knowledge but in opposition to the ideology of neuroscience have two further consequences. First, the notion of radical alterity, which was so crucial to modernist and post-modern narratives, must be revised. Contemporary neuroscience, to its credit, does not stigmatize neurological difference, in distinction with earlier totalizing biological theories of Lombroso, Goddard, Fernald, et al. Neurological "others" are not threats to be contained. Rather, neuroscience posits neurological spectrums on which people assume different and variable positions.[8] The radical other is not a necessary tool for critiquing the ideology of neuroscience. For neuroscience, alterity is relative.

At the same time, neuroscience describes a distinctly non-unified, non-Cartesian self, continually composed and amended through new and repeated synaptic connections, most of this happening beneath the connections that constitute conscious awareness. *Je est un autre.* The self is other to itself; the other also is other to itself. Self and other are, then . . . others, but share that internal alterity as a crucial commonality. To paraphrase Franzen: French symbolist poets knew this, but now we *really* know. But what does this knowledge of the shared quality of otherness entail?

For Haddon and Lethem especially, this revised sense of otherness entails a reexamination of metaphor—or, more properly, as I argued in chapter 1, of catachresis, the trope located just at the boundary between language and non-language. The defense of narrative must begin at the place where language encounters the world, where new linguistic expressions become possible. Look at Rimbaud's famous pronouncement. It takes the form of a literal statement. Is it a simple (or complex) statement of fact? Is it a metaphor? Is it a cliché—that is, a metaphor that has lost its novelty? Does an understanding of neuroscience or psychoanalysis transport the statement from the realm of metaphor to that of fact? Once we *know* that the center of consciousness has no center and is not knowable, what then are our obligations to others similarly unknowing? As Derrida transposed the dictum, *"l'autre que je suis"*: I am/is another. I follow the other (seek the other; or, come after, succeed, the other). These are literal statements. They are true. In Donald Davidson's compellingly contrarian essay on metaphor, a metaphor is not some alternative use of language. Metaphor is a literal use of language and is, literally, a lie. My love is not, in fact, a rose. But I am/ is another and I follow the other that I am. That is true, so that is not a metaphor. But what is meant by any of these terms? To ask this question is to chisel into the matter of the non-linguistic, the catachresis that Zizek nominates "the rock upon which every attempt at symbolization stumbles" (*Sublime Object* 169).

Is it possible to say something new? And once one says something new, how long does it stay new? How do we create the possibility for these possibilities? In Haddon's *Curious Incident*, the autistic subject's resistance to metaphor, his insistence on literal language, reveals the broader need for a release from language and from normative social relations, and the novel proposes that this need is valuable and should be fostered and cared for. Christopher's impairment renders him socially difficult, but marks a place on a neurological spectrum on which all people are neighbors. Christopher's relations with language and other people reveal a potential in everyone which deserves care and appreciation even though such care is difficult and can be only unevenly reciprocated. In Lethem's *Motherless Brooklyn*, the Tourretic subject's verbal tics are excesses that bring about new verbal forms. The tics are metaphors, and metaphors, in turn, can be theorized through this novel as tics. The work of linguistic innovation is, again, placed on a neurological spectrum, and the tic/metaphor is seen in relation to fixed or normalizing forms of expression, in particular, the work of genre.

But are there conceptual links between narrative, metaphor, language, ethics, and care? Recent discussions of narrative and care share important features. Both are opposed to totalizations. Morson's arguments regarding narrative as rooted in presentness, in incompleteness, in revealing not established beginnings and inevitable endings but possiblities of action and open places in time, resemble in important ways descriptions of care and compassion presented by philosophers Eva Kittay and Martha Nussbaum. For all these writers, an appreciation of incompleteness and vulnerability is essential to the practice either of narrative or of ethics. Just as Morson opposes the totalizing views of narrative proposed by Hayden White and other post-structuralists (views that emerge out of a Saussurean approach to language as self-referential system), so Kittay and Nussbaum (and we might add sociologist Arlie Hochschild and cultural theorist Sehyla Benhabib) oppose a universalizing, abstract ethics based in the thinking of John Rawls in which the ethical subject is necessarily a rational, language-using subject.[9] Rawls, of course, presents an odd intersection with Hayden White, but the oddness fits here, for even though Rawls would dismiss White's approach to ideological critique, both thinkers share the same point of reference: namely, the autonomous subject, which must be accepted (in Rawls's case) or replaced by some radical alterity (in White's). Kittay and Nussbaum, like James and Morson, want to avoid this dichotomy. In its insistence on the autonomous, rational, linguistically competent nature of the subject, Rawlsian ethics creates broad classes of—to use my term—dys-/disarticulated subjects who have no place in the social order. It ignores the fact that all people begin and end life as helpless, and that life as a whole requires interdependence at least as much as autonomy, and that life is characterized by its vulnerability and its openness to rapid change. Thus, to place ethics only in the hands of the autonomous and rational is, indeed, not to universalize ethics at all, but to eliminate it as a practical pursuit. We could paraphrase Morson: "One needs *care* because the world is imperfect. One needs *care* because there is no goal. And one needs *care* because things do not fit." And this is the reasoning, I think, behind Geoffrey Galt Harpham's statement that "language is not just an autonomous formal system but rather a medium whose formal elements permit an unformalized excess to become legible, a medium saturated with otherness, and thus with ethics" (*Getting* 61). The alterity that a totalizing—or anti-totalizing—view would place outside of selfhood and language would be located within these categories by thinkers like Nussbaum, Kittay, and Morson. As Eric Santner puts it (revising Levinas), ethics is the obligation to the other who is other to him- or herself—which is to say, the self that is vulnerable, not autonomous, not without fissures and inaccessibilities.

"I Want My Name to Mean Me"

Mark Haddon has said that Christopher, the protagonist of *The Curious Incident of the Dog in the Night-Time*, is not necessarily meant to be taken as a person with autism. The term never appears in the novel, and Haddon expressed his preference that future editions delete "autism" from their covers so that Christopher might be presented "with no labels whatsoever," either inside or outside the book (Interview). This preference is made, of course, in spite of Christopher's manifesting many of the classical or stereotypical evidences of autism: the love of routine, extreme attention to detail, dislike of physical contact, obliviousness to social cues, difficulty understanding what others are thinking and feeling, and possessing certain savant skills in mathematics. We should take Haddon's comments as both true and not true, both evasive and appropriate. Christopher clearly resembles what one thinks of as a high-functioning autistic person—as though his author had carefully studied popular accounts of autism by Temple Grandin, Donna Williams, Uta Frith, Simon Baron-Cohen, and Oliver Sacks and constructed Christopher accordingly. Christopher may well have supplanted Dustin Hoffman's Raymond in the film *Rain Man* as the most famous autistic character in fiction.[10]

At the same time, Haddon's demurral is appropriate. The refusal to provide a diagnostic label would certainly please the character, for every label is an imposition of meaning, and thus also of power. As disability advocates and theorists point out, the imposition of medical categories in particular is often a form of disablement. Christopher, after all, disputes even his name, which means "bearer of Christ." "'I want my name to mean me,'" he says (15). He wants not to be the bearer of any other meaning than what he might himself create. He will not *meta-pherein* for any purpose, including *Christo-pherein*. The metaphor is an act of transport, or of translation, made more difficult in that the bill of lading specifying exactly what is to be transported, and to whom, is never clear. Having demurred at the obvious diagnostic label, Haddon devotes his characterization of Christopher to exploring metaphor as a problem of connectedness. Christopher becomes a case study not of autism, but of the attempt to live without bearing another's meaning. And yet the evacuation from one discursive structure leads into another, whether intact, in ruins, or under construction. Christopher's search for semantic autonomy must be undertaken in overlapping social environments—a family, a city, a government school system, a particular moment in national and global political and economic histories—and in linguistic environments of written and spoken genres.

The fourth edition of the *Diagnostic and Statistical Manual of Mental Disorders* (*DSM-IV*) emphasizes the isolation experienced by people with Asperger's Disorder, the "impairment in reciprocal social interaction," and the degree to which people with Asperger's "lack understanding of the conventions of social interaction" (82). *DSM-IV* also refers to restricted and repetitive patterns of behavior and interests, while noting that, unlike more severe forms of autism, people diagnosed with Asperger's show normal cognitive and language development.[11] Many writers on autism have criticized what they regard as the categorical approach of the *DSM-IV* and speak instead of a spectrum of autistic features. There seems at present to be a broad consensus that, as Lorna Wing writes, "autism is not . . . a unique or separate condition . . . but is closely related to a range of developmental disorders" (312). Further, this spectrum may not be simply one that link diagnosable disorders, but one that extends through the whole human population. Temple Grandin, the noted animal scientist and memoirist with Asperger's Syndrome, argues that highly talented people in many fields share certain autistic traits, that "the genes that produce normal people with certain talents are likely to be the same genes that produce the abnormalities found at the extreme end of the same continuum," and that "there is no black-and-white dividing line between normal and abnormal" (179, 186). We see then in the autistic spectrum certain potentials that are deeply, essentially human. As Matthew Belmonte puts it, to be autistic is to be "human, but more so" (166). While linguistic ability in all its metaphoric range, the intimate social bond, the touch, emotional reciprocity all characterize human life, do they fully delineate it? Do these qualities complete the definition, and render all other qualities pathological? Or do the quest for literal, nominalist, Cratyllic language and the need for isolation also characterize human being?

Christopher in *Curious Incident* strives for an absolute literality in language. He cannot understand, and so tries always to avoid, metaphors, jokes, and lies. When his mother compliments him as a good boy because he is so honest, he tells us that he is not honest because he is good, but because he simply "can't tell lies" (19). Metaphors and jokes are incomprehensible to him because, like facial expressions, they have multiple meanings. Every case of figurative—that is, counterfactual—language seems to lead to more cases, unceasingly, leaving Christopher with a sense of cognitive vertigo, "shaky and scared," and this is why he dislikes "proper novels" (19). On the couple of occasions in the narrative when Christopher does employ a figure of speech, he quickly informs us that he has used a simile and not a metaphor. Thus, when he writes that a policeman's hairy nose "looked as if there were two very small mice hiding in his nostrils" (17), he assures us that this is literally true, that this is indeed what the man's nose looked like. Similes can be true, while metaphors—and jokes and novels—are always lies.[12]

Language, as Christopher perceives, threatens always to veer out of control. Even when referents are particular, the signs for them must always be general, and so the name can never mean only the thing—as Kenneth Burke put it, the thing becomes the transient embodiment for the word, rather than the word permanently marking the thing. The world, for Christopher, is a world of things, and there are so many of them but so few words available to name them. Christopher prefers the map, the diagram, the algorithm, for these represent the world in ways that slippery words cannot. The working of the model, which I criticized above, is to Christopher deeply satisfying. These forms are stable pictures of a particular moment of reality. Words are of a different order that refers in large part only to itself and clearly is in league with the impossible, shifting meanings of human faces and with a social world whose most prominent traits are concealment and untruth.

Christopher objects to language per se insofar as it is figurative and thus false, or at best ambiguous. It is inadequate as a tool to organize the world as he perceives it, and in this conclusion Christopher joins Temple Grandin, one of whose chief themes is the predominance in autistic people of visual over verbal thinking.[13] Christopher also objects to narrative, the most characteristic mode of organizing and giving meaning to human experience over time. Time, that universal medium of change and unknowability, "is not like space," Christopher tells us. One can construct a physical or mental map of an area of space which will be a true representation, and if "you put something down somewhere, like a protractor or a biscuit," the object will not change its position on its own, and your map will remind you of its position and its relation to other objects (156). With an adequate map, you can always find yourself in space.

Time, however, cannot be mapped in this way, for a great part of its terrain—the future—cannot be known, at least not in its most important features. For Gary Saul Morson, the ability to present time's contingency is narrative's chief epistemological virtue. But for Christopher, this temporal indeterminacy is terrifying, and this anxiety explains Christopher's preoccupation with always knowing exactly what time it is, and his obsessions about personal daily schedules and railway timetables. "I like timetables," Christopher explains, "because they make sure you don't get lost in time" (158). And yet, the timetable or the schedule is not like a map of space, for it does not represent an actual, current reality, but is more like a preliminary sketch of states of affairs that may or may not ultimately come to pass. A train might be late, or even cancelled.

Christopher's approaches to language and narrative remind us first of the Cratyllic or Adamic impulses discussed earlier; the quests for more and more effective conceptual systems and models are the modern and contemporary equivalents of attempts to conceive of a perfect language of correspondence.. The linking of such representational strategies to the autistic spectrum suggests that if this is indeed an autistic way of seeing the world, it is not pathological, but is part of an impulse to perfect language that may reach back to language's earliest epochs. Or, I should add, to perfect language and to do away with it, for the apocalyptic urges to smash the social-symbolic order coexist with the urges toward a perfect, systemic correspondence between language and the world. As we will see later, Christopher himself exhibits apocalyptic desires in what he calls his "favorite dream." Christopher's Cratyllic, anti-metaphorical impulse also resonates with the views of some evolutionary neurologists regarding the origins of language. The Cratyllic-Adamic-autistic vantage point would appear in this context to be *proto-linguistic* in that it seeks to employ signs without their full symbolic—that is, polysemic or ambiguous—range. A sign that always and only refers to one object or class of objects would be, Terrence Deacon argues, an index not a symbol. Drawing on Charles Saunders Peirce's semiotic categories of icon, index, and symbol, Deacon describes the meaningful cries and gestures of animals as indices. Vervet monkeys, for example, utter particular cries to indicate the approach of particular predators. Such indexical reference, Deacon argues, is not language proper because it is based on a "necessary association"; the vervet cries "rely on a relatively stable correlation with what they refer, in order to refer" (67). Conversely, genuine linguistic, or symbolic, reference is not based on direct association or contiguity, but on more general, systemic relationships. For Peirce, use of the symbol requires always a third term—not just sign and referent, but also an "interpretant," a sign that governs the interpretation of the relation between sign and referent, and subsequently itself requires an interpretant to facilitate its own interpretation. Thus, the use of symbols, in Peirce's view, can be understood only in the context of a semantic universe of symbols, each requiring the others to achieve its meaning. Deacon, echoing Peirce, asserts that the relation between symbol and object relies on the "complex function of the relation the symbol has to other symbols" rather than simply to the object to which it refers (83).

For Deacon, all animals with relatively complex nervous systems, certainly all mammals, are capable of indexical thinking. They can see objects not simply as themselves but can see one in relation to another. A dog or cat knows the meaning of the sound of a can being opened, for the sound is consistently followed by a meal. Indexical thinking, Deacon observes, is an enormously effective evolutionary adaptation. For every animal but ourselves, it has served admirably, and for our human-primate ancestors it was the only form of thinking until only about two million years ago. The evolution of human language, Deacon argues, is in essence the shift from indexical to symbolic thinking, a gradual "restructuring event" in which, over the course of nearly two million years (our current linguistic abilities were achieved between 200,000 and 100,000 years ago) "we let go of one associative strategy and grabbed hold of another, higher-order one" (93). But Christopher's example, and that of his mythological, philosophical, and scientific analogues, indicates that we have not let go of indexical thinking completely—that it is not only still an important part of our neural responses to the physical world, but that it still plays an important role in our uses of and attitudes toward language. Language qua language is symbolic. Ambiguity, irony, jokes, fictions, lies are essential to what it is, to the economy of having a limited number of signs mediate our relations to a world of infinite events, sensations, perceptions, etc. We are the "symbolic species," as Deacon explains, but part of us is indexical as well, and we are subject perhaps to a nostalgia for the indexical. Likewise, as Gerald Edelman argues, the consciousness of animals without language is "largely dependent upon the succession of events in real time" without a workable concept of the past (103). Only the emergence of language "provides the means of freeing animal behavior from the tyranny of ongoing events" (92). But part of us wants to get out of time, to get out of syntax and symbol, and to return to a life in the present, a life in the index. Thus, we can see Christopher's panic in the face of time and symbol use as evidence not only of his autism as a particular disorder but of the psychic, neural, and historical residue of a longstanding conflict between different modes of semiotic action.

As we see, then, open narrative of the sort Morson describes, the sort found in what Christopher calls the "proper novel," only compounds his problems with time. Fortunately, Christopher has access to two alternate genres that allow him to tell his story. First, his narrative is a memoir, a story of true events experienced by him, since, as he says, "I find it hard to imagine things that did not happen to me" (4). Second, his narrative will be a mystery story, and for Christopher, a story in this mode is a puzzle, resembling more an algorithm, model, or map than it does an open chronological narrative employing figurative language. A neighbor's dog has been murdered. Christopher himself came upon the dog's body. After having located the body in space, it remains for him to locate the murderer and place murderer and victim in a mappable spatial relation. A mystery, for Christopher, exists to be solved, for the crime has already been committed and its effects have been discovered. All that remains is the missing piece of a contemporaneous spatial puzzle, to which temporal narrative may be of assistance but is not essential.

As a person with what may or may not currently be called Asperger's Syndrome, Christopher makes an excellent detective. When a teacher compliments him on being clever, Christopher replies that he is merely "observant" (25). His powers of observation, moreover, rely on precise memories of things in their places: It is associative, indexical, and so it is made far more difficult by social interaction. As he says, "when I am in a new place and there are lots of people there it is even harder because people are not like cows and flowers and grass and they can talk to you and do things that you don't expect, so you have to notice everything that is in the place, and also you have to notice things that might happen as well" (143). His indexical mode of thinking is confused and threatened when it enters a world of symbolic action, and yet his observant, associative mind gives him advantages in activities that require logical thinking within strict regulations. "That is why I am good at chess and maths and logic," Christopher explains, "because most people are almost blind and they don't see most things and there is lots of spare capacity in their heads and it is filled with things which aren't connected and are silly, like 'I'm worried that I might have left the gas cooker on'" (144). Christopher's Asperger's mind focuses on a particular task to the exclusion of all others, notices all that is relevant to that task, but is overwhelmed if faced with too much information on other matters. Christopher surely would have noticed at once Poe's purloined letter sitting openly on the table.

Christopher models himself on Sherlock Holmes, a character in whom he sees strong resemblances to himself, both in his powers of observation and, quoting Conan Doyle, in "the power of detaching his mind at will" (73). Several writers on autism have remarked on the quasi-autistic qualities of Holmes's investigative style, and, in fact, many classic and hard-boiled fictional detectives share these features of acute observation, focused and logical thinking, and social isolation which characterize Christopher and which clinical and popular writers have attributed to those on the autistic/Asperger's spectrum. The detective is "an outsider socially and an eccentric psychologically," writes Richard Alewyn (71). He has, in Steven Marcus's view, no personal life "apart from his work. . . . Being a detective is the realization of an identity, for there are components in it which are beyond or beneath society—and cannot be touched by it—and beyond and beneath reason" (206–207). But these same traits that isolate the detective are the traits that enable him to see and think more clearly. And only in his isolation can the detective preserve the social order, which is, ultimately, every detective's goal.

In the mystery or detective genre, the crime, in particular the corpse itself, is a rip in the social fabric, and a revelation of a hidden reality of corruption. The camera's slow entry into the severed ear near the start of David Lynch's *Blue Velvet* is a figure for the genre's logic. Through a traumatic dismemberment, we are directed into a subterranean world in which the crime is revealed not as an aberration but as a symptom of a more pervasive criminality and as a threat to future stability. The detective genre at least gestures toward social critique. In some cases, the critique is limited and quickly disavowed. What may have seemed a wider threat is really the work of a single and uniquely perverted mind; when the criminal is apprehended, the threat vanishes and stability is ensured. The classic "whodonits" of the Agatha Christie branch of the genre exemplify this tendency toward ideological containment with its assurance that in the end nothing is seriously wrong with the social order. And, in narrative terms, the "whodonit," as is the case also with Christopher's imagination, relies on spatial mapping rather than chronological development; it is appropriate that the climactic scene of such mysteries often takes place in a single room in which all the suspects have been assembled. Conversely, the hard-boiled fictions of Dashiell Hammett, Raymond Chandler, Chester Himes, and others are very much concerned with revealing the symptomatic status of violent crime, and the pervasive, systemic nature of political and social corruption. (Conan Doyle is an ambiguous figure on this spectrum. Many of his stories indicate that crimes point toward deeper conspiracies of crime and are genuine threats to social order, yet in general the solving of crimes and punishment of criminals are sufficient to contain these threats.)

What social dysfunctions, then, are revealed, critiqued, or contained through Christopher's investigation with its Asperger's methodology? The body of the dog in *Curious Incident* provokes first a narrow question that can be investigated as a sort of puzzle: Who killed the dog? This is, as it stands, an isolated "whodonit" question, amenable to the detached, indexical thinking at which Christopher excels. It soon opens up, however, as in hard-boiled or *noir* versions, into questions and problems that are deeply embedded in the social-symbolic relationships of Christopher's life—that is, into the areas where he is most impaired. Haddon constructs his character so that a neurological condition overlaps with characterological conditions of genre. The fictional detective, now located on the autistic spectrum and so doubly outside normative social-symbolic relations, must investigate a crime which stands as symptom of a rupture in a social order that he is only marginally part of and is neurologically unequipped to understand.

What Christopher discovers however—or, more accurately, what we as readers discover through Christopher's investigation—is that the social order is itself firmly placed on the autistic spectrum. That is, the society that Christopher has lived in all his life, but now gradually comes to uncover with more care, is characterized by its members' isolation and inability to communicate with each other. He finds this first in his family. His mother is frustrated to the point of despair by her inability to have a normal maternal relationship with Christopher, and her marriage suffers, especially because her husband often blames her for her problems with their son. She leaves with another man, but from what we see in the novel, this relationship also does not seem especially close. Christopher's father embarks on a failed relationship with Mrs. Shears, and their emotional and communicative impasse leads to the murder of the dog. Christopher's father seems a solitary, brooding man given to violent outbursts. His strategy for explaining his separation from his wife to Christopher is to end her existence as a member of the family by telling Christopher she is dead.

The novel's depiction of social isolation extends beyond the family. As Christopher walks through his neighborhood, knocking on doors and interviewing neighbors about the dog's murder, we find that the neighbors barely know each other. The first person Christopher talks to wears a T-shirt that thematizes a lack of social connection: "Beer— Helping Ugly People Have Sex For Over 2,000 Years." Christopher asks him, "'Do you know who killed Wellington?'"

> I did not look at his face. I do not like looking at people's faces, especially if they are strangers. He did not say anything for a few seconds.
>
> Then he said, "Who are you?"
>
> I said, "I'm Christopher Boone from number 36 and I know you. You're Mr. Thompson."
>
> He said, "I'm Mr. Thompson's brother."
>
> I said, "Do you know who killed Wellington?"
>
> He said, "Who the fuck is Wellington?" (36)

Christopher has better luck with his two succeeding interviews. One woman, whose name he doesn't know, greets him, "'It's Christopher, isn't it?'" (36); and the next, whom he knows as Mrs. Alexander, says, "'You're

Christopher, aren't you?'" (39). These neighbors know who he is—he's the kid down the street with some kind of disability—but clearly they've never spoken to him. As Christopher tells Mrs. Alexander, "'I don't like talking to strangers,'" but as we see through the failures of communication that these interviews present, no one in the neighborhood likes talking to strangers much, and everyone is more or less a stranger to each other. And yet, people are not unfriendly to Christopher, and they try to be helpful. The unnamed woman warns Christopher, "'You be careful, young man'" (38); the man with the unusual T-shirt asks, "'Look son, do you really think you should be going around asking questions like this" (37); and Mrs. Alexander appears to want to engage Christopher in conversation and goes inside to prepare a soft drink and cookies for him though he leaves before she returns. There seems to be a desire for connection that is in conflict with a broader inhibition, and this broader inhibition, while not explained explicitly, appears to arise from social and economic factors.

Swindon, the city where Christopher and his family live, lies seventy miles west of London and has a population of about 180,000, with significant Asian and Caribbean communities. According to its Borough Council website, while its traditional manufacturing sector has declined, Swindon has developed thriving mid- and high-tech industries. Unemployment, however, has risen since the late 1990s, and the site expressed concern that long-term unemployment, in particular, had increased and that the Swindon workforce was less qualified for high-tech work than workers in comparable localities. Housing is also a problem in Swindon. In 2003, there were 1,600 abandoned houses in Swindon while eight hundred households live in temporary housing provided by the city (either in public facilities or in private facilities contracted by the city). A special report on homelessness prepared for the Borough Council in 2003 reported that the city had accepted three hundred homeless households for rehousing in that year, and that nine hundred other "non-priority" households (either single people or childless couples) could not be assisted by the city. The report estimated that the shortfall in affordable housing was 1,218 units in 2003 (*Swindon Borough Council*, 16). Both in reality and in Haddon's fictional portrayal, Swindon occupies a post-Thatcher England characterized by vibrant high-tech industries coexisting with declining social services and education and with rising unemployment and homelessness. It seems characterized also by a lack of social networks and civic, community, and class organizations of the sort that E. P. Thompson described as helping to form the basis of a distinct working-class culture in England from the eighteenth through the mid-twentieth centuries.[14] Nor do we see any evidence of extended families; the small detached houses of Swindon are inhabited only by nuclear families, or fragments of them. This is a social world that, for reasons Haddon does not investigate, has been flattened, atomized, with each household an isolated and fragile entity.

By means of Christopher's role as autistic detective, Haddon depicts a pervasive social autism. The administrative bureaucracy of this society is not malign; Christopher as detective does not uncover the sorts of corruption and police violence found by the hard-boiled detectives, Sam Spade and Phillip Marlowe, or even, to a lesser degree by his model Sherlock Holmes. The police, in fact, are always patient, helpful, and reasonable in *Curious Incident*. But the police and the contracting welfare state can do nothing to address the weakening of social and family bonds that Christopher's investigation reveals. At the same time, however, although Christopher can be read as a figure for a broader social autism, this novel is not primarily a work of social or political critique. Its political points are not developed, and the extended metaphor of a social autism is offered but then withdrawn. The novel's focus returns, at last, to the family, to human emotion, and to difficulties in personal relationships that appear to go beyond or beneath any particular social structures. In spite of his apparent critique of a specifically post-Thatcher social fragmentation, Haddon's deeper explanation of social dysfunction seems to rely more on neurology and notions of the autistic spectrum than on politics. In this reading, Christopher, as a person with Asperger's, is not a trope for a social autism that has political or economic causes; rather, the novel's instances of social disconnection, anomie, and violence are products of autistic tendencies that are wired, in some degree, into all human neural systems. Christopher—with his resistance to symbolic thinking and ambiguity, his abhorrence at being touched, his difficulties in understanding others' thoughts and feelings—is an extreme example of qualities possessed in lesser amounts by everyone.

Curious Incident ends with Christopher's triumph. Having passed his A-levels with honors, he writes that now he will attend university. "And then I will get a First Class Honors degree and I will become a scientist. And I know I can do this because I went to London on my own, and because I solved the mystery of *Who Killed Wellington?* And I found my mother and I was brave and I wrote a book and that means I can do anything" (221). But Christopher cannot achieve these goals without extensive social and familial support and care. At the same time, while both family and society display certain dissociative qualities that we would place on the autistic spectrum, Christopher's father and mother differ markedly from him in other respects. Christopher acknowledges that he has trouble with what philosophers and, more recently, writers on autism, call "theory of mind"—the ability to conceive of other people possessing separate minds and to imagine what they might be thinking or feeling.[15] But, significantly, Christopher provides these thoughts on theory of mind just after the most intense emotional and linguistic event in the novel up to that point—his discovery and reading of the letters from his mother that his father had hidden from him. In these letters, we witness for the first time a voice, a mind, unmediated by Christopher's consciousness, and the mother's voice breaks the novel apart. These letters show an extreme instance of another cognitive and emotional mode of being, and Christopher's Holmesian, Asperger's puzzle-solving method of apprehending this other mind proves to be inadequate.

The letters' sudden shift in voice and sensibility brings to the novel the complexity of adult emotions and social and sexual relations. These letters stand clearly in contrast both to the autistic tone and sensibility of Christopher's narration and to the broader social autism that the novel portrays. Simultaneously chatty and emotionally intense, the letters tell Christopher of the deterioration of her marriage and her decision to leave the home. His mother relates her frequent losses of temper as she reaches "the end of my tether" (107) or of having "lost my rag" (108) at some action of Christopher or her husband. She "cried and cried and cried" after one incident, and her decision to leave "broke my heart" (109). She tells of household violence, of hitting her husband and of throwing food during a failed attempt to get Christopher to eat, and of her sorrow over these actions: "and he told me I was being stupid and said I should pull myself together and I hit him, which was wrong, but I was so upset" (107). Christopher cannot understand these emotions, and responds physically. "It was as if the room was swinging from side to side, as if it was at the top of a really tall building and the building was swinging backward and forward in a strong wind" (112). This vertigo is the same feeling he described earlier when he wrote about his physical reaction to false statements. Thinking of things that aren't true, he wrote, "makes me feel shaky and scared, like I do when I'm standing on the top of a very tall building" (19). Apparently, his pain results from a terrible cognitive disruption: His mother is not dead; his father lied to him. The stability of clear, unambiguous signification has been lost, blown away by the winds of an emotional life that is steeped in, and can only be expressed in, the dangerous ambiguities of language. Christopher's difficulties in constructing a theory of mind with regard to other people—his difficulty imagining their perceptions, thoughts, and feelings—is, as Haddon portrays it, entirely of a piece with his difficult relation to language.

The emotional climax of the novel, however, is a moment of linguistic breakdown on the part of Christopher's mother—her reaction to the news that her husband had told Christopher that she was dead.

> And then Mother said, "Oh my God."
> And then she didn't say anything for a long while. And then she made a loud wailing noise like an animal on a nature program on television.
> And I didn't like her doing this because it was a loud noise, and I said, "Why are you doing that?" (193)

Christopher's mother's response is non-linguistic and non-symbolic; it is an immediate outburst of feeling. It could be called "indexical," in that it points toward or bears a causal relation to an emotion, although it does not, in any general, symbolic sense, represent the emotion. As Christopher notes, it links her to animals. In literary terms, her wailing places her in the lineage of Faulkner's Benjy and DeLillo's Wilder, whose emotional cries reinforce their separation from the symbolic realm. But in this case, the non-linguistic outburst is uttered by the character in this novel most thoroughly immersed in language use, whose letters, as we have seen, serve as counterpoint to Christopher's hostility to the resources and perspectives of language. Unlike Benjy or Wilder, Christopher's mother is not some "other," outside the loop of language. She is both a competent, indeed enthusiastic, user of language (even if ungrammatical and a poor speller) and a person capable of emotional loss of language that connects her with animal behavior—and also to her son, who is prone to screaming tantrums. Haddon's imagining of Christopher's mother's "loud wailing noise" as an emotional center for the novel indicates powerfully that, for Haddon, all symbolic and emotional activity falls on a broad spectrum of neurological response, with no clear break between the linguistic and non-linguistic. And the mother's wailing, we should note, is in response to a quintessential symbolic act: the father's lie, his denial of her existence.

And yet, Christopher cannot understand his mother's wailing. He regards it in terms of animal behavior, does not see it as similar to his own emotional outbursts, and, sadly, rejects the emotional connection that it invites. Immediately after her wailing, Christopher's mother asks him if she can hold his hand, "'just for once. Just for me. Will you? I won't hold it hard.'" But Christopher refuses, saying, "'I don't like people holding my hand'" (194). It is Christopher's affliction that, in a sense, *everyone* is other to him; every experience that is not his is other. The ambiguities, imprecisions, and necessary generalizations of symbolization are partly what make possible human contact and understanding— together with the emotional, physical forms of connection we share with animals. As the scene of his mother's wailing shows, Christopher's failure to understand his mother's wailing—a failure of empathy—lies along the same neurological spectrum as his inability to understand her letters (or, indeed, to catch the most ordinary linguistic nuances). Even with the strengths and resources that he displays throughout the novel, Christopher is terribly vulnerable; he is also desperately loved, but is unable to return that love in recognizable ways. He needs protection, and can never be protected enough, can never be loved enough. He is always, irreducibly, strange, irreducibly himself.

The novel places us, then, in a complicated situation. Christopher's social and emotional isolation reads as a terrible sadness, heightened by the irony produced by Christopher's incomplete awareness of it (which is, perhaps, what truly makes it isolation). This isolation, as a neurological given, can in part be ameliorated through education or medication, but it can never be entirely overcome. At the same time, as this novel presents it, no person truly is other to another. We all are connected by non-symbolic, indexical, and emotional bonds that we share with other animals, as well as by symbolic bonds. Moreover, our symbolic capacities are built upon and cannot exist apart from the earlier, non-symbolic cognitive structures; and all of us live, think, and interact along a spectrum of symbolic and non-symbolic capacities. As *Curious Incident* also suggests, this spectrum includes as well the autistic spectrum and its tendencies toward isolation. This tendency toward isolation is social and political, as we observed earlier, a product of the late capitalist, post-Thatcher weakening of social bonds. In other forms of social life, the novel appears to imply, social bonds would be stronger and tendencies toward isolation and anomie less pronounced. But, as the example of Christopher and his precisely observed neurological condition suggest, the tendency toward isolation is, finally, irreducibly neurological. Christopher is, on one level, a metaphor for the social autism that surrounds him. He is also, and for the purposes of this novel, more fundamentally an *instance* of an autistic tendency that has biological bases with manifestations that pervade individual and social life. To borrow again Belmonte's phrase, to be autistic is to be human, only more so.

Shortly after his mother's collapse into wailing, Christopher describes his favorite dream. The connection is crucial, but before pursuing it, I want to stress again that his mother's wailing is not an exit from the symbolic or the social realms. She had been banished by a symbolic act of betrayal: Her *letters* had been hidden and she was narrated out of her son's life. Her wailing is her first utterance on returning to the social and symbolic realms, at least with regard to her family. This animal sound is not an act of departure from the symbolic; quite the opposite, it is her re-entry into a social-symbolic world from which she had been erased. Her cry, emerging from her deepest organic and cognitive being, protests and rejects isolation and silence. Thus, the close juxtaposition late in the novel of the mother's wailing with Christopher's favorite dream emphasizes unequivocally Haddon's view that alterity is relative, not absolute. Everyone desires connection, community, and love. Christopher, after all, searches for his lost mother and has ambitions to succeed in school and university. Yet everyone maintains a sector of self that rejects social-symbolic contact and is terrified of touch.

Christopher's dream is an apocalyptic vision in which nearly everyone on earth dies of a virus. This virus, however, is not biological, but semantic. As Christopher says, "people catch it because of the meaning of something an infected person says and the meaning of what they do with their faces when they say it" (198). Because the virus can spread through televised images and dialogue as well as through personal contact, it spreads rapidly; soon, the only people left are people like Christopher who cannot understand facial expressions or the shifting meanings of all symbolic usage. In this new world, populated only by autistic people, devoid of symbols, meanings, and ambiguities, Christopher feels liberated. He knows that "no one is going to talk to me or touch me or ask me a question" (199). He can eat whatever he wants, play computer games all day, drive cars, and when he goes home, "it's not Father's house anymore, it's mine" (200). When the dream is over, he says, "I am happy" (200).

Christopher's deepest wish, it seems, is that the world as a site of meaning—the social-symbolic world—be obliterated. He wishes a reversion to an indexical world consisting only of objects in which signs, presumably, would be unnecessary or would be perfect, unvarying emblems for the things themselves. Perhaps, in this world, Christopher would lose his own false, metaphorical name and would discover his true one. In any event, through Christopher's dream, Haddon portrays the apocalyptic imagination as a violent opposition to ambiguity and symbolization—an interpretation very much in keeping with many of the central apocalyptic texts and commentaries, both biblical and modern.[16] Haddon further implies that the apocalyptic imagination is a form of autistic thinking, and that autistic thinking tends toward apocalypticism. The urge toward a symbolic reduction so complete that it requires global annihilation, in this view, is part of the human evolutionary-neurological inheritance. Just as, in Christopher's mother's case, we can never be sufficiently emotionally and symbolically connected to others, so as Christopher's dream implies, neither can we ever be sufficiently alone. Both these tendencies and desires exist together, in all people, and in this sense we might read *Curious Incident* as a neurological *psychomacheia*, a drama of the struggle within every soul between opposing positions on the neurological spectrum. Once again, if this interpretation is valid, the social and political conditions depicted in this novel become secondary to, or particular manifestations of, conditions and conflicts of our neurology. The ideology of neurology trumps traditional critique of ideology.

This struggle leads us back to the question of care. Why should Christopher be an object of care? And why especially should he be an object of care when he cannot reciprocate that care, at least not in ways that those who care for him would wish for? One cares, I think, for Christopher because of his vulnerability, his needs, his limits. The novel presents him continually in the context of this care, even though Christopher's narration seems oblivious to it. Haddon seems to present this care almost as a moral imperative. But rather than indicating reasons for this imperative, Haddon presents it as a fact: Christopher's parents care, and others who come in contact with him care, and the reader who encounters him, presumably, cares. One *must* care because one *does* care, rather than the reverse. His vulnerability, which manifests itself through his symbolic and social limitations, demands that one bestow care. Yet, as I have argued, these symbolic and social limitations render him both different from and similar to others. His autistic qualities locate him on a neurological spectrum shared by all people. One empathizes with him, and empathizes even with his inability to empathize; one cares even for his inability to care. And this is because, I think, all of us share, in part, this lack of empathy and care, this wish for isolation, even the urge to annihilate the social and symbolic world. It is, perhaps, the absolute self-sufficiency and absolute vulnerability and need in the case of the infant that ultimately demands this care.

But this care requires a social setting: families, communities, institutions. The urge to negate social and symbolic structures also has a place in those same structures. Although care for radical vulnerability may be based in our neurology, different social arrangements and institutions make possible different types and degrees of caring; and although the apocalyptic-autistic sensibility may be a neurological constant, again, different forms of social organization can channel urges toward social-symbolic negation in different directions and with different results—toward art, disciplined spiritual emptying, or other single-minded peaceful pursuits, or toward genocide, war, or greed-inspired destruction of the natural world. In this sense, Haddon's precise depiction of Christopher's social world may not be merely a realist red-herring that is subordinated to implacable neurological foundations. Caring for the most vulnerable, fostering their gifts and their agency, and learning from them are more possible in some societies than in others, and to identify obstacles to caring is a beginning of social critique.

Tics as Metaphors; Metaphors as Tics

Autism is not the only signifying neurological disorder in the age of neuroscience. Tourette's Syndrome, researchers Leckman and Cohen have written, has become "our hysteria" (3), the physical manifestation that seems best able to illuminate the relations between "brain and mind" in both health and disease. While Haddon in *Curious Incident* explores the possibility of eradicating metaphor, and the linguistic and social trans-ladings it implies, Jonathan Lethem, in his novel *Motherless Brooklyn*, presents Tourette's as a condition of excessive metaphor and returns to the central modernist question, How can there be aesthetic or societal innovation in the face of confining social-symbolic norms? Tourette's, for Lethem, appears as a neurological disruptor of the social-symbolic world as closed system, demonstrates how disrupted symbolic usage returns to a revised normal state, and explores how metaphor, genre, and trauma figure into these processes of disruption and normalization. As in Haddon's depiction of autism in *Curious Incident*, alterity is a central concern in *Motherless Brooklyn*; but the location of alterity is not outside and counter to a social-symbolic order. Alterity is, rather, a neurological function. We are never not other, and our social, ethical, and aesthetic gestures and relations must, ultimately, reflect on this condition that necessarily eludes our reflection.[17]

Lionel Essrog, the book's Tourettic narrator, describes an encounter on a city bus with a Tourettic person with highly visible symptoms. The person is poor, dirty, perhaps homeless, and his tics consist of grotesquely annoying belching and farting sounds. The other passengers, offended and uncomprehending, regard him with outrage. He feigns innocence till they look away; then he begins again. Lionel notes here, as with his own tics, the convergence of a physiological need to perform

the tic with a specific social setting in which the tic will be most disruptive and most humiliating both to the performer and the observ-
ers. While the bus passenger's tics are not intentional, neither are they
random. And though not linguistic, they are certainly symbolic, thrust-
ing themselves into wider contexts of social meaning in which they can
be interpreted. Neurological compulsion here seems to storm a social-
symbolic barrier like an incipient revolution. And yet, as Lionel completes his description of the scene, he insists that the rip in the social-
symbolic fabric will close almost instantly. "Consensual reality," he tells
us, "is both fragile and elastic, and it heals like the skin of a bubble." The
scene as a whole illustrates above all "the reality knitting mechanism
people employ to tuck away the intolerable, the incongruous, the disruptive" (43–44).

Lionel's own characteristic tics are explicitly and extravagantly verbal.
For the most part, they consist of novel combinations of words. In some
cases, the neologisms are created through phonetic shifts, more or less
at random—"echolalia salad," as Lionel describes it (4), with concoc-
tions such as "see that homosapien, homogenize, genocide, can'tdecide,
candyeyes, homicide cop?" (125). Mostly, the phonetic movement is
combined with a more motivated, conscious or unconscious, transformation of language that helps enact some idea of Lionel's identity, sexuality, or response to a particular social situation. He tics frequently, for
instance, on his own rather unusual name—"my original verbal taffy,"
he calls it (7)—and these naming tics generally express anxiety. "'Alli-
bybye Essmob . . . Lionel Arrestme,'" he shouts to a police detective
who questions him about the murder of Lionel's mentor and employer,
Frank Minna (109). He elsewhere proclaims himself "Viable Guessfrog"
(92), "Lionel Deathclam" (93), "Criminal Fishrug" (97) and, in other
moods, "Lyrical Eggdog," "Logical Assnog" (104), and "Valiant Daffodil"
(155). In a similar fashion, Lionel responds to a sexual experience with
"slipdrip stinkjet's blessdroop mutual-of-overwhelm's wild kissdoom"
(259), an astonishing, conflicted juxtaposition of joy, exhaustion, shame,
gratitude, and terror, a remarkably condensed love lyric. These verbal
figures seem to result from a disordering of structures of identity and
experience. When uttered, they first disorder conventions of language
use, and then reorient conventions so that, on second or third reading,
they prove no longer disruptive.

The verbal tics that Lethem creates for Lionel are metaphors—new terms that bridge various areas of discourse and feeling and that create new meanings and understandings. They are not, we should emphasize, metaphors *for* some previously existing term. That is, they are not substitutions, as Aristotle's theory of metaphor posits. Rather, they resemble catachreses, as discussed in chapter 1, terms that establish a semantic place for a meaning that previously had no term. This is the sense of metaphor suggested by Paul Ricoeur, who argues that genuine metaphor "does not merely actualize a potential connotation, it creates it. It is a semantic innovation, an emergent meaning" ("Word" 79). As I will argue, *Motherless Brooklyn* presents a conflict between opposing senses of metaphor, for the precise character of Lionel's semantic disruptions and emergent meanings is part of what is in question. Lionel speaks of his tics as "smoothing down imperfections, putting hairs in place, putting ducks in a row, replacing divots": that is, compulsively creating order and pattern. And yet, he continues, when the tics "find too much perfection, when the surface is already buffed smooth, the ducks already orderly. . . then my little army rebels. . . Reality needs a prick here and there, the carpet needs a flaw" (1–2). Lionel speaks of a "meta-tourette's," an overarching principle of symbolization, of ordering and disordering, disrupting and normalizing, for which the actual condition of Tourette's serves as figure and exemplar. The human use of symbols, as Lethem presents it, is precisely this dynamic of weaving, unweaving, reweaving.

But what exactly is there to be disrupted and reordered? It is clearly more than a particular word or utterance. Rather, as we saw in the example of the offensive ticcing on the bus, what is disrupted is a social-symbolic convention—an agreed-on mode of behavior and expression. When Lionel tics, or riffs, on his name, what is at stake is not a simple graphic or phonemic entity, but the convention of the proper name as a mark of identity. "Lionel Essrog" in his full personal and social being is disassembled and recreated as "Lyrical Eggdog," and his numerous other guises. In order to explore more fully the symbolic disruption of social practices, Lethem foregrounds the use of genre. *Motherless Brooklyn* is, of course, a variation of the detective novel and relies heavily on certain conventions of the *noir* or hard-boiled versions of this broad genre. Even its characters are self-conscious about their status as participants in a hard-boiled narrative. "'You're the jerk I gotta deal with, you're Sam

Spade,'" Lionel's colleague and rival, Tony, says to him. To which Lionel replies, quoting Dashiel Hammett, "'When someone kills your partner, you're supposed to do something about it'" (183). But *Motherless Brooklyn* is not just a novel that employs genre. It is a novel in which genre is itself a topic, as we see particularly in its treatment of jokes.

The novel makes clear quite early that we live and die within genre. When Frank Minna has been stabbed and is bleeding to death in the back seat of a car on the way to the hospital, he refuses to say who stabbed him; rather, he demands that Lionel tell him a joke. Lionel, reluctantly, agrees. "Guy walks into a bar," he begins, and Frank immediately interrupts him, praising his use of generic convention: "Best jokes start the same fuckin' way, don't they? The guy, the bar" (25). Lionel continues the joke, which is about a man accompanied by an octopus which can play any musical instrument. The bartender provides the octopus with a series of instruments—piano, guitar, clarinet—and as the octopus plays each one, Lionel embellishes the narrative of the performance. The octopus "lays out a little etude" on the piano and plays "a sweet little fandango" on the guitar. Frank comments on each embellishment. "'Getting fancy,' said Minna. 'Showing off a little'"; and later, "'He's milking it'" (26). Lionel understands that Frank is commenting both on the octopus's performance and on his own narration of it. The effectiveness of the joke as joke, then, depends on generally understood structural conventions and on the ability to expand and vary the narrative within the conventions. At the same time, Lionel struggles to restrain his tics, which threaten to destroy the joke's coherence and timing altogether. The joke begins a certain way, as Frank observes. Its middle is to a large degree open to the creative agency of the teller. At the center of the joke, the genre permits significant narrative fluidity. The joke also ends in a generically determined fashion—with a punch line. In this case, the octopus decides he wants to have sexual intercourse with a set of bagpipes ("Play it? If I can figure out how to get its pajamas off, I'm gonna fuck it!" (27). Interestingly, however, the punch line is rendered relatively insignificant in two ways. First, Lionel anticipates it prematurely with a tic—"fuckit, says gonnafuckit"—and second, Frank is unconscious at the moment it is properly delivered. As this joke is rendered by Lethem, it is the joke's narrative that is crucial, not its closure. Once the generic structure has been established, Lethem stresses its narrative fluidity, its detours and deviations, rather than its return to strict convention. Genre depends on its own violation.

This self-violating, fluid character of effective genre use helps explain Lionel's antipathy toward Loomis, the "garbage cop" and his clichéd, characterless one-liners. ("Why did the blonde stare at the carton of orange juice? Because it said, 'Concentrate.' Get it?" [122]). These jokes are nothing but setup and closure, with "no room," as Lionel observes, "for character or nuance" (123). Loomis's inability to explore the flexibility of genre, his restriction to only its rigid, "generic" features, is, for Lionel, also a moral, a perceptual, and, in a sense, a neurological failure:

> His imprecision and laziness maddened my compulsive instincts. . . his leaden senses refused the world, his attention like a pinball rolling past unlit blinkers and frozen flippers into the hole again and again: *game over*. He was permanently impressed by the most irrelevant banalities and impossible to impress with real novelty, meaning, or conflict. (121–22)

The tic as metaphor, as Lionel employs it, draws, as we have seen, on personal and social sources that can be identified and analyzed. Likewise, the tic as a function in genre directs analysis to particular social and ideological determinants. But Lethem adds another sort of verbal tic as well, one that seems to have no origin or remainder, a tic that is unreconcilable, that baffles symbolization. This is the name "Bailey," a proper name that functions as a contrary of Lionel's own name. While "Lionel" is infinitely malleable, a "verbal taffy," "Bailey" does not blend with other words. Bailey is Bailey. Nor can Lionel explain what Bailey is or why it became a characteristic tic for him. He conjectures that it may derive from George Bailey, the protagonist of *It's a Wonderful Life*, and so function as a sympathetic Everyman, or, as Lionel speculates, an ideal interlocutor, "my imaginary listener" who "bears the brunt" of his more violent verbal outbursts (10). But Bailey may also be himself, the imagined author of his tics. When Lionel, who is an orphan, periodically, and compulsively, phones an Essrog family in Brooklyn, who may be his parents, he can, when asked, identify himself only by ticcing "Bailey." Bailey is the constant mystery of Lionel's consciousness, the recurring "other" of the novel. It seems to stand for what cannot be translated or combined; it is the irreducibly radical tic, the single tic that continues to disturb, that refuses the process of normalization precisely because there is no other term that can stand in for it or with it. And yet, in the end, in keeping with the dominant logic of the novel, Bailey is normalized. At the novel's conclusion, Lionel has extricated himself from the criminal underworlds he had entered, and he and his fellow protégés of the late Frank Minna now manage a legitimate Brooklyn car service. At this point, Lionel returns one last time to the mystery of Bailey, but this time he demystifies the name. Bailey now is no irreducible other; he is just another "guy I never happened to meet" (311). His mystery thus is empirical, not conceptual. All that is disruptive, unknowable, is finally folded back into the known. Alterity is simply another, somewhat more distant point on a continuum.

Is metaphor, then, genuinely disruptive, or are its disruptive qualities merely apparent? And can metaphor be genuinely innovative if it is not also genuinely disruptive? Responses to these questions depend first on the contexts purported to be disrupted. It seems reasonable to assume, as Lethem's novel suggests and as writers in the field of cognitive science and literature argue, that metaphor exemplifies how mind works in all respects. Insofar as the mind takes in information from many sources and must then create schemas by which it evaluates and determines courses of action, it continually engages in processes of combination and blending. Mark Turner's notion of the "emergent space" that results from two or more cognitive spaces that have been joined is, for him, both a description of cognition per se and metaphor in particular. "Conceptual blending," Turner writes, "is a fundamental instrument of the everyday mind, used in our basic construal of all our realities" (93). Metaphor is simply the signal instance of this process of constructing new combinations of perceptual and linguistic material, and, as Patrick Colm Hogan writes, "for most cognitive scientists, there is no difference in kind between the practices of literature and those of ordinary thought" (87). Linguistic practice, then, in this view, is congruent with mental structure. Metaphor and its innovations are always happening and are relatively unproblematic. To be sure, Turner at one point refers to metaphoric blending as an "assault" on conventional symbolic practice (93), but his prevailing tendency is to regard the making of metaphor as normative and peaceful. One might suspect some violence in his descriptions of how categories of one mental space are "projected" onto another in order to produce the new, blended, emergent space, but, with the one exception mentioned, whatever violence maybe posited is tacit. Once the synthesis of the emergent blend has been achieved, the struggles or assaults that may have led to its production are discarded.[18]

The perspective on metaphor is quite different when we turn to theories influenced by post-structuralism. In writers like Ricoeur, Derrida, De Man, and Lacan, we see an enormous rhetorical emphasis on the violence of figurative language. These writers still posit a return to a norm, but the energies of their theories derive from their descriptions of disruptions of symbolic usages. For Paul Ricoeur, metaphor emerges "out of the ruins of the literal sense shattered by semantic incompatibility" ("The Metaphorical Process" 151), and all "movement toward the generic"—or, as we might put it in this discussion, toward normalization—"is arrested by the resistance of the difference . . . intercepted by the figure of rhetoric" (147). Jacques Derrida, in "White Mythology," is even more emphatic with regard to the violent processes of metaphor. Metaphor, he argues, is a category of catachresis, that is, a figure for which no other can be substituted and "that no semantic substitution will have preceded." It is a "forced" trope and is (we might add, like a Tourettic tic) "irruptive" in its entry into symbolic usage (255–56). Any new form of "proper sense," for Derrida, can be achieved only through "the violence of a catachresis" (256, n. 60). Moreover, for Derrida, the process of metaphor must be seen as endless, as each irruption of figurative language points toward other figures in an infinite sequence of semantic instability. "The metaphorization of metaphor, its bottomless overdeterminability," he writes, "seems to be inserted in the structure of metaphor" (243). In Lacan, and particularly in Zizek's reading of him, any symbolic order is inevitably shattered by the traumatic appearance of the "real," that is, the event or presence that cannot be symbolized; indeed, for Lacan, such a traumatic presence—or, more accurately, lack or absence—holds a constitutive place in the traumatic order, and the process of symbolization is in large part the effort to close, in however unsatisfactory a fashion, the ruptures in the symbolic continually opened up by the real. It is important to note that in all these cases, some normal or pacified version of symbolic use reemerges in the wake of these violent disruptions. The wounds to the symbolic, in

Lacan, are always healed, for one cannot live for long in the traumatic real—although these closures of symbolic gaps, as Zizek argues, form the basis for religion and political ideology, and, indeed, in Lakoff and Johnson's terms, for all the "metaphors we live by." For Ricoeur, out of the ruins emerges a new semantic "pertinence, a new congruence," such that the new utterance "'makes sense' as a whole" ("The Metaphorical Process" 144). Metaphor ultimately is "not the enigma but the solution of the enigma" (144). Even Derrida acknowledges a local or provisional normalization of language use. One uses the language one inherits, and while no original or final meanings can be determined, even as one deconstructs all pretenses to such meanings, one must employ the meanings at hand. This is Derrida's notion of the "double gesture": one simultaneously reveals and critiques the violence and infinite instability of language, and yet continues to use that language because there is, after all, no other. (And, of course, one recognizes that the linguistic processes one critiques are necessarily present also in the language of one's own critique.)

Yet, in spite of these normalizing gestures, the emphases on violence in these theories is striking and remains in contrast to the positions of such thinkers as Turner and Black. What is at stake in conceiving of metaphor or linguistic innovation as either normative or catastrophic? This tension in part continues the history of the question posed in chapter 2 regarding the totalizing (or systematizing) and anti-totalizing tendencies of modernity. Post-structuralist theories of metaphor follow from the premise of language as a self-referential and ideologically reinforcing system, a crucial component of an all-encompassing social-symbolic order. To escape from this totalizing, hegemonic space requires the imagining of a radical alterity, and this is the apocalyptic role metaphor plays in these theories. Structure as conceived by the cognitive theorists is not an agency of systematizing normativity that can be resisted only from outside. Rather, language and metaphor work in the ways they do because they express actual structures and processes of the mind. Alterity, in this view, would simply be another emergent space, a new thing blended from pieces of older things. What else could it be? The products of mind are as they are because the mind is as it is.

We might say, returning our attention to *Motherless Brooklyn*, that not only do tics function as metaphors, as vehicles of organization, disruption, and reordering, but that, from the perspective of post-structuralist theory, metaphors themselves are tics: they are uncontrollable eruptions from outside the symbolic order that disrupt that order enough to change it at least slightly, even though the oppressive norms, once disrupted, will always reassert themselves. The metaphor as tic, however, signals the possibility of freedom in the form of the disruptive, the unpredictable, the irreducible—in the form, at last, of Bailey as the other. If, on the other hand, one does not regard language as a system or the human social-symbolic world as a symbolic order; if one does not accept the premise that the cultural production of modernity has been, in its essence, a totalitarian foreclosure of human freedom; if, that is, one does not feel urgently the need for some other of language to penetrate and transform the language system—then, like Turner and Hogan (or, in different ways, like Wittgenstein or Bahktin), one will see the use of metaphor as part of the ordinary human cognitive-linguistic apparatus, indeed as an exemplary instance of how we negotiate our ways around and among our world, our fellow humans, and ourselves. Bailey, then, as we observed before, is not the other; he's just another guy we've not yet met. Or, if he is other, he is an alterity already contained in neurology or language.[19]

If we stick with the cognitive, or neuroscience, or dialogic, or ordinary language view, there seems to be no problem with either tics or metaphors. Is there still a problem? Is something missing from this picture which seems in many ways so adequate to most conceptual needs?

I still have a nagging sense that there is a problem, and that *Motherless Brooklyn*'s presentation of Tourette's can help us understand it. The problem, most broadly, is the problem of the negative—the problem of suffering, trauma, and injustice, and of the perceived need for a radical symbolic response to such conditions or events. These catastrophes are, as we say, parts of life, but when they occur, they seem unaccountable. They call into question customary forms of thought and representation, and alter symbolic landscapes. As we experience them, they do *not* fit. They seem to require some excessive, violent, quasi-apocalyptic mode of representation in that they seem, at least momentarily, to obliterate existing meanings, yet to demand interpretation in their aftermaths. The event negates signification; its retrospective representation resupplies it in excess. Seen in this way, through a perspective informed by trauma, the several theories of metaphor and language use as natural, normal, evolutionarily sanctioned, positions on an unbroken spectrum may still, finally, be correct, but they appear to lack the urgency required to be adequate to lived experience and to history.

It may seem a strange turn of argument to ally poststructuralist theory with history and lived experience, but let's return briefly to Derrida's thinking on metaphor. There is a Saussurean, or Peircean, slant to his description of the irruptive force of metaphor in "White Mythology." The creation of linguistic novelty is both violent and infinite, but it is seemingly without motive. There is never a final, stable position of meaning, but this unstable, limitless innovation is simply a function of how language works: it is *differance*. We can point to phonemic and graphic slippage, as in Saussure, or to the continual need for every interpretation to pass to a new position of interpretation, as in Peirce. In either case, the production of new utterances is a structural condition of language, or of how language is made. The moments of violence, the small apocalypses that result in metaphor turn out to be themselves systemic (a reading that can also be applied to the Lacanian real). In this way, the Derridean argument turns out to supplement the positions of Wittgenstein, Bakhtin, and Turner: the traumatic disruption is not some other of language; it is, rather, a constitutive element. But in making this turn, this assimilation, have we not elided trauma, or decided to ignore its actual, historical, experiential, contingent character *as* trauma.[20]

Derrida tries to address this problem in his 1986 essay on poetic language, "Shibboleth." Where "White Mythology" discusses the potentially infinite slippages of signification that characterize metaphor and language in general, "Shibboleth" tries to answer the question, Why does such slippage stop when an actual articulation is made? Why does any given articulation, any metaphor, take the particular form that it does when it is uttered? Derrida's account of the origin of metaphor here is, naturally, itself a metaphor. A painful, traumatic event acts as an incision or a wound in language. The event, in its temporal-historical occurrence, is unique, singular, and, as such, is unreadable and unrepresentable. For an event's *incision* to be repeated or normalized as *inscription*, it must become repeatable; it must lose its uniqueness. The incisive, wounding event, Derrida writes, "pays for its readability with the terrible tribute of lost singularity" (330). Its "date"—Derrida's term for historical-temporal particularity—is annulled at the moment of its entry into language. Poetic language, then, or metaphor, originates in the radically non-linguistic event of wounding, but at the instant that the wound becomes word, it simultaneously becomes available for all the varieties of linguistic transformation that Derrida and other theorists describe elsewhere. The wound itself is non-exchangeable, incommensurable, thus meaningless. The metaphor of the wound, the wound as language, is infinitely transformable, excessively meaningful. But this translation, the aboriginal carrying across, of cry into utterance, incision into writing, is never complete. Language still contains "the trace of an incision, which is at once both unique and iterable, cryptic and readable"; there is still "the date, there is the madness of 'when'" (336). Thus, the generalized "irruption" and continual variation of metaphor that Derrida wrote of in "White Mythology" here is localized at a particular moment of traumatic wounding, the date and particularity of which are then annulled as the wounded language renews its normal work of generalization and repetition. Furthermore, and finally, Derrida links this process of normalization with the working of genre. Genres, idioms, disciplines, and all customary, normative modes of utterance are made possible through "the effacement of the date" (333). Derrida cites as examples philosophy, hermeneutics, and poetics, and we could presumably add the lyric, the novel, the apocalyptic narrative, detective fiction, and the joke.

Genre, then, following this line of thinking, is a covering over of trauma, as, indeed, would be all normative symbolic use. Innovation in the use of symbols—the tic, in the context of *Motherless Brooklyn*—is the irruption of an event that cuts into customary usages. When customary usage, or genre, reasserts itself, we should not assume that the wound or incision or trauma has been healed, but rather that it has been effaced, written over. In being carried over into language, the trauma (the incision, the tic) becomes normal: no longer a singular injury that effaces language, but a repeatable word or trope whose traumatic character is blurred. Such, I would argue, is a possible reading of the ending of *Motherless Brooklyn*. Lionel has solved the mystery of Frank Minna's death and has extricated himself from the criminal underworlds he had uncovered. He now runs a *legitimate* car service, and thus is now within the law (which might indicate also being within the customary rules of language). "Bailey," his most singular and unreadable tic, is no longer a traumatic intrusion from his past as an orphaned or abandoned child, but is now just "another guy I never met."

But in reading this ending as the conclusion of a process of normalization in which metaphor and linguistic innovation are seen not as disruptive events but as positions on a cognitive-neurological spectrum, we encounter, I think, two obstacles. First, this return to the norm, or to a somewhat altered norm, is entirely a part of the hard-boiled detective genre. The detective always is forced to draw back from the labyrinthine corruptions he has unveiled. He solves a particular crime, but is powerless against the larger social networks of crime he has glimpsed. The detective replaces the veil and returns to private life. Even if he remains a detective and works on other cases, the process of unveiling and re-veiling will repeat itself. So, Lionel's retirement and withdrawal into normality—legitimacy—is a generic move, like the punch line that ends a joke. That's the first obstacle—that the normalizing gesture that ends the novel is already twice normalized, as part of the plot and as a feature of the genre, and this redundant normalizing in a novel so conscious of its generic identity should arouse some suspicion. The second obstacle to a straightforward acceptance of this ending that makes "Bailey" and all his metaphoric affiliates into just another point on a spectrum of normal language use is that Lethem has already cautioned us about generic endings. In the octopus joke, the end, the punch-line, although it is funny, doesn't matter. Frank enjoys the generic setup and the narrative variation, but has passed out by the end. Generic convention, in this case, accompanies death; and the joke, the genre, is demanded by Frank as a way of avoiding talking about his wound and the betrayal on the part of his brother who ordered his murder.

Trauma, then, begins this book; it may be that the effacement of trauma ends it. In the middle are the excessive, extravagant irruptions of ticcing metaphors. It still may well be that linguistic innovation, metaphors, figures of speech are all part of the normal functioning of mind and language. This novel illustrates the difficulty and violence—both semantic and actual—of establishing this norm.

"None Was as Strange as Care"

In Richard Powers's *The Echo Maker*, a neurologist and popular writer based clearly on Oliver Sacks is summoned to Nebraska to evaluate and, he assumes, later write about a young man suffering from Capgras Syndrome, a rare disorder in which a person becomes convinced that one or more of the people closest to him is not who he or she appears to be—is an impostor or android. The loved-one *looks like* him- or herself, but the patient *knows* that the appearance is a deception. The reference to Sacks in this text is important. The famous and eloquent neurologist is the person most responsible for bringing the ideas of modern neuroscience to wide audiences, and at the same time, Sacks is committed to a narrative understanding of neurological disorders. He has functioned, one might say, as the house theologian, the explicator of the soul, for the *New York Review of Books* and *The New Yorker*. Thus, Dr. Gerald Weber, the Sacks character, occupies a central place in Powers's defense of narrative: he is a scientist who conveys knowledge primarily through stories, but who finds his authority challenged by advances in neuroscience that he could not have imagined when he began his career as a popular writer.

The problem of Capgras, as Powers has Weber describe it, is a problem of recognition, which makes it a problem describable in neurological, narrative, and ethical terms. Can one tell the story of someone one cannot recognize? Can one care for someone one cannot recognize? What is involved, socially, subjectively, symbolically, and neurologically in recognition? Encountering another, what does one recognize? Conversely, encountering someone one knows intimately, what does one not recognize? As Powers takes pains to show, the question of recognition is inseparable from the question of misrecognition. Is there then an ethics of misrecognition? Clearly, there is a narrative mode of misrecognition; many of the central stories of many narrative traditions depend on key moments of misrecognition—in Genesis and Homer, in fairy tales, in Roman comedy and its Shakespearean adaptions. There are comedies and tragedies and tragicomedies of misrecognition.

Weber's first conversation with the neurologist treating Mark, the young man who cannot recognize his sister as his sister, sets out the terms of the debate between neuroscience and narrative. Dr. Hayes, the neurologist treating Mark, expounds an entirely neural description of the disorder, in which, as he concludes, "cortex has to defer to amygdula" (131). Weber, feeling himself "turning reactionary," suggests that "'we need to look for a more comprehensive explanation'"— to which Hayes responds with some incredulity, "'something more than neurons, you mean?'" (132). The neurologist treats neurons, and any narrative approaches to Mark's problems—Weber mentions the possibility of exploring "psychodynamic responses to trauma"—are simply outside the range of scientific clinical practice. As the novel proceeds, Weber comes increasingly to question his narrative methods as he acknowledges the enormous power and even greater promise of neuroscience's physical understanding of the brain. Weber concedes that as he was composing his colorful, anecdotal case histories, it was neuroscientists who had been making the "first real headway into the basic riddle of consciousness." Indeed, he feels that "every problem facing the species [is] awaiting the insight that neuroscience might bring. Politics, technology, sociology, art: all originated in the brain. Master the neural assemblage, and we might at long last master us" (226). Weber's doubts about his methods are exacerbated by negative reviews of his new book that accuse him of disregard for current research and of serious ethical failure—of a "sideshow exploitation" of his patients even while arguing for "tolerance for diverse mental conditions" (221).[21]

As Weber studies Mark's failures of recognition, he is increasingly unable to recognize himself. His wife's reassurances and admonitions to ignore the criticisms of his work—and to jettison the persona of "famous Gerald," the best-selling author—serve only to reinforce his sense that she does not recognize him, that they no longer recognize each other. Concurrently, other characters in the novel, particularly Karin (Mark's sister, and the main object of his misrecognitions), experience varieties of misrecognitions of themselves and others. The plot of the novel is in large part a dance of misrecognitions and revised cognitions, and readers are invited to conclude, with several of the characters, that Capgras is universal. "'No one on the planet was who you thought he was,'" observes Karin (296). Barbara, Mark's nurse whom Weber both misrecognizes and recognizes, laments that America has become "'a substitute. I mean: Is this country anyplace you recognize?'" (433). And Weber concludes, "The whole human race suffered from Capgras" (347).

At the basis of Powers's rethinking of an ethics and epistemology of narrative consistent with neuroscience is the function of mirror neurons. These are specialized brain cells, identified first in monkeys, then found in humans, which appear to facilitate both the imitation of others' actions and the ability to interpret or understand others' actions.[22] As Giacomo Rizzolati, one of the principal researchers of mirror neurons, writes, they are "a particular type of neurons that discharge when an individual performs an action, as well as when he/she observes a similar action done by another individual" (419). Powers's Gerald Weber, citing Rizzolati's work, concludes that mirror neurons provide two revelations: first, they make clear "the neurological basis of empathy," and second, they form the basis of symbol use and representation. "Images of moving muscles," Weber asserts, "made symbolic muscles move, and muscles in symbol moved muscle tissue" (355). Thus, we are meant to conclude, ethics and mimesis—recognition in all its senses—arise from the same neural systems. Intersubjectivity and genuine communication are not unattainable, utopian ideals. They are the norm. It is Cartesian or post-structuralist solipcisms that are fantasies—the thought that one is trapped in an intransitive subjectivity or an ideologically preclusive symbolic system, or, to cite the social darwinist fantasy, the thought that ethics is a thin veneer of socialization barely covering a primal barbarity. And this ethical and representational adequacy of the norm is due in large part to what have often been regarded as the inadequacies of natural language—its imprecision and availability to ambiguity, lying, and manipulation. As neuroscientist Gerald Edelman has observed, these features constitute language's strength, and are the legacy of neural systems that work through the recognition of patterns rather than through logic (90–91). Our minds are constructed to recognize, and recognition is the basis both of ethics and of art. As Weber again tries to situate his devotion to narrative in the context of a neuroscience that he feels has made him obsolete, he thinks, "lying, denying, repressing, confabulating: these weren't pathologies. They were the signature of awareness, trying to stay intact" (381). "Some part of us could model some other modeler. And out of that simple loop came all love and culture" (384).[23]

How, then, does care work in this context? What is it that we recognize or misrecognize in the object of care? Why do Weber's mirror neurons suddenly fail to fire at the sight of his wife of nearly thirty years, and then blaze into being when he is with Barbara, whom he barely knows? Why does Karin know that the devoted, saint-like Daniel does not know her, while Karsh, whom she knows as a cad, recognizes her entirely? What is recognized in recognition? In these cases, the self that recognizes its own division and alterity recognizes and can be recognized only by an other who is likewise divided and other. Care, as in Eric Santner's formulation, means care for the other who is other to himself, and so Levinas's account of the ethical relation to the other who takes on the single, impermeable face of a negative divinity must—like all mental products in the age of neuroscience—be secularized. The other is not unrecognizable; he or she is simply misrecognized, or, rather, recognized as being in a state of constant and necessary misrecognition. And here, we might add, parenthetically, that this is a point that Lacan knew, but that now, in the age of neuroscience, we really *know*.

But aside from these theoretical questions, we should note that Powers presents the care of an impaired subject in a professional, institutional setting, and this distinguishes *The Echo Maker* from its romantic, Victorian, and modernist antecedents. Though the principle caring relationship, between a sister and an impaired brother, is still familial, the novel presents relationships with two neurologists and, most important, I believe, with a nurse's assistant or care attendant, that is, with the lowest member of the professional caring hierarchy. The role of Barbara would seem to move this narrative beyond the impasse so definitively articulated in Conrad's *The Secret Agent*—that genuine care beyond the personal, familial realm would prove "difficult of application." Barbara's efforts on Mark's behalf are extraordinary and introduce the problem of the indebtedness that care implies. Karin tells her, "'I am in your debt. I'll never be able to thank you for this.'" To which Barbara replies, "'It's nothing. It's completely for me. . . . Who knows when we'll need someone looking out for us'" (243). This invocation of delayed reciprocity is a familiar formulation. It is what the peasant boy, Gerasim, tells Ivan Ilyich. But it is important and profound, for it implies a sense of shared frailty, the universal need for care that motivates, in these two fictional instances, as well as in the research of Arlie Hochschild and more recently, of Eileen Boris and Jennifer Klein, people to care for non-family members as if they were family. More specifically, this reciprocity is what motivates severely undercompensated, socially marginal workers to care for clients as if they were family members. The "social doulia" that Eva Kittay advocates finds some embodiment in these low-paid, often immigrant workers who provide care in hospitals and in home settings—with the major obstacle being that these workers find no reciprocal care or respect from the society. As Kittay insists, there can be no social care worthy of the name unless care in the form of adequate wages and social capital is also provided for the caregivers. Barbara, of course, is anomalous. She is a mystery, letting slip cultural and literary references that someone at her professional level would be unlikely to know. She has read Weber's work, for instance. As we learn, she, like Weber, experienced a radical crisis of confidence in her professional identity as a successful journalist; and through a series of accidents, she was responsible for Mark's injury. Her care for Mark is intended to pay a debt to him. Thus, while the novel introduces the question of the status of the care attendant, Barbara is not a typical example. She is a double for Weber, an instance of the internal mirroring that is so much a part of the novel's structure. The novel shows us that care *is* universal, that empathy and mimesis are parts of our neuronal nature, and that to tell someone's story is always a form of care, though it may be a distorted form—that is, a form that misrecognizes its object or that substitutes its own formulation for any actual assistance. But the question of how to move from personal, familial care to some broader, social form remains hinted but unposed.

And yet, this may, in fact, be the question Karin asks when she laments to Weber late in the novel, "'God, what is *wrong* with us? You're the expert. What *is* it in our brains that won't . . . ?'" (425). She is unable to finish the question. That won't what? That won't connect, that won't recognize, won't care? And the remedy is not the creation or rediscovery of some perfect language or a transcending leap outside of symbolization into the consciousness of the animal or angel, sacred fool or wild child. As Joseph LeDoux writes, with understatement, the evolution of language "was not a trivial process." The brain, already "fully booked," had to condense and relocate some existing functions as it expanded to allow for new ones (302–303). These changes, quite rapid in evolutionary terms, produced, in LeDoux's view, the problems of neural connection that characterize both our pathologies and our norms. Cognitive systems are not fully consonant with emotional and motivational systems. When such failure of connection occurs dramatically in an individual—in psychosis, Capgras Syndrome, or some other serious disorder—the individual is sick. When cognition, emotion, and motivation are not in accord on social and political levels, we find injustice, cruelty, war, exploitation, systems of thought that stigmatize difference—all the social failures of recognition that have so largely characterized human history.

Misrecognition, then, may be, most fundamentally, the misrecognition of desire: the misalignment of cognition with emotion and motivation. Narrative creates bridges among these areas of mental concern. Dr. Matthew O'Connor, the amateur gynecologist and psychoanalyst of Djuna Barnes's novel *Nightwood*, provides a relevant explanation of the function of narrative as necessary misrecognition.

> "Do you know what has made me the greatest liar this side of the moon, telling my stories to people like you, to take the mortal agony out of their guts, and to stop them from rolling about, and drawing up their feet, and screaming, with their eyes staring over their knuckles with misery which they are trying to keep off, saying, 'Say something, Doctor, for the love God!' And me talking away like mad. Well, that, and nothing else, has made me the liar I am." (135)

This is more or less what Weber proposes to do in his revised case study of Mark, to tell "just the story of invented shelter, the scared struggle to build a theory big enough for wetware to live in" (274). And yet this act is also one of pleasure, as O'Connor and Weber and their authors and Russian novelists and psychologists know very well. And so we see in *The Echo Maker* the rush of desire that accompanies a new encounter of recognition. What is "wrong" with us also is a function of how our sexualities are configured, through whatever constitutional and cultural means that occurs.

Traditionally—and certainly in modernist texts, following romantic and Victorian antecedents—care has been imagined as separate from sexual desire. The relation of care, particularly as it involves cognitive or linguistic impairment, is, as we have seen, typically between family members, either siblings or parents and children, often between a sister (who takes on the role of a mother) and her impaired brother—thus, in effect, doubling the incest prohibition. There is a rigorous chastity enclosing characters from Billy Budd to DeLillo's Wilder. To desire such characters or to attribute desire to them is to wound them, to hasten their dys-/disarticulation. Claggert's hidden desire for Billy leads directly to the fatal episode of Billy's stuttering. Benjy is castrated after a misattribution of sexual desire to him at a moment when he was, in fact, "trying to say." When desire does enter into a relation of care in *Nightwood*—the universal desire and care directed toward Robin—the result is a series of catastrophic psychic and social breakdowns into masochism and chaos. Countering, I would argue, early twentieth-century ideologies of degeneration and eugenics, modernist texts place the dys-/disarticulate in capsules of innocence and show them to require forms of premodern, Christian, familial care that prove ineffectual against totalizing forces of modernity. Again, Robin is fascinating in her distinction here: In *Nightwood*, innocence is itself a category of broader social degeneration.

In practical terms, this demarcation seems necessary, given the possible abuses of desire in a relationship of care. But the strict division serves also to limit the full potential range of the erotic and to foreclose areas of potential recognition in relations of care. In *The Echo Maker*, novel recognitions of changes in subjects—of Weber by Barbara or Karin by Karsh—are accompanied by disorienting jolts of desire. Those who care faithfully, unchangingly—Weber's wife, Karin's friend Daniel—misrecognize, and sexual desire is absent. Recognition of a change in subjectivity is accompanied by erotic force. This recognition is also the recognition of vulnerability, loss, and error. Karsh understands the dynamics of betrayal in ways that Daniel cannot. Barbara, in contrast to Weber's wife, understands the vertiginous crisis of facing professional failure and loss of faith in what one took to be oneself. Karin comments that "love was not the antidote to Capgras. Love was a form of it, making and denying others, at random" (268). "Of all the alien, damaged brain states this writing doctor described, none was as strange as care" (94). And yet, as Weber recognizes late in the novel, as he tries to tell and retell Mark's story and to care for him, "responsibility has no limits" (404). And what do these words mean—love, care, responsibility, desire—and how do they intersect? Our actual confusions, our ethical and cognitive failures, are played out in our vocabularies. Human being is social being, "being-with"; but everyone wants sometimes just to do what he or she wants. And to change an unjust social order whose injustices are so deeply grounded that they seem unchangable, an order in which professional care-providers are considered just above the level of slaves, would seem to require, as Herbert Marcuse wrote in 1969, some change in our instinctual gratifications!

But this might not be impossible. Marcuse held out some hope, as have writers like Jessica Benjamin and Martha Nussbaum.[24] And while the ideologists of neuroscience would like to see us locked into a closed system of consumerism and psychopharmaceuticals, the science of neuroscience seems to allow for the possibility of change. The encouraging message of contemporary neuroscience—at least, I'll take it as encouraging—is that new patterns of synaptic connection are always being formed and recognized, and that our thoughts themselves produce new patterns all down the neural pathways. In other words, we can learn, and our cultural products reshape our neural patterns and so contribute to our learning. The defenses of narrative undertaken by Powers and, in less explicit ways, by Haddon, Lethem, and others, are not really defenses against neuroscience itself, but against the ideology of neuroscience and all the related reductive, model-based ideologies of genetics, economics, and some of the other social sciences. Narrative is in accord with neuroscience not because narratives can be interpreted in terms of clearly understood brain functions (as some work in cognitive science approaches to literature would like to do), but because the way the brain works, particularly after the addition of language, and its sheer complexity result—organically, we might say—in ambiguity, indeterminacy, and the need for continual interpretation. Gerald Edelman makes this point repeatedly. "A fully reductive scientific explanation of [human] nature and its ethics and aesthetics is not desirable, likely, or forthcoming" (66). "[T]he necessary price of successful pattern recognition in creative thinking is initial degeneracy, ambiguity, and complexity" (83). And while in the sciences, we may arrive at "laws or at least strong regularities, in the case of historical analysis, qualitative judgement and interpretation are usually the most we can achieve" (84). Finally, he writes, "the ambiguity that is inherent in natural languages is not a critical weakness. . . . On the contrary, it is the basis of the rich combinatorial power that we recognize in imaginative constructions.

These properties are just what one would expect to result from the operation of a selectional [that is, one that works through complex pattern recognition] brain" (90–91).

The narrative, then, in neuroscientific terms is in fact a truer form of knowledge than the model and certainly a truer form than the ideology of neuroscience would allow. We do not *really* know anything now that we did not know before. We are creatures, let's say, endowed with/ selected for mimicry, empathy, desire, and ambiguous representation. Figures with cognitive or linguistic impairments in the age of neuroscience are not instances of radical otherness outside of social-symbolic understanding—though the *wish* that this be the case persists. Rather, these dys-/disarticulates stand at different points on a neurological spectrum and present to us social-ethical challenges to re-articulate them, to articulate and practice new forms of care. To understand these revised articulations is to recognize anew and again misrecognize the values and the scope of language.

Epilogue

"Language in Dissolution" and "A World without Words"

Two very different texts occur to me as forming the end to this book. One, Roman Jakobson's 1956 essay "Two Aspects of Language and Two Types of Aphasic Disturbances," I return to, having read it many times over the past decade. The other, David Goode's 1994 *A World without Words: The Social Construction of Children Born Deaf and Blind,* I've been reading for the first time. Jakobson's essay is a classic of rhetoric, linguistics, poetics, and literary theory that is remarkable also for its attempt to serve as an intervention into clinical practice. Goode's book consists of case studies of deaf-blind children which then serve as grounding sites for thinking about the phenomenology of human consciousness and social relations—that is, of consciousness without language and how those with language can form relationships with the non-linguistic. To read and think about these texts is to rehearse the themes and arguments of *The Disarticulate.* Taking them together, we see how figures with impaired language or cognition are placed in texts, generate speculation on impairment, on language as such, particularly on tropes, on subjectivity as linguistic or non-linguistic; we see the figures of the impaired serve also as indices pointing back toward those actual people with cognitive or linguistic impairments and so are obliged to think of the social and ethical conditions of their lives, their material and social needs, their potentials for agency, their requirements for care. As we see anew in these two final texts, scientific and clinical discussions of those I have termed dys-/disarticulate inexorably

move toward phenomenological, epistemological, and aesthetic considerations, and these, in turn, entail ethical and political questions.
Historical-ideological considerations condition all these discussions.
None of these are separable. For Jakobson, the proper understanding
of metaphor and metonymy is invaluable for the treatments of aphasias;
conversely, the consideration of aphasias leads toward a better understanding of tropes—and, specifically, of the use of tropes in a historical setting. For Goode, the ultimate or primal grounding of the human
world is located in non-linguistic consciousness, and the ultimate ethical relation is that between the speaking and the non-speaking subject.
The dys-/disarticulate is always the testing ground . . . with all the ethical problematics such a siting brings. And this appears to be regardless
of discipline: in fiction, philosophy, linguistics, sociology.

> Linguistics is concerned with language in all its aspects—language in
> operation, language in drift, language in the nascent state, and language
> in dissolution.

—Roman Jakobson, "Two Aspects of Language and Two
Types of Aphasic Disturbances"

Almost since I began writing *The Disarticulate*, Jakobson's famous
essay on figurative language and language impairment has lingered with
me. To grasp as a topic "language in dissolution" and to weld an analysis
of the greatest powers of language—metaphor and metonymy—together
with the partial and entire breakdowns of language in neurological aphasias seemed to me an awesome, inspiring endeavor. Jakobson aspired to
view the making and unmaking of language as based on the same components. Drawing on the neurology and speech pathology of his time—
largely on classic earlier work by John Hughlings-Jackson and Henry
Head, and on more recent work of Alexander Luria and Kurt Goldstein—Jakobson described two broad types of aphasia. One involved difficulty in selecting words or substituting one word for another. Patients
with this sort of aphasia could respond to contextual cues and complete
sentences that had been begun for them, but could not find the words to
begin their own. Jakobson called this a "similarity disorder." Conversely,
other patients could generate words, but lacked grammatical ability to

form them into sentences. They suffered from a "contiguity disorder," which led to the "degeneration of the sentence into a mere 'word heap,'" in Hughlings-Jackson's term (106). Jakobson's originality lay in connecting these two sorts of aphasia with two ancient terms of rhetoric and poetics: metaphor and metonym. Metaphor, as he described it, is the identification of similarities, and the selection of a proper term based on some similarity. Metonym is an expression of spatial or logical relation. Therefore, the "similarity disorder" entails a disabling of the metaphorical capacity of language while the "contiguity disorder" is a disabling of the metonymic. In Jakobson's argument, impairments of speech can now be understood in relation to the foundational components of language, and so linguistics—"the science of language"—can take its rightful place among the biological sciences and no longer be "passed over in silence, as if disorders in speech perception had nothing whatever to do with language" (96).

But the essay now becomes more puzzling. Having made this strong analogy between tropes and language disorders and stated his intention that his argument be received as an intervention into clinical discourses, Jakobson shifts the essay toward literary analysis. Different types of aphasia (similarity and contiguity) correspond to different basic tropes (metaphor and metonym). And these different tropes then correspond to different literary periods and genres. Metaphor characterizes romanticism and symbolism and, more generally, poetry; metonym characterizes literary realism and prose narrative. Modern literary theory as Jakobson saw it in 1956 neglected prose, metonym, and realism in favor of a focus on poetry, romanticism/symbolism, and metaphor. Thus, somehow, in the conditions of modernity, a language of plenitude that would employ both metaphor and metonym had become split and fallen. "The actual bipolarity [of language] has been artificially replaced . . . by an amputated, unipolar scheme" (114), which, as I take it, constitutes modernism—a dys-/disarticulated, "amputated," "word heap" that suffers, like an aphasic subject, from a contiguity disorder. Part of the amputation involves loss of the referent, which is the domain of "pragmatical prose." Poetry, on the other hand "is focused upon the sign" and so is deemed by modernists as the sole proprietor of all "tropes and figures" (114), which now must be regarded as empty of reference or context.

And what is this referent amputated from "pragmatical prose" in order to render the impeded symbolisms and metaphors of poetry? Jakobson cites instances from Tolstoy: Anna Karenina's handbag and Princess Bolonskaya's "hair on the upper lip" (111). Jakobson terms these typically realistic details synechdoches, that is, partaking of the contiguous logic of metonymy. In other words, for Jakobson, in presenting this image or shorthand for a character, one as good as names the character. But this seems inadequate. Synechdoche is generally a rather mechanical trope—the throne, the crown, what-have-you. These "parts" do not stand for the "whole" of these women. Rather, they evoke them emotionally; the flaw stands both for a physical and spiritual beauty, and for an emotional relation entered into both by other characters and by the reader. This seems to lie more in the realm of Barthes's "reality effect"—an idea developed a decade later. Like Barthes, Jakobson insists that the representation of reality is tropic. But Barthes seems to me more on the mark in arguing that these reality bytes are inserted into narrative, are actually non-contiguous, are, in fact, closer to metaphor. But—here we are again, as we began this book—metaphors for *what*? And what actually is the work of metaphor? Jakobson, we recall, proposes two functions. Metaphor indicates similarity and metaphor selects the correct term—presumably to indicate similarity. But both these tasks—and metonym as well—rely on the fact of representation per se. Whether there is a referent or not, or grammar or not, is not ultimately the issue. The trope brings not-language into language. That is the "reality effect," or metonym; and that is the language game of symbolism or romanticism—the work of metaphor, in Jakobson's terms. Both metaphor and metonym, then, work through catachresis—language that creates a reality that had not been there previously.

I can say then, that in reading Jakobson's "Two Aspects of Language," I'm all turned around. I'm troped. What does this essay stand for? What turn does it point toward? The gesture toward clinical aphasias is a pretext, perhaps a prosthetic. The real issue is "the bipolar structure of langauge," and this dichotomy, Jakobson tells us, derives from Saussure. Metaphor is the synchronic, systemic character of language. Metonymy is the diachronic, which is the contamination or the other of system, that which moves through historical time. Jaksobson's real plea is to bring time and history back into language—to rearticulate the dys-/disarticulated,the diachronic, the "reality effect," the Lacanian real, the traumatic, the other. Jakobson, in 1956, reiterates the linguistic tensions of modernism and anticipates the sublimes of contemporary neuroscience. And yet the essay has a fairy-tale quality to it as well. The development of language and the breakdown of language, for Jakobson, turn out to be exact reflections of each other. We come into language and out from language along the same route. But this is not true, as cognitive linguist Sheila Blumstein informed me. An adult with damage to language areas of the brain does not speak like a small child.[1] At the same time, work that has been important to me in this project has drawn similar implications. For Kristeva, Blasing, and Heller-Roazen, language sends its roots deeply into material, non-semantic grounds toward which the semantic may return again. All my historical and philosophical arguments about the dys-/disarticulate locate this figure on the boundary between meaning and non-meaning and contend that this site is central to our most enduring cultural fascinations. Jakobson's essay continues to fascinate me because it is there, too. It has no clinical value. Its arguments on metaphor and metonymy seem to me wrong turns. Ultimately, I take the essay to hinge on a critique of modernist aesthetics as a disabling of grammar and meaning.

"Two Aspects of Language" ends with the utopian sense that our modernist, metaphorical, dys-/disarticulated language can be reintegrated and healed. Language itself is the dys-/disarticulate for Jakobson—"language in dissolution." It is a new trope, unnamed by Jakobson: the part that stands for, or beside, what is missing, or what has been excluded. But how do we apprehend this missing part? Not on the basis of what we see or what we speak. We require a meta-statement, non-tropic, to show us both sides of the exclusion—something stationary, felt to be stationary, beyond the orbits in question. That would be the Jakobson text. I feel an odd combination of comfort and unsettlement each time I return to Jakobson's essay. What he does overlaps so powerfully with much of what I've tried to do. And so I return to it, feel uncomfortable with it, feel deeply how wrong it is, and return to it.

But my speculations on Jakobson should not have the last word. Instead, I'm turning to a book I should have discovered long ago, sociologist David Goode's case studies and accompanying and subsequent thinking about children who survived pre-natal rubella infections and were born deaf and blind. These children did not acquire language, and Goode's concern is with investigating how their families or institutions, and then he himself, develop non-linguistic relationships with them. Goode's findings and his argument, in the simplest terms, is that such relations are both quite possible and indispensible. Goode describes the profound experience of simply being with these children—playing with them, holding them, rocking them, guiding them and being guided by them, coming to know what they like and recognize their wishes, to regard them as conscious agents.

Goode contests the notion that human consciousness, subjectivity, and agency reside exclusively in language abilities and that people without language are not fully human. Linguistic and non-linguistic modes of apprehension, expression, and communication are different, but there are nevertheless baseline conditions of humanity that are deeper and more primary than language. The body, Goode argues, possesses a "lexicon" of expression, and one can interpret feeling and intention through its movements and responses. Through shared physical, proprioceptive responses and actions, we create a world or lived environment—an *umwelt*, as Goode puts it, employing a term put in use by the biologist Jakob von Uexküll. This world, created and experienced through the body, is mutual and social. It has the qualities of something primal, for there is nothing more deeply human than this social world of bodies. But it is, Goode insists, not primal in a mystical, archaic sense. It comes into being only in particular social settings and interactions. People together bring the *umwelt* into being through "joint projects in the world of daily life" (116), and these projects "take on concrete meaning through their essentially situated emergence" (107).

Goode wants to stress the ordinariness of these relationships between the speaking and non-speaking. The children he writes about have not been abused and damged, as in the cases of Kaspar Hauser or "Genie," the subject of Russ Rymer's fascinating and horrifying book. Though Goode draws on the thinking of Merleau-Ponty in his depictions of non-linguistic, bodily experience, and though his work has much in common with that of Oliver Sacks (with whom he corresponded and spoke when working on this book), his subjects are not exotic primal beings, wild children, sacred fools, or idiot savants. They are children, and the expressive bodily capacities they possess are held by all of us. This seems true to me, even obvious. The lived environment I created with my sisters certainly was based largely around physical activities and bodily contact. And my relationship with my daughters, who are now five years old, still is very corporeal. The body of Daddy—hanging on it, climbing it, tackling it, sitting on it, and hugging it—is a great focus of attention; and I return the attention in hugging, lifting, tickling, tossing in the air their little bodies. And, we should add, even among adults—in games and sports, in friendship, in lovemaking—our shared world is one of bodily gestures, intentions, touches, and responses. Still, if we accept the point that our bodies are central, even primary, in creating a human world, and that social relations, subjectivity, and agency are possible for subjects lacking language, we still must acknowledge that the human world or *umwelt* is also symbolic. For human beings, the primal, corporeal environment takes form in the equally shared and created world of symbols, culture, language, and history. And Goode, as I said, makes clear that the formation of the corporeal world is an "essentially situated emergence"—situated, that is, in a social-symbolic world. While there is no meta-text for considering the relations with the non-speaking about whom he writes, and while "the answers to our most important questions are found in the conversations with our bodies, and not in any text" (115), the answers to our *next* most important questions, we might say, *are* textual.

That translation, that carrying-across, from what we imagine to be the primary, not-linguistic, *most* important level of being into the symbolically apprehensible, historical *next* most important level—but the only level through which we can discuss any of this—constitutes the work of this book. "Translation," of course, is a mistranslation of "metaphor," which is a cousin of "metamorphosis," which returns us to the body. William Carlos Williams called for a poetry that would take its place in the world just like a physical object—just as tangible and uninterpretable. This was Keats's game with his spectral hand: "Look, I hold it toward you"; and it was Whitman's in "Crossing Brooklyn Ferry": "Who knows but I am as good as looking at you now, for all you cannot see me?" The symbolic is our lived world, with the continual sensation of echoing some lost world. It is sleight-of-hand, uncanny, but also ordinary—"something understood," as George Herbert said of prayer. It is always crossing and recrossing, never getting it right. And there at the crossing—in our oldest myths and in modern science, philosophy, fiction, and politics—serving both as boatman and judge, resides the dys-/disarticulate.

NOTES

NOTES TO CHAPTER 1

1. This material on Sinai, revelation, and Philo of Alexandria is indebted to Steven D. Fraade's "Hearing and Seeing at Sinai: Interpretive Trajectories."

2. I refer here to Martha Nussbaum's defense of compassion in *Upheavals of Thought*.

3. See my *After the End* for a discussion of the relations of revelation, apocalypse, historical and social trauma, and the sense of post-apocalypse—of living after some definitive ending.

4. See Svitlana Kobets for an account of both Russian and western European traditions of the sacred fool.

5. Scholars in cognitive science have worked with great ingenuity to link the study of literature to new understandings derived from neuroscience. I will discuss some of these efforts in chapter 4. At present, let me say that I find efforts to historicize neurology, as in Mary Crane's *Shakespeare's Brain* and Lisa Zunshine's *Why We Read Fiction*, more compelling than work that makes broader claims. Crane examines how the psychological portrayals in Shakespeare's plays are grounded in contemporaneous views in natural philosophy of how thinking and emotion work. Zunshine describes how narrative at different historical moments is able to portray different degrees of what she calls "mind reading," the ability to engage in processes like "I know that you think that Jane noticed Joe's expression of anger, but I think that Jane knows that Joe is not angry, and he knows she is observing him and may intend to mislead her." This process of mind-reading is different in Homer than in Jane Austen or in Virginia Woolf, and so we must look not just at brain functions but at histories of genre and of science in order to analyze it scrupulously.

6. See Avital Ronell's magnificent rhapsody on the cultural place of stupidity, a book so rich it would require a far longer book than this to explicate it, and to which I cannot possibly do justice here. In one of her formulations, Ronnell writes, "stupidity does not allow itself to be opposed to knowledge in any simple way, nor is it the other of thought. It does not stand in the way of wisdom, for the disguise of the wise is to avow unknowing. At this time I can say only that

the question of stupidity is not satisfied with the discovery of the negative limit of knowledge; it consists, rather, in the absence of a relation to knowing" (5).

7. Joanna Klink's gorgeous and important volume of poems, *Circadian*, provides something like a Rilkean sense of a poesis that emerges through the friction between a linguistically structured consciousness and a material alterity:

> To be outside the classifiable world,
> and having lost track, and having heard
> no message. As when a single existence
> vanishes and the flute does not warp,
> or sounds like the inside of a shell,
> and the word for shell means
> too many things. ("And Having Lost Track")

8. Cf. David Mitchell and Sharon Snyder's concept of the "material metaphor." For Mitchell and Snyder, the use of the disabled body in literary narrative is a way to provide for narrative "the one thing it cannot possess—an anchor in materiality" (63), and what Mitchell and Snyder see as the pervasive use of disabled figures as metaphors constitutes a narrative prosthesis, "a crutch upon which literary narratives lean for their representational power, disruptive potentiality, and analytical insight" (49). My thinking on catachresis engages more with the tropic character of language. All language, I will argue, is a carrying-across, a *meta-pherein*, from the non-linguistic, and it is the figure with a specifically linguistic impairment—not the disabled body per se—that most fully stands in for this process, which is both entirely ordinary and utterly problematic. Further, my argument is not as politically judgmental with regard to how tropes of impaired figures are employed. As I will discuss later in this chapter and in more detail in chapter 4, there is in Mitchell and Snyder, and in other writers in disability studies, an incipient iconoclasm, a resistence to all metaphoric usages, that poses significant theoretical difficulties.

9. In his playful and illuminating essay "What Are the Signs of What?" Kenneth Burke takes this thesis to its logical, or paradoxical, conclusion, demonstrating how words become condensations of social attitudes and things, their referents "material exemplars of the values which the tribal idiom has placed upon them" (361). Thus, Burke concludes, "in this sense, things would be the signs for words" (379). And so, in this same sense, the entire world would be a "material metaphor" in the way Mitchell and Snyder intend for disability.

10. Gayatri Spivak describes a shift away from politics over the course of McCullers's career (131), but we see the shift quite clearly within this book.

11. Antonopoulos is the most thoroughly dys-/disarticulated character in the novel. He is dys-/disarticulated even from McCullers's text and imagination, for he is the end-point of fantasy from whom no further fantasies of community are generated. He is structurally important, as my argument observes, in playing for Singer the role that Singer performs for the other characters. But Antonopoulos, unlike Singer or the others, is portrayed stigmatically, with an extravagant

overlay of grotesque and abject detail. He is, for McCullers, an idiot in the classical sense of complete self-enclosure. Existing primarily in relation to his own stomach and genitals, Antonapoulos, we might say, is not so much incapable of language as he is rejecting language and the social relations it entails. The degree of his mental impairment is unclear. What is certain is that he is self-sufficient in spite of all humiliation and pain, even to the point of death. And so he is radically unlike the other characters, all of whom strive for social connection even if they cannot achieve it. At the same time, the stigmatic and grotesque qualities seen in Antonopoulos seem to be functions of his cognitive impairments. See Heidi Krumland on Antonopoulos's status as a cognitively impaired person. Krumland argues convincingly that "representing a cognitively impaired man realistically was a challenge that McCullers could not meet due to the typical preconceptions about cognitive impairment in her time" (40).

12. There is a third site of textual instability in *The Heart is a Lonely Hunter*, namely gender and sexuality, and important readings of the past twenty years have identified the chief exclusion in this and other of McCullers's works as any non-normative sexuality. The universal social isolation in *Heart* is a function of a "compulsory heterosexuality," to use a term inaugurated by Adrienne Rich, and the text's unspeakabilities and grotesque protuberances are blossoming zones of queerness of all sorts. I am convinced by the arguments of Rachel Adams and Sarah Gleeson-White, among others, that a heteronormative consciousness and unconscious is crucial to *Heart*, but I would not want the sexual readings to replace social, political, and linguistic concerns that seem at least equally necessary to textual and historical understanding of the novel.

13. As Sedgewick writes, "There is a *homosexual* in this text—a homosexual person, presented as different in his essential nature from the normal men around him. That person is John Claggart. At the same time, *every* impulse of *every* person in this book that could at all be called desire could be called homosexual desire. . . . The intimate strangleholds of interrepresentation between that exemplar of a new species, the homosexual man, and his thereby radically reorganized surround of male erotic relations seem to make it irresistible to bring to *Billy Budd* all *our* intimate, paralyzing questions about the essential truths of 'homosexuality'" (92, italics in original). It is becoming notable that several of the texts I discuss as significant instances of dys-/disarticulation are also exemplary texts for queer theory—that the queer is disarticulated and the dys-/disarticulated is queer. We will see this again in chapter 2 with regard to *Nightwood*. Desire for the queer or dys-/dysarticulated figure in these texts is also a utopian desire for freedom from social normativities. But insofar as the queer remains dys-/disarticulated, any sexual component of love must be transformed into *caritas*, or brotherly love, or care, and lose the destabilizing force of sex. The dys-/dysarticulated figure—that is, the one with a clear impairment or disability—initiates a rethinking of care; but this ethical reconceptualizing comes at the cost of a denial of sexual and gender identities and desire. It is important,

then, that our thinking of dys-/disarticulation remain close to gender and queer theories. Robert McRuer attempts to work through some of these linkages in his book *Crip Theory*. See chapter 4 for a discussion of McRuer.

14. Marcel Wingate points out that by the mid- to late nineteenth century, stuttering was attracting significant scientific and medical study, with attention given to physiological, cognitive, and emotional factors. Melville, ignoring contemporaneous scientific thinking, refigures stuttering in a more traditional, religious sense as failed prophetic utterance.

NOTES TO CHAPTER 2

1. See also Harpham's *Language Alone* for a discussion of the modern notion of language as a closed system as constituting a kind of "critical fetish" which has "served as a proxy for other issues that resist resolution on their own terms" (65).

2. Michael Hardt and Antonio Negri make an important case for the political potentials of a multitude in pursuit of redefining what might be held in common. In arguing against the actuality of modern totalization, Hardt and Negri observe that freedom and resistance to power is, in reality, "prior to the exercise of power," and that the political, and anti-modern, resistances to capitalism on the part of subaltern or proletarian populations is not the search for a utopian or inconceivable outside to totalization, but is, rather, in the service of an already existing freedom. "In this context," they write, "the dream of an outside, an external standpoint or support for resistance, is both futile and disempowering" (82). Moreover, they continue, arguing against the closed "dialectic of enlightenment" scenario described by Horkheimer and Adorno, we need to recognize "how the positive, productive monsters of antimodernity, the monsters of liberation, always exceed the domination of modernity and point toward an alternative" (97). The key to their argument is the position that within the "monsters," the Calibans of the antimodern, lies the possibility of an emerging "altermodern"—not the radical alterity suggested in the modernist dys-/disarticulate—but a genuine, liberatory political power opposing modern forms of economic and ideological domination but sharing the same world with them; indeed, basing its politics precisely on the sharing of the world. "And yet within the traditions of antimodernity there always lives the possible emergence of altermodern forces and forms, especially, as we have seen, whenever the common appears as the basis and goal of strugles—not only the common as a result such as networks of social relations or forms of life" (117).

3. Bakhtin wrote explicitly against Saussure's view of language as system, arguing that a synchronic notion of language "does not correspond to any real moment in a historical process." The system "is merely an abstraction" (32). Rather, "the word is born in a dialogue as a living rejoinder within it; the word is shaped in dialogic interaction with an alien word that is already in the object" (76).

4. See also the important and challenging work of Gilles Deleuze and Felix Guattari and of Anthony Wilden. I read (as well as I can) the complex arguments

of *A Thousand Plateaus* and *System and Structure* as utopian interventions that propose ways out of totalizing ideologies. These texts seek to be both descriptive and prescriptive, showing how language actually works (as open even when it seems closed) and urging that this insight be put to use. Thus, Deleuze and Guattari critique existing forms of knowledge as "arbolescent," that is, presuming an organic structure of roots, trunk, branches, leaves, etc., which presupposes clear origins, hierarchies, and ends. They propose instead the rhizome, which "ceaselessly establishes connections between semiotic chains . . . like a tuber agglomerating very diverse acts, not only linguistic, but also perceptive, mimetic, and cognitive: there is no language in itself, nor are there any linguistic universals, only a throng of dialects, patois, slangs, and specialized languages." And "there is no mother tongue, only a power takeover by a dominant language within a political multiplicity" (7). Wilden, in a unique melding of systems theory, psychoanalysis, and post-structuralism, seeks to undermine the foundation of all forms of symbolic closure, and to explore how all significant forms of symbolic activity are open, that is, continually in a relation with an outside.

5. For historical accounts of the movements in the United States and United Kingdom in the early twentieth century to classify and institutionalize people having (or assumed to have) cognitive impairments, see Snyder and Mitchell's *Cultural Locations of Disability*, Soloway's *Demography and Degeneration*, Thomson on *The Problem of Mental Deficiency*, and various works by Noll and Trent, including their co-edited volume on *Mental Retardation in America*. See also Mark Jackson regarding the intersections of scientific and social thought concerning the "feeble- minded" in early twentieth-century England.

6. In early editions of *Criminal Man*, "atavism" was the chief term defining criminality. The criminal was "a relic of a vanished race" (135). Later, and in response to criticisms of this concept, Lombroso introduced degeneration as a second or parallel cause of criminality. In practice, it is often difficult to disentangle Lombroso's uses of the two terms. In either case, the criminal represents a lower place on a racially determined evolutionary ladder. Whether the criminal, or his parents or his "race," never evolved further, or evolved further but then degenerated is ultimately inconsequential.

7. It surprised me to learn that the term "moral idiocy" is still in common use, notably in political polemics. Cf. "Israel, Hamas, and Moral Idiocy" by Alan Dershowitz (*Christian Science Monitor*, Dec. 8, 2008); "Epidemiology Meets Moral Idiocy" by Christopher Hitchens (*Slate.com*, Oct. 16, 2006); "Sen. Robert Byrd's Moral Idiocy: Dog-Fighting, No!; Murder of the Unborn by Abortion, Yes!" (*TheAmericanView.com*, undated); "End the Moral Idiocy on Kashmir" (*AndrewBoston.org/blog/*, July 10, 2008). These odd usages seem to combine the archaic early twentieth-century medical sense of "idiot"with the more casual contemporary senses of a generally unintelligent or willfully ignorant person in order to make ad hominem arguments implying that one's adversary is

incapable of understanding rational or ethical truths. To use this term at all, with its extensive pseudo-scientific legacy, is to abdicate argument oneself.

8. Thus, from *Gatsby*:

> "Civilization's going to pieces," broke out Tom violently. "I've gotten to be a terrible pessimist about things. Have you read 'The Rise of the Colored Empires' by this man Goddard?"
>
> "Why, no," I answered, rather surprised by his tone.
>
> "Well, it's a fine book, and everybody ought to read it. The idea is if we don't look out the white race will be—will be utterly submerged. It's all scientific stuff; it's been proved."
>
> "Tom's getting very profound," said Daisy, with an expression of unthoughtful sadness. "He reads deep books with long words in them. What was that word we——"
>
> "Well, these books are all scientific," insisted Tom, glancing at her impatiently. "This fellow has worked out the whole thing. It's up to us, who are the dominant race, to watch out or these other races will have control of things."
>
> "We've got to beat them down," whispered Daisy, winking ferociously toward the fervent sun. (17)

9. "Juke" and "Kallikak" were pseudonyms for two families studied by late-nineteenth- and early twentieth-century sociologists to demonstrate the genetic transmission of criminality and low intelligence. Richard Dugdale published his study of the Jukes in 1877. Henry H. Goddard published his study of the Kallikaks in 1912.

10. Robert Baker's thinking on the "extravagant," the excessive wandering of modernist style, is the most thorough and innovative recent exploration of the relations between modernism and a perceived totalizing modernity. For Baker, literary and philosophical modernisms represent apocalyptic gestures trying to break outside "the conventional boundaries of experience established by the dominant social, scientific, and philosophical frameworks of capitalist modernity" (2). In response to modern pressures of instrumentalization, modernist literature aims toward "linguistic phosphorescence, the transformation of words into prisms that, appearing to take on something of the reified quality of the world around them, cut through the flattening of language endemic to modern societies, words made into things thus becoming words that move like currents again" (31). See also Astradur Eysteinsson who, drawing heavily on Adorno, describes very well the negative and critical energies of modernism, how its irrationality is the repressed other of capitalist/bureaucratic rationality (42).

11. Irving Howe and Thomas Mann both note the importance of Dostoevski in the conception of Stevie. He is the "literary cousin" of Myshkin, writes Howe; and for Mann, "without Dostoevski's *Idiot*, Stevie is unthinkable" (q. in McDonagh 311).

12. See Rod Edmond for an excellent discussion of Conrad's use of Lombroso's ideas. As Edmond notes, at the turn of the century, "biological themes of decline were becoming the dominant form of social critique, and the body was increasingly

used as a source of knowledge about society, rather than as simply a rhetorical figure for it" (44). Conrad, however, "simultaneously employs and satirizes such modes of description and their cultural and ideological assumptions" (48).

13. William Greenslade points out that by the 1890s, Lombroso was already losing favor among experts and academics, though his views retained considerable popular appeal (95). More broadly, the notion of degeneration, though its "diagnostic value . . . was shrinking in the eyes of the specialists, stubbornly refused to surrender its value as a generaizing shorthand currency" (128).

14. See Martin Halliwell and Patrick McDonagh for illuminating accounts of Stevie's antagonistic relations with the social order and the role of biologistic social theory in *The Secret Agent*.

15. Conrad may have been drawing on Lombroso's surprisingly sympathetic views on anarchists. Unlike other criminals, anarchists were not characterized by atavism or degeneration. Rather, they manifested honesty, altruism, and an "absence of misoneism," or fear of the new (313). Anarchists' views, Lombroso wrote, are "not so absurd as they are supposed to be" although their methods are "both absurd and dangerous." Moreover, those anarchists who were genuine idealists needed to recruit followers "from among ordinary criminals, lunatics, and insane criminals" in order to carry out their actions (305). The best way to combat anarchism, in Lombroso's view, was through political-social reform and creation of ways "to voice the grievances of the people" so that "just causes would not be abandoned exclusively to the advocacy of extremists" (306). Conrad, of course, was in no way as optimistic as the liberal Lombroso. But even as his narrative mocks the anarchists as absurd individuals and ineffectual political actors, their goals and ideals remain intact, as they do in Lombroso's analysis.

16. Aaron Fogel's critique of sympathy in *The Secret Agent* is a useful counterpoint to my argument. The problems with sympathy, pity, and compassion, for Fogel, are not merely practical—i.e., entailing "difficulty of application on a large scale." Rather, he writes, "sympathy cannot be the ground of community—not because it is too weak but because it is in essence a form of isolationist activity, mental disconnection. . . . The more intense it is, the more it explodes and divides . . . and actually bars connection by virtue of its intense and satisfying emotion" (162). Fogel points, rightly, to the violence of Stevie's responses to injustice and to the hollowness of the emotion of pity. Of the "Great Lady," Conrad writes, "she had a great capacity of pity for the more obvious forms of human miseries, precisely because she was such a complete stranger to them" (*Secret Agent* 97–98). But it is a mistake, first, to conflate, as Fogel does, the terms "compassion," "sympathy," and "pity." Pity may be regarded as an "isolationist activity," but this cannot be said of compassion, sympathy, or, as I have used it, empathy. As I have tried to argue, these emotions have experiential and even cognitive contents. One knows what one feels, knows that others feel similarly, and then thinks toward an ethical response. For an extended discussion of the moral emotions and their cognitive contents, see Martha Nussbaum's *Upheavals of Thought*.

17. See Janice Brockley, Penny Richards, and Leila Zenderland for accounts of the transition from religious and sentimental to scientific representations of cognitively impaired characters in American fiction. Richards notes that in the early nineteenth century, having a retarded child was not considered shameful, and mildly retarded children attended school along with other children. Popular fiction of the time often stressed the purifying spiritual influence of cognitively impaired family members (67–8), and, as Brockley observes, tales of parental devotion to their impaired children were common (136). Later in the century, stories portraying the cognitively impaired offspring as evidence of sin or divine judgement become more prevalent: "cursed with this living death," wrote a mother in 1873 (q. in Richards 75). Or the sentimental and judgemental views appeared together. As Edward Johnson, superintendent of the Training School for Feebleminded Girls and Boys in Vineland, NJ, wrote in 1906, "When the heart-broken parent asks why this affliction is placed upon him, let him realize that God makes no mistakes, and these children may be the means of uplifting the world" (q. in Zenderland 167). See also Klages, Patrick McDonagh, and James Trent for more thorough descriptions of nineteenth-century thinking about cognitive impairment.

18. In 1927, in the case of *Buck v. Bell*, the U.S. Supreme Court upheld a Virginia law permitting the sterilization of certain people with cognitive impairments. Indiana was the first state to pass sterilization legislation, and by 1926, twenty-three states had such laws covering both the insane and the feebleminded. Stanley Powell Davies points out that these laws were highly controversial and that in *Buck v. Bell*, the Supreme Court went against precedent. Before that decision, state and appeals courts had generally overturned state sterilization laws on constitutional grounds (Davies 99–110).

19. Eugenic panic and policy initiatives did not, of course, disappear in the United States. In 1934, Leon Whitney, executive secretary of the American Eugenics Society, wrote, "Many far-sighted men and women in both England and America have been working earnestly towards something very like what Hitler has now made compulsory . . . a constructive agency in the betterment of race" (q. in Noll 72).

20. See Gould regarding the connection between Goddard's and Yerkes's research by means of intelligence tests and immigration law (187, 261–62, 301).

21. See also Gerald Schmidt for an account of Faulkner's emphasis on heredity and genealogy. Schmidt aligns *The Sound and the Fury* with naturalist works like Norris's *McTeague* in showing an inescapability of hereditary precedents. The connection with literary naturalism's sense of determining hereditary forces is useful and interesting, but we must also recognize Faulkner's different uses of family history. For Faulkner, the decline of the Compson family is not primarily because of forces of nature or of social forces analogous to natural forces. Rather, historical change affects families, and individual character is shaped in relation to historical circumstance. The gothic-naturalist portrayal of hereditary degeneration is sensational but a diversion from the real problem.

22. All references to the appendix, introduction, and other documents pertaining to *The Sound and the Fury* are to the Norton edition of the novel.

23. Stacy Burton has written cogently on the dialogical relation between Benjy and Caddy. "Only Caddy," writes Burton, "speaks, listens, and responds to Benjy as though he has the capability to engage in verbal dialogue; she alone involves herself with him in a way that suggests his discourse and history matter" (219). Against the numerous readings of Benjy as entirely outside of social and symbolic contact, Burton argues that he too "is a character struggling to order and express his experience in the world" (215).

24. The third-person narrative, John Matthews writes, "explores the resources of conventional narrative discourse only to learn that they can compose no more authoritative telling of the story than the inside accounts that have gone before" (390).

25. David Minter suggests this relation of narrative to care when he observes, "in Benjy's need for tenderness we see something of the emotional confluence which precipitated the writing of *The Sound and the Fury*" (351).

26. This opposition between loss and absence refers, of course, to Dominick LaCapra's important critique of certain post-structuralist discourses for their eliding historical events with structural conditions so as to negate history's actual temporal and consequential working. See also Judith Butler's discussion of historical versus structural trauma in *Bodies That Matter* and my discussion of trauma as symptom-producing event in *After the End* (chapters 2 and 3).

27. Faulkner's again misleading and, in this case, romanticizing comment regarding Dilsey in the appendix is "They endured" (215).

28. For different views regarding the presence of fascism, sexuality, and Jewishness in *Nightwood*, see Jane Marcus, Licia Carlston, and Maren Tova Linett.

29. This is exactly the point of Carrie Rohman's insightful and well-argued essay, though its conclusions are, I believe, mistaken. Thus, while it is true that Robin "ultimately transgresses the symbolic as a limit upon her phenomenality" and that this then "troubles the very terms of human subjectivity" (58), I am not convinced that the novel celebrates this "privileging of being as nonidentity, as something therefore beyond humanism" (62). Robin certainly represents a liberation from the social-symbolic, but the political valences of her posthuman destination seem to me highly uncertain and not necessarily to be celebrated.

30. The passage continues: "(take away a man's conformity and you take away his remedy) who had to lie on his back in a box, but the box was lined with velvet, his fingers jewelled with stones, and suspended over him where he could never take his eyes off, a sky-blue mounted mirror, for he wanted to enjoy his own 'difference.' Robin is not in your life, you are in her dream, you'll never get out of it" (146).

31. Another analogy here, yes; but I would argue that the hypothetical "as if" clause refers to her appearance, the "sort of blue fluid under her skin," and that the second clause about the absence of "all transactions with knowledge" extends the analogy into an absolute claim, having nothing to do with either Robin's skin or the hide of time.

32. Habermas argues for an intersubjective, communicative form of reason (that is, not subjective and Cartesian) in which the "critique of Western 'logocentrism' . . . is diagnosed not as an excess but as a deficit of rationality" (310).

NOTES TO CHAPTER 3

1. The original language, in this account, was Hebrew, the only language that could "fully express the purpose of the heart" (Zohar 256). Umberto Eco glosses this commentary as meaning that language before the fall of the tower was what we might call an effective language, for it "not only 'said' but 'did'" and was able to activate supernatural forces (123).

2. Modernism—a set of aesthetic and philosophical responses to the technological, administrative, economic, quantifying, rationalizing conditions of modernity—is apocalyptic. The post-modern is post-apocalyptic. The definitive catastrophe has already taken place. Not only is the world broken—as imagined also in modernism—but the narrative links to the time before the catastrophe have been broken as well. Nor is any greater, possibly redemptive but at any rate conclusive, catastrophe to be anticipated. It's over, and we are where we are: depthless, unredeemed, without origin, demystified, post-historical, post-human. As an imaginative vision, this can be a source of deep, though ambivalent, misgiving, as in Fredric Jameson or Jean Baudrillard; or for ambivalent celebration, as in Jean-François Lytotard; or for more hopeful, liberatory appraisals, as in Donna Haraway or N. Katherine Hayles. See my *After the End* for a discussion of the apocalyptic/post-apocalyptic postures of post-modern and post-structuralist texts. All this, one might say, is fantasy, a poetry of theory, and a complex obverse of the modernist fantasies of a totalizing, rationalized, administered society. But fantasy has its corollary in fact, and the theoretical-poetical shoe often animates the empirical foot. Over the past century, we have seen both the state and corporate capital engage more and more deeply into aspects of life from the personal and domestic to the economic-political and the biological. We have also seen resistance to this political-economic order grow weaker and apparently emptier of political meaning. So, how could we not also encounter fantasies—theoretical and fictional—of surveillance, the eradication of subjectivity, the end of history, and various ecstatic ways out of these dilemmas? I say this with two caveats. First, the weakening of *grands recits* of liberation has been accompanied by new, more local liberatory narratives involving race, gender, sexual orientation. Second, social scientists like David Harvey and Saskia Sassen have provided enormously revealing accounts of the economics, geographies, and demographics of contemporary global capital—accounts whose ideological-political stances are clear, but in which ideological fantasy is minimal.

3. The end of the cold war helped make audible a number of discourses which had largely been drowned out in the militarism and vigorous denials of history of the Reaganist 1980s: the possibilities of genuine peacetime economies, disarmament, serious approaches to world poverty, a proliferation of political

visions released by the end of the political need for an anti-communist hegemony. There was also, of course, a renewed and newly triumphal discourse
of unchecked global capitalism that looked to the former Soviet bloc and the
developing world as places where goods could be produced more cheaply for
the American and European markets. This discourse of "free trade" served as
a euphemism for the search for cheap labor and the absence of environmental
standards. But by the mid-1990s, significant social movements were organizing
industrial and agricultural workers, students, and environmentalists to protect
political freedoms, national sovereignty, and labor and environmental regulations and to oppose the efforts of corporations and their allies in government to
impose on the entire world a new gilded age of outlaw capitalism. The destruction of the World Trade Center stifled much of this multiplicity of voices, as the
Bush administration and the corporate powers it represented used this traumatic event to help establish in the world "a unity with one single faith" which
would be articulated in a single language of "homeland security." These powers
are engaged, I would argue, in rolling back the dividedness, multiplicity, and
ambiguity that, according to my midrash, God authorized when the Tower of
Babel fell. Undivided absolutes of Good and Evil, which were exposed as politically untenable, if not ridiculous, as the cold war was ending were welcomed
back by the Bush administration with relief and delight. Every sign sought out
its proper referent and clung to it the way that Charlton Heston threatened to
hold onto his gun—never to be removed except from his cold, dead hand. This
is, of course, the characteristic post-apocalyptic symptomatic response: The
world of semantic and moral ambiguity has fallen and been swept away; the
world of simplicity and clarity has taken its place. Hallelujah! It may be that the
split in the signifier is all that holds the world together. The most significant
such splitting in recent years, in the realm of social theory, has been Michael
Hardt and Antonio Negri's project of elaborating the concept of a "multiude"
that might create forms of solidarity and political power to revive a new kind of
"common" in terms of natural resources, intellectual property, and social space.

4. In "Cratyllus," Socrates speaks of Cratyllus's position on a language of perfect
correspondence as "a kind of hunger" (100). Hermogenes, he implies, is probably
right in his analysis of language as we use it; but there nevertheless remains an
appetite, a desire that language be and do more. This "cratyllic hunger" continues
to this day. Maurice Merleau-Ponty, for instance, wrote, "We all secretly venerate
the ideal of a language which in the last analysis would deliver us from language
by delivering us to things" (4). See George Steiner, Umberto Eco, Gerard Gen-
nette, and Jonathan Ree for histories of, as Eco titled his book, "the search for a
perfect language." There is also, however, an opposing "Hermogenic" (or Saussurean) hunger that desires and delights in abolishing linguistic correspondence
and mimesis. Roland Barthes's exuberant political-linguistic critiques of the late
1960s seem to me the best examples of this Hermogenic hunger. "Writing constantly posits meaning," Barthes wrote in "The Death of the Author," "but always

in order to evaporate it," and so writing, "by refusing to assign to the text (and to the world-as-text) a 'secret,' i.e. an ultimate meaning, liberates an activity we may call countertheological, properly revolutionary, for to refuse to halt meaning is finally to refuse God and his hypostases, reason, science, and the law" (54).

5. See Fredric Jameson's *The Prison House of Language* and Geoffrey Galt Harpham's *Language Alone* for thorough accounts of the linguistic turn in relation to literary theory. Both Jameson and Harpham are critical of the philosophical and political consequences of the widespread and often uncritical adoption of Saussurean linguistics in literary theory. For Jameson, abandoning the signified and referent in favor of the signifier implies a withdrawal from political thinking, and Jameson concludes that the notion that "everything is language is as indefensible as it is unanswerable" (185). Harpham regards this emphasis on language as "the critical fetish of modernity" (57), and argues that since language can be described only by means of language, such description must use metaphors that exclude or repress essential elements, and that such exclusions are especially damaging when a linguistic model is extended to apply to social phenomena. The Saussurean model of language as a self-contained system of signs, writes Harpham, is "necessarily and extravagantly haunted by what it excludes" (34), particularly, for Harpham, notions of human nature and agency. Jameson's and Harpham's partly overlapping conceptions of the Saussurean inspired linguistic turns as totalizing and confining are compelling, but both writers neglect what I am calling the counter-linguistic turn—the important concurrent theoretical moves toward articulating an other of language, or a genuine alterity within language, that might provide an alternative to the prison and the fetish.

   For accounts of the linguistic turn in analytic philosophy (where the term originated), see Richard Rorty's introduction to *The Linguistic Turn* and his *Philosophy and the Mirror of Nature*. This intellectual trajectory is unrelated to Saussurean linguistics, but there are parallels between the two approaches. Consider, for instance, W. V. Quine's remark that "no particular experiences are linked with any particular statements in the interior of the [language] field, except indirectly through considerations of equilibrium affecting the field as a whole" (205), or Donald Davidson's view that meaning is determined "by assigning the sentence a semantic location in the pattern of sentences that comprise the language" (225) and that there is "no way to tell what the singular terms of a language refer to" (228).

6. The first academic responses I've seen to what I am calling a counter-linguistic turn have been a 1995 symposium in the journal *Common Knowledge* (vol. 4) entitled "A Turn Away from 'Language'?" in which Manfred Frank, Judith Butler, Drucilla Cornell, and others debated the possibility of a non-linguistic foundation of subjectivity, and a special issue of *SubStance* that featured evolutionary and neurological perspectives on the origins of narrative (vol. 30, 2001).

7. Jacques Derrida, who in "Violence and Metaphysics: An Essay on the Thought of Emmanuel Levinas" had critiqued Levinas's thinking on alterity as an attempt that

must ultimately think the other in terms of the same, has in more recent work moved closer to Levinas's position of positing an other that is "*tout autre*," wholly other (see *The Gift of Death*). The work of Alain Badiou is another instance of an ethics based on a relation to alterity outside of language. Badiou's ethics centers on the notion of the "event," an apocalyptic-traumatic occurrence that shatters existing symbolic frames and forces a radical reevaluation of ethics and history. Ethics consists of embracing an attitude of fidelity toward the truth that emerges from the event. This truth is discursive, but the event is not. Ethics, then, for these thinkers, is a response to an irruption of otherness rather than to a general ethical principle or to a pragmatic evaluation of a particular circumstance.

8. Julia Kristeva, of course, began her work on "semiotic" or pre-symbolic modes of subjectivity well before this broader shift in emphasis, showing again that the movement from linguistic to counter-linguistic is an ongoing tension in modern thinking rather than a single linear progression.

9. For recent contributions to and overviews of animal studies, see Kari Weil, *Thinking Animals*; Cary Wolfe, *Animal Rites*; and Dominic LaCapra, *History and Its Limits*.

10. See also Cary Wolfe's theorizations of "post-humanism," which is not, he cautions, a version of N. Katherine Hayles's thinking of a disembodied, partly cybernetic "post-human." Rather, post-humanism evokes modes of being outside of semiotic systems. It is strenuously counter-linguistic, committed to embodiment, and regards what Wolfe calls the "liberal humanist subject" as an entity constitutively divided against itself. These, of course, are linguistic categories. We must go through and beyond humanism in order to reach posthumanism, and doing so, we arrive at states that precede and underlie the human. As Wolfe writes, "that radically ahuman evolutionary emergence in turn makes possible language proper and the characteristic modes of consciousness and mentation associated with it, but remains tied (as in body language, kinesics, and more general forms of symbolic semiology) to an evolutionary substrate that continues to express itself in human interaction" (*What Is Posthumanism?* 120–21). This argument places in an evolutionary context what post-structuralism argues in terms of language, psychoanalysis in terms of the unconscious, dys-/disarticulation in terms of the collisions of impairment, symbol use, and social injury or trauma, and ways that disability studies, feminist scholarship, studies of race, and Marxian analysis all describe how particular marginalized or abjected categories of alterity—woman, queer, crip, proletariat, etc.—reveal the incoherence/non-identity of the dominant symbolic (i.e., hierarchical) structures. Each of us believes that we have found, if not the "ur-alterity," at least the "other" of most immediate political or theoretical importance, which is to say, the "other" that most profoundly befuddles a complacent yet all-pervasive neoliberalism. It is important, I think, not to take the radicalism of any of our claims too seriously. We are all products of the liberal humanism we claim to be deflating. Wolfe, even in his hyperbolic tone, is right. There cannot be a post-humanism (or a counter-linguistic turn) without humanism (or language).

This point repeats with less nuance Dominic LaCapra's arguments regarding the primal yet dependent character of post-human imaginings.

11. In *Writing History, Writing Trauma*, Dominick LaCapra points to a frequent confusion in literary and psychoanalytic theory between absence and loss—the first of which is structural, the second historical. To posit as an absence what is, in fact, a loss, is to deny a historical event and may also preclude taking steps toward healing the wounds produced by the loss. Identifying trauma only as an inevitable gap in the symbolic order rather than as a terrible and destabilizing event that happened seems to suggest that a condition of paralyzed irony is the most reasonable political stance.

12. For work on trauma theory, the Holocaust, and issues of witnessing, see Shoshona Felman and Dori Laub, Cathy Caruth, Dominick LaCapra, James Berger, Marianne Hirsch, Rothberg, Lawrence Langer, Young, and Geoffrey Hartman. For trauma theory as it relates to more contemporary political issues, see Greenberg, ed., Berger, and Farrell.

13. In 1970, a thirteen year old girl was found by social welfare workers in Temple City, California, locked in a room where she had apparently spent most of her life. She had not been introduced to language and so could not speak. The girl subsequently became an object of intense interest to psychologists and linguists—as, at the same time, battles over her legal custody were taking place. She is referred to as "Genie"; her true name was never divulged. Russ Rymer provides an excellent account of this awful affair.

14. The use of impaired or disabled characters to carry such symbolic weight has been explored and critiqued by scholars associated with disability studies, such as Lennard Davis, Rosemarie Garland Thomson, David Mitchell and Sharon Snyder, Ato Quayson, Robert McRuer, and Michael Davidson. This body of work is of great value in showing the pervasiveness of disability in our most important cultural narratives and as functioning as a kind of dys-/disarticulator with regard to prevailing discourses of human ability. For my engagements with and responses to disability studies, see chapter 4.

15. For the best evocation of the psyche of a Mets fan, see the work of my sorely missed late former colleague at Hofstra University, Dana Brand. Sadly, I never got round to discussing this scene with Dana. I know he would have loved it— and the whole scene in the Mill Luncheonette, since he too went to Columbia (as did Auster). Today, 2895 Broadway is the site of the Mill Korean Restaurant.

16. Compare this to a somewhat similar case, that of Pip in *Moby Dick*, who, having fallen off a whale boat and floated alone in the ocean overnight, loses his sanity. This madness Melville, or Ishmael, enthusiastically describes as divine wisdom:

> By the merest chance the ship itself at last rescued him; but from that hour the little negro went about the deck an idiot; such, at least, they said he was. The sea had jeeringly kept his finite body up, but drowned the infinite of his soul. Not drowned entirely, though. Rather carried down alive to wondrous depths, where strange shapes of the unwarped primal world glided to and

fro before his passive eyes; and the miser-merman, Wisdom, revealed his
hoarded heaps; and among the joyous, heartless, ever-juvenile eternities, Pip
saw the multitudinous, God-omnipresent, coral insects, that out of the firma-
ment of waters heaved the colossal orbs. He saw God's foot upon the treadle
of the loom, and spoke it; and therefore his shipmates called him mad. So
man's insanity is heaven's sense; and wandering from all mortal reason, man
comes at last to that celestial thought, which, to reason, is absurd and frantic;
and weal or woe, feels then uncompromised, indifferent as his God. (322)

17. LaCapra makes the point repeatedly that the hyperbolic quality of much post-
structuralist writing is an acting out/working through of the historical traumas
of modernity. His essay on absence and loss in *Writing History, Writing Trauma*
sets out this argument most succinctly. See also chapter 2 in my *After the End*.

18. For the best recent comprehensive history of the 1960s, see Maurice Isserman and
Michael Kazin's *America Divided*. For a history of the American Left, its utopian-
egalitarian aspirations, achievements, and failures, see Kazin's *American Dreamers*.

19. We see this dynamic even in contemporary evolutionary anthropology where
so much seems at stake as to the ratios of cooperative and nurturing versus
competitive and aggressive behaviors in apes and, more speculatively, extinct
hominids. No less than entire political worldviews hang in the balance as scientists evaluate a primate's capacity for sharing or for murdering. See, for example,
Frans de Waal, Richard Joyce.

20. See Mary Lazar for a discussion of how the film version of *Being There* differs
from the novel, particularly in its unambiguously salvific ending.

21. Popular and non-academic responses to Sacks's writing are almost invariably
enthusiastic. Walter Clemons in *Newsweek*, for instance, wrote that Sacks's
"humane essays . . . are deeply stirring because each of them touches on our own
fragile 'normal' identities and taken for granted abilities" (63), and Brina Caplan
in *The Nation* praised Sacks for "a romantic spirit worthy of William Blake or D.
H. Lawrence" (212). Criticisms of Sacks come mainly from two sources: scientists
and medical professionals who take him to task for his lack of rigor (see Daniel
X. Freedman, Jerome Bruner); and writers from the field of disability studies
who consider Sacks's approach a condescending appropriation of his subjects'
lives. For the latter, see Thomas Couser, whose treatment of Sacks is the most
thorough and judicious to date, and, more polemically, Tom Shakespeare, who
wrote that Sacks "mistook his patients for a literary career" (137). For an account
of Sacks that considers him as a religious writer, from a perspective different but
somewhat parallel to mine, see Mark A. Schneider. Scheider, a sociologist who
takes as his point of departure Weber's theory of modernity as disenchantment,
considers Sacks as part of a contemporary or post-modern phenomenon of re-
enchantment of the world. Schneider argues that, contra Weber, the bureaucratic
and technical procedures of modernity have not banished enchantment, that
enchantment is "part of our normal condition" and simply takes new forms just
beyond whatever might be the prevailing rational paradigms (x).

22. Sacks has recently published an entire book on the neurology of music, largely without, I should note, the theologizing tendencies I am discussing here. See *Musicophilia* and, for another perspective on music and neuroscience, Daniel J. Levitan's, *This is Your Brain on Music*.

23. See Antonio Damasio and Gerald Edelman for evolutionary-neurological accounts of consciousness prior to language.

24. This sense that all cultural products derive from a pre-cultural substratum resembles Rousseau's argument that spoken language and poetry derive from the kinesthetic qualities of song, that "verse, singing, and speech have a common origin" and "the first discourses were the first songs" (*On the Origin of Language* 50). It resembles as well the theories discussed in chapter 1 (of Kristeva, Heller-Roazen, and Blasing) which treat poetic language as the most embedded in prelinguistic, physical and sonic qualities.

25. See Dorothy Hermann's biography of Helen Keller and my Editor's Preface to Keller's *The Story of My Life: The Restored Edition*.

26. For Julia Kristeva, the "semiotic" is a mode of expression rooted in biological and psychic drives. It is separate from and opposed to symbolic and linguistic expressions and can be seen in "the child's echolalia before the appearance of language, but also the play of colors in an abstract painting or a piece of music that lacks signification but has a meaning" (*Interviews* 21; see also *Revolution in Poetic Language*). Paul Ricoeur, and other theorists such as David Carr and Andrew Norman, argue that narrative is not an arbitrary structure imposed on an intrinsically formless reality (as is, for instance, Hayden White's view), but is rather a fundamental human mode of apprehending and organizing the world.

27. Language is a central concern in all of DeLillo's work, and he has on several occasions has used impaired characters to explore the relations between language and some other of language. In *Great Jones Street* (1973), the protagonist, Bucky Wunderlick, ingests a drug that disables the brain's language centers and thereby becomes a double of the novel's mentally retarded character who is said to represent "the beauty and horror of wordless things" (52). When his language abilities return, Bucky is nostalgic for that unmediated experience in which "nothing erodes in the mad weather of language" (265). In *The Body Artist* (2001), we encounter a mysterious figure, possibly autistic, or retarded, or a kind of idiot savant—or perhaps a projection of the protagonist's imagination—who seems to exist outside of any normal chronological sequence and who, perhaps for that reason, cannot properly use language. The protagonist, traumatized by the sudden death of her husband, seeks finally to emulate this condition outside of time and language. It is possible even to identify the character of Lee Oswald in *Libra* (1988) as a linguistically impaired quasi-wild-child character whose dyslexia becomes a figure both for the general senselessness of cold war America and for the difficulties of historical representation. David Cowart's *Don DeLillo: The Physics of Language* is the most thorough and consistently perceptive treatment of DeLillo's attitudes toward language. Cowart notes

astutely that DeLillo likes to "tease the reader with what one might call intimations of essentiality" (180), but loses sight at times of the extent to which this
is a tease, the portrayal primarily of a desire, and not a truth. Cowart's DeLillo
comes to resemble at times my reading of Oliver Sacks.

28. "The Cloud of Unknowing" is the title of an anonymously composed four-
teenth-century English text of mystical negative theology that describes the
ecstatic relation to a God that surpasses all attempts to understand or articulate
Him in language.

29. Joseph Dewey, Arnold Weinstein, and Paul Maltby in various ways regard Wilder
as genuinely salvific, arguing that through Wilder, as Weinsten writes, DeLillo
"reveres that ultimately opaque language that is prior to all codes and grammars"
(306), or that, in Maltby's words, Wilder illustrates DeLillo's romantic belief in
"some primal, pre-abstract level of language which is naturally endowed with
greater insight, a primitive order of meaning that enables unmediated understanding, community, and spiritual communion with the world" (264). David
Cowart is skeptical of such assertions, though he then argues persuasively that
Wilder as "cloud of unknowing" functions as antidote to the toxic cloud of the
novel's second section and to the "nebulous mass" that forms in Jack's body (280).

30. Kenneth Burke was right to call the invention of the negative one of the defining features of human language use (*Language as Symbolic Action*, 9–13), and one
can conceive of death only in terms of negation—or the elaboration of negation
by means of tropes of the sublime and varieties of catechresis. So, elimination of
the concept of death—the goal of the drug dylar—brings with it, as its necessary "side effect," the elimination of signification, since there is no signified
to correspond to the signifier "my own death." Death, an essential piece of a
Saussurean language of systemic relations and sliding signifiers, cannot be part
of a language of perfect correspondence. For another perspective on death and
language, we can look to evolutionary linguistics. The development of the brain
that made possible the use of symbols occurred together with the development
of long term memory, and any reasonably sophisticated symbol use is impossible without an extended memory. Thus, language evolved together with the
awareness of time and, concurrently, we must assume, the knowledge of death.
See Damasio, Deacon, and Edelman for discussions on the relations between
language and memory.

31. The critical reception of *White Noise* (the novel of DeLillo's which has received
the most critical attention) recapitulates the theoretical trajectory this essay
has described, moving from perspectives oriented by a linguistic turn to readings that suggest turns against language. For Cornel Bonca, *White Noise* was
celebrated initially "because it seems to illuminate the [then] reigning theories
of cultural post-modernism, as if it were written as an example of what Fredric
Jameson, Jean-François Lyotard, or Jean Baudrillard [had] been saying about
our socio-cultural condition" (25). Earlier interpretations, such as those by
Leonard Wilcox, John Frow, and Frank Lentricchia, often focused on the "most

photographed barn in America" as an instance of Baudrillardian simulation, the autonomy of symbols and the loss of the referent. Later interpretations (e.g., Weinstein, Maltby, and Cowart) have tended to focus more on Wilder and on levels of existence or consciousness that transcend or negate symbolization.

32. Paula Bryant notes that the cult seeks "the binding of symbol and object into one-to-one correspondence through a terminal act of connection" (18), and David Cowart describes the murders as an "expression of a desire . . . to arrest the lexical fullness that gives rise to ambiguity" (167) and to institute "a violent return to the Adamic state of language" (171). Neither, however, recognizes sufficiently the broader political implications the novel draws from these acts of terror. Dennis Foster is explicit on this point, seeing in the cult murders "a demystifying parody of civilized systems" which are likewise, according to Foster, designed to produce "terror, ecstasy, and death" (106). Foster has written a brilliant and provocative analysis of *The Names*, in which he interprets the novel's various anti-Saussurean moves in terms of a Kristevan pre-linguistic level of consciousness that motivates all cultural production. This pre-linguistic "language" (Kristeva's *chora*) is, for Foster, the origin of what he calls a "perversity" that is a universal and implacable feature in human nature. Foster's perversity resembles Kristeva's notion of abjection, Lacan's idea of the real, and Bataille's of the heterogenous. This pre-linguistic perversity that we see in the cult's alphabetic murders and Tap's glossolalic novel is non-rational, non-productive (in economic terms), equally creative and destructive, and is the force that inevitably derails all social efforts toward rational or progressive goals. Thus, for Foster, all efforts the subject may pursue in order to understand or, in psychoanalytic terms, work through his perverse impulses will fail, for the perverse thoroughly inhabits rationality and language, and therapy is merely another form of perverse enjoyment. Foster's readings, although brilliant, are, I think, marred by the tendentiousness with which he maintains his thesis. All literature, it would seem, indeed all culture, all human thought, is for Foster *nothing but* the enactment of perversity—an "institutional complicity with some more primal need" (96). He begins with this premise, and every example simply proves it further. One is tempted to ask, how does Foster *know* these things, and to wonder whether his views on human nature and culture, however interesting, are, finally, more matters of personal temperment than of evidence, interpretation, or argument.

33. The practice of speaking in tongues derives from the following passage from Acts:

Now as the day of Pentecost had come, they were all together in one place; and suddenly there came from the sky a noise like the blowing of a great wind, and it filled all the house where they were sitting. And they saw what was like separate tongues of fire, and one settled on each of them, and they were all filled with the Holy Spirit, and they began to speak in different languages according as the Spirit gave each one the gift of speaking them. (2:1–4)

DeLillo has commented that glossolalia "could be viewed as a higher form of infantine babbling," and that "we feel, perhaps superstitiously, that children have a direct route to, have direct contact to the kind of natural truth that eludes us as adults" (q. in DeCurtis 64). Thus, David Cowart may be correct to say that DeLillo "leaves open the possibility that a relation persists between the linguistic and the divine" (174). I would emphasize, however, the extremely hypothetical quality of DeLillo's remarks and observe again that what we see in *The Names* is an instance of failed glossolalia reworked into a doubled form of literary art: that is, an extremely sophisticated production of a naive text. And yet, like Cowart, and like those involved in the various theoretical turns toward physicality, trauma, and alterity under discussion in this essay, I too want to "leave open the possibility" that something beyond language is being tapped by a successful literary artist.

34. There is another possibility DeLillo proposes in these texts: that one simply use language in its ordinary ways, regarding the catachretic, transcendent potentials I have focused on as simply another thing that language can do. As Winnie, the chemistry professor, wisely advises Jack Gladney concerning Dylar, "'There is no medicine, obviously'" (230). One must live one's life with the knowledge of death and with the separation of signifier and signified. In *The Names*, in more extended fashion, DeLillo extols the virtue of ordinary, social speech. "Conversation is life, language is the deepest being" (52). "What pleasure in the simplest greeting," he continues. "These familiar things . . . bridge the lonely distances" (52–53). See Amy Hungerford for an illuminating argument placing this return to the ordinary in language in relation to the glossolallic or catachretic urge to transcend language. As Hungerford writes, "it is small talk, rather than any weighty conversation about ultimate questions, that is most powerfully transcendent in *The Names*" (68).

35. Mark Osteen offers a compelling reading of the failed glossolalia as an invitation, indeed an obligation, to dialogue. "By immersing readers in heteroglossia, Tap's tale throws off the objections and obstructions to dialogic interplay" (*American Magic and* 140), and in that way, "though we cannot return to Adamic speech, we may take comfort in the proliferating richness of human talk" (136). Osteen's extended reflection and analysis of the prefix "ob" (and Tap's secret "ob" language) is a marvelously playful and brilliant contribution to understanding the role of language in this novel.

36. In addition to the earlier reference to Kenneth Burke's more general comments on the negative in language, I mean "negation" in roughly the senses proposed by thinkers of the Frankfurt School, as a fundamental rejection of prevailing modes of thought, a quasi-apocalyptic mental clearing away of the ideological terrain so as to make room for genuine freedom, whose precise forms cannot yet be known. Herbert Marcuse, for instance, called for "interpretation of that-which-is in terms of that-which is not, confrontation of the given facts with that which they exclude" (447), and placed negation in the context of a damaged world as "the effort to contradict a reality in which all logic and all speech are false to the extent that they are part of a mutilated whole" ("A Note on Dialectic" 449). Utopia is negation's unarticulatable motivating force, whether

expressed in philosophy or art. "Utopia remains the negation of what exists," wrote Theodor Adorno, and yet "art is no more able than theory to concretize utopia, not even negatively. A cryptogram of the new is the image of its collapse; only by virtue of the absolute negativity of collapse does art enunciate the unspeakable: utopia" (*Aesthetic Theory* 32). Or, expressing this incommensurability in other terms, "what differs from the existent will strike the existent as witchcraft" (*Negative Dialectics* 33).

37. A group of rabbis are arguing about a passage of Torah.

Again Rabbi Eliazer said to them: "If the *halachah* [Jewish law] agrees with me, let it be proved from Heaven!" Whereupon a Heavenly Voice cried out, "Why do ye dispute with R. Eliazer, seeing that in all matters the *halachah* agrees with him!" But Rabbi Joshua arose and exclaimed, "It is not in heaven."

What did the Holy One do in that hour? He laughed with joy, saying, "My sons have defeated Me, My sons have defeated Me." (Babylonian Talmud vol. I, 353 [BT BM 59b])

Rabbi Joshua refers to the following Biblical passage:

Surely, this instruction which I enjoin upon you this day is not too baffling for you, nor is it beyond reach. It is not in the heavens, that you should say, "Who among us can go up to the heavens and get it for us . . . ?" Neither is it beyond the sea, that you should say, "Who among us can cross to the other side of the sea and get it for us . . . ?" No, the thing is very close to you, in your mouth and in your heart." (Deuteronomy 30:11–14).

NOTES TO CHAPTER 4

1. The "normate," writes Garland-Thomson, "names the veiled subject position of cultural self, the figure outlined by the array of deviant others whose marked bodies shore up the normate's boundaries. . . . Normate, then, is the constructed identity of those who, by way of the bodily configurations and cultural capital they assume, can step into a position of authority and wield the power it grants them" (8).

2. I should emphasize that my experience and position vis à vis disability studies is literary and cultural. I cannot comment on clinical or administrative directions in the field.

3. Amy Vidali has made a valuable contribution toward reorienting the understanding of metaphor from a disability perspective. Critiquing Lakoff and Johnson's argument situating the origins of metaphor in the experience of a body necessarily—that is, ideologically—imagined as whole and able, Vidali calls not for the abandonment, but for a rethinking of metaphor that "engages the diversity of disability; refrains from policing metaphor; encourages transgression from the disability community; and invites creative and historic reinterpretaions of metaphor" (34). One shortcoming of the essay is that Vidali accepts Lakoff and Johnson's premise regarding the origin of metaphor in the body and so tries to imagine new metaphors using terms more congenial to disabled bodies—metaphors of scent, for instance, rather than sight or grasping. Thus, both

Vidali and Lakoff and Johnson fail adequately to consider metaphor's status as a part of language which is both conventional and innovative. Each metaphor is part of the history of language, and so part of social and ideological histories, and so it is reductive to think only in terms of the metaphor's relation to the body, which would seem to give metaphor the status of some primal, gestural signification.

4. As in the formative periods of various ethnic and gender studies, disability scholarship has identified itself closely with political goals. As Garland-Thomson put it, her intent was to shift descriptions of disability "from a form of pathology to a form of ethnicity" (6). Likewise, Siebers puts political goals at the forefront of disability scholarship, asserting that "the most urgent issue for disability studies is the political struggle of people with disabilities, and this struggle requires a realistic conception of the disabled body" (*Disability Theory* 68).

5. Bérubé writes, "it is altogether queer that disability studies might suggest that the literary representation of disability *not* be read as the site of the figural" and so, in effect, render itself "incompatible with the enterprise of professional literary study, dedicated as so much of it is to the interpretation of the figural" ("Disability and Narrative" 570). Ultimately, though, Bérubé reintegrates literary and disability studies, concluding that "rereading narrative from the perspective of disability studies leads us to reread the role of temporality, causality, and self-reflexivity in narrative and to reread the implications of characters' self-awareness. . . . [T]o reread in this way is to try to learn what makes all reading and self-representation possible" (576).

6. Darryl A. Smith provides an illuminating discussion of the uses of disability in African American "dozens" humor. Physical disability, especially in exaggerated form, Smith argues, is used in these jokes to ridicule the social stigma of race. The dexterity and hyperbole of the ridicule prevents the humor from doubling back to restigmatize the disability. As Smith writes in a forthcoming article, "Dis-/ability as manifest in the comedic *agon* of the dozens is a report on both the semantic and somatic experience of a dexterity-in-disability" (no pagination).

7. What form this new ethical-aesthetic would take is, of course, difficult to say. Quayson does not address the question. Lennard Davis's notion of "dismodernism" suggests one way of thinking of a universality based around disability as a shared sense of the finitude and vulnerability of all human life, and thus the abandonment of disability as a term of political identity. "What is universal in life if there are no universals is the experience of the limitations of the body," and this in opposition to current dominant ideologies whose common touchstone is "the perfection of the body and its activities" (*Bending* 32). In terms of aesthetic production, we might look to Michael Davidson's depictions of a wide range of counter-hegemonic artistic products coming from seemingly paradoxical disability perspectives: ASL poetry by deaf poets that alludes in fascinating ways to the perceived immediacy of the oral poetry of pre-literate societies;

photographic images constructed by blind photographers; the brilliant, unsentimental cinema of the West African film maker Jibiril Diop Mambety, which portrays the disabling impact of global capital on the developing world; the meticulous, expansive poetry of Larry Eigner, a poet who lived with cerebral palsy and whose medical condition provided an unstated condition of possibility for his poetic vision. This poetics of limitation—far more radical, I would argue, than, say, the more arbitrary, purely formal poetics of the French Oulipo tradition—goes well beyond the moralizing over metaphor that characterized earlier critical work in disability studies and lays a groundwork for a true broadening of the possibilities of a disability hermeneutics.

8. McRuer's critique of normativity draws a great deal from Michael Warner's *The Trouble with Normal*. Warner, like McRuer, argues against mainstream gay politics, maintaining that a true politics of difference must endorse a new, perhaps paradoxical, notion of universal dignity grounded in the shared indignity of sex. The shame of corporeality, of sweat, fluids, penetrations, etc., is part of sexual life and should not be neutralized through the normativities of marriage, home ownership, service on the PTA, and so on. Warner's position is not a reworking of Marcuse's in *Eros and Civilization*, that the affluence and enlightenment of late capitalism will allow us to jettison sexual repressions and live in Edenic innocence. Rather, Warner's point is that we should embrace repression and its erotic consequences as intrinsic to any human sexuality. Repression, and thus perversity or transgression, are not opposed to human dignity; they are inseparable from it, and can only be detached at great social cost. "Only when this indignity of sex is spread around the room," Warner writes, "leaving no one out, and in fact binding people together, that it begins to resemble the dignity of the human," which, he continues, is "a dignity in shame" (36).

9. See Zizek's *First as Tragedy, Then as Farce*. Communism must reemerge, Zizek argues, as the privatization of what had been enjoyed in common divides the world more and more definitively into the Included and the Excluded. The contemporary proletariat of the Excluded has more to lose than just their chains. "We are in danger of losing *everything*: the threat is that we will be reduced to abstract subjects devoid of all substantial content, dispossessed of our symbolic substance, our genetic base heavily manipulated, vegetating in an unlivable environment. This triple threat to our entire being renders us all proletarians" (92). The Excluded is the crip, and is the dys-/disarticulate. The goal of global capital, as both Zizek and McRuer would argue, is to exclude the Excluded (the crip, the dys/dis) from thought itself. *Crip Theory*, then is more about revolution than transgression. While its rhetoric aims toward transgression, its actual politics may be revolutionary—which, as I am suggesting, in the current political climate is more transgressive than the gender- or disability-based politics that McRuer invokes.

10. Another crucial but unmentioned intertext for McRuer is Leo Bersani's 1987 essay, "Is the Rectum a Grave?" In it, Bersani first criticizes the political pretension of sexual transgression, the idea that in gay sado-masochism, for example,

we see "subversive parodies of the very formations and behaviors they appear to ape" (206). Bersani then goes on to describe sexuality as rooted not in domination but in powerlessness and the desire to dissolve the rigid boundaries of the self. Domination, submission, and other "transgressions" are, for Bersani, symptomatic of the wish to deny the longing for self-negation. He argues that the "value of powerlessness" is not found in an idealized sexuality of gentleness or even passivity, but rather in "a more radical disintegration and humiliation of the self" (217). Sex, Bersani concludes, is irredeemable, and "the value of sexuality itself is to demean the seriousness of efforts to redeem it" (222). Thus, "jouissance," for Bersani, is "a mode of ascesis" (222), and the destruction of selfhood through sexuality returns one to a deeper understanding of what it means to be a human animal and so to a more responsible politics. Something like this logic, I think, informs McRuer's idea of the transgressive crip.

11. See Simo Vehmas's discussion of the controversy following the publication of *Disability Rights and Wrongs*. He quotes Shakespeare's former ally Mike Oliver's scathing and *ad hominem* comment that Shakespeare is "'a relatively affluent person with a minor impairment who is never going to be at the sharp end of personal support services' and who thus writes 'well intentioned but meaningless platitudes'" (21).

12. Two books that did much to define their respective fields, Cathy Caruth's *Unclaimed Experience* and Rosemarie Garland-Thomson's *Extraordinary Bodies*, appeared in 1996 and 1997.

13. In his latest book, *Disability Aesthetics*, Tobin Siebers seeks to begin this process of creating links between trauma and disability. Siebers's larger project is to read modernist art in terms of disability—to argue, in fact, that modernism is at its heart an attempt to come to terms with and represent disability. His argument, it seems to me, is reductive and historically dubious. As I argue in this book, modernism is deeply implicated with a variety of approaches to physical and cognitive impairment, but it seems more productive and more accurate to look at the complex relations that emerge between discourses of impairment and other contemporaneous scientific, aesthetic, and philosophical discourses. Siebers's approach to trauma, unfortunately, is likewise limited. Since he has no sense of trauma as event, he is unable to theorize representations as symptoms, or as ways both of acting out and working through the memories of traumatic events—points made with great clarity by Zizek and LaCapra. Siebers makes the confusing and, I believe, inaccurate argument that "there is no perceivable difference" between fictional depictions of violence and images of actual violence through journalistic media (104), and proceeds on this basis to reconceive contemporary works of "trauma art" as forms of ritual. Without a notion of symptom, Siebers's theory of trauma as ritual strikes me as a confused mystification. Far more promising is a recent essay by Daniel R. Morrison and Monica J. Casper which examines the conceptualizations of war-time brain injuries and obstetric fistulas suffered by women in impoverished environments. Morrison

and Casper bring together clinical practices, popular representations, and historical and contemporary social contexts in ways that greatly illuminate how in these cases trauma, disability, and social practice cannot be thought separately. Although the focus in this study is primarily clinical, it has rich implications for studies in the humanities as well, and its sense of trauma draws both from clinical and literary models.

14. See LaCapra's *Writing History, Writing Trauma*, and especially the chapter "Trauma, Absence, Loss."

15. See Zizek's *The Sublime Object of Ideology*, one of the absolutely essential texts on trauma and symptom as social forces. See also Fassin and Rechtman's recent *Empire of Trauma* for a compelling historical account of how trauma has come to occupy the central place it now holds with regard to contemporary understandings of violence, how discourses of trauma have "created a new language of the event" (6).

16. See Dominick LaCapra's work since the early 1990s for insightful commentaries on the hyperbolic language of post-structuralism, which he regards as often an acting out of trauma which the text cannot address directly. See also my *After the End*, chapter 3.

17. The discourse it most resembles is that of apocalypse and post-apocalypse. The formation of symptoms, the narrative working through of these symptoms, and the ideological narrative fetishes that permit the denial of the symptoms' existence and power all become, in effect, the constitution of a new symbolic order, a new heaven and new earth. Thus, however obscurely, in the post-traumatic, post-apocalyptic landscape of symptoms and signs, the catastrophe becomes revelation. All that preceded it and all that follows after now take meaning from that single moment; the historical rupture now functions also as a distorting-revealing conduit, and transmission is renewed. See *After the End* for a discussion of the relation between the languages of apocalypse and trauma.

18. It is ethically important, however, to insist that trauma is not sacred. Trauma is utterly secular. It is simply something that happens. It has causes, which are both social and personal; and it has consequences, again both social and personal. Its devastating impacts challenge existing symbolic resources, and thus it may appear, or seem best described in terms of the sublime, the sacred, or the apocalyptic. But it is not. The value of trauma as a descriptive term for historical catastrophe, it seems to me, is its lack of connotation, its negativity or blankness. It is what has happened; it brings with it no frame. It is not "tragic," has no connotation of sacrifice, does not redeem. And yet, terminologies, narratives, and histories must change their shapes in order to accommodate the new realities that events such as wars and genocides have brought into being. Insofar as the trauma *also* results from a crime, survivors feel ethically and legally compelled to bear witness; and their audiences feel likewise compelled to bear witness to the oral or textual witnessing through which the trauma has been transmitted.

19. Notwithstanding my criticisms of these elisions of trauma, *Narrative Prosthesis* is a fascinating and important book. The central concept continues to be useful in itself and as it provides a focus for debating disability studies' approaches to literature.

20. Mark Osteen is right to observe in disability studies a "tendency to overlook or minimize tensions in the field's guiding principles" (Introduction 2).

21. Toni Morrison transposes this impulse into sexual terms in Sula's fantastical admonition that she will be rearticulated into her community after "'all the old women have lain with the teen-agers; when all the young girls have slept with their old drunken uncles; after all the black men fuck all the white ones; when all the white women kiss all the black ones; when the guards have raped all the jailbirds and after all the whores make love to their grannies; after all the faggots get their mothers' trim; when Lindbergh sleeps with Bessie Smith and Norma Shearer makes it with Stepin Fetchit; after all the dogs have fucked all the cats and every weathervane on every barn flies off the roof to mount the hogs . . . then there'll be a little love left over for me. And I know just what it will feel like'" (145–46).

22. Again, see Eileen Boris and Jennifer Klein for a history of how the labor market of home care-workers evolved.

23. Michael Davidson, whose work is consistently a vanguard in disability studies, makes a valuable contribution to the discourse of care, dependency, and disability with his special edition of the *Journal of Literary and Cultural Disability Studies* (vol. 1, no. 2, 2007) devoted to these questions. As he points out, the recent work by Nussbaum and Kittay has had a strong effect on disability studies scholarship, but has "touched a sensitive nerve among disability activists over the issue of whether foregrounding dependent relations violates hard won virtues of independent living" (Introduction, i).

24. For Nussbaum's argument regarding animal rights and her responses to Peter Singer, et al., see chapter 6 of *Frontiers of Justice*. See also the important discussions in Kittay and Carlson, eds., *Cognitive Disability and its Challenge to Moral Philosophy*.

25. Lennard Davis has been critical of Nussbaum, arguing that the debate with Rawls is of interest only to professional philosophers and not germane to disability studies, and that Nussbaum is a *parvenue* to disability studies who advances arguments without real familiarity with the theoretical field in which she has encroached. While Davis on the whole agrees with Nussbaum's arguments—they contain "nothing to sneer at," he praises faintly—he concludes that "we might not need a philosopher to get us to them" ("Dependency and Justice" 4). The problem seems to be one of turf. Davis trivializes Nussbaum's arguments, especially in that he ignores the case she made in her earlier book *Upheavals of Thought* for an active political role for compassion, which provides an enormously valuable support for Davis's own thesis of a universality based on shared vulnerability.

26. Why, then would one not act on the basis of compassion? This is a terrain
    explored in different ways by Lee Edelman and Dennis Foster. Compassion, for
    Edelman, always obeys a totalizing, narcissistic logic whose function is always
    politically conservative, "always intent on preserving the image in which the ego
    sees itself" (173). The way out is to merge oneself fully with one's desire which,
    at its deepest level, is desire for *jouissance*, or the death-drive—the wish to have
    no self, or a self without borders or defenses. Foster similarly describes subjec-
    tivity as fundamentally perverse. In essence, this critique implies that compas-
    sion is impossible or inauthentic because we are not compassionate by nature.
    But anthropological evidence is mixed on this point. Human beings appear to
    be capable of selfish, tribal, generous, compassionate, altruistic, and sadistic
    behaviors. It is difficult to judge which is more essential, but compassion is at
    the least an important part of the mix.

27. In this regard, I particularly appreciate Tobin Siebers's comment to his read-
    ers to "remember what you already know about people with disabilities, so
    the knowledge will be useful to you when you join us. The blind do not lead
    the blind. The lame do not walk alone. We do not love only our own kind or
    ourselves. You others are our caregivers—and we can be yours, if you let us"
    (*Disability Theory* 52).

28. Michael Bérubé and Lennard Davis also have commented on the need and,
    indeed, the value of disability studies taking a closer interest in cognitive
    impairment. For both, the condition of cognitive impairment calls for a more
    sustained examination of autonomy and voice. "If mindedness is so obviously
    a necessary condition for self-representation," Bérubé writes, then damage to
    the mind can serve as impetus for "meditation on the possibility of narrative
    representation" ("Disability and Narrative" 572; cf. Davis, "Disability" 530). See
    also Licia Carlson's important intervention in ethical philosophy, in which she
    critiques the consistently pejorative use of cognitive disability as limit case for
    various theories of ethics.

29. My own experience clearly is relevant here to how my argument has evolved.
    As I mentioned in the introduction, my two sisters both have a recessive gene
    condition (probably Angelman's Syndrome) which caused serious cognitive
    impairments. Susan and Claudia are very sweet, loving women and, I think, are
    for the most part happy; but they certainly cannot live independently. They can-
    not speak. I am quite certain that they do not understand political discourses
    and so cannot act as full civic agents. Each lives in a group home in a suburban
    neighborhood, and they both go to work each day packing meals for a meals-
    on-wheels program. I believe they like their jobs; they like the idea of having
    a job, of some purposeful activity. They need a good bit of supervision on the
    job, and frequent breaks. One of my parents visits them every couple of weeks,
    and I visit about twice a year—not enough, but it's what I can do at this point.
    Of course, our parents won't live forever, and when they're gone, the responsi-
    bility for making sure my sisters' lives go as well as possible will be mine. My

one real regret about their upbringing is that when they were small children and it was becoming apparent that they were not learning to speak, it occurred to no one that we might try teaching ASL. Claudia has been able to pick up a few signs over the years, but I'm sure we would have had more success had we started when she was at the language acquisition stage. I am not saying, *pace* Stubblefield and Savarese, that Claudia is a person with unimpaired cognition who simply never developed speech; but I think it is true that she does have communicative abilities that we never found ways to properly encourage. At any rate, given my family experience, I am far more sympathetic to positions like those of Kittay that acknowledge the reality and consequences of cognitive impairment.

NOTES TO CHAPTER 5

1. In distinguishing between science and ideology, I do not want to suggest that science can exclude ideology, any more than can any discourse. But I will try to describe in this chapter an enormously influential ideologizing of neuroscience that is, in fact, rejected by most practicing neuroscientists. These scientists, of course, accept the premises of empirically based, quantitatively describable research, but they reject the notion that their research will ever result in any conclusively explanatory or predictive results regarding how the mind works or the relation between brain physiology and social relations or cultural products. The brain's complexity, scientists like Jean-Pierre Changeux, Gerald Edelman, and Joseph LeDoux insist, will always prevent complete understanding, and so there will never come a time when particular mental or cultural functions will be reducible to some cerebral mechanism. Indeed, as Edelman, LeDoux, and Terrence Deacon argue, the indeterminacy of symbolization is itself a result of how the brain is constructed.

2. See Catherine Malabou's *What Shall We Do with Our Brain?* in which she describes the ideological conflation of the notion of the brain's "plasticity," i.e., the neural capacity to receive and transmit impressions, and thus to adapt and learn, with the neoliberal notion of "flexibility," in which a docile global labor force copes with decreases in pay, health care, pensions, workplace safety, and jobs themselves. Is this "flexibility" really what the brain is for, she asks, and, if not, to what uses ought we to put its amazing plasticity?

3. See economist Joseph Stiglitz's Nobel Prize acceptance speech (2001) for a compelling critique of the predictive powers of econometric models. These models, he wrote, "virtually made economics a branch of engineering," possessing transparent diagnostic and predictive powers (482). By "knowing preferences and technology and initial endowments," these models could claim to "describe the time path of the economy" (484). But this presumption of complete information, Stieglitz argues, is illusory. First, possession of knowledge in any economy is asymmetrical, and economic models ignore inequalities of power that grant some participants more information than others (490). Second, Stieglitz

emphasizes, events will happen that no model can anticipate. Random events will occur and "have consequences that are irreversible." Even the smallest failure of information will destroy a model's predictive power, and such failures are inevitable. The world as it is manifests "a high level of indeterminacy," and "one cannot simply predict where the economy will be by knowing preferences and technology and initial endowments" (521).

4. Barbara Hernnstein Smith makes a similar point in discussing the knowledge claims of evolutionary psychology. At issue, she writes, "is whether such explanations trump the understandings of the human scene, interior and exterior, developed by myriad other social scientists (ethnographers, psychologists, sociologists and so forth) over the past century and by myriad chroniclers (historians, diarists, diplomats, journalists, travelers, essayists, poets, novelists, playwrights and so forth) over the past two or three millennia" (146). As Franzen might have put it, what they thought might be true, we can now know, in a newly privileged vocabulary, is really *true*. Consider also the biologist R. C. Lewontin's observations on the determinism characteristic of an overly broad belief in genetics: "Genes make individuals, individuals have particular preferences and behaviors, the collection of preferences and behaviors makes a culture, and so genes make a culture" (14). "We will understand what we are when we know what our genes are made of" (13).

5. For Roland Barthes, once language is released from its ideological imperative to create interpretable meaning—its "totalitarian ideology of the referent," conveyed most typically through narrative—it will then "liberate an activity we may call countertheological, properly revolutionary, for to refuse to halt [the infinite proliferation of] meaning is finally to refuse God and his hypostases, reason, science, the law" (13, 54). Hayden White regards the reliance of historiography on narrative as a form of institutional discipline that forecloses the imagining of radical social change in that it "deprives history of the kind of meaninglessness that alone can goad living human beings to make their lives different for themselves and their children" (72). Thus, in answering the question "Is narrativity itself an ideological instrument?"in the affirmative, White calls for "a conception of history that would signal its resistance to the bourgeois ideology of realism by its refusal to attempt a narrativist mode for the representation of its truth" (81).

6. Paul Ricoeur here states very simply what he develops over the course of an essay and then a three-volume book: "Narrativity and temporality are closely related—as closely related as, in Wittgenstein's terms, a language game and a form of life. Indeed, I take temporality to be that structure of existence that reaches language in narrativity and narrativity to be that language structure that has temporality as its ultimate referent" ("Narrative Time" 169). David Carr builds his argument on Ricoeur's with particular emphasis on the subject or writer's attitude toward the future. Both action and narrative involve "a kind of oscillation" between two points in time, and so in life as in writing, "we are

constantly striving . . . to occupy the story-tellers' position" (145). Thus, the act of narrative "is practical before it becomes cognitive or aesthetic" (146). Louis Mink, in contrast, and in closer alignment with Barthes and White, regards narrative as distinct from events in life and the world, but argues, *pace* both poststructuralists and positivists, that it is our most valuable form of knowledge of events. Narratives, Mink writes, "are not imperfect substitutes for more sophisticated forms of explanations and understanding, nor are they the unreflective first steps along the road which leads toward the goal of scientific of philosophical knowledge. The comprehension at which narratives aim is a primary act of mind, although it is a capacity which can be indefinitely developed in range, clarity, and subtlety" (135).

7. This selection of recent fiction is roughly the terrain delineated by Marco Roth in his discussion of the "neuronovel." Roth's critique of this fiction is that it shares and reinforces the ideology of neuroscience at the expense of the expansive, epistemologically and ethically rich understandings of narrative described in this chapter. I believe Roth gets this exactly wrong, and I argue that the "neuronovels" under discussion are critiques of the ideology of neuroscience and defenses of narrative. The novels tend to be ambivalent. They recognize the practical and theoretical force of neuroscience as science at the same time as they respond to the usurpations threatened by neuroscience as ideology; and they are deeply concerned with both the powers and limits of narrative and language. Thus, in McEwan's *Saturday*, the neurosurgeon protagonist Henry Perowne believes firmly both in the practical applications of neuroscience and in its more totalizing ideological implications. "It isn't an article of faith with him," we read, "he knows it for a quotidian fact, the mind is what the brain, mere matter, performs." Dismissing literature, and the books his poet daughter inflicts on him, Henry pleads, "no more magic midget drummers . . . please, no more ghosts, angels, satans, or metamorphoses. When anything can happen, nothing matters" (66–67). The neurosurgeon concludes, "this notion of Daisy's, that people can't 'live' without stories, is simply not true. He is living proof" (67). And as for Baxter, the small-time criminal with Huntington's Disease, with whom Henry has a minor car accident mid-novel and who then invades Henry's home, "no amount of love, drugs, Bible classes or prison sentencing can cure Baxter or shift him from his course. It's spelled out in fragile proteins, but it could be carved in stone or tempered steel" (217). Yet, by the end of the novel, altered by the events of his day, Perowne performs a life-saving operation on Baxter and vows to ensure he is given all the care he requires to navigate through his incurable condition. Perowne has changed both their stories.

And it is in the contexts both of neuroscience and history that we may understand McEwan's use of Matthew Arnold's "Dover Beach" to save the day in *Saturday*: as recited by the young, naked, pregnant poet to bizarrely disarm the neurally diseased criminal Baxter, who has commandeered Perowne's home. "Dover Beach," that old chestnut, loping along with all the "best that has been thought and said," here used explicitly for the edification and conversion of the dangerous working-class subject in order to defend the lives and property of the ruling class . . . just as Arnold intended! But here we have Arnold's "ignorant armies" and "let us be true to one another"—as recited in 2003 on the eve of the Iraq War? A famous lyrical depiction of private melancholia, care, and muted eroticism in the shadow of traumatic political events has an unpredictable effect on a person suffering irreversible neurological damage. Baxter, given to uncontrolled twitches, unable to move his eyes and gaze, is increasingly prone to violent outbursts; America and its coerced allies descend into war with Iraq, a kind of Baxter among nations—or, a war among several Baxters, some more prosperous and technologically capable than others, with the inhabitants of the more prosperous realms able to retreat into their domestic pleasures, beauties, and melancholies. What is "Dover Beach" then—this most hackneyed canonical artefact, and very beautiful poem? How did it get into this "neuronovel" whose credo is biological determinism? Its function is that it *undetermines*. In its disguised mimesis (i.e., of the present, our present), in its musical-emotional affectiveness, it transforms a previously determined situation. The recitation of the poem by the naked, pregnant young poet is an *event*, in the midst of trauma, that disrupts a traumatic social and neurological determination.

See also in this regard, Jonathan Greenberg's "Why Can't Biologists Read Poetry: Ian McEwan's *Enduring Love*."

8. The disability community and writers in disability studies might contest this sympathetic depiction of neuroscience's view of neurological impairment, citing both the continued widespread stigmatization of neurological difference by "neurotypicals" (or, in Rosemary Garland-Thomson's term, by "normates" of all kinds) and the continued use of a "medical model" of disability to appropriate the experience, subjectivity, and voices of the disabled. Neuroscience would be yet another instance of viewing all physical and psychological impairments as primarily medical conditions rather than viewing them in the context of dominant social and institutional attitudes, practices, and structures. In addition, some might point to the persistent use of disability as metaphor—a "narrative prosthesis," in David Mitchell and Sharon Snyder's term—by which the experience of disability is subordinated to more general social concerns (as, for instance, might be said of the present study). I would point out that the idea of a neurological spectrum derives from neuroscience (the diagnosis of autistic spectrum disorders, for instance—with the implication that all minds find some place on this spectrum), and emphasize that this idea of the inclusiveness of disability is of vast importance. Disability theory stresses the universality of disability—the fact that all people lack certain abilities at different points in their lives—as well as stressing the particular group identity of the disabled as a minority facing discrimination. These two emphases, I would argue, sometimes appear to be in conflict. The research, as opposed to the ideology, of neuroscience, I believe, encourages a sense of human commonality that *should* work

against the stigmatization of those occupying particular places on a neurological spectrum. For a discussion of the significance of metaphor in disability theory, see chapter 5.

9. In contrast to what she calls the "universal other" of liberal moral theory (in Kant and Rawls), Seyla Benhabib proposes a notion of a "concrete other" who engages more fully with socio-economic status, emotion, and physical vulnerability or disability. Rather than moral norms of "right, obligation, and entitlement," relations with the concrete other demand norms of "responsibility, bonding, and sharing" (159). For Martha Nussbaum's and Eva Kittay's responses to Rawls, see chapter 4.

10. Stuart Murray is right to note and to question the current fascination with autism. His comprehensive and insightful survey of representations of autism in fiction, nonfiction, film, advertisements, etc., argues that it is partly autism's elusiveness that provokes such a plethora and range of portrayals, the goals of which, in large part, are not understanding but rather embody "the complex desires of a society that wishes to be fascinated with a topic that seems precisely to elude comprehension" and represents "the allure of potentially unquantifiable human difference and the nightmare of not somehow being 'fully' human" (*Representing Autism* 4, 5). See also Mark Osteen, ed., *Autism and Representation* for more thinking on autism in aesthetic, political, and clinical contexts. And see Murray's more recent book, *Autism*, for an excellent overview of historical, sociological, and scientific perspectives.

11. Most readers will be aware that the most recent *DSM* (*DSM-V*) removed Asperger's as a separate condition, blending its characteristics in a broader spectrum of autism. Nevertheless, the term continues to be used, especially by people who identify themselves as people with Asperger's. The split between higher- and lower-functioning people on the autistic spectrum has significant and troubling consequences in terms of political representation and forms of care, as it seems that these two groups (though the boundary between them is often indistinct) have different interests and needs. I will also continue to use the term Asperger's in this chapter since it was still part of the popular and clinical lexicons when the texts I am discussing were written.

12. Again, see Donald Davidson's argument that metaphors do not have some hidden, alternative meaning that is either substituted for a surface meaning or links two previously unrelated meanings, or that radically disrupts an established meaning. A metaphor, for Davidson, simply means what it says. There is no such thing as "metaphorical meaning"; there is only literal meaning. Christopher would entirely agree with Davidson's statement that "most metaphorical sentences are *patently* false, just as all similes are trivially true. . . . For a metaphor *says* only what it shows on its face—usually a patent falsehood or an absurd truth. And this plain truth or falsehood needs no paraphrase—its meaning is given in the literal meaning of the words" (258; Davidson's emphasis). Insofar as metaphors can be distinguished from lies, Davidson argues, their difference "is

not a difference in the words used or what they mean . . . , but in how the words are used" (259). Whether one uses words in order to lie or to make a metaphor depends on an understanding of a linguistic—that is, a social—situation—and here, of course, in the realm of social understanding, is where Christopher's competence most falters. For Davidson, the act of thinking about the untruth or absurdity of the metaphor's literal meaning can lead to productive new ways of thinking; but these new ways of thinking are not produced by a special kind of metaphorical meaning. The metaphor means what it says.

13. This linguistic incapacity along the autistic spectrum varies. Dawn Prince-Hughes, in her memoir, stresses that social difficulties can coexist with verbal fluency, an observation supported by the research of Tager-Flusberg, who reported that the social and communicative impairments of autism may "not have any identifiable influence on the course of grammatical development" (175).

14. The decline of working-class social institutions and practices is portrayed compellingly in post-Thatcher films like *The Full Monty* and *Brassed Off*. See also sociologist Robert Putnam's analysis of the decline of comparable American social practices in *Bowling Alone*.

15. Temple Grandin makes similar remarks regarding her struggles to pick up cues that would indicate what other people are thinking, comparing herself to *Star Trek*'s android crewman, Lt. Commander Data. Simon Baron-Cohen argues that this difficulty in "mind-reading" is an important component in the consciousness of people with autism. Many in the Asperger's community have been critical of this diagnosis and the tests that led Baron-Cohen, Uta Frith, and others to arrive at it. See, for instance, http://www.journeyswithautism.com/2009/04/02/a-critique-of-the-theory-of-mind-tom-test/. For a thorough review of recent scientific literature on autism and theory of mind, see Lars Sorensen.

Lisa Zunshine argues that the mind's ability to speculate regarding others' thoughts, feelings, motives, and intentions is *the* key component in the writing and reading of fiction. "Intensely social species that we are," Zunshine writes, "we thus read fiction because it engages, in a variety of particularly focused ways, our Theory of Mind" (162). Zunshine recognizes—as she must—that this formulation comes across as a most reductive depiction of the imaginative range of the novels we love and return to. But she responds that, in fact, theory of mind is so commodious a faculty as to take in all the important emotional, historical, political, aesthetic, ethical, etc., concerns that we find in fiction—though we must wait for neuroscientific confirmation of this thesis. I remain skeptical here, and still find hers a reductive conclusion to a book filled with fascinating and innovative readings. See also H. Porter Abbott's fascinating essay on minds in fictional texts purposely constructed so that they cannot be read—for instance, Melville's Bartleby. Abbott adopts a Levinasian position such that the unreadable mind in a fictional text precludes empathy and in doing so highlights "the humility and respect" one must bring "before the human unknowable" (463). I would argue that the dys-/disarticulate figures under discussion stand on a border between readable and unreadable, on an outer ledge of social-symbolic status—beyond it, but showing the impossibility of being beyond it. And so the ethical obligations they initiate are both Levinasian (based on a presumption of absolute alterity) and more familiar (based on empathy, on their commonness as human, and suffering, beings, or as I suggested earlier, on their common status as other who is other to himself).

16. The Book of Revelation contrasts the purity and incommensurability of the New Jerusalem with the economic and sexual exchanges that characterize Babylon. Slavoj Zizek glosses the "second death" referred to in Revelation 20:6 and 14, as the extinguishing of the symbolic order that completes the destruction of the physical world (*Sublime Object*, 132–34; *Looking Awry*, 22–23). See also Frank Kermode as well as my *After the End* for interpretations of apocalyptic desire as a wish to end ambiguity.

17. See Ronald Schleifer's thorough and insightful essay describing a poetics of Tourette's Syndrome. In Tourette's, Schleifer argues, we find a melding of biology, the material (that is, gestural, sonic, emotive, pre-semantic) nature of language, and conscious and unconscious motivations, with verbal tics "hovering between meaning and meaninglessness" (570). As Schleifer writes, "echoing, repetition, puns, punctuated language—erasing in its barks and noises the distance between signifier and signified even as it excites the emotions and passions: this description of Tourette might help us see some of the resources of language poetry attempts to 'reachieve'" (571). Schleifer and I begin with the same premises, which he describes in a more complete scientific context. My argument moves more specifically toward the metaphoric-catachretic character of the tics Lethem invents for Lionel in *Motherless Brooklyn* and then toward the problem of novel utterance in the context of genre, or how to create a new word among the "current words" that Conrad refers to (see chapter 2). Schleifer's argument more resembles those of Blasing, Heller-Roazen, and Kristeva (discussed in chapter 1) which link poetry to pre-linguistic origins. It is important to note with regard to both our discussions of verbal Tourettic tics that tics of the poetic level of Lionel's would be extremely rare if not unprecedented.

18. The traditional theory of metaphor that Turner's most resembles is the interactionist theory of Max Black. Black describes each of the two terms in a metaphorical utterance as a system of standard or commonplace views—the typical associations placed on "wolf" or "rose" or "moon," etc. When these word-systems are placed together, each of them shifts its meaning somewhat. A new understanding emerges—as in Turner's emergent spaces. And again, as in Turner, there is in Black no implication (or metaphor) of violence. The commonplace understanding is not overturned or burst. Genre remains intact. Black rejects definitions of metaphor as merely substitution, comparison, or decoration. Metaphor, for him as for Turner, advances cognition. But for both these thinkers, in contrast to post-structuralist thinking on metaphor, language never can be thrown into a state of critical, traumatic unsettlement.

19. See Ellen Spolsky's intriguing and pertinent effort to read cognitive science and Derrida through each other's perspectives. Both, she argues, propose semantic instability, i.e., metaphoricity, as a cognitive advantage. Innovation is possible because misunderstanding is possible, and yet, in most contexts, we understand each other well enough to get by. "The gap between signifier and the signified is no tragedy," she writes; "it builds in the flexibility to allow the system to meet the challenge of new contexts and to use old words in new combinations with new meanings." Indeed, human evolutionary success "would actually be compromised by an entirely rigid, that is, dependable, representational system" (52)—or, we might say, by a perfect Adamic language. Spolsky understands "system" in a less confining sense that I have used it. I would distinguish social-symbolic senses from biological ones, and would argue that the social-symbolic system is always a construct whose properties depend on the ideological stance of the person describing it (see chapter 2).

20. Dominick LaCapra makes this point very clearly in his distinction between absence and loss. Reference to absence indicates a structural condition, a condition of possibility, such as *differance* or Heidegger's "appropriation." Loss, on the other hand, suggests a fundamental change, an event, a traumatic—and thus, a historical—transformation. LaCapra argues that it is a characteristic of much post-structuralist theory to elide these categories—especially to deny trauma by mislabeling loss as absence, event as structure.

21. Some of these criticisms of Weber clearly echo Tom Shakespeare's criticisms of Sacks in his review of *An Anthropologist on Mars* in which he labeled Sacks "the man who mistook his patients for a literary career" (137). See Thomas Couser, Leonard Cassuto, and chapter 4 of this book for further considerations of Sacks's work.

22. See Giacomo Rizzolati and Laila Craighero (esp. 169).

23. This is very much the position of neuroscientist V. S. Ramachandran, for whom the importance of mirror neurons is "difficult to overstate." They may, he writes, "be central to social learning, imitation, and the cultural transmission of skills and attitudes. . . . By hyperdeveloping the mirror-neuron system, evolution in effect turned culture into the new genome" (23). See cognitive psychologist Allison Gopnik for a more skeptical appraisal of mirror neurons' significance. She argues that such uncritical celebration ignores the role of experience and environment, places too much confidence in the ability to interpret brain images, and mistakes congruence or overlap for causation. Such criticisms can be found also in the work of philosopher Alva Noe.

24. Marcuse writes:

> But the construction of such a society presupposes a type of man with a different sensitivity as well as consciousness: men who would speak a different language, have different gestures, follow different impulses; men who have developed an instinctual barrier against cruelty, brutality, ugliness. Such an instinctual transformation is conceivable as a factor of social change only

if it enters the social division of labor, the production relations themselves. They would be shaped by men and women who have the good conscience of being human, tender, sensuous, who are no longer ashamed of themselves. (*Essay on Liberation* 21)

Shame at our status as corporeal, vulnerable, mortal beings is also crucial to the ethical visions of Martha Nussbaum and Jessica Benjamin.

NOTES TO THE EPILOGUE

1. Personal conversation, August 22, 2012. See also Alfonso Caramazza, "Parallels and Divergences in the Acquisition and Dissolution of Language."

WORKS CITED

Abbott, H. Porter. "Unspeakable Minds and the Captive Reader." *Style* 42 (2008): 448–67.

Acts and Letters of the Apostles. Trans. Richard Lattimore. New York: Farrar, Straus, and Giroux, 1982.

Adams, Rachel. *Sideshow U.S.A.: Freaks and the American Cultural Imagination*. Chicago: University of Chicago Press, 2001.

Adorno, Theodor. *Aesthetic Theory*. Ed. Gretel Adorno and Rold Tiedemann. Trans. Robert Hullot-Kentor. Minneapolis: University of Minnesota Press, 1997.

———. *Negative Dialectics*. Trans. E. B. Ashton. New York: Continuum, 1973.

———. "On the Fetish-Character in Music and the Regression of Listening." *The Essential Frankfurt School Reader*. Ed. Andrew Arato and Eike Gebhardt. New York: Continuum, 1982. 270–99.

———. "What Does 'Coming to Terms with the Past' Mean?" In *Bitburg in Moral and Political Perspective*. Ed. Geoffrey H. Hartman. Bloomington: Indiana University Press, 1986. 114–29.

After Communism: What? Special Issue, *Daedalus* 123.3 (1994).

Alewyn, Richard. "The Origin of the Detective Novel." *Poetics of Murder: Detective Fiction and Literary Theory*. Ed. Glenn W. Most and William W. Stowe. San Diego: Harcourt, Brace, Jovanovich, 1983. 62–78.

Arnold, Matthew. *Culture and Anarchy*. Ann Arbor: University of Michigan Press, 1965.

Artaud, Antonin. *The Theater and Its Double*. Trans. Mary Caroline Richards. New York: Grove Press, 1958.

Attridge, Derek. *The Singularity of Literature*. London and New York: Routledge, 2004.

Auster, Paul. *City of Glass. The New York Trilogy*. New York: Penguin, 1990. 1–158.

Awakenings. Dir. Penny Marshall. Columbia Pictures, 1990.

Babylonian Talmud; Seder Nezikin, in Four Volumes. Trans. I. Epstein. London: Soncino Press, 1961.

Badiou, Alain. *Ethics: An Essay on the Understanding of Evil*. Trans. Peter Hallward. London and New York: Verso, 2001.

Baker, Robert. *The Extravagant: Crossings in Modern Poetry and Modern Philosophy*. Notre Dame, IN: University of Notre Dame Press, 2005.

Bakhtin, M. M. *The Bakhtin Reader: Selected Writings of Bakhtin, Medvedev, Voloshinov*. Ed. Pam Morris. London and New York: E. Arnold, 1994.

Barker, Claire. "Disability Theory (Review)." *Journal of Literary and Cultural Disability Studies* 4 (2010): 105–107.

Barnes, Djuna. *Nightwood*. New York: New Directions, 1961.

Baron-Cohen, Simon. *Mindblindness: An Essay on Autism and Theory of Mind*. Cambridge, MA: MIT Press, 1995.

———, Helen Tager-Flusberg, and Donald J. Cohen, eds. *Understanding Other Minds: Perspectives from Developmental Cognitive Neuroscience*. Oxford and New York: Oxford University Press, 2000.

Barthes, Roland. *The Rustle of Language*. Trans. Richard Howard. Berkeley and Los Angeles: University of California Press, 1989.

Bataille, George. *Visions of Excess: Selected Writings, 1927–1939*. Ed. Allan Stoekl. Trans. Allan Stoekl, Carl R. Lovitt, Donald M. Leslie, Jr. Minneapolis: University of Minnesota Press, 1985.

Baudrillard, Jean. *Simulations*. Trans. Paul Foss, Paul Patton, and Philip Bleitchman. New York: Semiotext(e), 1983.

Beckett, Samuel. *The Letters of Samuel Beckett, vol. 1: 1929–1940*. Cambridge, UK: Cambridge University Press, 2009.

Benhabib, Seyla. *Situating the Self: Gender, Community and Postmodernism in Contemporary Ethics*. New York: Routledge, 1992.

Benjamin, Jessica. *The Bonds of Love: Psychoanalysis, Feminism, and the Problem of Domination*. New York: Pantheon, 1988.

Benjamin, Walter. "On Language as Such and on the Language of Man." *Reflections: Essays, Aphorisms, Autobiographical Writings*. Ed. Peter Demetz. Trans. Edmund Jephcott. New York: Schocken, 1978. 314–32.

———. "Theses on the Philosophy of History." *Illuminations: Essays and Reflections*. Ed. Hannah Arendt. Trans. Harry Zohn. New York: Harcourt Brace Jovanovich, 1968. 253–64.

Berger, James. *After the End: Representations of Post-Apocalypse*. Minneapolis: University of Minnesota Press, 1999.

———. "Editor's Preface: Documents of an Education." Helen Keller. *The Story of My Life: The Restored Edition*. Ed. James Berger. New York: Random House Modern Library, 2003. Vii–xxxv.

———. "Falling Towers and Postmodern Wild Children: Oliver Sacks, Don DeLillo, and Turns against Language." *PMLA* 120 (2005): 341–61.

———. *Prior*. Kenmore ,NY: BlazeVox, 2013.

———. "Trauma without Disability, Disability without Trauma: A Disciplinary Divide." *JAC: A Quarterly Journal for the Interdisciplinary Study of Rhetoric, Writing, Multiple Literacies, and Politics* 24 (2004): 563–82.

Berlant, Lauren. "Compassion (and Withholding)." *Compassion: The Culture and Politics of an Emotion*. Ed. Lauren Berlant. New York and London: Routledge, 2004. 1–13.

———, ed. *Compassion: The Culture and Politics of an Emotion*. New York and London: Routledge, 2004.

Berlin, Isaiah. *The Roots of Romanticism*. Princeton, NJ: Princeton University Press, 1999.

Belmonte, Matthew. "Human but More So: What the Autistic Brain Tells Us about the Process of Narrative." *Autism and Representation*. Ed. Mark Osteen. New York: Routledge, 2007. 166–79.

Bersani, Leo. "Is the Rectum a Grave?" *October* 43 (1997): 197–222.

Bérubé, Michael. "Disability and Narrative." *PMLA* 120 (2005): 568–76.

———. *Life as We Know It: A Father, a Family, and an Exceptional Child*. New York: Pantheon, 1996,

Bewell, Alan. *Wordsworth and the Enlightenment: Nature, Man, and Society in the Experimental Poetry*. New Haven, CT: Yale University Press, 1989.

Black, Max. "Metaphor." *Proceedings of the Aristotelian Society* New Series 55 (1954–1955): 273–94.

Blake, William. *Complete Writings*. Ed. Geoffrey Keynes. New York: Oxford University Press, 1972.

Blasing, Mutlu Konuk. *Lyric Poetry: The Pain and the Pleasure of Words*. Princeton, NJ: Princeton University Press, 2007.

Bloch, Ernst. *The Utopian Function of Art and Literature: Selected Essays*. Trans. Jack Zipes and Frank Mecklenburg. Cambridge, MA: MIT Press, 1988.

Bloom, Alexander, ed. *Long Time Gone: Sixties America Then and Now*. Oxford and New York: Oxford University Press, 2001.

Bloom, Allan. *The Closing of the American Mind*. New York: Simon and Schuster, 1987.

Blue Velvet. Dir. David Lynch. De Laurentiis Entertainment Group, 1986.

Bonca, Cornel. "Don DeLillo's *White Noise*: The Natural Language of the Species." *College Literature* 23 (1996): 25–44.

Boris, Eileen, and Jennifer Klein. *Caring for America: Home Heath Workers in the Shadow of the Welfare State*. New York: Oxford University Press, 2012.

Brand, Dana. *Mets Fan*. New York: McFarland, 2007.

Brassed Off. Dir. Mark Herman. Miramax, 1997.

Brockley, Janice. "Rearing the Child Who Never Grew: Ideologies of Parenting and Intellectual Disability in American History." *Mental Retardation in America*. Ed. Steven Noll and James W. Trent, Jr. New York and London: New York University Press, 2004. 130–164.

Bronfen, Elisabeth. "The Body and Its Discontents." *Body Matters: Feminism, Textuality, Corporeality*. Ed. Avril Horner and Angela Keane. Manchester and New York: Manchester University Press, 2000. 109–23.

Bruner, Jerome. "Hole in the World." *New York Review of Books* 31 (September 27, 1984): 39–41.

Bryant, Paula. "Discussing the Untellable: Don DeLillo's *The Names*." *Critique* 29 (1987): 16–29.

Burke, Kenneth. "What Are the Signs of What? A Theory of 'Entitlement.'" *Language as Symbolic Action: Essays on Life, Literature, and Method*. Berkeley: University of California Press, 1966. 358–79.

Burks-Abbott, Gyasi. "Mark Haddon's Popularity and Other Curious Incidences in My Life as an Autistic." In *Autism and Representation*. Ed. Mark Osteen. New York: Routledge, 2008. 289–96.

Burton, Stacy. "Benjy, Narrativity, and the Coherence of Compson History." *Cardozo Studies in Law & Literature* 7 (1995): 207–28.

Butler, Judith. *Bodies that Matter: On the Discursive Limits of "Sex."* New York and London: Routledge, 1993.

Callahan, Raymond E. *Education and the Cult of Efficiency: A Study of the Social Forces that Have Shaped the Administration of the Public Schools.* Chicago; University of Chicago Press, 1962.

Cameron, Sharon. *Impersonality: Seven Essays.* Chicago and London: University of Chicago Press, 2007.

Caplan, Brina. "Orders of Wisdom." *The Nation.* 242 (February 22, 1986): 211–13.

Caramazza, Alfonso. "Parallels and Divergences in the Acquisition and Dissolution of Language." *Philosophical Transactions in Biological Sciences* 346 (1994): 121–27.

Carlson, Licia. *Faces of Intellectual Disability.* Bloomington: Indiana University Press, 2010.

Carlston, Erin. *Thinking Fascism: Sapphic Modernism and Fascist Modernity.* Stanford, CA: Stanford University Press, 1998.

Carr, David. "Narrative and the Real World: An Argument for Continuity." *History and Theory: Contemporary Readings.* Ed. Brian Fay, Philip Pomper, and Richard T. Vann. Malden, MA, and Oxford, UK: Blackwell, 1998. 137–52.

Caruth, Cathy. *Unclaimed Experience: Trauma, Narrative, and History.* Baltimore: Johns Hopkins University Press, 1996.

Cassuto, Leonard. "Oliver Sacks and the Medical Case Narrative." *Disability Studies: Enabling the Humanities.* Ed. Sharon L. Snyder, Brenda Jo Breuggermann, and Rosemarie Garland-Thomson. New York: MLA, 2002.

Clemons, Walter. "Try a Little Tenderness: New Books Dissect Modern Medicine." *Newsweek* 106 (December 30, 1985): 63.

Cloud of Unknowing, and Other Works. Trans. A. C. Spearing. London: Penguin, 2001. 11–101.

Changeux, Jean-Pierre. *Neuronal Man: The Biology of Mind.* Trans. Laurence Garey. Princeton, NJ: Princeton University Press, 1997.

Coetzee, J. M. *Life and Times of Joseph K.* New York: Penguin, 1983.

Conrad, Joseph. *The Secret Agent.* New York and London: Penguin, 1984.

Couser, G. Thomas. *Vulnerable Subjects: Ethics and Life Writing.* Ithaca, NY: Cornell University Press, 2004.

Cowart, David. *Don DeLillo: The Physics of Language.* Athens and London: University of Georgia Press, 2002.

Crane, Mary Thomas. *Shakespeare's Brain.* Princeton, NJ: Princeton University Press, 2000.

Damasio, Antonio. *The Feeling of What Happens: Body and Emotion in the Making of Consciousness.* New York: Harcourt, Brace, 1999.

Davidson, Donald. "What Metaphors Mean." *Inquiries into Truth and Interpretation.* Oxford and New York: Clarendon Press, 1984. 245–64.

Davidson, Michael. *Concerto for the Left Hand: Disability and the Defamiliar Body.* Ann Arbor: University of Michigan Press, 2008.

———. "Introduction." *Journal of Literary and Cultural Disability* 1 (2007): i–v.

Davies, Stanley Powell. *Social Control of the Mentally Deficient.* Second ed. New York: Crowell, 1930.

Davis, Lennard J. *Bending Over Backwards: Disability, Dismodernism, and Other Difficult Positions.* New York: New York University Press, 2002.

———. "Dependency and Justice." *Journal of Literary and Cultural Disability* 1 (2007): 1–4.

———. "Disability: The Next Wave or Twilight of the Gods?" *PMLA* 120 (2005): 527–32.

———. *Enforcing Normalcy: Disability, Deafness, and the Body.* London and New York: Verso, 1995.

Deacon, Terrence W. *The Symbolic Species: The Co-evolution of Language and the Brain.* New York and London: W. W. Norton, 1997.

DeCurtis, Anthony. "'An Outsider in This Society': An Interview with Don DeLillo." *Introducing Don DeLillo.* Ed. Frank Lentricchia. Durham, NC: Duke University Press, 1991. 32–66.

Deleuze, Gilles, and Felix Guattari. *A Thousand Plateaus: Capitalism and Schizophrenia.* Trans. Brian Massumi. Minneapolis and London: University of Minnesota Press, 1987.

DeLillo, Don. *The Body Artist.* New York: Scribner, 2001.

———. *Great Jones Street.* Boston: Houghton Mifflin, 1973.

———. *Libra.* New York: Viking, 1988.

———. *The Names.* New York: Knopf, 1982.

———. *White Noise.* New York: Viking, 1985.

De Man, Paul. "The Rhetoric of Temporality." *Blindness and Insight: Essays in the Rhetoric of Contemporary Critcism."* Second ed,., rev. Minneapolis: University of Minnesota Press, 1983. 187–228.

Dennett, Daniel C. *Brainchild: Essays on Designing Minds.* Cambridge, MA: MIT Press, 1998.

———. *Brainstorms: Philosophical Essays on Mind and Psychology.* Cambridge, MA: MIT Press, 1981.

———. *Consciousness Explained.* Boston: Little Brown, 1991.

Derrida, Jacques. *Acts of Religion.* Ed. Gil Anidjar. New York and London: Routledge, 2002.

———. "Force of Law: The 'Mystical Foundation of Authority.'" *Deconstruction and the Possibility of Justice.* Ed. Drucilla Cornell, Michel Rosenfeld, and David Gray Carlson. New York: Routledge, 1992.

———. "Differance." *Margins of Philosophy.* Trans. Alan Bass. Chicago: University of Chicago Press, 1982. 1–28.

———. *The Gift of Death.* Trans. David Wills. Chicago and London: University of Chicago Press, 1995.

———. "Shibboleth." *Midrash and Literature.* Ed. Geoffrey H. Hartman and Sanford Budick. New Haven and London: Yale University Press, 1986. 307–47.

———. "Structure, Sign, and Play in the Discourse of the Human Sciences." *Writing and Difference.* Trans. Alan Bass. Chicago: University of Chicago Press, 1987.

———. "Violence and Metaphysics: An Essay on the Thought of Emmanuel Levinas." *Writing and Difference*. Ed. and trans. Alan Bass. Chicago: University of Chicago Press, 1978. 79–153.

———. "White Mythology: Metaphor in the Text of Philosophy." *Margins of Philosophy*. Trans. Alan Bass. Chicago: University of Chicago Press, 1982. 207–72.

De Waal, Frans B. M. *Good Natured: The Origins of Right and Wrong in Primates and Other Animals*. Cambridge, MA: Harvard University Press, 1996.

Dewey, Joseph. *In a Dark Time: The Apocalyptic Temper in the American Novel of the Nuclear Age*. West Lafayette, IN: Purdie University Press, 1990.

Dickstein, Morris. *Gates of Eden: American Culture in the Sixties*. New York: Penguin, 1989.

"A Discussion about Theory of Mind: From an Autistic Perspective." Autism Europe's Congress, 2000. www.autistics.org/library/AE2000-ToM.html.

Dostoevsky, Fyodor. *The Idiot*. Trans. Alan Myers. Oxford and New York: Oxford University Press, 2008.

DSM-IV: Diagnostic and Statistical Manual of Mental Disorders. Washington, DC: American Psychiatric Association, 1994.

Dugdale, R. L. *The Jukes: A Study in Crime, Pauperism, Disease, and Heredity*. New York: Putnam, 1910.

Eco, Umberto. *The Search for a Perfect Language*. Trans. James Fentress. Oxford, UK, and Cambridge, MA: Blackwell, 1995.

Edelman, Gerald M. *The Remembered Present: A Biological Theory of Consciousness*. New York: Basic Books, 1989.

Edelman, Lee. *No Future: Queer Theory and the Death Drive*. Durham, NC, and London: Duke University Press, 2004.

Edmond, Rod. "Home and Away: Degeneration in Imperialist and Modernist Discourse." *Modernism and Empire*. Ed. Nigel Rigby. Manchester, UK: Manchester University Press, 2000. 36–63.

Eysteinnson, Astradur. *The Concept of Modernism*. Ithaca: Cornell University Press, 1990.

Faulkner, William. *The Sound and the Fury*. New York: Vintage, 1990.

Fassin, Didier, and Richard Rechtman. *The Empire of Trauma: An Inquiry into the Condition of Victimhood*. Trans. Rachel Gomme. Princeton, NJ: Princeton University Press, 2009.

Felman, Shoshona, and Dori Laub. *Testimony: Crises of Witnessing in Literature, Psychoanalysis, and History*. New York: Routledge, 1992.

Fisher, Seymour, and Roger P. Greenberg. "A Second Opinion: Rethinking the Claims of Biological Psychiatry." *The Limits of Biological Treatments for Psychological Distress: Comparisons with Psychotherapy and Placebo*. Ed. Seymour Fisher and Roger P. Greenberg. Hillsdale, NJ: Lawrence Erlbaum Associates, 1989. 309–36.

Fitzgerald, F. Scott. *The Great Gatsby*. New York: Scribner, 2004.

Flack, Jessica C., and Frans B. M. de Waal. "'Any Animal Whatever': Darwinian Building Blocks of Morality in Monkeys and Apes." *Journal of Consciousness Studies* 7 (2000): 1–29.

Fogel, Aaron. *Coercion to Speak: Conrad's Poetics of Dialogue*. Cambridge, MA: Harvard University Press, 1985.

Forster, E. M. *A Passage to India*. New York: Harcourt, Brace, and World, 1952.

Foster, Dennis A. *Sublime Enjoyment: On the Perverse Motive in American Literature*. Cambridge, UK, and New York: Cambridge University Press, 1997.

Foucault, Michel. *Madness and Civilization: A History of Insanity in the Age of Reason*. Trans. Richard Howard. New York: Vintage, 1965.

———. *The Order of Things: An Archaeology of the Human Sciences*. New York: Vintage, 1973.

Fraade, Steven D. "Hearing and Seeing at Sinai: Interpretive Trajectories." *Sinai Revisited: Jewish and Christian Interpretations*. Ed. George J. Brooke, Hindy Najman, and Loren T. Stuckenbruck. Leiden: Brill, 2008. 247–68.

Franzen, Jonathan. *The Corrections*. New York: Picador, 2001.

Freedman, Daniel X. "Where the Rest of Him Was." *New York Times Book Review* (November 11, 1984): 11–12.

Freud, Sigmund. *Beyond the Pleasure Principle*. Trans. James Strachey. New York: W. W. Norton, 1990.

———. *Civilization and Its Discontents*. Trans. James Strachey. New York: W. W. Norton, 1989.

———. "Fetishism." *The Standard Edition of the Complete Psychological Works of Sigmund Freud*. Trans. James Strachey. Vol. 21: 149–57.

———. *Moses and Monotheism*. Trans. Katherine Jones. New York: Vintage, 1967.

———. *Totem and Taboo: Resemblances between the Psychic Lives of Savages and Neurotics*. Trans. A. A. Brill. New York: Vintage, 1946.

Friedlander, Saul. "Themes of Decline and End in Nineteenth-Century Western Imagination." *Visions of Apocalypse: End or Rebirth?* New York: Holmes and Meier, 1984. 61–83.

Frith, Uta. *Autism: Explaining the Enigma*. Oxford, UK, and Cambridge, MA: Basil Blackwell, 1989.

Frow, John. "The Last Things before the Last: Notes on *White Noise*." *Introducing Don DeLillo*. Ed. Frank Lentricchia. Durham, NC: Duke University Press, 1991. 175–91.

The Full Monty. Dir. Peter Cattaneo. Fox Searchlight Pictures, 1997.

Garber, Marjorie. "Compassion." *Compassion: The Culture and Politics of an Emotion*. Ed. Lauren Berlant. New York and London: Routledge, 2004. 15–28.

Garland-Thomson, Rosemarie. *Extraordinary Bodies: Figuring Disability in American Culture and Literature*. New York: Columbia University Press, 1997.

Genette, Gerard. *Mimologics*. Trans. Thais E. Morgan. Lincoln, NB, and London: University of Nebraska Press, 1994.

Gilmore, Glenda Elizabeth. *Defying Dixie: The Radical Roots of Civil Rights, 1919–1950*. New York: W. W. Norton, 2008.

Gleeson-White, Sarah. *Strange Bodies: Gender and Identity in the Novels of Carson McCullers*. Tuscaloosa: University of Alabama Press, 2003.

Goddard, Henry Herbert. *Feeble-Mindedness: Its Causes and Consequences*. New York: McMillan, 1926.

———. *The Kallikak Family: A Study in the Heredity of Feeble-Mindedness*. New York: Macmillan, 1923.

Goldstein, Kurt. *The Organism: A Holistic Approach to Biology Derived from Pathological Data in Man*. New York: Zone Books, 1995.

Goode, David. *A World without Words: The Social Construction of Children Born Deaf and Blind*. Philadelphia: Temple University Press, 1994.

Goodey, C. F. *A History of Intelligence and "Intellectual Disability": The Shaping of Psychology in Early Modern Europe*. Farnham, UK, and Burlington, VT: Ashgate, 2011.

Goodman, Paul. *Growing Up Absurd: Problems of Youth in the Organized System*. New York: Random House, 1960.

Gould, Steven Jay. *The Mismeasure of Man*. New York and London: Norton, 1996.

Gopnik, Alison. "What the Myth of Mirror Neurons Gets Wrong About the Human Brain." *Slate.com*, April 26, 2007.

Grandin, Temple. *Thinking in Pictures and Other Reports from My Life with Autism*. New York: Vintage, 1995.

Greenberg, Jonathan. "Why Can't Biologists Read Poetry? Ian McEwan's *Enduring Love*." *Twentieth Century Literature* 53 (2007): 93–124.

Greenberg, Judith, ed. *Trauma at Home: After 9/11*. Lincoln: University of Nebraska Press, 2003.

Greenslade, William P. *Degeneration, Culture, and the Novel: 1880–1940*. Cambridge, UK: Cambridge University Press, 1994.

Habermas, Jurgen. *The Philosophical Discourse of Modernity: Twelve Lectures*. Trans. Frederick Lawrence. Cambridge, MA: MIT Press, 1987.

———. *The Theory of Communicative Action*. Trans. Thomas McCarthy. 2 vols. Boston: Beacon Press, 1983.

Haddon, Mark. *The Curious Incident of the Dog in the Night-Time*. New York: Doubleday, 2003.

———. "The Curiously Irresistable Literary Debut of Mark Haddon." Interview with David Weich, 2003. www.powells.com/authors/haddon.html.

Halliwell, Martin. *Images of Idiocy: The Idiot Figure in Modern Fiction and Film*. Aldershot, UK, and Burlington, VT: Ashgate, 2004.

Haraway, Donna. "A Cyborg Manifesto: Science, Techonology, and Socialist-Feminism in the Late Twentieth Century." *Simians, Cyborgs, and Women: The Reinvention of Nature*. New York: Routledge, 1991. 149–81.

Hardt, Michael, and Antonio Negri. *Commonwealth*. Cambridge MA: Harvard University Press, 2009.

Harpham, Geoffrey Galt. *Getting It Right: Language, Literature, and Ethics*. Chicago: University of Chicago Press, 1992.

———. *Language Alone: The Critical Fetish of Modernity*. New York and London: Routledge, 2002.

Hartman, Geoffrey H. "On Traumatic Knowledge and Literary Studies." *New Literary History* 26 (1995): 537–63.

Harvey, David. *A Brief History of Neoliberalism*. Oxford and New York: Oxford University Press, 2005.

Hayles, N. Katherine. *How We Became Posthuman: Virtual Bodies in Cybernetics, Literature, and Informatics*. Chicago: University of Chicago Press, 1999.

Head, Henry. *Aphasia and Kindred Disorders of Speech*. Cambridge: The University Press, 1926.

Heaney, Seamus. *The Cure at Troy: A Version of Sophocles' Philoctetes*. New York: Noonday Press, 1991.

Heller-Roazen, Daniel. *Echolalias: On the Forgetting of Language*. Cambridge, MA: Zone Books, 2008.

Hermann, Dorothy. *Helen Keller: A Life*. New York: Knopf, 1998.

Hirsch, Marianne. *Family Frames: Photography, Narrative, and Postmemory*. Cambridge, MA: Harvard University Press, 1997.

Hochschild, Arlie. *The Managed Heart: Commercialization of Human Feeling*, updated with a new preface. Berkeley: University of California Press, 2012.

Hogan, Patrick Colm. *Cognitive Science, Literature, and the Arts: A Guide for Humanists*. New York: Routledge, 2003.

Hughlings-Jackson, John. *Selected Writings*. Edited for the Guarantors of Brain by James Taylor, with the advice and guidance of Gordon Holmes and F. M. R. Walshe. New York: Basic Books, 1958.

Horkheimer, Max, and Theodor W. Adorno. *Dialectic of Enlightenment*. New York: Continuum, 1969,

Hungerford, Amy. *Postmodern Belief: American Literature and Religion since 1960*. Princeton, NJ, and Oxford, UK: Princeton University Press, 2010.

Hyman, Steven E., and Eric J. Nestler. *The Molecular Foundations of Psychiatry*. Washington, DC: American Psychiatric Press, 1993.

Isserman, Maurice, and Michael Kazin. *America Divided: The Civil War of the 1960s*. New York: Oxford University Press, 2012.

Jackson, Mark. *The Borderland of Imbecility: Medicine, Society, and the Fabrication of the Feeble Mind in Later Victorian and Edwardian England*. Manchester, UK: Manchester University Press, 2000.

Jakobson, Roman. "Two Aspects of Language and Two Types of Aphasic Disturbances." *Language in Literature*. Ed. Krystyna Pomorska and Stephen Rudy. Cambridge, MA: Harvard University Press, 1987. 95–114.

James, William. *A Pluralistic Universe*. Cambridge, MA: Harvard University Press, 1977.

Jameson, Fredric. *The Prison-House of Language: A Critical Account of Structuralism and Russian Formalism*. Princeton: Princeton University Press, 1982.

——. "Reification and Utopia in Mass Culture." *Social Text* 1 (1979):130–48.

Johnson, Barbara. "Melville's Fist: The Execution of *Billy Budd*." *The Critical Difference: Essays in the Contemporary Rhetoric of Reading*. Baltimore: Johns Hopkins University Press, 1985. 79–109.

Joyce, Richard. *The Evolution of Morality*. Cambridge, MA: MIT Press, 2006.

Kartiganer, Donald M. "'Now I Can Write': Faulkner's Novel of Invention." *New Essays on The Sound and the Fury*. Ed. Noel Polk. Cambridge: Cambridge University Press, 1993. 71–98.

Kazin, Michael. *American Dreamers: How the Left Changed a Nation*. New York: Knopf, 2011.

Kelley, Robin. *Hammer and Hoe : Alabama Communists during the Great Depression*. Chapel Hill: University of North Carolina Press, 1990.

Kermode, Frank. *The Sense of an Ending: Studies in the Theory of Fiction*. London: Oxford University Press, 1968.

Kevles, Daniel J. *In the Name of Eugenics: Genetics and the Uses of Human Heredity*. Cambridge, MA, and London: Harvard University Press, 1995.

Kierkegaard, Søren. *Fear and Trembling*. Trans. Alistair Hannay. New York: Penguin, 1985.

Kimball, Roger. *Tenured Radicals: How Politics Has Corrupted Our Higher Education*. New York: Harper and Row, 1990.

Kittay, Eva Feder. *Love's Labor: Essays on Women, Equality, and Dependency*. London: Routledge, 1999.

Klages, Mary. *Woeful Afflictions: Disability and Sentimentality in Victorian America*. Philadelphia: University of Pensylvania Press, 1999.

Klink, Joanna. *Circadian*. New York: Penguin, 2007

Kobets, Svitlana. "Foolishness in Christ: East vs. West." *Canadian-American Slavic Studies* 34 (2000): 337–64.

Kosinski, Jerzy. *Being There*. New York: Bantam, 1970.

Kramer, Peter. *Listening to Prozac: A Psychiatrist Explores Antidepressant Drugs and the Remaking of the Self*. New York: Viking, 1993.

Kristeva, Julia. *Interviews*. Ed. Ross Mitchell Guberman. New York: Columbia University Press, 1996.

———. *Revolution in Poetic Language*. Trans. Margaret Waller. New York: Columbia University Press, 1984.

Krumland, Heidi. "'A Big Deaf Mute Moron': Eugenic Traces in Carson McCullers's *The Heart is a Lonely Hunter*." *Journal of Literary Disability* 2 (2008): 32–43.

Lacan, Jacques. *Ecrits: A Selection*. Trans. Alan Sheridan. New York: Norton, 1977.

———. *The Four Fundamental Concepts of Psycho-Analysis*. Ed. Jacques-Alain Miller. Trans. Alan Sheridan. New York: Norton, 1981.

LaCapra, Dominick. *History and Its Limits: Human, Animal, Violence*. Ithaca: Cornell University Press, 2009.

———. *Writing History, Writing Trauma*. Baltimore, MD, and London: Johns Hopkins University Press, 2001.

Lakoff, George, and Mark Johnson. *Metaphors We Live By*. Chicago: University of Chicago Press, 2003.

Lane, Harlan. *The Wild Boy of Aveyron*. Cambridge, MA: Harvard University Press, 1976.

Langer, Lawrence L. *Holocaust Testimonies: The Ruins of Memory*. New Haven, CT: Yale University Press, 1991.

Lazar, Mary. "Jerzy Kosinski's *Being There*, Novel and Film: Changes Not by Chance." *College Literature* 31 (2004): 99–116.

Lecercle, Jean-Jacques. *The Violence of Language*. London: Routledge, 1990.

LeDoux, Joseph. *Synaptic Self: How Our Brains Become Who We Are*. New York: Penguin, 2002.

Lefebvre, Henri. *Introduction to Modernity: Twelve Preludes, September 1959–May 1961*. Trans. John Moore. London: Verso, 1995.

Lentricchia, Frank. "*Libra* as Postmodern Critique." *Introducing Don DeLillo*. Ed. Frank Lentricchia. Durham, NC: Duke University Press, 1991. 193–215.

———, ed. *Introducing Don DeLillo*. Durham, NC: Duke University Press, 1991.

LeMahieu, Michael. "Nonsense Modernism: The Limits of Modernity and the Feelings of Philosophy in Wittgenstein's *Tractatus*." *Bad Modernisms*. Ed. Douglas Mao and Rebecca L. Walkowitz. Durham, NC: Duke University Press, 2006. 68–93.

Lethem, Jonathan. *Motherless Brooklyn*. New York: Vintage, 1999.

Levinas, Emmanuel. *Otherwise Than Being or Beyond Essence*. Trans. Alphonso Lingis. The Hague: Martinus Nijhoff, 1981.

———. *Totality and Infinity*. Trans. Alphonso Lingis. Pittsburgh, PA: Duquesne University Press, 1969.

Levitan, Daniel J. *This is Your Brain on Music: The Science of a Human Obsession*. New York: Plume/Penguin, 2007.

Lewontin, R.C. *Biology as Ideology: The Doctrine of DNA*. New York: HarperPerennial, 1991.

Linett, Maren Tova. *Modernism, Feminism, and Jewishness*. Cambridge , UK ,and New York: Cambridge University Press, 2007.

Linton, Simi. *Claiming Disability: Knowledge and Identity*. New York: New York University Press, 1998.

———. *My Body Politic: A Memoir*. Ann Arbor: University of Michigan Press, 2007.

Lombroso, Gina. *Criminal Man, According to the Classification of Cesare Lombroso, Briefly Summarised by Gina Lombroso Ferrero*. New York: Putnam, 1911.

Luhmann, Niklas. *Essays on Self-Reference*. New York: Columbia University Press, 1990.

Lukács, Georg. *The Meaning of Contemporary Realism*. Trans. John and Necke Mander. London: Merlin Press, 1963.

Lumpkin, Katherine Du Pre. *The South in Progress*. New York: International, 1940.

Luria, Alexander. *The Man with a Shattered World: The History of a Brain Wound*. Trans. Lynn Solataroff. New York: Basic Books, 1972.

Lyotard, Jean-François. *The Differend*. Trans. George Can Den Abbeele. Minneapolis: University of Minnesota Press, 1988.

Malabou, Catherine. *What Shall We Do with Our Brain?* Trans. Sebastian Rand. New York: Fordham University Press, 2008.

Maltby, Paul. "The Romantic Metaphysics of Don DeLillo." *Contemporary Literature* 37 (1996): 258–77.

Marcus, Jane. "Laughing at Leviticus: *Nightwood* as Woman's Circus Epic." *Silence and Power: A Reevaluation of Djuna Barnes*. Ed. Mary Lynn Broe. Carbondale: Southern Illinois University Press, 1991.

Marcus, Steven. "Dashiell Hammett." *Poetics of Murder: Detective Fiction and Literary Theory*. Ed. Glenn W. Most and William W. Stowe. San Diego: Harcourt, Brace, Jovanovich, 1983. 197–209.

Marcuse, Herbert. *The Aesthetic Dimension*. Boston: Beacon Press, 1978.

———. "The Affirmative Character of Culture." *Negations*. Boston: Beacon Press, 1968. 88–133.

———. *Counter-Revolution and Revolt*. Boston: Beacon Press, 1972.

———. *An Essay on Liberation*. Boston: Beacon Press, 1969,

———. "A Note on Dialectic." *The Essential Frankfurt School Reader*. Ed. Andrew Arato and Eike Gebhardt. New York: Continuum, 1987. 444–51.

Marks, Herbert. "On Prophetic Stammering." *Yale Journal of Criticism* 1 (1987): 1–20.

Marx, Karl, and Friedrich Engels. *The Communist Manifesto*. Trans. Samuel Moore. New York: Penguin, 1967.

Masson, Jeffrey Moussaieff. *Lost Prince: The Unsolved Mystery of Kaspar Hauser*. New York: Free Press, 1996.

Matthews, John T. "The Discovery of Loss in *The Sound and the Fury*." *The Sound and the Fury: A Norton Critical Edition*. Ed. David Minter. New York: W.W. Norton, 1994. 370–93.

———. *The Play of Faulkner's Language*. Ithaca and London: Cornell University Press, 1982.

McCullers, Carson. *The Heart is a Lonely Hunter*. Boston and New York: Mariner, 2004.

———. "Author's Outline of 'The Mute' (*The Heart is a Lonely Hunter*)." *The Mortagaged Heart: Selected Writings*. Ed. Margarita G. Smith. New York: Mariner, 2005. 124–52.

McDonagh, Patrick. *Idiocy: A Cultural History*. Liverpool: Liverpool University Press, 2008.

McEwan, Ian. *Saturday*. Garden City, NY: Anchor, 2006.

McRuer, Robert. *Crip Theory: Cultural Signs of Queerness and Disability*. New York: New York University Press, 2006.

Melville, Herman. *Billy Budd, Sailor*. New York: Washington Square Press, 1999.

———. *Moby Dick; or, The Whale*. Ed. Hershel Parker and Harrison Hayford. New York and London: W. W. Norton, 2002.

———. Pierre: or, the Ambiguities. Evanston, IL: Northwestern University Press, 1972.

Merleau-Ponty, Maurice. *The Prose of the World*. Ed. Claude Lefort. Trans. John O'Neill. Evanston, IL: Northwestern University Press, 1973.

Midrash Rabbah, Genesis. Ed. H. Freedman and Maurice Simon. Condon and New York: Soncino Press, 1983.

Mizruchi, Susan L. *The Science of Sacrifice: American Literature and Modern Social Theory*. Princeton, NJ: Princeton University Press, 1998.

Million Dollar Baby. Dir. Clint Eastwood. Warner Brothers, 2004.

Mink, Louis O. "History and Fiction as Modes of Comprehension." *History and Theory: Contemporary Readings.* Ed. Brian Fay, Philip Pomper, and Richard T. Vann. Malden, MA, and Oxford, UK: Blackwell, 1998. 121–36.

Minter, David. "Falkner, Childhood, and the Making of *The Sound and the Fury.*" In *The Sound and the Fury: An Authoritative Text, Backgrounds and Contexts.* Ed. David Minter. New York: Norton, 1994. 343–58.

Mitchell, David T., and Sharon L. Snyder. *Cultural Locations of Disability.* Chicago: University of Chicago Press, 2006.

———. *Narrative Prosthesis: Disability and the Dependencies of Discourse.* Ann Arbor: University of Michigan Press, 2000.

Morrison, Daniel R., and Monica J. Casper. "Intersections of Disability Studies and Critical Trauma Studies: A Provocation." *Disability Studies Quarterly* 32 (2012).

Morrison, Toni. *Sula.* New York: Knopf, 1973.

Morson, Gary Saul. "Narrativeness." *New Literary History* 34 (2003): 59–73.

Murray, Stuart. *Autism.* New York and London: Routledge, 2011.

———. *Representing Autism: Culture, Narrative, Fascination.* Liverpool: Liverpool University Press, 2008.

Nell. Dir. Michael Apted. 20ᵗʰ Century Fox, 1994.

New English Bible, with the Apocrypha. New York: Oxford University Press, 1971.

Nielsen, Kim. *The Radical Lives of Helen Keller.* New York: New York University Press, 2004.

Noe, Alva. *Out of Our Heads: Why You Are Not Your Brain, and Other Lessons from the Biology of Consciousness.* New York: Hill and Wang, 2009.

Noll, Steven. *Feeble-Minded in Our Midst: Institutions for the Mentally Retarded in the South, 1900–1940.* Chapel Hill: University of North Carolina Press, 1995.

———, and James W. Trent, eds. *Mental Retardation in America.* New York and London: New York University Press, 2004.

Nordau, Max. *Degeneration.* Lincoln and London: University of Nebraska Press, 1993.

Norman, Andrew P. "Telling It Like It Was: Historical Narratives on Their Own Terms." *History and Theory: Contemporary Readings.* Ed. Brian Fay, Philip Pomper, and Richard T. Vann. Malden, MA, and Oxford, UK: Blackwell, 1998. 153–71.

Nussbaum, Martha C. *Frontiers of Justice: Disability, Nationality, Species Membership.* Cambridge, MA: Harvard University Press, 2007.

———. *Hiding From Humanity: Disgust, Shame, and the Law.* Princeton, NJ: Princeton University Press, 2004.

———. *Poetic Justice: The Literary Imagination and Public Life.* Boston: Beacon Press, 1995.

———. *Upheavals of Thought: The Intelligence of Emotions.* Cambridge, UK: Cambridge University Press, 2001.

On the Origin of Fictions: Interdisciplinary Perspectives. Special Issue, ed. H. Porter Abbott. *Substance* 30 (2001): 3–253.

Osteen, Mark. *American Magic and Dread: Don DeLillo's Dialogue with Culture.* Philadelphia: University of Pennsylvania Press, 2000.

———. "Autism and Representation: A Comprehensive Introduction." *Autism and Representation.* Ed. Mark Osteen. New York and London: Routledge, 2008.

———, ed. *Autism and Representation.* New York and London: Routledge, 2008.

Parker, Patricia. "Metaphor and Catachresis." *The Ends of Rhetoric: History, Theory, Practice.* Ed. John Bender and David Wellbery. Stanford, CA: Stanford University Press, 1990. 60–73.

Parsons, Talcott. *Social Systems and the Evolution of Action Theory.* New York: The Free Press, 1977.

Peirce, Charles S. *Selected Writings: Values in a Universe of Chance.* Ed. Philip P. Wiener. New York: Dover, 1958.

Pick, Daniel. *Faces of Degeneration: A European Disorder.* New York and London: Routledge, 2004.

Pinker, Steven. *The Language Instinct: How the Mind Creates Language.* New York: HarperCollins, 1995.

Plato. "Cratyllus." *The Dialogues of Plato.* vol. 3. Trans. B. Jowett. Oxford, UK: Clarendon Press, 1953. 1–106.

Polk, Noel. "Trying Not to Say: A Primer on the Language of *The Sound and the Fury.* *New Essays on The Sound and the Fury.* Ed. Noel Polk. Cambridge: Cambridge University Press. 139–76.

Powers, Richard. *The Echo Maker.* New York: Farrar, Straus and Giroux, 2006.

———. *Gain.* New York: Picador, 1998.

———. *Galatea 2.2.* New York: HarperCollins, 1995.

———. "An Interview with Richard Powers," with Jim Neilson. *Review of Contemporary Fiction* 18 (1998): 13–23.

Presley, Delma E. "Carson McCullers and the South." *Critical Essays on Carson McCullers.* Ed. Beverly Lyon Clark and Melvin Friedman. New York: Hall, 1996.

Prince, Michael. *Philosophical Dialogue in the British Enlightenment: Theology, Aesthetics, and the Novel.* Cambridge, UK, and New York: Cambridge University Press, 1996.

Prince-Hughes, Dawn. *Songs of the Gorilla Nation: My Journey through Autism.* New York: Harmony, 2004.

Putnam, Robert D. *Bowling Alone: The Collapse and Revival of American Community.* New York: Simon and Schuster, 2000.

Quayson, Ato. *Aesthetic Nervousness: Disability and the Crisis of Representation.* New York: Columbia University Press, 2007.

Quine, W. V. "Two Dogmas of Empiricism." *Perspectives in the Philosophy of Language.* Ed. Robert J. Stainton. Peterborough: Broadview Press, 2000. 189–210.

Quintillian. *Institutes of Oratory.* Trans. John Selby Watson. http://rhetoric.eserver.org/quintilian/8/chapter6.html.

Rain Man. Dir. Barry Levinson. MGM/UA, 1988.

Ramachandran, V. S. *The Tell-Tale Brain: A Neuroscientist's Quest for What Makes Us Human.* New York and London: W. W. Norton, 2011.

Rawls, John. *A Theory of Justice*. Cambridge, MA: Harvard University Press, 1999.

Ree, Jonathan. *I See a Voice: Deafness, Language, and the Senses—A Philosophical History*. New York: Metropolitan Books, 1999.

Rich, Adrienne. "Compulsory Heterosexuality and Lesbian Experience." *Blood, Bread, and Poetry: Selected Prose, 1979–1985*. New York: W. W. Norton, 1994. 167–87.

Richards, Penny L. "'Beside Her Sat Her Idiot Child': Families and Developmental Disability in Med-Nineteenth-Century America." *Mental Retardation in America*. Ed. Steven Noll and James W. Trent, Jr. New York and London: New York University Press, 2004. 65–84.

Ricoeur, Paul "The Metaphorical Process as Cognition, Imagination, and Feeling." *On Metaphor*. Ed. Sheldon Sachs. Chicago: University of Chicago Press, 1978. 141–57.

———. "Narrative Time." *Critical Inquiry* 7 (1980): 169–212.

———. "Word, Polysemy, Metaphor: Creativity in Language." *A Ricoeur Reader*. Ed. M. J. Valdes. Toronto: University of Toronto Press, 1991. 65–85.

Rizzolati, Giacomo. "The Mirror Neuron System and Its Function in Humans." *Anatomical Embryology* 210 (2005): 419–21.

———, and Laila Craighero. "The Mirror-Neuron System." *Annual Review of Neuroscience* 27 (2004): 169–92.

Rohman, Carrie. "Revising the Human: Silence, Being, and the Question of the Animal in *Nightwood*." *American Literature* 79 (2007): 57–84.

Ronell, Avital. *Stupidity*. Urbana and Chicago: University of Illinois Press, 2003.

Rorty, Richard. *Contingency, Irony, and Solidarity*. Cambridge, UK: Cambridge University Press, 1989.

———. *Philosophy and the Mirror of Nature*. Princeton, NJ: Princeton University Press, 1979.

———, ed. *The Linguistic Turn: Recent Essays in Philosophical Method*. Chicago: University of Chicago Press, 1967.

Rose, Martha L. *The Staff of Oedipus: Transforming Disability in Ancient Greece*. Ann Arbor: University of Michigan Press, 2003.

Roszak, Theodore. The Making of a Counterculture: Reflections on the Technocratic Society and its Youthful Opposition. [1969]. Berkeley: University of California Press, 1995.

Roth, Marco. "Rise of the Neuronovel." *n+1* (September 14, 2009). http://www.nplusonemag.com/rise-neuronovel.

Roth, Philip. *The Ghost Writer*. New York: Farrar, Straus, and Giroux, 1979.

Rothberg, Michael. *Traumatic Realism: The Demands of Holocaust Representation*. Minneapolis and London: University of Minnesota Press, 2000.

Rousseau, Jean-Jacques. *A Discourse on Inequality*. Trans. Maurice Cranston. New York: Penguin, 1984.

———. "Essay on the Origin of Languages." *On the Origin of Language: Two Essays. Jean-Jacques Rousseau and Johan Gottfried Herder*. Trans. John H. Moran and Alexander Gode. Chicago and London: University of Chicago Press, 1966. 1–74.

Rymer, Russ. *Genie: An Abused Child's Flight from Silence*. New York: HarperCollins, 1993.

Sacks, Oliver. *An Anthropologist on Mars*. New York: Vintage, 1995.

———. *Awakenings*. New York: HarperCollins, 1990.

———. *A Leg to Stand On*. New York: Summit, 1984.

———. *The Man Who Mistook His Wife for a Hat, and Other Clinical Tales*. New York: Touchstone, 1998.

———. *Musicophilia: Tales of Music and the Brain, Expanded and Revised Edition*. New York: Vintage, 2008.

Salmond, John A. *Gastonia 1929: The Story of the Loray Mill Strike*. Chapel Hill, NC: University of North Carolina Press, 1995.

Santner, Eric L. *On the Psychotheology of Everyday Life*. Chicago and London: University of Chicago Press, 2001.

Sassen, Saskia. *Global City: New York, London, Tokyo*. Princeton, NJ: Princeton University Press, 2001.

Saussure, Ferdinand de. *Course in General Linguistics*. Ed. Charles Bally and Albert Sechehaye, in collaboration with Albert Riedlinger. Trans. Wade Baskin. New York: McGraw-Hill, 1966.

Savarese, Ralph. *Reasonable People: A Memoir of Autism and Adoption*. New York: Other Press, 2007.

Scheerenberger, R. C. *A History of Mental Retardation*. Baltimore, MD: P. H. Brookes, 1983.

Schleifer, Ronald. "The Poetics of Tourette Syndrome: Language, Neurobiology, and Poetry." *New Literary History* 32 (2001): 563–84.

Schmidt, Gerald. "Fictional Voices and Viewpoints for the Mentally Deficient, 1929–1939." *Mental Retardation in America*. Ed. Steven Noll and James W. Trent, Jr. New York and London: New York University Press, 2004. 186–206.

Schneider, Mark A. *Culture and Enchantment*. Chicago and London: University of Chicago Press, 1993.

Scott, Bonnie Kime. *Refiguring Modernism (volume two): Postmodern Feminist Readings of Woolf, West, and Barnes*. Bloomington and Indianapolis: Indiana University Press, 1995.

Sedgewick, Eve Kosofsky. *Epistemology of the Closet*. Berkeley and Los Angeles: University of California Press, 1990.

Shakespeare, Tom. *Disability Rights and Wrongs*. New York: Routledge, 2006.

———. Review of Sacks' *An Anthropologist on Mars*. *Disability and Society* 11 (1996): 137–39.

Shattuck, Roger. *The Forbidden Experiment: The Story of the Wild Boy of Aveyron*. New York: Farrar Straus Giroux, 1980.

Shelley, Mary. *Frankenstein*. New York: Penguin, 1992.

Shine. Dir. Scott Hicks. New Line Home Entertainment, 1996.

Shklovsky, Victor. "Art as Technique." *Russian Formalist Criticism: Four Essays*. Trans. Lee T. Lemon and Marion J. Reis. Lincoln: University of Nebraska Press, 1965. 3–24.

Siebers, Tobin. *Disability Aesthetics*. Ann Arbor: University of Michigan Press, 2010.
———. *Disability Theory*. Ann Arbor: University of Michigan press, 2008.
Smith, Barbara Herrnstein. *Scandalous Knowledge: Science, Truth, and the Human*. Durham, NC: Duke University Press, 2005.
Smith, Darryl A. "Handi-/Cappin' Slaves and Laughter by the Dozens: Divine Dismemberment and Disability Humor in the U.S." *Journal of Literary and Cultural Disability Studies* (forthcoming).
Soloway, Richard A. *Demography and Degeneration: Eugenics and the Declining Birthrate in Twentieth-Century Britain*. Chapel Hill: University of North Carolina Press, 1990.
Sontag, Susan. "Fascinating Fascism." *Under the Sign of Saturn*. New York: Picador, 2002. 73–108.
Sorensen, Lars. "Autism, Aspergers, and Theory of Mind: A Literature Review." *Cognition and Children's Thinking Seminar* 295.590 (2009). http://www.cs.rutgers. edu/~biglars/Lit-Rev-Autism-ToM.pdf
Spivak, Gayatri Chakravorty. "Can the Subaltern Speak?" *Marxism and the Interpretation of Culture*. Ed. Cary Nelson and Lawrence Grossberg. Urbana and Chicago: University of Illinois Press, 1988. 271–313.
Spolsky, Ellen. "Darwin and Derrida: Cognitive Literary Theory as a Species of Post-Structuralism." *Poetics Today* 23 (2002): 43–62.
Stein, Gertrude. "Composition as Explanation." *A Stein Reader*. Ed. Ulla E. Dydo. Evanston, IL: Northwestern University Press, 1993.
Steiner, George. *After Babel: Aspects of Language and Translation*. Second ed. Oxford and New York: Oxford University Press, 1992.
Stiglitz, Joseph. "Information and the Change in the Paradigm in Economics." http:// nobelprize.org/nobel_prizes/economics/laureates/2001/Stiglitz-lecture.pdf
Stikker, Henri. *A History of Disability*. Trans. William Sayers. Ann Arbor: University of Michigan Press, 1999.
Stoddard, Lothrop. *The Rising Tide of Color against White World-Supremacy*. New York: Scribner, 1920.
Stubblefield, Anna. "The Entanglement of Race and Cognitive Dis/Ability." *Metaphilosophy* 40 (2009): 531–51.
Swindon Borough Council Review of Homelessness Services. March 2003. www.swindon. gov.uk/homelessness_review_-_March_2003-2.pdf
"Symposium: A Turn Away From 'Language'?" *Common Knowledge* 4.2 (1995): 24–85.
Tager-Flusberg, Helen. "Dissociations in Form and Function in the Acquisition of Language by Autistic Children." *Constraints on Language Acquisition: Studies of Atypical Children*. Ed. Helen Tager-Flusberg. Hillsdale, NJ: Lawrence Erlbaum, 1994.
Tanakh, The Holy Scriptures. Philadelphia and Jerusalem: The Jewish Publication Society, 1985.
Thomson, Mathew. *The Problem of Mental Deficiency: Eugenics, Democracy, and Social Policy in Britain, c. 1870–1959*. Oxford: Clarendon Press, 1998.

Trent, James W., Jr. *Inventing the Feeble Mind: A History of Mental Retardation in the United States.* Berkeley: University of California Press, 1994.

Turner, Mark. *The Literary Mind: The Origins of Thought and Language.* New York and Oxford: Oxford University Press, 1998.

Vehmas, Simo. "Philosophy and Science: The Axes of Evil in Disability Studies?" *Journal of Medical Ethics* 34 (2008): 21–23.

Vidali, Amy. "Seeing What We Know: Disability and Theories of Metaphor." *Journal of Literary and Cultural Disability Studies* 4 (2010): 33–54.

Villey-Desmeserets, Pierre. *The World of the Blind.* New York: Macmillan, 1930.

Voloshinov, V. N. *Marxism and the Philosophy of Language.* Trans. Ladislav Matejka and I. R. Titunik. New York: Seminar Press, 1973.

Warner, Michael. *The Trouble with Normal: Sex, Politics, and the Ethics of Queer Life.* New York: Free Press, 1999.

Weil, Kari. *Thinking Animals: Why Animal Studies Now?* New York: Columbia University Press, 2012.

Weinstein, Arnold. *Nobody's Home: Speech, Self, and Place in American Fiction from Hawthorne to DeLillo.* New York: Oxford University Press, 1993.

Weinstein, Philip. *Unknowing: The Work of Modernist Fiction.* Ithaca, NY: Cornell University Press, 2005.

Whalen, Robert Weldon. *"Like Fire in Broom Straw": Southern Journalism and the Textile Strikes of 1929–1931.* Westport, CT: Greenwood Press, 2001.

White, Hayden. *The Content of the Form: Narrative Discourse and Historical Representation.* Baltimore, MD, and London: Johns Hopkins University Press, 1987.

Whitman, Walt. *Leaves of Grass: The First (1855) Edition.* Ed. Malcolm Cowley. New York: Penguin, 1986.

Wilcox, Leonard. "Baudrillard, DeLillo's *White Noise*, and the End of Heroic Narrative." *Contemporary Literature* 32 (1991): 346–65.

Wilden, Anthony. *System and Structure: Essays in Communication and Exchange.* Second ed. New York: Routledge, 2011.

Williams, Donna. *Nobody Nowhere: The Extraordinary Autobiography of an Autistic.* New York: Avon, 1994.

Williams, Raymond. *Culture and Society: 1780–1950.* New York: Columbia University Press, 1983.

———. *Politics of Modernism.* London: Verso, 1989.

Williams, William Carlos. *Spring and All.* New York: New Directions, 2011.

Wing, Lorna. "Autistic Spectrum Disorders." *British Medical Journal* 312 (1996): 327–28.

Wingate, Marcel E. *Stuttering: A Short History of a Curious Disorder.* Westport, CT, and London: Bergin and Garvey, 199

Wittgenstein, Ludwig. *On Certainty.* Ed. G. E. M. Anscombe and George Henrik von Wright. Trans. Denis Paul and G. E. M. Anscombe. New York: Harper and Row, 1972.

———. *Philosophical Investigations.* Trans. G. E. M. Anscombe. Cambridge, MA: Blackwell, 1997.

————. *Tractatus Logico-Philosophicus*. Trans. C. K. Ogden. London and New York: Routledge and Kegan Paul, 1986.

Wolfe, Cary. *Animal Rites: American Culture, the Discourse of Species, and Posthuman Theory*. Chicago: University of Chicago Press, 2003.

————. *What is Posthumanism?* Minneapolis: University of Minnesota Press, 2010.

Zenderland, Leila. "The Parable of *The Kallikak Family*: Explaining the Meaning of Heredity in 1912." *Mental Retardation in America*. Ed. Steven Noll and James W. Trent, Jr. New York and London: New York University Press, 2004. 165–185.

Zizek, Slavoj. *First as Tragedy, Then as Farce*. London and New York: Verso, 2009.

————. *Looking Awry: An Introduction to Lacan through Popular Culture*. Cambridge, MA: MIT Press, 1991.

————. *On Belief*. London and New York: Routledge, 2001.

————. *The Sublime Object of Ideology*. London: Verso, 1989.

————. *Tarrying With the Negative: Kant, Hegel, and the Critique of Ideology*. Durham, NC: Duke University Press, 1993.

The Zohar. Trans. Harry Sperling and Maurice Simon. London and New York: Soncino, 1984.

Zunshine, Lisa. *Why We Read Fiction: Theory of Mind and the Novel*. Columbus, OH: Ohio State University Press, 2006.

ABOUT THE AUTHOR

James Berger is Senior Lecturer in American Studies and English at Yale University. He is author of *After the End: Representations of Post-Apocalypse* (1999) and a book of poetry, *Prior* (2013). He is also editor of Helen Keller's *The Story of My Life: The Restored Edition* (2003).